Economic Growth and Structure

Economic Growth and Structure

Economic Growth and Structure

Selected Essays

Simon Kuznets
Harvard University

W · W · Norton & Company · Inc ·

New York

Contents

Preface

THE ESSAYS in this volume were written over the last twelve years as a by-product of quantitative analysis of the modern economic growth of nations. These papers, and the data on which they are based, draw comparisons over a wide geographic area and a long time span. Unlike the nine papers published in *Economic Development and Cultural Change*,[1] those assembled here, with few exceptions, do not include the relevant statistical evidence; rather they are essays on larger themes. They either unfold a broad preliminary view—as does the first essay, "Toward a Theory of Economic Growth"—or deal with the general implications of one aspect of the complex process of modern economic growth.

Because the discussion in many of the essays is not based upon adequately organized empirical evidence, the conclusions drawn are only suggestive and tentative. Two conclusions, both in the first essay, need to be specifically noted here because in rereading the papers I found that they are subject to qualification. The first relates to the retardation in the rate of growth of per capita product (see pp. 20–23); the other, to the tendency of major wars to depress economic growth in the participating countries (see pp. 54–57). The first trend is an algebraic necessity in the very long run, but

---

[1] These appeared under the general title *Quantitative Aspects of the Economic Growth of Nations*. The first was published as the October 1956 issue of *Economic Development and Cultural Change*, V, 1, and the most recent one appeared as Part II of the October 1964 issue of that journal.

it is less observable and imminent than suggested in the discussion. The second conclusion, while clearly true of World War I, is less clearly applicable to the post-World War II experience,[2] and perhaps should not be asserted as bluntly as it was. Other changes in emphasis could have been made, but the essays were, and are, intended to pose questions and advance suggestions for further research, not to provide definitive answers.

Since the papers were originally published in a wide variety of journals, and two only in French, their publication in this volume makes them more accessible and useful. Only stylistic changes have been made in the original versions.

Much of the research underlying these papers was based on work initiated under the auspices of the Committee on Economic Growth of the Social Science Research Council. I am indebted to Miss Lillian Epstein, who assisted me in the original preparation of the papers as well as in the review for republication. I am also grateful to Professor James S. Duesenberry of Harvard University for his suggestions on the papers to be included. Finally, thanks are due to various publishers, as noted in footnotes to each article, for permission to reprint.

September 1964   SIMON KUZNETS

[2] See my *Postwar Economic Growth: Four Lectures* (Cambridge, Mass.: Harvard University Press, 1964), particularly Lecture III.

Economic Growth and Structure

Economic Growth and Structure

Toward a Theory of
Economic Growth

THE CURRENT interest in and extensive discussion of the economic growth of nations stem from several sources. A brief review may indicate the major questions that are being raised and point the directions that an approach to a theory may follow.

The Current Interest in Economic Growth

The first recent stimulus was concern over possible secular stagnation in the industrially developed nations. The decline in the rate of population growth of many Western European nations and of European settlements in the New World is not a new phenomenon; it has been commented upon since the late nineteenth century, when the marked and sustained decline in birth rates gave rise to lurid discussion of "race suicide." The reaching of the limits of external expansion, the disappearance of the free frontier, is also an old theme—in fact, an integral element in the economic theory of the long run evolved by the Classical School in the early nineteenth

I am indebted to Professors Moses Abramovitz, John Maurice Clark, Wilbert Moore, and Joseph J. Spengler for many comments made on the first draft of this paper and utilized in revising it.

The discussion draws heavily upon statistical data summarized in an appendix, which has been omitted because of limitations of space.

Reprinted by permission of the Trustees of Columbia University in the City of New York, from Robert Lekachman, ed., National Policy for Economic Welfare at Home and Abroad, Columbia University Bicentennial Conference Series (New York: Doubleday and Company, 1955), pp. 12–85.

1

century. But the great depression of the 1930's and Keynesian economics, with its emphasis on threatening shortages of private investment opportunities and on their implication in terms of dragging levels of national output and of chronic unemployment, lent new vigor to the stagnation theory. Particularly important, these events served to substitute for the equanimity with which John Stuart Mill, for example, viewed the prospect of a stationary state, a deep anxiety arising from the conviction that secular stagnation meant chronic unemployment and hence a marked failure of the economic system.[1]

With World War II and its aftermath, this concern about economic stagnation receded, but a new source of emphasis on economic growth arose. In its present form this interest is in secular prospects and problems of "underdeveloped" countries, by which we mean countries that have been unable to utilize the opportunities afforded by modern material and social technology and have failed to supply minimum subsistence and material comfort to their populations.[2] This too is no new problem; under-

[1] It is instructive to compare Mill's comments in Chapter 5 of Book IV of his *Principles* (in which the stationary state is viewed favorably as relief from the competitive struggle and from overemphasis on material attainments of a "progressive" economy) with the recent anxious discussion in this country of the problem of secular stagnation. True, Mill envisaged the stationary state as operating under a system of greater distributive justice than did the growing state that he and the Classical economists knew, and the policy orientation of modern economists who emphasized the threat of secular stagnation was not unlike Mill's in that they wished to avoid the injustice implied in chronic unemployment. Yet the strong conviction of the indispensability of growth in recent discussion of *industrially advanced* countries is in sharp contrast with Mill's view that "it is only in the backward countries of the world that increased production is still an important object." John Stuart Mill, *Principles,* 5th London ed. (New York: Appleton and Co., 1878), Vol. II, p. 338.

[2] Three definitions of underdevelopment can be suggested. First, it may mean failure to utilize fully the productive potential warranted by the existing state of technical knowledge—a failure resulting from the resistance of social institutions. In this sense, all countries in the world are underdeveloped and have, perhaps, become increasingly so with the rapid growth of technical knowledge during the last century. Second, it may mean backwardness in economic performance, compared with the few economically leading countries of the period. In this sense, the vast majority of countries are underdeveloped at any given time. Third, it may mean economic poverty, in the sense of failure to assure adequate subsistence and material comfort to most of a country's population. The problem of underdeveloped countries in current discussion reflects elements of all three definitions; its acuteness arises largely out of the material misery stressed in the third definition, it is sharpened by realization of a lag compared with other, economically more advanced countries, and it is generally viewed as a social problem originating in the failure of social institutions rather than in a lack of technical knowledge.

developed countries have always been with us. Indeed there is hardly a stretch of human history in which a substantial proportion of mankind has not lagged behind the more advanced communities in utilizing its material potential and therefore experiencing misery and suffering. But the recent emphasis on the problem of economic growth stems from the realization that the nineteenth-century theory of international division of labor, with its promise of the inevitable and rapid spread of the benefits of modern economic civilization to all corners of the earth, is hardly tenable. Further, there is pressure for more rapid economic growth in many underdeveloped countries which, having achieved political freedom recently, are confronted with urgent problems of economic sufficiency and security; and there are increasingly close international ties, which suggest that lack of freedom from want in some countries, with the attendant political and social perturbations, may well mean lack of freedom from fear in others that are economically more advanced.

The third and probably most important reason for the recent interest in economic growth is the emergence of a different social organization which claims greater efficiency in handling long-term economic problems—the authoritarian state of the Soviet type. This offshoot of Western European civilization is again not completely new. Many elements in its organization can be seen, if in rudimentary form, in the histories of Germany and particularly of Japan during periods of rapid industrialization, and in a sense, the organization of the USSR can be viewed as a further transformation or deformation of the social institutions in the break from the preindustrial to the industrial phase that, for somewhat similar historical reasons, was foreshadowed in German and Japanese experience. On the spiritual side the Soviet case represents ideas and tendencies that have a long history. As I. L. Talmon shows, the roots of "totalitarian democracy" go back to the eighteenth century, and its glorification of the state, controlled by the elect in accordance with a preconceived theory that fits society into a Procrustean bed of some notion of what is good for man, is hardly a new element in Western thought.[3] What is new is the emergence and existence, alongside the economically successful, relatively free democracies, of new authoritarian states whose professed secular religion lies in material achievement and whose theories of orthodoxy and heresy impede free and peaceful intercourse with the rest of the world.

[3] I. L. Talmon, *Origins of Totalitarian Democracy* (London: Secker and Warburg, 1952).

The question immediately raised bears upon the potentialities of such an authoritarian system for the economic growth of both the countries that are and those that are not under its sway.

This recent division of a large part of the world into two camps—both offshoots of the same stream of thought and all the more hostile because of a common belief in the importance of material achievements—lends particular strength to another source of recent interest in economic growth: armed conflict as a major channel of expenditures of economic resources and a powerful accelerator and modifier of long-term trends in the economic and social organization of nations. Here again is an old problem, but the economic aspects have been modified beyond recognition by recent technological and political changes. It is not customary to include wars in discussion of economic growth, and perhaps they should be excluded if a reasonably acceptable theory is to be evolved. But it seems rather dangerous to do so at the start: a substantial proportion of the last two centuries has been accounted for by major wars; preparation for these wars, their conduct, and their aftermaths have significantly transformed long-run economic changes; and armed conflict is to some extent an ultimate expression of the ever-present divisive tendencies among nations.

Can we hope to formulate a theory of economic growth that would indicate the factors in the development of the industrially advanced nations and thus illuminate the problem of possible secular stagnation; to frame the factors so that a testable analysis of obstacles to the economic growth of underdeveloped nations and hence a basis for intelligent development policy become possible; to consider the operation of these factors under a system of free enterprise, as well as within the authoritarian system, so that the potentialities in both and their interplay become clear; and to distinguish the factors that make for peaceful and warlike behavior, so that the bearing of each on economic growth can be perceived? To put the question in this way is to predetermine a negative answer—provided that by a theory we mean a statement of testable relations among empirically identifiable factors, such relations and factors having been found relatively invariant under diverse conditions in time and space. Such a theory of economic growth of nations may never be within our reach. Obviously we do not have it now, and what is more important, we are not yet ready for it. The very concern about economic growth is recent, and it is hardly an exaggeration to say that since the mid-nineteenth century, when the Classical and Marxian schools had already formulated their economic theories of the long run, no significant theoretical work has been done in this field, excepting the attempts to revise Marxian theory in the light of subsequent events. Meanwhile, with the passage of time, our experience in the economic growth of nations has broadened and empirical records have accumulated, but no significant attempt has been made either to utilize these data within a theoretical framework or even to organize, extend, and test them preparatory to theoretical analysis.

These statements are not made as an apology for the limitations of what follows. Nor is it my purpose to provide yet another illustration of the conditions under which economists (and perhaps other social scientists) usually operate—confronted by urgent problems that rapid and complex historical changes bring forth, with no adequate theoretical tools or data for handling them, and under pressure to provide answers in situations in which some intelligence, no matter how limited, is vitally needed. More important in the present context are two implications of the foregoing statements. First, they clearly suggest the need for a long-time and wide-space perspective in the empirical foundation of any theory of economic growth—the body of observations from which it must be derived and by which it must be tested. The very understanding of the problems involved, let alone a theoretical formulation and solution, is hardly possible if we limit our view to one country or to a relatively short period of historical experience. Therefore, the following pages summarize the outstanding features of the empirical record of economic growth for a minimum range of time and space.

Second, it is apparent, and will become increasingly striking as we reflect on the variety of growth experience suggested by the empirical evidence, that an explicitly formulated theory of economic growth would at present be of limited usefulness, at least as a tool for research and prediction. Under the present circumstances, such a theory would be either an expression of dogmatic belief in some "self-evident" trait of human nature and corresponding "principle" of social organization; an exercise in the philosophy of history operating with vague terms and elusive units; or a formalistic model of the mechanism of economic growth, lacking assurance that it is complete, that the relations are correctly drawn, and that we can ever have the data required for the empirical constants in the formulas.[4] Interesting as such attempts might be, it seemed preferable to limit ourselves to a less ambitious task: to draw some suggestions from the empirical record about the identity and relative importance of and interconnections among the determining factors, as guides to the further study of the data and particularly to the directions in which testable theoretical analysis must be pursued. In this sense, the title of this paper is truly descriptive; it is *toward* a theory of economic growth that we are attempting to proceed. We may avoid walking off in the wrong direction if we are not required to give explicit answers where no adequate basis for them exists.

Specifications of the Summary

The summary of empirical evidence presented below attempts to bring into view as much of the world as possible, organizes the data around the nation-state as the unit of observation, emphasizes quantitative data, and limits the time range to the last two centuries, although it occasionally forays into earlier times and at many points must, for lack of data, cover a shorter recent period. A brief explanation of these specifications may prevent misunderstanding of the findings.

Statistical data are emphasized because economic growth is essentially a quantitative concept. Much as we are aware, without statistics, of obvious differences in the rate of growth and economic position among the communities that comprise mankind, some notion of the magnitudes is indispensable for clear understanding and analysis. For the purposes of measurement, the economic growth of a nation may be defined as a sustained increase in its population and product per capita.[5] These rates of increase, their pattern over time, and the differential changes of groups within the population

[4] This is not meant to deny the value of such hypotheses, nor to claim that it would be possible to forego tools of this type in the immediate future in further organization and analysis of data. All we urge here is the need for a wider view of the phenomena being explored and a recognition of their variability among countries and over time, with proper emphasis on testable empirical evidence.

[5] A combination of secular stagnation or decline of population with a sustained rise in per capita product has been observed only rarely in the last two centuries. Insofar as a definition of economic growth must reflect common experience, it seems best to include a sustained increase in both the total population and the per capita product.

or of components within the product, when compared among nations, are an indispensable record of the basic quantitative aspects of economic growth, of the *results* of the process whose determining factors we would seek to identify in any prospective theory. Sustained movements are those which extend beyond a period so short that they may be confused with transient disturbances, either roughly recurrent and associated with business cycles or more irregular and often associated with calamities, natural or man-made. For practical purposes a period not much shorter than half a century is desirable.

The choice of the nation-state as the unit of observation is partly dictated by the way statistical (and much historical) data, particularly on economic product, are organized; they are ordinarily given for states, largely because states have the power to produce such data and are the foci of interest which these data serve. But there is more here than meets the eye. Modern history suggests that each of these sovereign political units into which mankind is divided identifies a group that claims a distinctive period of common history—a distinct heritage of the past that strongly conditions the process of economic growth—and that the state mechanism, among its many functions, serves as a tool of economic growth, designed to assure the economic security and growth of the society that it organizes. Hence, at least as the first approximate way of ordering the data, there is much to be said for grouping them around the sovereign state as a unit, even though on occasion it may be more convenient to use some larger entities, or at some later stage of analysis it may be concluded that another unit may prove more effective in establishing generalizations.[6]

The limitation to the last two centuries is the result partly of inadequate data for earlier times and partly of the desire to concentrate on a historical period close to us, in which we can more easily orient ourselves. But there are even more fundamental reasons for this choice. The recent centuries subsume all of the human

[6] For a more detailed discussion of this point, see sections contributed by the author to *Problems in the Study of Economic Growth* (National Bureau of Economic Research, July 1949), mimeographed, pp. 3–20 and 118–135, and "The State as a Unit in Study of Economic Growth," *Journal of Economic History*, XI (1951), pp. 25–41.

For larger countries, intracountry regional units may also prove useful since they provide an opportunity to study similarities and differences in growth experience under conditions where cultural and political differences are much narrower than in intercountry comparisons.

past and are a more complete canvas than any earlier period. More specifically, during the last two centuries the potential of economic growth has become particularly large, in both absolute and relative terms; and hence any observable similarities and differences will be of special interest, since they will have developed under conditions more conducive to economic growth than those in the more distant past. Thus, even if data were abundant for, say, the last two centuries B.C., even if we could claim adequate understanding of the material and social conditions of that time, even if we were not concerned with relevance to current problems, we might still argue against that period and for the recent two centuries, largely because, given the state of human knowledge in the earlier period, potentialities for economic growth were narrow and the possible diversity of experience more limited. It is in observing similarities and differences of growth experience where wide diversity is possible that we can form the more tenable notions concerning the factors at play.

Given the choices and emphases just indicated, the effort must be made to bring as much of the world as possible within view. If we are to focus on a period in which potential diversity in rate, pattern, and structure of economic growth is wide, the danger in attempting to generalize from observations for any limited part of the world is all the more obvious. Granted that this goal of a world-wide record is unattainable, particularly for quantitative data, it still should be the desideratum—if only as a goad and as a warning.

We begin the summary with the growth of population, go on to the growth of total and per capita economic product, outline briefly the major changes in the shares of the various components of national product and their implications for the grouping of populations, and conclude with some observations concerning trends in external relations among national units.

Trends in Population Growth

World population increased from about 700 million in 1750 to about 2,400 million in 1950, more than tripling in 200 years. This increase is unusually high when viewed against the known long stretches of human history. The rate of growth from 1750 to 1950 is 6.4 percent per decade, or 85.2 percent per century. If we assume this cumulative rate of growth for the 17.5 centuries between the beginning of the Christian Era (the year 0) and 1750 and start with the 694 million estimated for 1750, the derived world total for year 0 would be about 15,000. Obviously, the rate of growth of world population per century for this period must have been much lower than 85 percent. Indeed, a rough estimate sets world population in year 0 between 200 and 300 million. With 250 million as the base, the average rate of growth per *century* from 0 to 1750 is 6 percent—in sharp contrast with a rate of 85 percent for the last two centuries.[7]

Two aspects of this recent upsurge in population growth deserve note. First, with few exceptions,[8] the increase in population has been widespread, particularly since 1850, by which date the economic and social factors that made it possible began to penetrate to the far corners of the earth. From 1850 to 1950, the population of Asia (excluding the USSR) and Africa almost doubled; of Europe, including Asiatic USSR, more than doubled; of Latin America almost quintupled; of North America more than sextupled. Despite the obvious differences among these continental groups in rates of growth over the last century (they are somewhat more pronounced for the period 1750–1950), the significant fact is that even in the many areas in which current per capita income is quite low, population growth since 1850 has been substantial. On the longer scale of past human history, an increase of 70 to 100 percent over a century is quite high.

Second, the rate of growth of world population has been accelerating. The rate of increase from 1750 to 1850 is 4.6 percent per decade; from 1850 to 1950, 8.2 percent. The rate of growth from 1850 to 1900 is 7.6 percent per decade; from 1900 to 1950, 8.9 percent per decade. This acceleration will not necessarily continue; there is no inevitable law about it. But it does indicate that during recent centuries increasing reservoirs of population growth have been tapped. In considering the implications for the future we must examine the rate of spread of the factors that may explain this recent upsurge in population.

[7] World population by continents is from United Nations, *The Determinants and Consequences of Population Trends* (New York, 1953), Table 2, p. 4. The contrast between the rates of growth is even more striking if we set the dividing point at 1650. On that date, world population is estimated to have been 470 million, and the rate of growth from 1650 to 1750 is 4 percent per decade, much lower than the 6.4 percent for 1750 to 1950 but still much higher than in the earlier period. From the beginning of the Christian Era to 1650 the rate of growth in world population is only 3.9 percent per century, compared with over 72 percent per century for 1650–1950, a ratio of 1 to 18.

[8] See footnote 9.

For this purpose the population-growth experience of individual countries must be taken into account. Although we can hardly do more here than skim the surface, even the most general impressions are important, since individual countries are the proper units of observation and the similarities and differences in their experiences are most revealing.

First, there is a marked diversity in the rates of growth of individual countries. True, for most of them, population grew at much higher rates during the recent century or two than in the long stretches of their historical past.[9] But the rates of growth were substantially different. The differences between the older and the younger countries are hardly surprising: the rate of population increase during the last century in North America was about three times as high as in Europe. The interesting and revealing findings are the differences among countries that are similar in size, age, and many cultural characteristics. Between 1800 and 1900 the rate of growth of population in Sweden was 8.1 percent per decade; in Norway, 9.8 percent; in Denmark, 10 percent; in Finland, 12.2 percent.[10] The differences in the decade rates look small; but they mean that over a century while Sweden's population little more than doubled, Finland's more than tripled.

The records of individual countries also reveal substantial differences in the patterns of growth over time. World population as a whole shows an accelerating rise beginning in the seventeenth century, and, in broad terms, continuing through recent decades. Among individual countries, there are differences in the *timing* of the upward swing in rates of population growth, depending largely upon the population position of the country and the time

[9] Three types of exceptions may be suggested. One, exemplified by Ireland and China since the mid-nineteenth century, represents a sharp break in population growth, leading to a decline or stagnation in total numbers. Another, of which France is an example, represents a late stage in population growth, a phase of retardation yielding rates distinctly below those of some earlier long periods of vigorous growth. A third, comprising the "young," originally relatively "empty" countries of the New World, may not show within the recent centuries *percentage* rates of growth higher than in earlier times, because in these earlier times the bases to which the percentages are calculated are so low. This last group constitutes an exception in a formal rather than substantive sense; and if the comparison were extended far enough back to cover long periods of slow growth in the aboriginal population, it might no longer be an exception.

[10] Underlying data are from R. R. Kuczynski, "Population," in the *Encyclopaedia of the Social Sciences* (New York: Columbia University Press), Vol. 12, pp. 243–245.

when the factors of increased growth came into play. There are also the obvious differences in the time pattern of rates between the young and initially "empty" countries and the older and more densely populated countries. In the former, a high rate of natural increase and substantial immigration made for a high rate of growth in early history; and then, with natural increase and immigration slackening, the rate of growth began to decline long before the recent decades. Thus, in the United States, the rate of increase per decade, adjusted for changes in area, ranges from 33 to 35 percent between 1790 and 1860 and drops to 20 percent or less beginning in 1890.[11] One gets the impression of a truncated swing in the rate of population increase, with the retardation phase quite prominent but the acceleration phase not clearly perceived unless one goes further back in time. In the older countries (mostly in Europe) for which records are sufficiently long, one can observe both the rising and the declining phases in the long swing in rates of population growth. Thus for Europe as a whole, including Asiatic USSR, the increase per decade is 3.4 percent for 1650–1750; 6 percent for 1750–1800; 7.3 percent for 1800–1850; 9.1 percent for 1850–1900; but then it declines to 7 percent for 1900–1950. Finally, in a third group of countries the rate of population growth has not yet begun to decline. The population of Brazil, for example, increased 131 percent from 1840 to 1890 and 190 percent from 1890 to 1940 [12]; in several other countries in Latin America and Asia the rate of population growth has been accelerating within recent decades. This variety of time patterns in the rate of growth for individual countries reveals that a sustained acceleration in the rate of increase of world population is not typical of most countries but is due to the successive entries of additional parts of the world into the orbit of the modern population growth pattern.

In considering the forces that made for both the rapid growth of world population and the diverse experience of individual countries during the recent two centuries, we first note the immediate determinants. For world population they are the crude birth and death rates, the excess of the former over the latter yielding the rate of increase in number. For individual countries there are in addition the rates of immigration and emigration. Although these rates are in a sense components of total change rather than causa-

---

[11] See Walter F. Willcox, *International Migrations* (New York: National Bureau of Economic Research, 1931), Vol. II, p. 98.

[12] From *The Determinants and Consequences of Population Trends*, p. 15.

tive factors, they reflect distinct substantive groups of actions and provide direct leads to the underlying forces at play.

Despite the inadequacies of data and analysis, the connection between the immediate determinants—birth and death rates—and the accelerated rate of increase of world population in recent centuries can be easily summarized.

1. The rise in the rate of population growth was due largely to the reduction in the death rate, *not* to any increase in the birth rate. True, in those countries where the medieval organization inhibited early marriages, birth rates increased for a while as guild and agricultural tenancy restrictions were relaxed and as new industries grew apace. Also, with the changing geographic distribution of world population, the world birth rate (a weighted average) may have risen because of a shift toward more prolific groups. But these are minor qualifications and for the recent century are more than offset by the *decline* in the birth rate in many countries.

Premodern death rates were well above 25 per 1,000 annually in "normal," nonepidemic, nonfamine, nonwar years; and birth rates were ordinarily somewhat above 30 per 1,000. However, the gap (i.e., the rate of natural increase) was much narrower than about 5 per 1,000, as suggested by these figures, because of epidemics, famines, and wars: only 0.6 per 1,000 per year since the rate of increase in population per *century* was about 6 percent. In the advanced countries the death rate has fallen to 10 or less per 1,000. The birth rate has not risen during any period within the last two centuries more than 2 or 3 points above the premodern level and recently declined in the more advanced countries to between 15 and 20 per 1,000.

It is particularly important to note that for centuries mankind lived under conditions in which deaths could easily outpace births. Annual crude birth rates have a fairly low biological ceiling, well below 100 per 1,000 (actually observed rates of as high as 50 are quite rare) because women in childbearing ages can constitute only a limited fraction of any normal population, because the number of children these women can bear during a year is limited by natural laws that govern the number of single and multiple births, and because the total number of children born to a woman is invariably fewer than the number of years in her childbearing period. Annual crude death rates can be much higher, as numerous experiences during earlier centuries indicate, and not only during years of plague or famine. It is the success of modern material and social technology in lowering death rates that has improved so markedly the conditions of population growth that characterized human history for centuries.

2. The forms of the reduction in the death rate are of particular bearing upon economic growth. The age-specific mortality curve is U shaped, with very high rates at the two ends—the infant and very young ages and the more advanced ages past 50. The decrease has been particularly large in the rates at infant and preadult ages, with the result that the enormous waste of breeding children who never reach productive ages has been reduced and the ratio of working-age groups to total population has increased. Furthermore, the factors that make for a decline in deaths have gradually become effective in controlling epidemics and thus have curbed the incidence of the major uncertainties of human life, with possible important effects on the time horizon of individual and social planning. Also, the improvements in medical practice and material conditions of life must have curbed the incidence of nonfatal disease and thus markedly reduced economic losses associated with the latter. Finally, greater control over the death rate meant, even if with some lag, greater control over health conditions in large and densely settled human aggregates, and made the modern large cities possible without catastrophic drains through increased death incidence. Before modern times, death rates were much higher in the cities than in the countryside; this difference was wiped out by the increased knowledge and advanced technology that made for the over-all reduction in mortality.

3. If birth rates had declined as rapidly as death rates, there would have been no acceleration in the growth of world population. In fact birth rates remained constant or declined, either with a lag after the decline in death rates or at a significantly lower rate. This lag and lesser rate of decline in birth rates was due, at least in part, to the slowness with which population either was subjected or reacted to changing conditions of social life. Slowness is, of course, a relative concept. In other words, changes in medical arts, public health measures, and the standard of living could, at least for a long while, act more rapidly and effectively on the death rates than any modification of social conditions could on the birth-rate habits that had such a long history.

That the lag and disparity are necessarily temporary is revealed by the experience of countries that entered the modern phase of population growth early and where the process had a longer time to develop. In these countries, mostly in Western Europe (disregarding the New World where immigration played an important part), the decline in birth rates began to outpace that in death rates in the 1890's. Since the lower limit to crude death rates is significantly above 0—all people must die some time—rates of less than 10 per 1,000 leave a narrow absolute margin for further reduction. If at the same time birth rates are about 20 per 1,000, the absolute reduction in birth rates can easily exceed that in death rates. The position during the 1890's was somewhat different, with birth rates at 30 and death rates at 20 per 1,000; but by halving both birth and death rates the rate of natural increase is reduced from 10 to 5 per 1,000.

Against this oversimplified but roughly valid picture of major movements in birth and death rates that account for the amazing growth of world population in recent centuries, the records of individual countries suggest a bewildering variety of combinations of immediate determinants. In addition to births and deaths, we must consider here emigration and immigration—flows of considerable importance in both the European countries and the areas of the New World into which the migrants moved—from the eighteenth century until the recent restrictions. We must also consider the chronology of the movement of the death rates and birth rates, the levels at which the declines in both begin, and the magnitude and timing of these declines, all of which differ so much from country to country. The movements are of course similar in that, as time passes, one country after another adopts the modern population growth pattern, with its decline in death rates, eventual decline in birth rates, and replacement of violent temporal fluctuations by a steadier course free from the impacts of epidemics and famines. Yet there still are marked differences among countries in their initial positions and in the subsequent combinations of the immediate determinants of birth, death, and migration; and it is these differences that should be the important raw material for analyses leading to a theory of economic growth.

For any given historical period, the population growth of a given country is arithmetically determined by the initial levels of its crude birth, death, and external migration rates, the timing as well as the magnitude of the declines in birth and death rates, and the course of the rate of external migration. There is room here for a variety of combinations productive of a great diversity of average rates of population growth, as well as of the pattern of such growth over time—let alone of different impacts upon the sex and age structure of the population, which have further consequences for economic growth. High birth and death rates may continue for the larger part of a historical period and be affected by factors making for declines only toward the end; yet, if combined with some net immigration, the result may be a high rate of total population growth. On the other hand, birth and death rates may decline rapidly, with the rate of natural increase also declining; but if the rate of immigration is rising, a high rate of population increase may be sustained. There is the case, typical of many older European countries, where fairly early in the modern period death and birth rates were already somewhat lower than they are today in many underdeveloped countries; where the rate of natural increase accelerated because of a rapid decline in death rates and a lag in the decline of birth rates; but where the overall increase was limited by substantial losses through emigration.

A complete typology of countries for the last two centuries, or even the last century—dividing them by groups with distinctive combinations of levels and movements of birth, death, and migration rates—is impossible here. Indeed, judging by the discussion in the United Nations, *The Determinants and Consequences of Population Trends*, such an attempt would be extremely difficult even for a demographic expert, partly because of scarcity of basic data and partly because of great lacunae in the analysis of data already available, which would have to be studied systematically country by country for long periods of recent history. We can only point to the obvious variety of population growth experience, even among countries that are not too different with respect to size and character of economic and social institutions, and emphasize that such differences are relevant to the similarities and differences in economic growth. Birth, death, and migration rates have a direct impact on the absolute number of population, on its sex and age structure and the consequent ratio of producers to dependents, on the adaptability of the labor force connected with accession of the younger generations and retirement or migration of the older, on the general processes of internal mobility caused by disparities between the differential rates of natural increase and the rate of increase of economic and other opportunities. More elusive, but perhaps even more important, is the indirect association between population growth patterns and economic growth, through the impress that stability (or instability) of human life and freedom (or lack of freedom) to migrate put upon the whole economic and social order. One may assume that the premodern population movement, characterized by high birth and death rates, probably limited the time horizon of an individual and resulted in a pattern of family organization, cultural response, and social ideology which could hardly favor the individual self-reliance that was such an important factor in economic growth during the past two centuries, or at least before World War I. Likewise, the possibilities of gains and losses through free migration, the freedom with which groups in the prime of their working life can move to countries offering better opportunity, create conditions that, however they threaten the countries of origin with direct loss, may benefit even them in the long run, as they do the recipient countries. It is this variety of interconnections between population and economic growth that makes it difficult to envisage an adequate theory of economic growth as long as the record and analysis of the diverse population experience of the countries of the world are so incomplete.

Trends in the Growth of National Product

Among the most effective measures of the economic performance of a nation is its total net product, or national income—the sum of all goods produced during a given period, adjusted for duplication, and net of any commodities consumed in the process of production. If available for a long period, measured in constant prices, and accompanied by estimates of significant components, such measures provide an invaluable picture of the broader aspects of a nation's economic growth. But even disregarding questions of detail that concern components, estimates of national income for a period sufficiently long to permit observation of growth, and acceptable even by lenient standards of statistical reliability, are now available for only fourteen countries, almost all economically developed and with high per capita income. For recent years, however, we have estimates for some 70 to 75 countries. Although many are exceedingly crude, these current estimates, combined with the few available for long periods, can yield a basis for some reasonable inferences about national income trends over the last century.

CHANGES IN PER CAPITA INCOME · Of the 2 billion people in the countries for which estimates of national income were available for

1949, over 30 percent had per capita income of less than $50, and almost one quarter more, between $50 and $100. These were countries in Asia, Africa, the Middle East, and Central and South America. At the other extreme were the United States, the United Kingdom, the Scandinavian countries, Switzerland, Canada, Australia, and New Zealand, which together accounted for 11 percent of the population covered and in which per capita income was $600 or more. The 400 million for whom no national income estimates are available would be mostly in the lower income brackets. One may, therefore, conclude that more than 60 percent of the world's population had per capita incomes of $100 or less; that less than 10 percent had per capita incomes of $600 or more; and that the rest ranged in a spectrum with the older Western European countries at the upper end and several Latin American countries and Japan at the lower end.[13]

As the compilers themselves recognize, such per capita income estimates tend to understate the economic levels of the less developed countries if only because the large volume of nonmarket-bound activities may be inadequately covered. There are many other reasons, whose exploration is out of place here, why statistical comparisons of this type tend to exaggerate the contrast between industrially advanced and underdeveloped countries.[14] But even if we make generous allowances for biases, striking differences in per capita income remain. Granted that the true ratio of per capita income in the United States to that in China is not 54 to 1, as the United Nations figures indicate, but only 10 or 15 to 1, this difference is still large. Such a large gap in per capita income must mean vast differences in the structure of the productive apparatus of the countries, in the extent to which they have adopted modern economic and social technology, in the health, education, and urbanization of their populations, and indeed in the whole set of social values. Manipulation of figures too often obscures the fact (and not only to statisticians) that differences in quantities,

[13] Underlying data are from W. S. and E. S. Woytinsky, *World Population and Production* (New York: Twentieth Century Fund, 1953), Table 185, pp. 389–390; and United Nations, Statistical Papers, Series E, No. 1 (New York, 1950), entitled *National and Per Capita Incomes, Seventy Countries, 1949*, Tables 1 and 4.

[14] See "National Income and Industrial Structure," *Proceedings of the International Statistical Conferences 1947* (Calcutta, 1951), Vol. V, pp. 205–239; reprinted in Simon Kuznets, *Economic Change* (New York: W. W. Norton and Co., 1953).

once they pass beyond a certain range, are symptomatic of cardinal differences in quality, an observation that should be kept in mind also in considering changes over time.

Our long records of national income are with some exceptions (Italy, Japan) for countries at the top of the income pyramid. The rates of growth in per capita income range mostly from about 10 percent to over 20 percent per decade. These rates are extremely high; an increase of 10 percent per decade means a rise over a century to over 2.5 times the initial value; and an increase of 20 percent means a rise over a century to more than 6 times the initial value. In fact, the rise per century in per capita income varied, for the countries for which we have fairly long records, from about 2.5 times (in France and the United Kingdom) to over 7 (in Sweden, and excluding the exceptionally high but statistically dubious rate for Japan between the 1870's and World War II).[15] Here again biases in statistical estimation tend to undervalue earlier periods compared with more recent ones and thus exaggerate the rate of growth. These biases, however, are less pronounced than those in cross-section comparisons among developed and under-developed countries. And again, even if we allow for the biases, the rises are sufficiently large to signify major changes in the underlying organization of life.

From the evidence relating to the international comparisons for 1949 and the limited number of long-term records on total and per capita income, several tentative inferences can be drawn. First, the *current* income levels in many countries with less than $100 per capita income are desperately low—low to a point where the means of subsistence are hardly adequate. In these countries, the per capita income could not have grown much over the last hundred years, since this would imply incomes too low at the beginning of the century to allow the population to survive, particularly since an insufficient quantity of goods could not be offset as well then as today by sanitary and medical controls. In China, India, Indonesia, Indochina, most of the Middle East, Africa, and many parts of Latin America, the population could hardly survive on half or perhaps even three quarters of current income levels. Yet we know that population has increased in almost all of them, in many substantially. It follows that if any secular rise in per capita

[15] See the author's "Quantitative Aspects of the Economic Growth of Nations: I. Levels and Variability of Rates of Growth," *Economic Development and Cultural Change*, V, 1 (October 1956), Tables 1 and 2.

income did take place in these countries over the last century, it must have been much smaller than the rise observed among the developed countries.

Second, for most of the *older* countries in this category (excluding some Latin American countries, Java under Dutch rule, Egypt in recent decades), population growth over the last century, while substantial, was at an appreciably lower rate than in countries that enjoyed a rapidly rising per capita income. It follows that growth of *total* national income, in constant prices, during the last century was also at a much lower rate in most currently underdeveloped countries than in countries now in the upper levels of the income pyramid. Third, since the countries with currently high per capita income (with some exceptions such as Japan) displayed the high rates of growth in per capita income during the last century, one hundred years ago international differences in per capita income must have been narrower, certainly absolutely and probably relatively, than they are today.

A fourth inference, somewhat less firm than the other three, can be drawn concerning per capita income levels in underdeveloped countries today compared with those in the developed countries before their industrialization. The current contrast between underdeveloped and more advanced countries appears to result only in part from differences in the rates of growth in per capita income during the last century; part results from differentials already existing in earlier days. This conclusion is suggested first by the contrast between the range of rates of growth in per capita income and the range of present *cross-section* differences in per capita income. Thus, for purposes of illustration, let us assume that the per capita incomes of China and Sweden are currently in the ratio of 1 to 10. A hundred years ago, well before the industrialization of Sweden began, Swedish per capita income, which grew faster than that in almost any other Western country, was about a seventh of its present level. If the per capita income of China had been the same a hundred years ago as it is today, it follows that even in 1850, well before Sweden entered its period of industrialization, per capita income was at least 1.4 compared with 1 in China; and if there has been any increase in the per capita income of China, the ratio was higher. Some corroboration of this inference is provided by Colin Clark's crude figures. His estimates of international units per worker for the presently developed countries, at the time before their industrialization—Great Britain in 1800 or even 1688, the United States in 1830, Sweden in the 1860's, Germany in 1854, Belgium in 1854, France in the 1840's—are all above 300. The same measure is 138 for China in 1935; 230 to 250 for British India in the 1930's and the 1940's; 153 for Brazil in 1928, but rising rapidly to 297 in 1946; 100 for Japan in 1887, and only 190 as late as 1920.[16]

If per capita income in many parts of the world is today significantly lower than it was in the currently developed countries before their industrialization, some fascinating questions arise upon which our data shed no light at all. Before the nineteenth century, and perhaps not much before it, some presently underdeveloped countries, notably China and parts of India, were believed by Europeans to be more highly developed than Europe, and at that earlier time their per capita incomes may have been higher than the then current incomes of the presently developed countries. If so, per capita income in these original economic leaders, now underdeveloped countries, declined substantially or, what is more likely, per capita income of the European countries and their settlements overseas rose substantially *before* industrialization. These speculations point up the need for an analysis of the phases of growth in developed countries before their industrialization and for information on the effects for many underdeveloped countries of today of the heritage of past economic superiority in the way of a large population and a social mechanism which, however effective in the past, and perhaps *because* it was so effective, has become obsolete and now constitutes a serious obstacle to the adoption of modern economic and social technology.

Turning now to the pattern of change over time revealed by the long period estimates of national income (and population), mostly for the economically advanced countries proper, we observe in most a *retardation* in the rate of growth of population, total income, and per capita income. If we could follow the historical record back far enough, we should find in all countries a period of *acceleration* in the rate of growth: in the older and already settled countries, such as the United Kingdom, in population, total income, and income per capita, since the high rate of growth of population and income per capita are modern phenomena and in fact were initiated within the two centuries under review; in the younger and initially "empty" countries, such as the United States, Canada, and Australia, in per capita income but not neces-

[16] The figures are from Colin Clark, *Conditions of Economic Progress*, 2d ed. (London, 1951).

sarily in population and total income, since their rates of population growth may have been high from the very beginning. The picture thus suggested for countries that were well settled by 1750 is that of a long swing from low rates of growth in population, total income, and per capita income to much higher ones, then to declining rates. For countries that were relatively empty at the beginning of the period, we observe a truncated swing of rates of growth in population and perhaps, although less likely, in total income, with high rates at the very beginning, then lower ones; and a complete swing in the rates of growth of per capita income, with low rates of growth, succeeded by higher rates as industrialization begins, then followed by retardation.

The statistical records for delineating the periods of growth before industrialization are quite scanty. There is a suggestion (in the record of the United States before 1840, of Sweden before the 1880's, even of Great Britain before the 1820's) that the acceleration in the rate of growth of population is initiated before that in growth of per capita income: the swarming of population, to use the demographers' term, is such that despite the technological changes the rise in total income can barely keep up with or only slightly exceeds the increase in numbers. It is only with some lag, as the high rate of population growth becomes stabilized or begins to decline and as the process of industrialization gets into full swing, that a significant increase in the rate of growth of per capita income is attained. This early phase, rapid rates of growth of population and total income but not of per capita income, is in many ways crucial. To this phase belong the early shifts in structure of the economy, away from agriculture and toward industry. It is in this phase that rapid adjustments must be made to the changing conditions constituted by the differential impact on the several classes of population swarming and of the technological changes made possible by the same factor that made for larger numbers. It is, therefore, in this phase that many "secular" decisions are made that have a lasting effect on the rate, pattern, and character of economic growth unfolded through the later decades.

Although no statistical analysis of this phase is presently possible, historical records indicate an important aspect of economic growth. This early phase of transition to the modern industrial economy is characterized by great internal strains and conflicts, consequences of the shifts in relative economic position and power of various groups affected differently by the increases in numbers and by the opportunities of the new technology. These accelerations of the rate of growth of population and total income appear, when viewed statistically, as rather placid movements of steadily climbing lines. But under the surface there are major shifts among social groups, some of which will be touched upon in the next sections, and the very change in the rate of increase over time may inolve serious strains in the pre-existing framework of society geared to a much slower rate of growth. Historical records of this phase, which we cannot date exactly—about 1780 to 1820 in Great Britain, 1810 to 1860 in the United States, 1820 to 1870 in Germany—reveal the many conflicts and strains, even to the point of bringing on a civil war (as in this country). They also reveal the scores of basic secular decisions and adjustments that were made on land tenure, immigration and emigration, the disposition of land in the public domain, the treatment of industry with respect to subsidies and tariffs, the relation of government to the necessary internal improvements, and the like. These adjustments and decisions are clearly important in their effects on the economic growth that followed; the presence of these strains and conflicts, and their resolution, as the concomitant of the changes in rate of growth, must be kept in view. By doing so we can avoid treating the statistical trend lines as mysteriously inevitable paths. If conflicts and strains arose and secular decisions had to be made, the implication is that there were several possible decisions, and that the choice of one, explicable perhaps in terms of a variety of conditions, was not inevitable in the sense that feasible changes in such a decision could not have substantially modified the outcome.

This observation can be repeated about the deceleration phase in the growth of the over-all totals of population, income, and per capita income observed in many industrially advanced countries. A decline in the rate of growth is inevitable only as an abstraction, in the bromidic sense that nothing can grow forever, but forever is a long time and permits unretarded growth for thousands of years. If retardation is observed within decades, it can hardly be interpreted as inevitable; it must be due to specific historical circumstances. Because they were specific, arising out of particular constellations of historical factors, they left room for alternative decisions in the sense that at any given time a different combination of factors, either as to identity or weight, was possible. As later discussion suggests, one important factor in retardation within the historically observed period was the organization of the world into separate sovereign units and the recurring transformation of international competition into armed conflict. In this light, the slowly retarding trend lines of the statistical record are not inevitable in the sense that they will run their full course along set paths. There are serious breaks in many of the records—for Germany, Japan, Russia, and Austria, among others. Thus both internal and external strains and conflicts are an almost continuous accompaniment of the process of growth which, when viewed statistically, appears so consistent and steady for long periods. One of the most difficult and intriguing tasks of a theory of economic growth is to combine both the disruptive and the integrative, the qualitatively changing and the quantitatively steady, aspects of the process.

Shifts in Industrial Structure

The component structures of a nation's aggregate product or income that are ordinarily distinguished include: (1) the industrial sectors in which product originates; (2) the income streams—wages, salaries, entrepreneurial income, dividends, interest, and so forth—that flow to the several productive factors engaged (labor, property, enterprise); (3) the origin of income in economic entities with different forms of organization—individual firms, ordinary business corporations, public utility corporations, nonbusiness corporations, and governments; (4) the allocation of income payments among recipients grouped either by the size of income or according to institutionally distinguishable social groups; (5) the distribution of national income, viewed as congeries of final products, between flow into consumption and capital formation, with numerous categories within each of these two main components; (6) the distinction between products originating and retained at home and the inflows and outflows across the nation's boundaries. An adequate study of even the quantitative aspects of economic growth requires consideration of all these component structures for as many countries and for as long a period within the last two centuries as data permit. Lack of space and particularly scarcity of data prevent such full treatment. We limit our brief discussion to two main distributions: by industrial origin and between flow into consumption and capital formation.

Changes or difffferences in the industrial structure of economies can be studied through the distribution of the labor force, capital, and income originating. Of these it is the first for which the richest stock of data is available and the one for which conceptual difficulties are least formidable. Data on capital by industrial categories are quite scanty. Although information on the industrial distribution of national income is more plentiful, the derivation of totals in *constant* prices is beset with difficulties. The adjustment for price changes, when we try to estimate *net* income originating in the several industrial sectors, must take account either of their differing cost structures and differential changes in prices affecting the elements of cost payments to other industries and gross product, or of the different living conditions of people attached to the several industries and hence the different levels and trends in the purchasing power of the money incomes they receive. It is, therefore, most practicable to summarize shifts in industrial structure primarily in terms of changing distributions of the labor force, with only secondary reference to changes in the industrial distribution of national income.[17]

THE SHIFT AWAY FROM AGRICULTURE · Because the trends are similar and cross-section differences well established, the summary can be brief.[18] First, in the countries where per capita income grew significantly, the proportion of the labor force engaged in agriculture declined and that engaged in nonagricultural industries increased. The shifts have been quite marked. Thus in the United States the share of the labor force in agriculture was over 70 percent in 1820 and less than 20 percent in 1940. In Japan, this share was 72 percent in 1870 and less than 30 percent by the mid-1930's. Second, in comparing the industrial structure of countries at a recent date, we find a close negative association between per capita income and the share of the labor force in agriculture: the higher the former, the lower the latter, and vice versa. Thus, the share of the labor force in agriculture in India, China, Indonesia, and many of the poorer countries in Latin America is between 60 and 70 percent; that in countries with high income per capita, even

[17] We should note, however, some of the limitations of analysis based upon the labor force. These data reflect only part of the input, neglect quality differences among various groups, including those due to training, and do not ordinarily record changes in hours. But they are adequate for the broad picture sought here, and are particularly illuminating for the changes in the whole mode of life of the population associated with changing industrial structure.

[18] Underlying data are largely from Clark, *op. cit.*

those that are great exporters of agricultural products (Canada, Australia, New Zealand), is usually well below 30 percent. Third, since the share of the labor force in agriculture in the underdeveloped countries is so high today, it could not have been much higher in the past: if it is 70 percent now, its absolute decline over the past century could not have begun to approach the decline of 50 percentage points in the United States. It follows that there must have been an association between the moderate rise (if any) over the last century in per capita income of the presently underdeveloped countries and the moderate decline (if any) in the share of labor in agriculture. Fourth, product per worker in agriculture is generally lower than in all nonagricultural industries combined, and its rate of growth is not as high as that in many nonagricultural industries such as mining, manufacturing, transportation, and communication utilities. It follows that the share of agriculture in national income is generally lower than its share in the labor force, and that over the long run, its share in national income may have declined more than its share in the labor force. This inference, however, should be qualified because of difficulties involved in imputation of the net income of industries in constant prices, and because of questions relating to long-term trends in product per worker in most service industries.

For the more advanced countries, in which nonagricultural industries grew to dominate the labor force and the product, we should also note some significant trends in the distribution of the nonagricultural sectors proper. The shares of mining and manufacturing in the total labor force grew significantly, but the increases have ceased or slowed down during recent decades. The shares of the transportation and communication industries in the labor force also grew but became stable after World War I or even before; yet they never reached sizable proportions because of the extremely high capital intensity and product per worker and the remarkably high rate of growth in per worker product. The shares of trade and other service industries, a miscellaneous group including business, personal, professional, and government services, have grown steadily and have continued to grow in recent decades. The distribution in the United States in 1940 shows less than 20 percent of the labor force in agriculture; somewhat over 30 percent in mining, manufacturing, and construction, primarily in manufacturing; only 6 percent in transportation and communication; and about 43 percent in trade and other services. In general, trends in the nonagricultural sectors' shares in national income followed the trends in their shares in the labor force, except for the greater rise in productivity per worker in such technologically advanced sectors as mining, manufacturing, and the public utilities. It is, of course, in dealing with net product, in constant prices, originating in the service industries, that the conceptual difficulties in estimation are at their perplexing worst.

This capsule summary contains little that is unfamiliar. The shift away from agriculture is perhaps best known and has led to the widespread identification of modern economic growth with industrialization, by which is usually meant the growing absolute and relative volume of industry as contrasted with agriculture. The causes, implications, and corollaries of these shifts in industrial structure are also for the most part familiar. But we mention them briefly, with primary emphasis on the shift from the agricultural sector to the nonagricultural sectors and on the interrelations of the implications and corollaries of the shifts.

If in country A the share of agriculture in the labor force declines from 70 to 20 percent while per capita income increases significantly, and if, to simplify the argument, we assume a constant ratio of population to the labor force (say 2.5 to 1) and no international trade, the trend means that each group of 250 in total population was supplied at the end of the period by only 20 workers in agriculture instead of the original 70. How could such a change be attained? There are two possibilities: (1) Despite the increase in income or consumption per capita, population used a lower *absolute* per capita volume of products of agricultural labor. This may have been due to either (*a*) substitution or (*b*) absolute reduction in per capita use, without substitution. (2) The rate of increase in per worker productivity in agriculture may have been higher than the rate of expansion of per capita demand for agricultural products. With such a differential, the ratio of agricultural workers to total population would drop; under the assumption of a constant ratio of population to labor force, the ratio of agricultural workers to all workers would also decline. If we now assume that the country engages in international trade, we introduce a third implication: (3) It may have reduced the share of exports in the total product of agriculture or increased the share of imports in the total use of agricultural products.

Implication (1*b*) is unrealistic and can be rejected: countries with rising income and rising consumption per capita do not reduce per capita use of the aggregate product of agriculture. Implication (3), however relevant in dealing with the economic growth of any one country, is of limited usefulness on a world-wide scale. With no absolute reduction in world-wide per capita use of agricultural products and the prevalence of declines in the share of agriculture in the labor force, reduced exports or increased imports of agricultural products of country A only shift the question to countries B, C, D, and so forth. How can these countries adjust to decreased imports from or increased exports to country A, while their own per capita use of agricultural products does not decline and agriculture's share in labor does? This is not to deny that international division of labor in agriculture (and in other sectors) and shifts in it are not important in the study of economic growth. The only point here is that it cannot be used (without additional considerations concerning shifts of weights in many world-wide totals, which cannot be pursued here) to explain trends in the distribution of the labor force and product away from agriculture, observed in so many countries and not offset by opposite movements in any. Under these conditions, only implications (1a) and (2) are relevant.

Examining them against the historical background of an advanced country, we find that both explanations are important. The substitution for products of agricultural labor assumes two forms. First, direct replacement results from technological changes and changes in taste: when firewood, a farmer's product, is replaced by coal, a product of nonagricultural labor, the case is clear, as are the cases of cotton being replaced by nylon and some foodstuffs by vitamin pills. Second, there is substitution only in the sense of a shift in the *locus*, not necessarily the nature, of the service. When 70 percent of the labor force, and of the population, was attached to agriculture, it performed many services in addition to agricultural cultivation—baking, spinning, soapmaking, and building—both as a family unit and in cooperation with neighbors. Such services, even if rendered in this fashion, would be classified as the product of agricultural labor. In fact, most of them have now been commercialized, and before they were commercialized few were covered in our national income estimates. The point to be noted is that labor attached to agriculture turns out something in addition to agricultural products, and substitution for the latter is a shift of place, not of product.

But implication (2) is far more important: the combination of a high rate of growth of productivity per worker in agriculture with a lower rate of growth in the per capita use of agricultural products. The former is largely a result of major technological changes, based on growth of tested knowledge and made possible by a proper social adjustment. The latter is partly the result of substitution just noted, partly the result of the basic structure of human wants in which, even in the long run, the need for agricultural products is satiated sooner than the need for nonagricultural products; and partly the result of the changes in mode of life and character of economic and social organization that are corollaries of this shift away from agriculture—urbanization and a more elaborate economic and social structure.

It seems clear that the marked shifts in the structure of the labor force and national product away from agriculture imply not only an industrial revolution, in the sense of major technological changes that provide the basis for increasingly effective use of resources in the nonagricultural sectors, but also an agricultural revolution, in the sense of marked changes in the technology and form of organization of agriculture itself. True, during the period under discussion, thanks to the new revolutionary means of transportation and communication, the expansion of agricultural civilization to hitherto unused, relatively empty areas added to world agricultural production and to agricultural product per worker—an addition that might have occurred even without revolutionary changes in agricultural technology. But since the latter took place in some older countries even before extensive expansion of agriculture to new lands, and since agricultural product per worker in all countries that showed a rise in income per capita also displayed a marked upward trend, changes in agricultural technology and organization must have been heavily responsible for and permitted the shift of the labor force and income structure away from agriculture. The rather obvious fact that industrialization supplies a new technological base for *both* agriculture and industry is to be stressed, if only because some recent statistical manipulations of product per worker in agriculture and in other sectors suggest that economic growth is just a matter of easy transfer of labor from "backward" agriculture to "progressive" industry. At the cost of repeating the obvious, it must be stressed that a technological revolution in agriculture is an indispensable base of modern economic growth; that this means, particularly in the older countries, a major dislocation of people settled on the land for centuries; and that one of the crucial problems with respect to currently underdeveloped countries is how such a costly shift—costly in terms of equipment required and of the destruction of established patterns of life for large groups in the population—can be carried through without social and political deformations that may stunt or distort economic growth in the longer run that follows.

THE SHIFT TOWARD URBANIZATION · If the shift in industrial structure implies technological revolutions in both agriculture and industry, with whatever different costs they involve in the older and more settled countries compared with the younger and emptier countries, the corollaries of this shift must also be noted. A whole complex of changes is embraced under the term "urbanization," in which a large proportion of labor and population in nonagricultural pursuits results, for technical reasons, in the concentration of population in densely settled, relatively large aggregates with numerous consequences to the mode of life. The reason is largely the economy of scale in nonagricultural pursuits permitted by a technology that separates the productive process from land area, an economy that produces increasing optimum-scale units as the technical means of transportation, communication, and organization grow more effective. This economy of scale also means that *pari passu* with urbanization there is a marked change in the scale and nature of the managing unit, whether for organizing economic activity or for organizing social activity at large—from the individual firm to the corporation, from private enterprise to public organization—as the complexity of problems and their impact on society as a whole increase. The growth of the large corporation, public utilities, and government means in turn an increase in the weight of those areas in economic life in which free competition in the usual sense of the term must give way to complete or partial monopoly.

All these processes affect the grouping of population by social and economic status and transform the basic patterns of life. As already indicated, there are the effects on the patterns of consumption which go far toward explaining the rise of service industries that has continued relatively unabated through the recent decades. There are also the effects on population-growth patterns, since it is the urbanization of the population, the growth of the wage-earning and salaried groups and the decline in the relative weight of small individual, nonprofessional entrepreneurs, and the emphasis on individual attainment through long and intensive training that play so great a role in the decline in the birth rate.

Above all it is the interplay of the shifts in industrial structure, urbanization, the character of economic and social organization, consumption (and savings) patterns, and population increase which provides the key to an understanding of the process of economic growth. The emphasis is on the indissoluble tie-in among all of these which renders the sustained rise of population and per capita income more than a matter of a few more industrial plants or a few more railroad miles. The transformation of an underdeveloped into a developed country is not merely the mechanical addition of a stock of physical capital; it is a thoroughgoing revolution in the patterns of life and a cardinal change in the relative power and position of various groups in the population. With the old and persistent patterns in the older underdeveloped countries (which include the earlier stages in those now developed) representing equally close interrelations between population movements, industrial structure, the mode of life, the character of economic and social organization, and the like, the growth to higher levels of population and per capita income involves a revolutionary change in many aspects of life and must overcome the resistance of a whole complex of established interests and values.

Trends in Capital Formation

The accumulation of capital is ordinarily viewed as an important factor in economic growth. Indeed, one has only to look at the physical evidence in industrially advanced countries and recognize modern technology's needs for machinery and apparatus to house and channel its driving powers, to admit that without the heavy capital investment in buildings, roads, bridges, railways, power stations, machine tools, and blast furnaces, high levels of total and per capita product are unobtainable. Capital accumulation must, therefore, be examined and, if possible, its bearing upon economic growth specified.

The most effective statistical approach is by means of estimates of capital formation as one component in national product, either net or gross of current consumption of durable capital. The other component, as used here, is the flow of finished products to the individuals and households that constitute the nation's ultimate consumers. True, this concept of capital omits irreproducible natural resources, which may be a major factor affecting the *direction* of a country's economic growth. But every country has some nat-

ural resources, and one may argue that the natural-resource potential is a function of the changing stock of technological knowledge,
the very same force whose application calls for the accumulation
of reproducible capital. The factors that induce formation of reproducible capital adequate as a basis for economic growth are unlikely
to be inhibited by an absolute lack of natural resources.[19]

Capital formation as ordinarily measured includes net or gross
additions to the stock of construction (including residential and
related housing) and of producers' equipment and net additions
to nonhousehold inventories within a country. As a component of
total national product, it also includes net changes in claims against
foreign countries (excess of exports over imports of all goods and
net factor receipts). There is some question of the treatment of
consumers' durable commodities other than houses—furniture, pas-
senger cars, and so on—and of military construction and equipment.
By and large, the figures underlying the summary below omit
consumer durables and include military construction and equipment.

For countries for which long-term data are available (largely the
more developed countries, excluding the recently established authoritarian nations as well as most underdeveloped countries, for which
data are lacking), the statistical evidence may be summarized under
three broad heads.[20]

First, the proportion of gross capital formation to gross national

[19] This is an inadequate comment on a major problem. But the brief
discussion reflects a judgment that the supply of natural resources is a secondary factor in economic growth, in the sense that growth can be attained
despite poverty in resources (as in Japan and some smaller countries); that
in the underdeveloped countries even known natural resources are exploited
at a much lower rate than in the developed; and that many countries, with a
wealth of valuable natural resources, such as Brazil through much of the
nineteenth century and Venezuela today, are still underdeveloped. This position does not imply a denial that, once a combination of factors favorable to
growth exists, the availability or lack of certain natural resources would affect
the *direction* of growth, the distribution of its emphasis among various industrial sectors of the economy; nor that the dependence of modern technology
upon certain natural resources creates a drive, on the part of rapidly growing
large states, to acquire control over the supply of such resources, with effects
on external relations among units to be discussed below; nor that the availability of economically valuable natural resources is a factor, although not of
the first rank, in the constellation that affects economic growth, with consequences for the geography of the spread of the industrial system during the
nineteenth and twentieth centuries. But in this brief sketch, it seemed justifiable
to set this problem aside as less crucial than the others discussed.

[20] See the author's "International Differences in Capital Formation and
Financing," in Moses Abramovitz, ed., *Capital Formation and Economic Growth*
(Princeton, N.J.: Princeton University Press, 1956).

product ranges from over 10 to over 20 percent; that of net national capital formation to net national product, from about 5 to about 15 percent. The upper limits suggested are particularly firm in the sense that no higher shares are found for periods of two decades or more. Even in Japan, where the proportions have been particularly high within the period covered by available data, these limits have not been exceeded. This means that flow of goods into ultimate consumption has been by far the dominant proportion of current product: not much less than 80 percent of product gross of current consumption of durable capital and more than 85 percent of net national product.

Second, while estimates reaching back into the early phases of industrialization or before are scanty and their margins of error naturally wide, there is a suggestion of a phase in modern economic growth in which capital formation proportions were rising. One could argue with some conviction that they must have risen from preindustrial levels when per capita incomes were low and their rate of growth moderate. Indirect support for this contention lies in the fact that in many presently underdeveloped countries, gross capital formation is less than 20 percent of current gross national product, and net capital formation is well below 10 percent of national income. If the surmise is true, there is an acceleration phase in the rate of growth of the capital stock similar to the acceleration phase in the rate of growth of population, national income, and per capita income. The timing of this upward phase in the rate of growth of reproducible capital, for comparison with the timing of accelerations in the rates of growth of the other magnitudes, would be of particular interest. Unfortunately, the current data and analysis do not permit comparison.

Third, for the countries for which long records are available (and they are the ones with particularly rapid rises in per capita and total income), the increase in capital formation proportions, if observable, ceases well before the recent decades. In some countries even a long record shows no upward trend in these proportions and, in fact, shows a decline in the *net* capital formation share in national income. Thus in the United States, for which we have estimates back to 1870, the ratio of gross capital formation to gross national product has been, on the whole, stable, and that of net capital formation to national income has declined. This difference in trends is due to the increasing share of charges for capital consumption in gross national product, and the latter is due in part to a temporary rise in the ratio of the stock of capital to current product and in part to a shift in the composition of capital away from the longer-lived types (e.g., buildings) toward the shorter-lived (producers' equipment).

These observations have some bearing upon the ratio of the stock of capital to output, a ratio that has recently been widely used in economic analysis. If we deal with net output and with capital net of accumulated depreciation, the relation between the capital-product ratio and the current proportion of net capital formation to national income can be easily seen. If we assume that national income (in constant prices) grows 4 percent per year and that net capital formation is 12 percent of national income, then on the assumption of stable proportions over a long period, the ratio of accumulated capital stock to annual output will be 3 to 1. To put it differently, a persistent capital-output ratio of 3 to 1 and a growth of 4 percent per year in national income imply a net capital formation proportion of 12 percent.

The capital-product ratios for a few countries suggest several findings in addition to those mentioned above.[21]

First, the ratio of net capital stock to annual national income varies from about 3 to 1 to about 7 to 1. But it is not necessarily higher in the countries with high per capita income. In those countries which are among the younger and have grown most rapidly (United States, Canada, Australia) the ratio is about 3 to 1 or slightly higher. In Great Britain and France it was about 6 or 7 to 1 just before World War I; in Germany, 4.6 to 1; in the Netherlands about 5.0 to 1 (in 1939).

Second, the ratio rose in the two or three countries for which long records are available (United States, Great Britain, France). In the United States it rose from 2.8 to 1 in 1879 to almost 3.8 to 1 in 1919; in Great Britain from 4.6 to 1 in 1865 to about 6.2 to 1 in 1895. But the rise ceased well before the recent decades.

Third, since countries with lower per capita income can have higher capital-output ratios than those with higher per capita income, the ratio of even reproducible capital to output in some underdeveloped countries may well be high. Even if a country's total product grows only 0.5 percent per year, a sustained net capital formation proportion of 3 percent of current product would,

---

[21] Underlying data except for the United States are from Clark, *op. cit.*; those for the United States are from Simon Kuznets, ed., *Income and Wealth*, Series II (Cambridge, England, 1952).

in the long run, yield a capital-output ratio of 6 to 1. Paradoxically, the slowly growing, low-income countries may be more capital "intensive" than the more advanced, rapidly developing ones, if we measure intensity by the magnitude of capital supply per unit of final output.

Some intriguing aspects of the evidence just summarized are of bearing upon the role of capital accumulation in economic growth. The first is suggested by the relatively low capital formation proportions even in the most advanced countries: on a gross basis, the upper limit seems to be 20 to 25 percent. It must be remembered that capital formation includes residential and related housing, which may account for three to four tenths of the total, and net changes in inventories, which are hardly a productive tool that embodies the benefits of technical progress. If capital formation is limited to the strictly productive tools that embody modern technology, that is, to industrial plant and equipment, the proportion of annual additions in national product may be no more than 5 to 7 percent; and the capital-product ratio with such capital as the numerator may be little higher than 1.

True, capital formation estimates are subject to a downward bias even in terms of the concept used here. In the early decades of a growing economy, considerable additions to capital stock may be provided by labor within the enterprise (e.g., the clearing of land by farmers) which escape measurement; in later decades, outlays on research and market development are treated as current expenses and do not enter the capital formation totals. A more important source of understatement is the difficulty of allowing for quality changes in passing from outlays in current prices to those in constant prices. Since quality changes are most marked in capital goods embodying the fruit of technical progress, the understatement is particularly important in that category of capital. But with all these qualifications, the proportion of *resources* devoted to increasing the capital stock that forms the material basis of the highly productive economic civilization of advanced countries is still surprisingly low.

Two answers to this puzzle may be suggested. First, technical progress consists not only of inventions and innovations that require heavy capital investments but also of a stream of relatively cheap changes and improvements whose cumulative effect is a drastic reduction in input of resources accompanied by increases in output. The major capital stock of an industrially advanced nation is not its physical equipment; it is the body of knowledge amassed from tested findings of empirical science and the capacity and training of its population to use this knowledge effectively. One can easily envisage a situation in which technological progress permits output to increase at a high rate without *any* additions to the stock of capital goods.

Second, if technological changes permit huge additions to output with only minor additions to reproducible physical capital, it may be that the essential investments are largely in human beings, the active agents in society, not in sticks, stones, and metal. Even if we disregard the essential social inventions and consider only the material flows, the concept of capital used above is probably much too narrow for an analysis of economic growth. If by capital formation we mean the use of any current resources that adds to future output, many categories now treated under flow of goods to ultimate consumers should be included under capital. Certainly significant fractions of outlays on education and training, travel and recreation, improvement of health, and even on living, insofar as they contribute to the greater productivity of the population, are among these categories. Perhaps this new dividing line cannot be drawn with assurance, but it does seem that if capital is what capital does—contributes to increased productivity—much of what is now classified under consumer outlay in advanced economic societies rightfully belongs under capital. With this change in classification, the proportion of capital formation in national income would be much larger than it is now in the developed countries, but *not* in underdeveloped societies. And instead of a difference in net capital formation proportions between 10 percent in advanced and perhaps 3 percent in underdeveloped countries, the true difference may well be between 30 percent or more and 3 percent.

That the stock and formation of physical capital has meaning only within the full context of economic life and that much of high level ultimate consumption functions similarly to capital formation makes it easier to understand other statistical findings. These findings indicate that some countries with a higher per capita income have lower or about the same capital formation proportions as others with lower per capita income; thus from the 1870's to World War I, net capital formation proportions in the United States were not significantly higher than those in Great Britain, although through much of the period the per capita income of the former was significantly above that of the latter. Even more puzzling is the finding that in all countries for which we have long records, capital formation proportions either do not rise at all or cease to rise after a while, although the upward trend in per capita income continues. These results are the direct opposite of those found in all cross-section analyses within a country at any given time: in such comparisons we invariably find that higher incomes per capita are associated with higher savings proportions.

As already indicated, technological change may make it possible to produce much greater volumes of final product with the same or lesser volumes of *all* resource input or may minimize the need for large stocks of physical capital by substituting training and education of human beings and improvement in the whole fabric of social organization for more machines. In that sense, the high consumption proportions in intercountry comparisons, and their maintenance or rise in long-term growth, may be associated with high or rising shares of categories within consumer outlay that are functionally similar to capital formation. High and rising consumption per capita is usually associated with high and rising proportions of outlay devoted to education and training, improve ment in health, and all types of goods beyond basic necessities that contribute to the skill, morale, and efficiency of the population. Finally, in addition to these permissive conditions on the techno- logical side that do not compel high capital formation proportions, there are more directly limiting factors on the savings side. On a country-wide scale, capital formation is identical, *ex post facto*, with savings, and limitations of the former proportion may, in the final analysis, be reducible to limitations of the savings proportion, in other words, to the spending habits of individuals who, in the society under discussion, are the main source of country-wide savings. It can be shown that under conditions that stimulate a continuous rise in the level of living, the savings proportions of the masses of income recipients are severely limited if they are calculated rationally to provide for old age and contingencies; and that the contribution to savings of the groups at the top of the income pyramid, the "automatic" savers, is limited by their small numbers and by their share in country-wide income. The savings proportions may be more limited in the younger and rapidly growing societies than in the older societies since the size distribution of income is less unequal in the former. (Compare the United States, Canada, and Australia with Great Britain or France between the 1870's and World War I.) In long-term changes, the savings proportions may be stable or may even decline slightly because the pressure toward higher levels of living keeps pace with growth of total income per capita; because the shift in class structure may be from those with higher saving propensities (farmers and small individual entrepreneurs) to those with lower (urban wage-earners and salaried workers); because a rise in the share of the top income groups is prevented by high mobility, today's captains of industry giving place to different captains of industry tomorrow; and because in recent decades the size distribution of income has definitely changed toward lesser inequality.[22]

The technicalities of the interplay between the factors determining the country-wide savings proportions and the use of these savings in various types of capital formation can hardly be discussed here. But one aspect should be noted because it bears closely upon the relation of capital formation to economic growth. If savings are limited by the responses of human beings, the effectiveness of capital formation permitted by such savings depends at least in part upon the way these savings are channeled into capital investment. One earmark of an advanced economic society is the variety of organizational forms of capital users and the variety of financial institutions which assemble and channel the savings. This is but another aspect of the thesis already urged that the effectiveness of a given stock of resources, embodied in physical capital, in increasing total output is partly a matter of its uses in combination with other resources and partly a matter of availability of such other resources and of the organizational arrangements for bringing them together. The new illustration reveals that the very choice of particular forms of physical capital, of quality rather than quantity of capital formation, depends upon the existence of institutions that can assure the most effective flow of savings so that they will reach those foci in

[22] This is a highly condensed summary of various hypotheses relevant to a complex and still inadequately explored aspect of economic growth of industrially advanced countries. Further discussion is contained in two papers: "Proportion of Capital Formation to National Product," *Proceedings of the American Economic Association* (May 1952), pp. 507–526, and "International Differences in Capital Formation and Financing," *Capital Formation and Economic Growth.*

Furthermore, as Moses Abramovitz has indicated, the point concerning the productivity-raising function of much of modern consumption expenditures implies that they are also substitutes for savings in the narrower sense of the term. Outlays on education and related activities are in a way provision for a future income and reduce the pressure for savings in the form of property claims; and of course they reduce the true level of disposable income and so cut into the amounts available for saving as ordinarily defined.

the productive economy in which additions to capital stock will yield the greatest contribution to long-term growth. Without such an organization some part of savings may be stagnant and lead to no capital formation and hence to no countrywide savings; or some may be invested in ways that are far from optimal for economic growth.

In making these comments one does not deny the importance of physical capital accumulation as a prerequisite of economic growth. A certain minimum stock is indispensable to the productive operations that form the content of advanced economic performance: one cannot conjure up railroad services without a roadbed and rolling stock. But this minimum stock is a *necessary*, not a *sufficient*, condition; with just a roadbed and rolling stock one gets no transportation services, and even with the addition of labor and fuel, there is a world of difference between efficient and inefficient performance. Furthermore, beyond this indispensable minimum, physical capital is not even a necessary prerequisite. Far more important in retrospect are the economic and social characteristics that reside in the capacities and skills of an economy's population, that determine the efficiency of the institutions which direct the use of accumulated physical capital, and that guide the current product into the proper channels of consumption and capital investment. These factors make the problem of economic growth so much more difficult than it would be if the stock of physical capital were the one really strategic factor in the process. If the latter were the case, given the ability of the more advanced countries to produce large stocks of capital equipment, the attainments of economic growth would have been far more widespread than they are.

Trends in International Flows

Relations among countries, relevant to problems of economic growth, are reflected in material flows: either peacetime, "normal" flows of population, goods, and capital funds across the boundaries or wartime flows, implied in cold war or hot conflict. There is also the spread of knowledge, ideas, tastes, and preconceptions that is in some ways even more important. These reveal in part the existence of transnational resources, of which the findings of empirical science and the stock of social inventions are the most conspicuous examples, and in part the community of human nature, which expresses itself in the tendency of discrete human societies organized in sovereign states to imitate, attract, or repel each other.

Our findings, which are largely statistical, relate to material flows. Before considering them, one should note that the volume of peacetime flows, at least, is partly a function of the way the world is divided into separate jurisdictions among which *external* relations can arise. If the world were one unit, there would be no external flows unless connections were established with other planets and their inhabitants (or with migrants to them, founding sovereign communities). By analogy, if there were only two or three sovereign states, the volume and character of these external flows would also be different. Furthermore, the different sizes of these units, the character of their boundaries, and a host of other geographic factors are all significant for both the economic development of the states and for the flows among them.

In its current (early 1950's) population estimates the U.N. distinguishes 85 independent states. For the sake of simplicity, we disregard the numerous dependencies here; their population is only 0.3 billion of total world population of 2.4 billion, and the economic independence of a political dependency is questionable. Four sovereign states—China and India, the two great underdeveloped countries, the USSR, which is just going through its phase of industrialization, and the United States, the economic leader—account for well over half of the 2.1 billion people living in the 85 independent units. At the other extreme, 39 states, each with a population of less than 5 million, account for less than 70 million, and 31 more states, each with a population between 5 and 20 million, account for less than 350 million. Thus by far the great majority of states, 70 out of 85, account for barely over 20 percent of the total population of independent states.

This somewhat bizarre distribution raises the question whether problems and study of economic growth for these small units, the majority of those in the world, are similar to those for the few large states with populations of 100 million or more today (and whose relative position on the population scale was the same a century ago). True, some characteristics of economic growth are universal. But surely the tasks of organization and integration, sharply posed by the disruptive character, at least in the older countries, of some of the processes involved in modern economic growth, are quite different in a huge country like the USSR or India from those in a small country like Norway or Sweden today, or in Uruguay or Venezuela in the future. The minimum or optimum scale of some modern industries is also of relevance. Finally it is clear that the volume of external flows is affected by the distribution among small and large states, for the proportion of foreign trade and often that of capital flows tend to be inversely related to the size of the country, measured by population or total income.

It would require a separate study to establish whether the current state distribution is very different from that of one or two centuries ago, and particularly whether any trend can be discerned in the structure of states. General impressions are not a safe guide, because there have been movements in opposite directions. Within the two centuries under view there were unification and reduction in number in some states, of which Germany and Italy are conspicuous examples. But there were also many separations and breakdowns: emergence into independence of the numerous sovereign states in the Western Hemisphere, Asia, Africa, and Oceania; dissolution of multinational monarchies of the Austro-Hungarian and Turkish types; and a peaceful separation of closely related but distinct national groups, exemplified by Norway and Sweden or Holland and Belgium. The general impression is that the number of sovereign units is increasing, if one disregards such statistical oddities as the princely states in India or the jurisdictions in early nineteenth-century Germany and Italy (some of which, however, did not bar close economic relations and coherence).

Although this suggestion of an increase in the number of sovereign entities is subject to further statistico-geographical tests, the trend over the last two centuries toward intensification of national organization and feelings has become quite evident. Recent historical research has properly emphasized this trend, to the point of concluding that the cult of nationalism has become the secular religion of modern times, a religion that has rapidly spread from its origin in Western Europe to much of the rest of the world. The relevance of this trend to economic growth and to international relations is of particular interest here. We can only note here the whole complex of influences on economic growth of strong national governments, through the enlargement of the internal trading area, the promotion of the security of economic activity, and its assistance to groups that constitute the spearhead of economic advance, as well as the reciprocal influence of technological progress and of a rise in economic productivity on the effective powers of central governments. But one may stress that intensification of nationalism is both the result of pressures generated by economic growth and a tool for overcoming them. For if modern economic growth, like any major change in the social order, requires some groups to make sacrifices and some to face risks, if it requires the dissolution of established positions and values in older countries and independent action in younger countries, there will be a natural tendency to strengthen the integrative ties of nationalism, either in the struggle for political independence or in the attempt to persuade the population to accept the sacrifices and dislocation that seem necessary to achieve the goals of economic growth. This does not mean that as a result of some deliberate calculation there has been a conscious plan to intensify national loyalties for the expressed purpose of inducing people to bear the burdens of economic growth. Yet it is hardly an accident that the first carriers of nationalism have also been among the leaders in the economic growth of their nations; the nationalist creed was adopted by the industrial entrepreneurial classes of the European countries and of some colonies in the late eighteenth and through most of the nineteenth century. Nor is it an accident that in recent decades, the strenuous attempts by authoritarian states to foster nationalist feelings by cultivating the myth of an ever vigilant and powerful enemy accompanied the call for sacrifices at home that were considered necessary to the effort to force the pace of economic growth. Finally, given this interrelation between economic growth and the intensification of the cult of supremacy of the nation (sometimes passing over into the ideal of the monolithic state), the consequences for peaceful and, even more, for warlike external relations are obvious.

It is against this background of the increasing political division of the world that the trends in external relations should be considered. For the peacetime flows, satisfactory data exist as far back as the mid-nineteenth century. Although it is difficult to summarize the evidence without oversimplification, the trends are so conspicuous that the danger of being misled is minimized.

MIGRATION · In the movement of men we are concerned exclusively with emigration and immigration. Tourist movements are included under flow of goods; and temporary border crossings by workers are not too important for economic growth, nor can they be measured reliably over long periods. As for international migration for permanent residence, the nineteenth century saw an increasing volume of *voluntary* movement of people to foreign countries that reached its climax in the two decades preceding World War I and grew to magnitudes, both absolute and relative, hardly to be found in any *free* migrations of earlier times. Intercontinental migrations estimated since the late 1840's were at an *annual* level of over a quarter of a million in 1846–1850 and rose to a peak of about 1.5 million per year in 1906–1915.[23] The addition of intracontinental migration would raise the annual volume of international migration in the decade before World War I to close to 2 million. If total migration was about 0.3 million in the 1840's and 2 million in 1906–1915, it grew more rapidly than total world population, which increased from about 1.1 billion in the mid-nineteenth century to about 1.7 billion in the first decade of the twentieth century. Although annual international migration was not much more than 0.1 percent of the total population, the cumulation of migration over a decade raises this to 1 percent and in evaluating such figures we must recognize the importance of free migration to marginal groups in the populations, most of the latter, for various reasons, being firmly attached to their countries of residence.

The character and function of this migration become clear as we examine the countries of origin and destination. The preponderant portion of intercontinental migration, and even of total migration, was from the older countries of Europe to the younger and emptier countries, particularly the United States. The record for this country reveals that while in the short run of business cycles, migration flows may have been more responsive to the pull of better conditions in the United States than to the push of transiently worse conditions at the source, in the longer run the push has been more important. The national origins of the European flow into the United States, in the succession from the British, to the German, to the Scandinavian, and then to the South and Southwestern European reveal the progressive impact of the dislocation in Europe produced by changes in agriculture and by industrialization (the only major interruption in the sequence was due to the collapse of the Irish economy in the famine of 1842). This largely European migration seemed to have served not only to man the economies of North America as well as some of those of Latin America and the European outposts in Oceania and Africa, but also to provide an escape valve during some critical phases in the modern economic growth of several older European countries. By contrast there was

[23] The underlying data are from Walter F. Willcox, *International Migrations* (New York: National Bureau of Economic Research, 1929), Vol. I, and Woytinsky, *op. cit.*

little international migration of the populations of Asia, when considered in relation to their huge size or even absolutely. And when dislocating impacts of the transition phases to the modern economy did reach some of them, as in Japan, legal barriers prevented large scale emigration to areas with higher living standards and greater economic opportunities.

The abrupt reduction and then almost complete cessation of international migration during and after World War I are fairly well known. Willcox's estimates show a drop in the volume of intercontinental migration to 0.8 million for the rather favorable period of 1921–1924. The tightening of restrictions during the depression decade of the 1930's resulted in a net migration loss in the United States. In 1949, to take a recent year, international migration was about three quarters of a million, abnormally high since it included a flow of over 200,000 Jews into Israel. The reduction of international migration to a trickle, and its shift from a relatively free to a highly restricted process after World War I, is but one manifestation of a violent break in the trends of international relations. Similar changes will be found in flows of goods and of capital funds.

COMMODITY FLOWS · In considering the trends in the flow of goods, our attention will be centered on commodities, since data on services (earnings in international activities of merchant marine, insurance companies, financial institutions, and tourists) are scanty. However, foreign commodity trade is by far the dominant component.

Taking a cross-section view for 1938, for example, we find that the ratio of commodity imports or exports to the available relevant country-wide totals (national income plus imports) varies from a low of less than 1 percent for the USSR, to about 5 percent for a large country like the United States, to as much as 30 percent for countries like Norway and New Zealand.[24] The ratio is biased for several reasons: it is too low because the numerator excludes international flows of services; it is too high because the denominator should be *gross* national product (not national income) plus imports; but most important, it is too low because it should be related not to total national product plus imports, but only to that part

---

[24] Underlying data for income are from U.S. Department of State, *Point Four*, Publication 3719 (January 1950); and for imports and exports are from the League of Nations, *Network of World Trade* (Geneva, 1942).

which can flow across boundaries. Neither the labor of construction workers nor the labor of physicians and others serving the resident population of a country can be exported or imported; and there are other similar goods. The proportion of such goods to total output is sizable, so that a ratio of commodity exports or imports to national product of 20 percent or more is likely to represent a country's close involvement in and dependence upon the network of international trade. It is primarily the smaller countries that are so involved. The correlation between the export-import ratio to national product and the size of the country, measured either by population or by national income, is negative: for 53 countries in 1938 the coefficient of rank correlation is between -0.4 and -0.5.

If it could be calculated, the world-wide ratio of commodity foreign trade to total output would be dominated by the low rates for the few larger countries, and it would therefore be highly untypical in the sense that it would combine these with the high ratios for a multitude of small countries. But it seems likely that through most of the nineteenth century, certainly since the second quarter and up to World War I, the volume of foreign commodity trade (and probably of services also) grew more rapidly than the volume of world output; and therefore an over-all ratio of the volume of foreign trade to unduplicated world output would have shown a significant rise. The quantum of world commodity trade tripled between 1850 and 1880, and then tripled again between 1880 and 1913, thus rising to nine times its original level.[25] During this period, world population increased only about 60 percent, so that the ratio of world commodity trade to population must have risen from 1 to about 5.5. Per capita income rose only in the most advanced countries. On the generous assumption that world per capita income doubled over the period, the ratio of world commodity trade to total output would have almost tripled from 1850 to 1913, and the increase was probably greater than that.

This rise in the ratio of the volume of foreign trade to world output before World War I did not necessarily result from the rise in the ratio in all or even in most countries. The records indicate that in a country already in the network of foreign trade and entering the phase of rapid growth of population and of industri-

[25] Underlying data are from Loreto M. Dominguez, *International Trade, Industrialization and Economic Growth* (Washington, D.C.: Pan American Union, 1953), mimeographed.

alization (with consequent large rises in total and per capita income), the ratio does not necessarily rise. In the United States, for example, it has in fact drifted downward slightly but perceptibly since 1870. The movement of the world-wide ratio was very likely the result of the extension of the orbit of world trade to countries that had not participated previously; and this in turn resulted from improvements in transportation and communication facilities. The *absolute* volume of flows of goods across boundaries increases with a country's economic growth and industrialization, barring the drastic changes in policy involved in an Iron Curtain. But it may well be that in the process of growth, the rising proportion of goods that cannot enter into international flows, and the effects of shifts of activity away from the country's boundaries may offset the effects of improved transportation and communication and result in a downward rather than upward trend in the ratio of international flows of goods to national output.

The implication of the consideration just advanced is that even if there had not been any violent disturbances in international relations, the marked rise in the ratio of world foreign trade to world total output might not have continued, but the retardation in this rise, and the possible decline, would have been gradual over many decades. What in fact happened is that the rate of growth in the absolute volume of foreign trade dropped abruptly beginning with World War I, and the ratio to world population and output must have declined. In 1913, the index of foreign trade was close to 300 (with 1880 as base year), and by 1947–1951 it was close to 400. Thus from 1913 to 1947–1951, a period of three and a half decades, world trade increased about a third, whereas in the three decades before World War I it tripled. Since World War I, world population has grown 40 percent, and world per capita income has also probably grown somewhat. Therefore the ratio of world trade to world production has probably declined significantly since 1913–1914.

CAPITAL MOVEMENTS · External flows of capital funds (foreign capital investments, short- and long-term) are largely a function of the international flows of goods: a country accumulates credits either by exporting more than it imports or by leaving earnings of existing investments abroad. It is, therefore, not surprising to find parallelism in the trends in international capital flows and in the flows of goods. The major difference is in level: capital funds are *net* balances resulting from *gross* flows of goods across boundaries and the relative proportions of the former in national product (or wealth) are much lower than those of the latter.

The ratios of capital imports or exports to domestic capital formation were, in some cases, sizable.[26] In the United Kingdom the share of net capital exports in net domestic capital formation for the period from 1870 to World War I ranged from one third to nine tenths, and in gross domestic capital formation, from one fifth to two thirds. In France, the other major creditor country of the nineteenth and early twentieth centuries, the share of capital exports in domestic net savings ranged from one third to four tenths. In some debtor countries (Sweden, Canada, Denmark) capital imports accounted for substantial shares of domestic capital formation, but this was not true of a large country like the United States nor, as far as the records indicate, of Japan. Since capital formation is a relatively limited share of national product, the proportions of capital flows to the latter are quite low. About the highest ratios shown are 6 to 7 percent for capital exports in the United Kingdom in the decade before World War I, and over 9 percent for capital imports in Canada in 1901–1910. But most shares in national income or gross national product are well below 5 percent.

From 1870 to 1914, international capital flows were at their highest, and international indebtedness in 1914 was the result of capital imports and exports during a period that, historically speaking, was most favorable to international movements. At the end of that period total international debt (short- and long-term, adding only net credits for creditor countries) was somewhat short of $50 billion. Whether this is a large or small amount depends upon the base with which it is compared. In 1912 the value of total reproducible capital of the United States alone was $94 billion, and the rate at which foreign capital was being loaned from 1870 to 1914 was clearly a small fraction of world capital formation, and even less of total output. There were just a few creditor countries—the United Kingdom, France, the Netherlands (to a smaller relative extent), Germany, and a few smaller countries—and their number and economic magnitude were limited vis-à-vis the potential debtor countries. Furthermore, their capital exports were kept down, partly

[26] Underlying data are from the author's "International Differences in Capital Formation and Financing," and from United Nations, *International Capital Movements During the Inter-war Period* (New York, 1949).

by the limitations on their *total* savings and partly by demands for the latter within the country.

A goodly share of the total capital exports was channeled into destinations justified by political rather than economic considerations. Of the total foreign investments of Great Britain, almost half were within the empire; of French foreign investments, close to half were in Russia, Turkey, the Balkan states, Austria-Hungary, and her colonies; and of Germany's investments, about one third went to Austria-Hungary, Turkey, Russia, and the Balkan states. Although in some cases economic and political considerations may have coincided, and in others the line of distinction cannot be drawn sharply, a sizable proportion of foreign capital investments was probably motivated by political considerations. Hence the amount available for countries in which conditions were conducive to economic growth was smaller than the over-all amount.

Before 1914, the trends in the proportional importance of capital exports and imports seem clear. In the two major creditor countries, the United Kingdom and France, the share of capital exports rose to a peak in the two decades just before World War I. In the debtor countries, capital imports tended to become less important as the country grew (Sweden, Canada, the United States, and Australia) and there were definite indications of a coming reversal to creditor position. The upward trends in the outflow proportions from the creditor countries are not inconsistent with the downward trends in the inflow proportions in each debtor country for which a long record is available: the total incomes of the latter were growing at a significantly higher rate than those of the former, and the number of debtor countries was increasing.

World War I had particularly marked effects on three major creditor countries, the United Kingdom, France, and Germany, and the whole network of foreign investments was drastically transformed by rapid drafts upon balances, cancellations, war debts, reparation obligations, and other financial claims. Although it is difficult to summarize post–World War I developments, several aspects seem clear. First, the disturbance of international conditions meant a sharp reduction in the response of capital funds to economic needs. Second, the isolation after World War I of a sizable sector of the world community in the USSR and the shift in the role of the United States to that of main creditor, with its lesser dependence upon and involvement in the network of world commerce and international division of labor, meant radical changes that were adverse to sustained growth of international trade and foreign investments. Third, no matter where the line is drawn between economic and political demands for the flow of funds, the relative importance of political demands has definitely increased since 1914, and the total volume of economic flows of capital across the boundaries has probably failed to keep pace with the growth of world population or output since 1914.

Aggression and Warfare

The abrupt reversal since 1914 of trends in world migration, trade, and capital flows, associated with the international dislocations of which the two world wars were the culminating points, brings to the fore the role of armed conflicts in the economic growth of nations. We have already suggested a relation between the intensification of national organization and feelings, on the one hand, and the pressures and strains of economic growth, on the other, and thus a relation between economic growth and the divisive tendencies that provide a favorable climate for war. But regardless of this and other possible relations, the quantitative importance of such conflicts prevents us from putting them into the pound of *ceteris paribus* or of exogenous factors, and any discussion of economic growth that disregards them is unrealistic. Major wars and their aftermaths have been with us since 1914, and even if we view the period from the Napoleonic Wars to 1914 as an interregnum of peace, and disregard the rather sizable conflicts that punctuated it—the Crimean War, the Franco-Prussian War, our Civil War, the Boer War, and the several Balkan conflicts—a large proportion of the two centuries since 1750 was dominated by wars that affected many members of the advanced economic community of the world. And even in the "peaceful" decades many warlike elements operate in the external relations among nations. Any covert or overt threat of the use of a nation's force in external relations is a form of attack, aggressive or defensive, and armed conflict is only the culmination. Such elements of aggression were widespread throughout the two centuries under review, as evidenced not only by the colonial policies of the major countries but also by sharp breaks and clashes of policies among the European states (and their descendants) themselves. The reversal spoken of above is not so abrupt after all; there were similar strains earlier in the political distortions of capital and of trade flows and in emigration and immigration policies.

It is impossible to summarize here the long-term trends in the use of aggression in international relations; whole libraries have been written on the subject, and it does not lend itself to condensation in the form of statistical totals or unequivocal qualitative statements. Perhaps a summary is not even necessary, since only the broadest outline is needed, and the reader is familiar with the historical record of the major European communities and their offshoots in the New World, in their relations among themselves and with other nations. Instead of attempting a summary I shall consider three questions: What is the association between economic growth and the tendency of a nation to introduce aggressive elements into its relations with the rest of the world? What factors make it likely, if not inevitable, that elements of aggression culminate in wars of major proportions? What are the effects of such wars on the economic growth of the nations engaged in them and of those that are neutral?

AGGRESSION AND GROWTH · Rapid economic growth of a country, once it is of a certain size, seems to be associated with extensive expansion (which often means aggression) or with the exertion of pressure on other reluctant nations to accept changes desirable to it. Great Britain, the rapidly growing economic leader in the late eighteenth and through most of the nineteenth century, thus extended its power and enforced a pax Britannica through much of the world. The United States extended its territory by purchase or by minor wars in the nineteenth century, opened up Japan by the Perry mission, and acquired control over the Philippines. Japan, once opened up, displayed aggressive tendencies through much of its modern history. Germany used wars as stepping stones to further expansion. This association does not mean that aggressive elements exist only in external relations of sizable countries experiencing rapid economic growth; they easily arise out of other conditions. But there do seem to be some almost compulsive factors in a rapidly growing country, provided it is of some minimum size, to display aggressive elements in its external relations with others.

There are cases that seem almost opposite: a retardation in economic and social growth, the decay of once powerful or leading societies, that tends to give rise to aggression because of the power vacuum created. Through much of the nineteenth and early twentieth centuries, the Turkish Empire, the "sick man of Europe," was a chronic source of quarrels, intrigues, and aggressive actions on the part of its would-be heirs among the European powers. And clearly, an indispensable condition for the imperialist policy of economically advanced countries is the "backwardness" of the to-be-dominated societies, their different social structures, which, from the point of view of the aggressive powers, must be modified to favor the proper level of economic intercourse.

In short, large disparities in economic and social conditions among nations that are within reach of each other are often associated with elements of domination by the economically advanced units over the others. Shifts in these disparities, because of rapid growth of new units or because of relatively rapid decay of others, often produce elements of aggression by which the new leaders attempt to claim the perquisites of economic power, or the old and surviving leaders attempt to deal with the new weakness that may have arisen.

A multitude of factors produce the association just indicated, but we are interested primarily in those involved in the process of economic growth. They can be seen most clearly in cases of rapid economic rise. There is first the purely permissive element; aggression means the threat of force, and the latter is largely a matter of the ability to transport power to the area threatened. Rapid economic growth often means rapid increase in this power disposable outside the country, a result both of accumulation of resources within the country and of concurrent changes in means of transportation and communication. But if aggression becomes possible, it does not therefore become necessary; and it is the compelling factors that are crucial. Here we must look for elements of attraction in the use of aggression. The basic one is, of course, that extension of the area over which economic resources of a given country can be used, in proper combination with outside resources, natural or other, is likely to result in a greater per unit product and reduce the risks involved in economic growth.[27] Economic growth is a risky process; for the individual firm it may mean commitments difficult to achieve and for a country it may involve specialization and the need for resources not available within its own boundaries. The leaders of a rapidly growing country may try to minimize such risks by using the power of the state to

[27] See the emphasis on the economic value of sovereignty in R. G. Hawtrey, *Economic Aspects of Sovereignty* (London, 1930). The discussion here uses several of Hawtrey's ideas.

assure access either to raw materials or to markets outside its boundaries.

Two corollaries deserve emphasis. Rapid economic growth usually means a more intensive international division of labor; the leader countries obtain raw materials from areas where natural conditions favor their production and give in exchange industrial products. Such intensification of international trade and capital flows, which is possible only with a higher level of economic performance in leader countries, may require that countries formerly outside the orbit of international trade and investment adopt arrangements that would make more intensive connections with the rest of the world feasible. Nations could "live at home," but only by sacrificing the advantages of close economic intercourse, advantages for both advanced and underdeveloped countries. Since such advantages are greatly enhanced by a given nation's rapid economic growth, we can say that extension into "empty" contiguous territory or the imposition of open-door arrangements upon a "backward" country is a positive function of the economic level. We thus have the natural sequence of attempts to impose rules of economic behavior upon countries that are reluctant to enter the orbit of world foreign trade, from protection of the traders of the advanced countries and the foreign planters of raw materials, to concessions for building railroads to transport the raw materials, to pressures for political changes to assure the safety of the long-term foreign investments represented by railroads, and so on.

Pari passu with this real increase in the advantages of a larger base (either to rule over or to trade with) that is the usual consequence of a country's rapid economic growth, there is the emergence of a "theory" that may easily dominate the views of the country and its leaders. Rapid growth is evidence of success which lends assurance to the country and its leaders that their economic and social practices have proved right, that their views on organizing society for economic functions have met the test of success, and that if adopted in other countries, they would be equally successful. Further, this success persuades them that they have a responsibility to widen the scope of application of this successful type of economic organization, to urge adoption of some of its basic features by those countries that have not been successful and for their eventual benefit. There is a strong feeling of economic and social superiority in the doctrine of the white man's burden and in Point Four activities, as well as an element of the obligation of the successful to the unsuccessful. Such a point of view, if held with sufficient intensity, may easily lead to aggressive action, despite the best of intentions.

All this need not add to a compelling necessity of rapidly growing nations to extend the base of their operations by the threat of force. But the pressures toward such action, combined with the very process of rapid economic growth both in the way of increase of prospective real advantages and the widely held theory of benefits to all from the spread of the successful form of organization, are strong indeed. If in addition such aggression is viewed in the historical context as a correction of past wrong (because non-beneficial) aggressions, that is, as "liberation"; or if it is viewed as preclusive in that if it is not committed by one country, it will be undertaken (presumably in much worse form) by others, the pressures become all the greater. Finally, as already suggested, rapid economic growth may often be the outcome of internal struggles over the problem of industrialization, with intensive nationalist feelings created to help some groups of the population to accept the burdens of economic dislocation. Aggression may seem more justifiable in the spirit of such nationalism and in a sense as a relief from the continuing strains and resentments.

AGGRESSION AND MAJOR CONFLICT · We may now ask why these elements of aggression result in major wars. They need not do so, because the threat itself may produce the desired changes, or even if the conflict actually breaks out, it may be minor in terms of the economic resources that are committed and wasted. A detailed discussion would require a more precise definition of a major war, and it is difficult even to specify what a war is, since conflicts range from a few casual brushes of frontier guards to the protracted deployment of mass armies equipped with all the awesome weapons of advanced military technology.[28] But it is sufficient for our purpose to define a major war as one in which several large countries of relatively advanced economic position are involved over a period of time; the extent of commitment is exemplified by the two recent world wars and by the Napoleonic Wars.

When so defined, the question of major wars can be answered in broad terms. In general, overt conflicts occur when there is disagreement about the relative power positions of the rivals, when the

---

[28] A valuable compendium on the subject is Quincy Wright, *A Study of War* (Chicago: University of Chicago Press, 1942).

eventual outcome of the possible struggle is viewed differently by the several camps. For when there is agreement on the result of the use of force and the conviction that force will be used, there is little incentive to engage in war. This is not to deny the possibility that a conflict may be begun by some countries without strong conviction of success, but even these may prove upon closer inspection to have been entered upon in the hope, no matter how slender, that the resultant change in the combinations and alliances of power may bring effective help from major sources previously unengaged.

Indeed, the rationale for many wars lies in just this difficulty of measuring the power potential of the contestants to be devoted to the struggle, and even more in the difficulty of forecasting the effects of the conflict, once initiated, upon the alliance of power in the several camps. Hindsight wisdom is dangerous, but in retrospect it does seem that many wars began with quite opposite views of the contending forces about their true relative power: the Franco-Prussian War, our own Civil War, and the Israeli-Arab war are three examples. Clearly, both contestants could not be right, and one was proved wrong; if true knowledge had existed in advance of the conflict, there might not have been a conflict. Likewise, some hopeless struggles have been entered upon by the weaker camp in the belief that assistance would be forthcoming as the struggle progressed, or at least that the cost of direct surrender would be minimized. Of course in some cases the commitment to a conflict may have been truly irrational, with practically no hope of benefit. But, again, it is the uncertainty that surrounds calculations of relative potential power which breeds warlike policies in an atmosphere of Wagnerian splendor.

If this is the explanation of the development of aggressive elements in external relations into overt conflicts, the preconditions of major wars become clearer. Like all conflicts, major wars will be initiated because of uncertainties about relative strength, measured against the losses in position that may be sustained without conflict; in short, they occur because of errors in judgment on the part of one contesting group. But the conflict cannot be a major one unless several large advanced economic societies are engaged, and unless these units in the opposing camps view the struggle as one in which the costs of defeat are so high that the utmost exertion is warranted to avoid it. The assumptions are that there are several large advanced economic units in the world, that they have available means of transportation and communication by which they can come to grips with each other in armed conflict, and that their scales of social and other values differ enough so that they will be ready to strain their advanced economic power to the utmost.

Against this background, the chronology of major wars during the recent two centuries assumes a semblance of order. The Napoleonic Wars appear as a drawn-out contest in which the protagonists were the two major advanced economies of Europe: France, which was already losing its relative position despite its political revolution, and rapidly growing England. The following interregnum of "peace" appears as a period in which the new rising industrial powers—the United States, Germany, and later Japan—attained a position that challenged British leadership and eventually led to World War I, and later, with the addition of the newly risen power of Russia, to World War II. The rapid growth of the modern economy, of industrial power and technology, the rise and intensification of nationalist feelings, the combination of industrial power with progressively different systems of social values, all contributed to the two protracted and exhausting world wars.

If the economic cost of major wars is largely a function of economic power already attained, the remarkable economic growth of the advanced countries is, *ipso facto*, an explanation of the enormous growth in the economic costs of major conflicts. The permissive relation is obvious; there is much more economic power to waste. But it is the compulsive relation that is more important and perhaps less clearly perceived. Given the intensity of the struggle, human resources are more valuable because of their higher productivity in the advanced countries than more easily reproducible physical capital; and it is possible, within limits, to substitute expensive machinery for the more precious human beings. The greater propensity, in wars between the more and less developed nations, is for the former to have a higher ratio of physical equipment per unit of combatant personnel and a lower human casualty loss. The consequences in the way of high economic costs for advanced countries and wide physical destruction in the less developed countries are also easily observed.

EFFECTS OF WAR ON ECONOMIC GROWTH · The question of the effect of major wars on economic growth is answered to some extent by the comment just made on the enormous rise in costs of major conflicts. Since the positive returns on these costs are at best changes in relative position rather than absolute gains in economic output, the effects upon economic growth are likely to be negative.

A more penetrating view of the problem can perhaps be secured by distinguishing three types of costs involved. First, there is the direct waste of resources, represented by the destruction of human lives and economic goods, varying in absolute and relative magnitude with the extent of participation, the vulnerability to armed attack, and the destructive power of current technology. The tremendous increase in these direct costs, as a function of higher levels of economic technology and of the greater intensity of the overt conflicts, was emphasized in the comments just above. Second, there is the opportunity cost of war, caused by the interruption of the advance of technological knowledge and efficiency in the production of peace-type goods that accompanies diversion of resources to military uses. In wartime, production of some civilian goods ceases altogether and market conditions for the civilian goods still in production do not demand higher levels of efficiency than have already been attained. Third, there is the dislocation cost of wars, their disruption of the international framework of the world economy. The postwar adjustment to the new international situation is neither easy nor quick. The prewar growth of many countries may have been geared to an established and properly functioning network of international economic relations; and because the restoration of this network after a major war is protracted and perhaps never completely successful, depressing effects on growth may be substantial and lasting.

Although measures are not available (except for direct costs), all three types can be illustrated by the experience of the United States in World War I. This country's direct participation in the conflict was relatively short; yet the outlays, both in war casualties and materials and in unrequited assistance to allies, were substantial. The opportunity costs seem to have been even greater. The diversion of resources from the production of consumer and peace-type goods after 1914, well before the country entered the war, led to low construction levels, undermaintenance of the peacetime production apparatus, and an accumulation of gross inefficiency in the economy at large, the consequences of which were felt at least until 1923. Still more sizable in the longer run were the costs of major dislocation in international relations caused by World War I. The whole period from the early 1920's through the Great Depression of the 1930's was probably dominated by the violent disruption of international relations between 1914 and 1923.

Prompt recognition of and adjustment to the changed situation would have dictated different policies from many that were followed. The latter, in retrospect, were sound only in terms of the prewar, more "normal" framework of world economic flows. Because a major war means drastic and rapid breaks in established international relations, many of the costs of the unsound developments in the 1920's and the 1930's must be charged to World War I. To put it differently, if the war had not occurred, there would probably not have been the sharp breaks in international migration, volume of trade, and capital flows; the economic growth of this country would probably not have slowed down as markedly as it did after the first decade of the twentieth century; and there would probably not have been the severe international depression that occurred in the 1930's. The argument that these consequences should be charged to the failure to appraise the changed situation and make the proper postwar adjustments is specious, since this failure was itself a function of the rapid and extensive dislocation that a major war implies.

The offsets sometimes noted in discussions of war impacts, when viewed against these three types of costs, are of uncertain value. It has been argued that a war absorbs otherwise involuntarily unemployed resources of men and machines. This can hardly be significant, since a major war effort requires resources far exceeding any idle reserves and usually is an enormous strain on an economy, even in a country not in the area of combat. It has also been argued that major wars in modern times have accelerated, albeit for purposes of destruction, the application of some basic scientific and technological findings, and thus have reduced the period of gestation of important inventions. But it is difficult to appraise the net contribution of such an acceleration. We do not know what might have happened, nor can we properly evaluate wartime technology in peacetime terms. In the absence of a basis for measurement and because the comparison involves some hypothetical alternatives, the conclusion must necessarily contain a large element of judgment. In the light of the protracted economic difficulties faced by many advanced countries after both major wars and of the deceleration of the rate of growth in this country after World War I and probably also after World War II (certainly compared with pre-World War I rates), the judgment here is that major wars tend to depress economic growth in the participating countries. This means that for a country that has already slowed down in its growth and entered the phase of decline in relative position, participation in a major conflict, on the winning or the losing side, strengthens the trend toward retardation. For a country that is still in the phase of vigorous economic growth, participation in a major war may mean a sharp break in the upward course of its economy.

The opportunity and international dislocation costs are relevant also to the economic growth of nonparticipating countries. Unless these are isolated, a major war brings them a period of high, almost feverish economic prosperity. Combatant countries increase the demand for the neutrals' products and because restrictions on international competition are temporarily lifted, the neutral countries will find additional markets in other countries. But at the same time the supply of important producer and consumer goods ordinarily turned out only by the advanced economies virtually ceases. This combination of abnormal conditions tends to make for a rather distorted and costly economic structure in the nonparticipating countries. The cessation of war and the gradual return of the former combatants to world markets may then produce a reversal in which the neutral countries' economic gains prove to be largely illusory. On net balance the opportunity cost of the war years and the dislocation costs of the postwar period may far outweigh the larger production and greater money returns during the war years proper.[29]

Theoretical Proposals

The summary of empirical findings and related explanatory conjectures presented above is incomplete in that it omits some pos-

---

[29] I am aware of the inadequate treatment here of the possible positive contributions of war to technological and other advances, and of the bias that may have crept into my judgment of the net balance, but in our present state of knowledge and with the present analytical tools, no fully defensible conclusion can be reached.

However it did seem to me that in much of the discussion, scholarly or popular, the more conspicuous cases of war-induced technological changes, as well as the apparently energizing effects of war effort, tended to blind the observers to the manifold ways in which wars represent losses from the standpoint of peacetime economic growth. In this connection much of the analysis in John U. Nef, *War and Human Progress* (Cambridge: Harvard University Press, 1950) is relevant.

sibly important observations; it is perhaps too venturesome in that it advances speculations without adequate qualification; and it is probably unbalanced in that it devotes too much space to external relations among nations compared with that devoted to long-term changes in their internal structure. But our aim was to survey the similarities and diversities of economic growth during the last two centuries in order to indicate the task of any adequate theory, rather than to offer a complete summary of empirical findings; and to suggest the interrelations and implications that some of the findings convey, not to present completely tested and qualified explanations. If we have discussed at too great length the external relations among nations, particularly the aggressive elements, it is because we feel that they have been unduly neglected—given their importance in past history and the close ties between them and other factors directly involved in the economic growth of nations.

In order to point up the contribution of the preceding discussion toward a theory, we now restate with a possible change of emphasis the lines of approach that are indispensable in any theoretical construction. This can be done best by listing the groups of processes, the strands that seem to be woven always into the fabric of economic growth and seem sufficiently distinct on the surface, even though they are basically interrelated through the factors behind them. At least five such topics, for which there are subtheories, should eventually be united into one theory of economic growth; these are population growth, growth of the stock of knowledge, long-term processes of internal adaptation to growth potentials, external relations of national units, in both cooperation and conflict, and interrelations among all these complexes and whatever components within each can be distinguished. A brief comment on each should indicate the major questions that would be the concern of a possible theory.

POPULATION GROWTH · The task of the theory of population growth seems clearest, perhaps because our stock of organized empirical data is among the richest. To put it simply, we know, in broad outline, the trends that have occurred and the list of relevant factors, but we have little tested knowledge of the relative weights of these factors. Without such weights, we have no theory in the sense of a body of relations to which we can attach coefficients tested for the limits of their variance under diverse conditions in space and time. It is such a theory that must be sought.

The ultimate test of theoretical analysis is in the extrapolative value of its conclusions. Can they be transferred outside the body of empirical observations from which they have been derived and be proved valid under other conditions? In this connection it is relevant to emphasize that purely empirical extrapolation or projection, even in a field like population growth, which we all tended to view as much more stable than the purely economic magnitudes and relations, is a poor substitute for such a theory. A striking revelation of misplaced confidence in empirically observed "stabilities" has been the recent experience with projections of population growth in this country. That these projections, based on extrapolation of our records of birth and death rates for different age and sex groups, proved to be, within a decade or less of their release, so far off the mark is clear evidence that the temporal variability of empirically observed trends is far greater than was generally believed before World War II.[30]

In attempting to develop a theory of population growth, even one limited to natural increase and thus avoiding the complex questions of international migration, we face two major difficulties. First, the decline in death rates, complex as the set of forces producing it is, can occur without an accompanying improvement in economic and social conditions that will assure at least a stable product per capita, let alone a higher one. Death rates in British India declined from about 26 per 1,000 in the 1920's to below 20 per 1,000 in the 1940's; yet there is little evidence of any increase in the low real product per capita. Death rates can apparently be changed by factors exogenous to and relatively independent of economic development; hence this aspect of a theory of population growth must take into account the rather difficult and complex range of possibilities in the realm of medical and public health progress, relatively unbound by the limitations of an economic potential.

The second group of complexities is related to the birth rates. It has in general been assumed that once initiated, their long-term decline, associated with a variety of economic and social transformations, is bound to continue until all groups of society have been affected. The recent upsurge in birth rates in the economically advanced societies is still somewhat of a puzzle with respect to

[30] In this connection see H. F. Dorn, "Pitfalls in Population Forecasts and Projections," *Journal of the American Statistical Association* (September, 1950), and several articles by J. S. Davis published since 1949.

size, duration, and impact. However, it suggests the possibility that in the advanced societies where changes in birth rates play a greater role than changes in death rates in affecting the rates of natural increase, the birth rates have become a more sensitive and variable phenomenon than they were in the past. In other words, in the underdeveloped societies where death rates may be more important in the near future, it is their relative independence of the limits set by economic performance that makes the prospective task of theory so difficult. In the advanced societies where birth rates are more important, it is their recent departures from downward trends and their greater sensitivity to changes in economic and social conditions that constitute an obstacle to the formulation of an adequate theory.

GROWTH IN THE STOCK OF KNOWLEDGE · That the accumulation of empirical and tested knowledge is at the base of the enormous growth of population and economic production during the recent two centuries is a truism. If evidence is required, a glance at the productive structure of any advanced economy will quickly reveal the huge proportion of its activities carried on in industries and by techniques that were completely unknown one or two hundred years ago, and that represent the practical application of much of the basic work in the natural sciences. Indeed, because this relation is so obvious, we referred to it only casually in discussing economic growth as manifested in per capita income, in the shift of industrial structure, and in the division of product between consumption and capital formation.

But no such omission is possible when we consider a theory of economic growth and of the determining factors and their interrelations. For the rate at which additions are made to the stock of tested knowledge will affect the rate at which that knowledge will be applied in economic production, and the latter may spell important differences in the rate as well as structure of economic growth. And this difference, which we cannot measure in our present state of ignorance, between modern times and the earlier centuries in the rate of additions to scientific knowledge must account, in large part, for unusually rapid rates of economic growth in recent centuries. What is true of this comparison over longer spans may easily be true of comparisons within the recent period. We cannot, therefore, take the stock of knowledge for granted; we must learn whatever we can about the causes of additions to and changes in it; we must have some theory of its production and accumulation.

The wide scope of this task must be emphasized for the proper understanding of what is involved. In separating the application of technical knowledge from the stock of useful knowledge, we distinguish between the stock available and stock used and concentrate here on the former. But *all* empirical knowledge, all scientifically tested information, no matter how abstract and remote it may seem, is potentially applicable in economic production. Science, no matter how abstruse, is analysis of the world around us, and economic production is one type of manipulation of this world. This obvious identity of the object of concern explains the chain of connection between the most "useless" cogitations and experiments of scientists often completely unaware of the practical potentialities of their work and revolutionary transformations of the basis of economic production that sometimes flow from them. All empirical knowledge is thus potentially relevant to economic production.

It follows that the very classification of types of relevant empirical knowledge, ranging from historico-geographic specific observations to experimental data, to principles, theories, and generalizations, and to combinations of all of these in inventions, improvements, and practices, is a major task in itself. There are gradations here from the broadest principles to the more specific inventions which may still require protracted testing and pilot plant tryouts before they can be applied on a significant scale in economic practice; from the collections of the most specific data in geology, meteorology, astronomy, and anthropology, to the most general type of abstract tool for operating in the field of theoretical analysis. The institutional conditions under which these bodies of knowledge are produced are vastly different; the patterns of cumulation and "laws" that govern their growth are not likely to be the same in theoretical work on basic principles and in work on accumulation of experimental data, such as boiling and melting points and molecular structure of organic compounds. Yet in the long run, social decisions that affect these conditions may have the most profound effect on economic growth. One need only consider the policy that authoritarian states display toward biology and the social sciences, or the domination of research by the needs of emergency warfare, to recognize that continuation of such practices for a sufficiently long period may have far-reaching consequences for the progress of human knowledge and hence for the potential of growth.[31]

We, therefore, need a theory of the production and accumulation of empirical knowledge, even if for years to come this may mean nothing more than an attempt to learn about the processes involved and the factors that seem important. We already have some hypotheses and reflections; any student who has concerned himself with the economic growth of nations to the point of deriving prognoses or policy conclusions almost inevitably makes assumptions concerning the progress of knowledge and its effects on economic production. It may be better to call explicitly for a theory of production of such knowledge as an indispensable focus for direct and continuous concern with the complex of forces involved here and with their effects on economic growth.

INTERNAL ADAPTATIONS TO GROWTH POTENTIALS · The internal adaptation of a society to growth potentials afforded by the population or by the stock of knowledge has been the chief concern of economic theory in connection with problems of growth. It is in this area that the discipline of economic analysis has made its greatest contribution.

To begin with, the earliest and basic task of economic theory was to demonstrate the interrelation joining individuals and groups in society to the origin and distribution of the social product. The most important function of the economic discipline was to show how a social phenomenon results from individual acts—how market, quantity, and price flow from the behavior of thousands of buyers and sellers in accordance with rules of economic rationality. It is no accident that the main contribution of the Physiocratic School, recognized as the founder of modern economics, takes the form of a *tableau économique,* that the distinctive features of economic analysis are various schemata of "reproduction," demand-and-supply schedules, and similar constructions, which are models intended to show both the connections between units, grouped by their mode

[31] To suggest even further complexities of the task urged in the text, one should note that there is not only growth of knowledge, but also destruction of it by the continuous substitution for inadequate data and theories of others better geared to rising standards of reliability or to more tenable analyses of expanding bodies of tested observations. Any attempt at measurement of the stock of knowledge must, therefore, be made in cognizance of the continuous changes in standards that shift the qualitative characteristics of existing knowledge. But this is no reason for not urging more emphasis on direct study of the complex of activities and results involved in the accumulation of knowledge.

of action, and the results in the form of either a market or national product, price, and allocation of resources and returns.

This emphasis on the interconnection of the various elements in the total economy of a country (usually classified according to their particular function, e.g., supplies of labor and of other productive factors, consumers, sellers, buyers, and savers) is what makes economic theory so relevant to the analysis of policy problems. It creates an awareness of the effects of any policy decision on *all* groups in society, not merely on some special interests that may be backing it. But it also makes economic theory an indispensable background in the consideration of problems of change, of which economic growth is one. The interconnections among labor, land, and capital in production and the interplay in distribution of units in the market (which is the mechanism by which the interconnections are effected) are basic for a theory of economic growth as long as the economy remains a system of interdependent parts in growth, as it does when viewed for the sake of simplicity in terms of static circuit flows. But in using the concept of the economy as a system of interrelated parts, we must avoid transferring to economic growth the limiting assumptions of static theory.

One way of adapting the articulated analysis of static interaction among the components in an economy to the problem of economic growth is to identify certain carriers of the latter within the system; the addition of capital via savings can thus be viewed as a passive condition and the dynamic function of the entrepreneur (the profit-maker) as the energizing element. Given such an entrepreneurial group, responsible for making the proper choice in the combination of productive factors, given a propensity for savings by which additional resources can be made available to the entrepreneurs, and given the interrelation between supply and demand for capital goods (savings) identical with that for other goods, economic growth can be visualized as a rise in total output within the framework of an interdependent system that moves forward to higher levels.

Entrepreneurs and capital formation are the minimum elements that must be added to the static conception of a circuit flow to make economic growth possible. But there can be marked variations in emphasis, as well as in the extent to which these additional elements in the theoretical system will be permitted to effect continuous changes on the interrelations. There are significant differences among the views of Adam Smith on the growth process as caused by the expansion of the market which results in increased division of labor and the competitive action of entrepreneurs watched over by the state to prevent the collusion to which they are prone; those of Malthus and Ricardo, who shared the conviction that pressure of population growth and exhaustion of land would make the entrepreneurs (profitmakers) helpless against a progressive reduction of their share in the nation's product, and hence against the arrival (considered fairly imminent) of the stationary state; of Karl Marx, whose labor theory of value provides the basis for the theory of exploitation, and who conceived of capitalists as a historical class driven toward greater and greater capital accumulation by the unavoidable decline in the rate of surplus value (the base of their profits) and toward the destruction of competitors and the increase in the proportion of the proletariat in the population, all eventuating in a revolutionary debacle; and of Schumpeter, who views the entrepreneurs as an elite group of innovators capable of overcoming the resistance to change of the traditionalist and numerically preponderant groups in the economy, and are likely to fail in the end only because their very success tends to strengthen the elements of society that inhibit their actions and provide an increasingly unfavorable social climate for their operation.

We indicate these differences—and they are so large as to produce different prognoses and different policy bases—to show that it is not enough to have a hypothesis that explains how economic growth is *possible*, as each of these theories does. It must also demonstrate how such growth *occurs* in the real world, and what factors in what combinations produce the particular adaptations of the economic systems in various countries to the potentials of economic growth. If entrepreneurial action and capital accumulation are to be stressed, the theory must still show how the factors determining these elements produced similar or different results, in the broad terms of a given background of historical experience.

In this connection, it is illuminating that the views just noted can be traced to somewhat different historical backgrounds. Granted that the whole intellectual climate, the basic *Weltanschauung*, of these authors differed from the rationalist background of Adam Smith to the inverted Hegelianism of Marx to the partly "hero in history," partly "elite" ideas of Schumpeter, yet one may argue that the historical canvas of the major technological changes whose application required the innovating type of entrepreneur and the institutions of banking that could finance him, which are given prominence in Schumpeter's theory, did not exist or were in embryo in Adam Smith's time and could hardly have played an important part in his analysis. Similarly, Smith could not have observed the disruptive effects of the Industrial Revolution in England, which colored so much of Marx's and Engels' study; nor could these effects loom as large to the twentieth-century economists, who are more concerned with the current problems of their day. Likewise we have noted the effect of the isolation of England during the Napoleonic Wars as well as the growth and mobility of its population upon the original and rigid (and it is the one that persisted) formulation of population and diminishing returns theory in the Classical economics of Malthus, West, and Ricardo. Such tracing of general theories to their historical background can only be suggestive at best. But it does seem that important differences in emphasis on the interrelation between the dynamic entrepreneur and his environment in producing economic growth reflect different phases of the growth experience itself. As long as economic theory is largely a response to current problems, it is likely to be affected by the immediate historical background. It follows that the construction of an adequate theory of internal adaptation of an economy to the potentialities of growth must be made with cognizance of the danger of concentrating on too limited a segment of history and must face the challenge of dealing with an adequate variety of growth experience. Such a theory must, in particular, reach beyond establishing the *possibility* of economic growth to formulate the important factors, with due effort to bring some testable order into the sequence and variety of phases that an internal adaptation of an economy to the potentialities of growth may display.

This leads to the question of parts of the economy and society other than those selected as the dynamic carriers of change or the providers of additional tools for them. Some of the comments made in the summary of empirical findings indicate that these elements are important in a theory of internal adaptation of a country, for it is in their gradual (or sometimes rapid) modification that the key to possible growth may lie. The theories noted above contain some references, explicit or implicit, to these other sectors in the economy. The Malthus-Ricardo analysis of longer-term trends in the distribution of national product points to the expected changes in the position of labor and in the share of landlords. The Marxian prognosis specifies the proletarianization of the masses of society, their increasing misery, and so on. One could go through the theories also in search of statements or inferences concerning the role of the state and find again significant differences ranging from its role in Classical economic theory in the way of enforcing competition and rationalizing the system of justice, education, welfare, and services, to the Marxian concept of the state as a tool in the hands of the capitalist classes, to some of Schumpeter's suggestions concerning the role of the state as a possible carrier of some survivals of precapitalist times and the organ through which the growth of elements inimical to the innovating entrepreneur may find expression. Such observations on the trends in the role of the "passive" elements are indispensable.

The reasons for specific emphasis upon this segment of the theory of internal adaptation is that here may lie the greatest contrast between the explanation of how economic growth is possible and the explanation of how it is actually realized. Given the dynamic elements, the carriers of change, we can demonstrate how economic growth is possible. To demonstrate how it is realized, we need in addition the interplay of these elements with all the other major groups and forces in the economy. Indeed, closer examination and more thoroughgoing study of the interrelations in the process of economic growth may show that the distinction between active and passive elements is false in its very sharpness. The literature on the entrepreneur as the focus of economic change suggests too much tautology; all change is enacted by human beings, and if we identify those that make changes as entrepreneurs (or profitmakers) without at the same time specifying the group apart from their actions, we explain economic change by definition rather than by substantive analysis. Yet a study of the origin and performance of entrepreneurs—defined substantively as all decision-makers, not tautologically as carriers of change—might reveal that the conditions that produce them and determine their effectiveness are intertwined with the conditions and factors that govern the behavior and the capacity for change of all other groups and institutions in society. Of particular relevance here are our earlier comments on the role of the state in its decisions for relieving the strains produced by economic growth, and on the role of physical capital and savings proper in relation to the consumption patterns and attitudes of the masses of consumers and workers. If this interconnection among all components in the process of economic growth persists, it is indispensable to incorporate in the theoretical analysis all the factors, passive and active, that determine the pace and structure of growth, factors that may be reflected in the changing functions of the state, the trends in character and composition of the labor force, the evolution of financial and other institutions, and the long-term changes in business structure. In concentrating on the presumably strategic elements, for instance the entrepreneur, we risk neglecting the other elements, particularly since some of them are believed by many economists to be outside the proper concern of the economic discipline.

If the theory of internal adaptation must weigh fully the factors involved both in the dynamic elements that provide the primary motive power and in the willing or unwilling response of all other important groups and institutions in society, and in the process test the validity of the distinction, the most feasible approach may be by explicit and comprehensive attention to the sequence of structural changes accompanying economic growth. The discussion of empirical findings conveys an impression of relative persistence and uniformity in the character of such changes, be they "industrialization," "urbanization," increase in scale of operation, greater degree of impersonal organization, or those changes connected with the distinction between consumption and reproducible capital formation. Some structural changes not specifically discussed (e.g., changes in the size distribution of income) may also reveal significant association with economic growth defined as the sustained increase in per capita product. Furthermore, because at least some of these shifts reflect either persistent traits of human wants or a common complex of technological knowledge, they may be found in economic growth under different forms of social organization, in the authoritarian states as well as in the libertarian democracies.

In any theoretical analysis, such a close association between the rate of economic growth and the changes in structure may become an important explanatory link. If per capita product grows, and if simultaneously certain structural shifts occur, the latter may explain the next stage of economic growth and some of its corollaries, both internal and external to the national unit. A *stage* theory of invariable sequences need not necessarily be attempted. But if such sequences recur often, the empirical data accumulated can perhaps be best organized with the help of a theory that uses changes in structure to set up phases in modern economic growth and attempts to formulate and test both active and passive factors and their interrelations against the background of what might be called typical *reference* phases of economic growth during the recent epoch, or, even more ambitiously, of similar phases distinguishable in several epochs of economic growth.

EXTERNAL RELATIONS OF NATIONAL UNITS · The theory of external relations is an extension of the theory of internal adaptation. If the latter can establish the ties among various factors that determine economic growth within a country, the analysis should presumably have some validity for the flows among nations. The industrial and other changes accompanying economic growth within a country usually mean shifts in relative rates of growth of the several regions and changes in location of industry. Thus any theory which, in accounting for the internal adaptation of a country to the potentialities of economic growth, explains shifts from agriculture to industry and the mechanism of the flows of labor, goods, and capital by which this is accomplished should also shed light on the flows of labor, goods, and capital among nations at different phases of their development.

This observation seems particularly valid for the theoretical analysis of peaceful types of external flows, with international migration analogous to internal migration, the flow of commodities and services across boundaries analogous to such flows among regions or industries within a country, and flows of capital funds in foreign investment analogous to domestic flows of capital investment. Indeed, much of the contribution of economic theory to the understanding of problems of world trade and capital investment lies in its service in explaining the basic features of economic processes within a country and then in applying these explanations, with such simple but concrete modifications as the assumption of relative immobility of labor and the emphasis on diversity of natural resources among the nations, to international flows.

A similar observation has bearing even upon a theory of aggressive external relations. For if the analysis of internal adaptation assigns, as it must, some role to the state, its performance within the country will suggest some inferences concerning external relations. If the major function of the state is to provide security and justice within the nation, as a basis for the beneficial effects of free competition and division of labor (under compulsion, if necessary), its role on the international scene is likely to be to protect the nation and strive for international division of labor, even if the latter entails an element of aggression. If the state is viewed as a repressive mechanism, a tool in the hands of the dominant classes, it is likely to be viewed as such outside the country's boundaries. It is significant that Classical economics, which interprets the state as a benevolent watchman and assistant at home, presents a relatively peaceful picture of external relations, whereas the Marxian School, which views the state as a tool in the hands of capitalist classes within the country, stresses imperialist aggression and exploitation.

Conceived as an extension of the theory of internal adaptation, the analysis of external relations naturally becomes an analysis of the spread, peaceful or violent, of the patterns of economic organization and growth from the more to the less advanced countries. If the same factors drive a given country forward to its more advanced stages and determine its relations with other countries, they are also likely to act on the "other" as they did on the less advanced sectors within the given economy. Thus Classical economic theory implies the inevitable spread of industrialization and economic growth across the world, radiating via international trade and capital movements from the leading national units, and the Marxian theory implies the spread of exploitive imperialism with the absorption of precapitalistic countries into the network of world capitalism.

Limitations of the theory of internal adaptation will therefore be reflected in limitations of the theory of external relations. One should note in this connection the underemphasis on the roles of various political and social institutions in the process of economic growth within the country, a natural consequence of the tendency of economists to concentrate on their own discipline and to carry these "noneconomic" variables as qualifying exceptions or as "special" doctrines not incorporated into the body of theory (note the treatment of noncompeting groups, the general view on the nationalistic doctrine of the protective tariff, and the like). Paralleling this underemphasis is a conspicuous neglect in the field of international relations. Thus, the assumption of internal mobility of labor or capital in response to purely economic differentials, which, however qualified by references to social, racial, and other barriers, does not incorporate them into the corpus of analysis, is likely to be paralleled by a similar difficulty in dealing with the much wider legal, cultural, and other obstacles in the international flow of labor and capital. Incorporation of these obstacles, if they are sufficiently important, may lead to an assumption of complete immobility rather than one of unrestricted mobility. But neither oversimplified model provides the basis for fruitful theoretical analysis. There are obvious analogies too between the underemphasis and overemphasis of aggressive elements in the role of the state within the economy and in external relations.

Earlier comments concerning the general direction of further work on the theory of internal adaptation—a more explicit consideration of the roles of all major economic and social institutions, and particularly of the state, and an attempt to distinguish their interrelations against the background of some recognized framework of phases in the recent epoch of economic growth—bear with equal force upon the theory of external relations. There is no need to repeat them here. We only add that neither theory will be complete without the other. Given the technological possibility of material (and hence of spiritual) flows among nations, the internal adaptation of any country, advanced or backward, cannot be explained without some understanding of its relations with the rest of the world. The sequence of structural stages in the process of growth and any associated changes in the level and time patterns of the rate of increase in total or per capita product must involve the competitive and cooperative relations in the spread of an economic epoch from one nation to the next. The internal adaptation of a country to the potentialities of the modern economic epoch, whether we call it "industrial capitalism" or, more properly, the "industrial system," is at the same time an adjustment to its existence or absence in other parts of the world. By the same token, external relations can be understood only as an extension of the processes of internal adaptation, modified by the cleavages that are greater among than within nations.

INTERRELATIONS · That the four distinct aspects of economic growth and the various components within them are interrelated need hardly be mentioned. This interrelation has been stressed in discussing internal adaptation and external relations; it certainly applies to population growth, which is related to accumulation of knowledge and to the structural changes that constitute the essence of internal adaptation which in turn affects external relations; and it is implied in treatment of the economy of any given country, or of a large part of the world, as a system of interrelated parts, in growth as well as in static-flow analysis. Even in the case of accumulation of knowledge, perhaps the freest variable among those outlined, economic and social institutions may determine, if not the direction and rate of progress in basic scientific theory, at least the chain of processes by which basic scientific discoveries are translated into a stock of tested knowledge which in turn becomes the basis for inventions and applications. Indeed, since empirical knowledge can be fully tested only by ramified application, and since such application is part and parcel of economic and other activity of large groups in society, the production of the stock of tested knowledge can hardly escape being linked in the whole chain of interconnections and reciprocal determination that binds together population growth, economic development, and the structural changes within the country and in the framework of international relations.

Hence, a discussion of the theory of interrelations as a separate topic in the outline of a prospective theory of economic growth is artificial and unnecessary. It is artificial because it would hardly be possible to treat one of the four topics without continuously referring to the others, which at some junctures appear as determinants and at others as effects. It is unnecessary because one could hardly add anything to the suggestions bearing upon such interconnections already made in the discussion of empirical findings, unless the scope of the empirical findings were broadened or our probing were made more intensive by means of additional data. We can only state more explicitly the questions we must face in trying to synthesize into a unified theory of economic growth the wide range of processes and factors hinted at above. These questions bear upon the possibility of formulating a unified theory for nations of different sizes, nations at different stages of the spread of a specific type of economic system, and nations with distinct characteristics of social and political organizations. This possibility leads immediately to problems involved in distinguishing one major epoch or type of economic system from another, and the question whether a unified theory of economic growth can apply to more than one epoch in the long history of society.

Whether one should devise variants of a theory of economic growth for the many small nations different from those for the few large ones is a question that has already been raised. It may well be that analysis would indicate that growth in the smaller countries, particularly in the more advanced ones, depends upon close economic ties with some large country, and that the changing fortunes of the latter determine the growth of its smaller satellites. It is granted that no nation, however large, is completely independ-

ent and also that the smaller units may remain relatively more independent, as long as they also remain underdeveloped. Further
analysis may show, however, that the advance of the small nations
is contingent upon their becoming members of a larger economic
constellation and that for them the recent methods of relative
isolation and forced industrialization under self-contained, authoritarian auspices are not conducive to economic growth. Without
prejudging the answer, one may stress that at the point of syn-
thesizing the different strands in the analysis of economic growth,
the problem raised by the contrast in size in the present (and past)
distribution of national units must be posed explicitly.

There is a difference in patterns of growth between the nation
that is the pioneer in a new economic epoch and those that follow,
just as there are differences among followers in the sequence of
their entrance. In our modern epoch, the simple listing of England,
the United States, Germany, Japan, and Russia suggests marked
differences in the pattern of growth as these countries entered the
phase of industrialization, and there seems to be significant association between at least some of these differences and the fact that
each entered the industrialization phase with a different number of
predecessors already in the field.

The possibility of variants in the theory of economic growth is
suggested by the different questions that one tends to ask in dealing with a pioneer country and its followers: for the former, why *it*
was the pioneer; for the latter, what obstacles had to be overcome
in following the example. Another relevant observation, already
made, is that the very increase in the number of large units that
have attained fairly high levels of economic growth is likely to have
taken place under, and in turn produced, conditions favorable to
increased incidence of major wars.

The question posed by differences in social and political structure
is closely associated with the sequence in the spread of an economic
system from one major country to the next. If a new phase in
economic history emerges, its appearance in the pioneer country
will occur in a specific historical setting, a given social and economic
structure, and will produce some important changes in it, as the
agricultural and industrial revolutions did in England. The follower
countries have a different historical heritage; it is this difference
that makes them followers rather than pioneers. Hence, as the new
system spreads it will affect countries that are significantly different
in their social and economic structure from the pioneer at the

time it entered the new era. Furthermore, the time lag between the pioneer and the followers will be some function of the difference between the political, social, and cultural heritages: the wider the difference, the longer the time lag. In addition, the latecomers will be adjusting to the potentialities of the new system under historical conditions quite different from those of the pioneer or even of the early followers.

It is, therefore, likely that the changes that accompany the shift will also be radically different. The late entrance of Japan and Russia is to some extent associated with the differences between their historical heritage and that which produced the early entrance of England and the United States, and the different political and social structures that evolved in them are a result partly of the differences in historical heritage, partly of differences in the world scene. In oversimplified terms, the authoritarian character of late industrialization may be rationalized as the response of a backward country that is not concerned with new inventions and discoveries since a rich stock is ready for adoption by imitation; that has as its most plentiful resource human labor, unskilled and unaccustomed to the individualistic cooperation which results from a long investment in education, political democracy, and the like; and that uses human labor to pay for the primary capital accumulation necessary for industrialization. Whatever the explanation, a question arises concerning the variants in the theory of economic growth needed to treat adequately the variety of political and social characteristics that may accompany the growth process, as a given system spreads to national units with historical heritages different from those of the pioneers and early followers.

The consideration of differences in political and social structure and their effect on economic processes leads directly to the definition of an economic epoch, of a type of economic system. Thus, if we shape our theory to account for growth of nations within the system of "industrial capitalism," it is to be questioned whether the USSR is a unit of the species and whether our theory should account for its growth experience. If we deal with the "industrial system," by which we mean an economic organization that applies extensively the results of modern science to the problems of economic production, but not necessarily under private business auspices, the USSR definitely belongs to the category and the theory must account for its growth experience. This question whether or not the projected theory should cover the growth of nations under industrial capitalism or under the industrial system or, for that matter, should also encompass such earlier epochs as merchant capitalism, the agrarian empires of the East, and the medieval town economy—is surely a major one and influences both the organization of empirical findings and the eventual attempt at synthesis of the various sections in the theoretical analysis.

The empirical evidence summarized here has been limited to the last two centuries and, largely for lack of data, to countries that operated under the auspices of libertarian democracy and the business system. As suggested above, there is good reason for limiting the organization of evidence and the formulation of a theory of economic growth to the experience of the last two centuries. One common thread in the empirical findings reinforces this decision: the rates of growth of both population and per capita income were exceptionally high; the shifts in the internal structure of the economies that have led in economic growth were rapid and widespread; the impact upon the country and the reactions of political and social institutions within the country and in international relations were far-reaching and violent; the diversity in growth experience among various countries was marked and the resulting differences in economic levels were striking. Even allowing for the myopia that may afflict the contemporary or near-contemporary observer, there is ground for viewing the last two centuries as a distinctly new epoch, an epoch that in the acceleration of the rates of economic and social change seems exceptional. As a matter of intellectual strategy, we might limit the immediate task to a theory of growth of nations under the industrial system (this does not preclude supplementation by similar attempts to distinguish the persistent relations and sequences in earlier epochs since much of the recent past cannot be clearly understood without them). But in this limited period of the last two centuries, the theoretical frame of reference should not be confined to countries that experienced economic growth under the business system. It is more useful to take the view that the authoritarian latecomers also are adapting themselves to the potentialities of technological and social invention for greater command over economic goods or economic weapons.

Ultimate Uses of the Theory

This bare outline of a theory of economic growth of nations under the industrial system of the last two centuries covers an extremely wide area, transcends the usual limits of the discipline of economics, and may seem so demanding as to be impracticable and useless. In a sense, nothing is easier than to prepare overambitious blueprints, and few intellectual exercises may be as futile. Likewise, given the division of labor among disciplines, it is easy to chide economics for neglecting related social phenomena which, however important in economic growth, may be viewed by economists as beyond their professional competence. Furthermore, criticism of faults of omission may be gratuitous if the omission is compelled by a structure of the discipline that has advantages for the treatment of other problems. These dangers were always lurking in the background during the writing of the preceding section. But they were offset by the hope that the goals set would encourage rather than inhibit the search for relevant empirical evidence and for more adequately formulated and closely knit theoretical analysis. In discussing the limitations of past economic analysis in the field, there was no intent to deny that these theoretical constructs rendered an immensely useful service in dealing with other, chiefly short-term problems, or that they suggested approaches to the analysis of economic growth proper, particularly to growth questions that were in the forefront of attention at that historical conjuncture.

It may help, if not to avoid, at least to limit misunderstanding and disagreement if we conclude with some brief observations concerning the crossing of the limits of the discipline of economics, the attainability of the theory to which the discussion has been directed, and the practical significance of the related work.

RELATED FIELDS · The major observation on the extension of analysis to areas beyond economic discipline proper—to population movements, accumulation of knowledge, political structure, and the like —is that in fact economic analysis does make assumptions, often explicit, concerning trends and relations in these fields. This is a matter of necessity, if the analyst wishes to infer something determinate either about the causes of economic growth in the past or about the prognosis for the future.

A most conspicuous illustration is the treatment of technological change in Classical and Marxian economics. Both systems contain a generalization to the effect that technical progress cannot be counted upon to overcome effects of diminishing (relative to growing population) supplies of irreproducible natural resources, particularly land. In Classical economics it is explicit in the law of diminishing returns from land, formulated as a *historical* or empirical generalization. In the Marxian doctrine, it is implicit in the law of diminution of the rate of surplus value, which is based in turn on the assumption that the reduction in time necessary to produce workers' subsistence *will* lag behind the effects of rise in the organic structure of capital. The plausibility of that assumption is linked to the role of land as a limiting resource in the production of food and other major sources of a worker's subsistence. The stagnation theory of the 1930's assigned a similar key role to technological change. Its proponents claimed that the demand for private capital arising out of new inventions and changes *not* associated with extensive expansion of population and area would fall short of the flow of savings *ex ante*. If such substantive statements about technological changes are a prerequisite for determinate statements about economic growth, surely it is better to recognize this area and the related area of accumulation of knowledge as deserving of major and explicit concern and study, empirical and analytical, than to continue to make assumptions based on general and untested impressions, no matter how obvious they may seem.

The argument applies, indeed, beyond the field of economic growth, to the validity of results of analysis in application to even short-term changes. It is hardly an exaggeration to say that economic analysis faces a difficult choice: either it must admit that none of its results has validity until they are supplemented by findings of other disciplines on the processes impounded in *ceteris paribus;* or it must state where, in real life, *ceteris paribus* begins and ends. The former alternative is hardly palatable; the latter involves an uncomfortably speculative decision. If this view is at all valid, much of the contribution of economic analysis of short-term problems must perforce completely disregard the long-term concomitants and consequences. Whatever the case in the treatment of short-term changes and problems, in the analysis of long-term trends, of economic growth, little in the way of testable results can be expected without explicit treatment of all the areas noted above. Much as one may regret leaving the shelters of an accustomed discipline, it does seem as if an economic theory of economic growth is an impossibility if by "economic" we mean staying within the limits set by the tools of economic discipline proper, even within the broader limits of Classical and Marxian economics and all the more within the much narrower limits that have prevailed since the middle of the last century.

THEORETICAL OUTLOOK · But what is the hope of attaining a comprehensive theory of economic growth which has to be built upon the contributions of so many disciplines in the social sciences and humanities and even in the natural sciences, some of which, like the history of science and technology, are in their embryonic stages? Can one work effectively toward so distant a goal? This question must be faced since the desired theory is not limited to some seemingly axiomatic general principles for policy guidance, or to mathematical and quasi-mathematical models demonstrating by a simple combination of a few variables how economic growth is possible. The theory implies a constant search for empirically identifiable variables and their relations, tested under as great a diversity of conditions as the evidence, available and securable, can reveal.

Two major reasons for working toward this goal come to mind. First such a theory provides an effective framework for classifying and organizing a vast number of relevant findings already accumulated on observed trends and their relationships in time and space. It is illuminating, and suggestive of directions for further research, to see the major lines of economic growth in a variety of countries and the relations between the sustained movements in their populations, total and per capita products, industrial structures, characters of business organization, the role and magnitude of the state, and international flows. In an attempt to pinpoint the major focus of such a theory in further organization of data and analysis, we could begin with the statement that economic growth is a combination of transnational, international, and intranational elements; that among the former the stock of knowledge of mankind and its persistent characteristic as *Homo sapiens* are major; that economic growth within a nation during any historical period is the result of an interplay between the institutions and patterns of behavior it inherits from the past and the strains and tensions created by the potential implied in the stock of knowledge, whether or not this potential is already being utilized by another nation; that economic growth is a costly process, both in the breakage it produces in the inherited complex of institutions and interests and in the opportunity cost of resources it requires; and that because economic growth is so costly (and although resolving the tension created by the opportunities inevitably gives birth to other strains and conflicts) the role of the state and other social institutions is of strategic importance. This statement, which is a capsule repetition of much of the discussion, does provide a base, a cogent and integrated view of a vast field of empirical findings and their relations. It should, therefore, serve as a stimulus toward a more explicit analysis of a variety of data until now kept apart and examined largely by specialists in the various disciplines. In short, if a theory of economic growth is to be not just a mechanical assembly of unrelated parts but is to imply some closely woven relations among the parts, it seems to offer an effective goal in that the acceptance of a central focus in a wide field forces attention to all its parts, stimulates the organization of an increasing body of empirical evidence, and inhibits the easy retreat to oversimplified schemes within the confines of a single discipline.

The second argument is related to this one. We do not need clear assurance that an acceptable theory, useful for predictive purposes, would result. Such a theory calls for variables that are empirically identifiable and testable and that also move in a relatively invariable pattern over time, despite major variations in conditions. It may well be that these variables cannot be found. We may never be able to attain specific measures of the distinguishable factors involved and may be forced to treat the various complexes as indissoluble *Gestalts,* constructs in which the very configurations of the identifiable elements are so important that no weights can be assigned to the elements themselves. But it should be sufficient if the theory at any given stage of its development, from the bare and vague sketch of its embryo beginning to the much richer and more articulated structure of later phases, permits the user to orient himself properly among the variety of data reflecting the diversity of experience, to see the relations, even though of limited persistence, among the various strands in the process, and to evaluate the successive notions or theories which are continuously elicited by changing historical circumstances and which, because they are designed to produce hard and clear answers to current problems, almost inevitably claim greater validity than they possess. The value of the theory lies not in its promise to yield precise predictions eventually but in its capacity to bring an ever-growing body of empirical data into analytical relationships which bind together various processes, and thus provide a continuous revision and extension of our notions concerning the important factors that determine economic growth.

PRACTICAL CONTRIBUTIONS · This leads directly to the practical value of the work guided by the broad theory suggested, whose specific outlines are subject to constant revision. Economic growth, and for that matter other aspects of economic life, are affected greatly by secular decisions made by society, decisions of the type already mentioned, concerning, for example, land, labor, capital, and their disposition within the given society or in relation with other societies. In such decisions, the conflict of group interests, the experience of other countries, and a variety of other forces all play their parts. But the very process by which such decisions are reached involves some theory of economic growth. Thus a particular group tries to pave the way toward acceptance of its policy recommendation by relating it to the long-term prospects of the society at large, by claiming that this specific decision (i.e., for disposition of the public domain in one way rather than another), will yield greater benefits to society as a whole, even though it may also be of particular value to the special claimant group. This type of argument, whether advanced by one of the articulate groups usually found in an overt democracy, or by a dictator who despite his powers finds it necessary to justify his decisions proclaimed from on high, contains a theory of economic growth, the latter defined as the most desirable sustained course of long-term changes for the country.

Frequently these notions are a simplified version of some theory propounded earlier by the professional economist or the professional student of social affairs. This is only natural since the "professional" theory is often an articulate, sophisticated answer to some current problems, developed within the intellectual framework of the basic concepts of economic theory. It is not necessarily based on a variety of empirical findings since such variety would almost inevitably make the task of generalization and of unequivocal formulation of policy impossibly difficult. It is this extremely valuable function that much economic writing and theorizing performs: the formulation of an articulate and broad view of a problem, geared to the current conditions and oversimplified to the point of yielding a determinate answer. Unfortunately, such theories, whether in the corpus of economic doctrine or in the simpler form of widespread beliefs, tend to persist far beyond the time of their relevance, and because of the overgeneralization inherent in them, they tend to claim validity far beyond the limits that would be revealed by an empirical test. Yet these views and notions have practical effects, since they may serve as the basis for important social decisions that have far-reaching consequences. To cite one example, the notion of the relation between international free trade and economic growth certainly facilitated the policy that nineteenth-century England pursued with respect to China. It led to the expectation that the opening of the ports would almost automatically draw the millions of Chinese inhabitants into the framework of international trade and thereby eventually introduce in China the higher levels of economic performance associated with modern economic life. It would be easy to repeat examples of widespread notions that are reflections of theories justified in their original historical setting for a relatively narrow area of application, but indefensible in application to other areas or other times.

If this is the case, the practical value of an ambitiously conceived and almost by definition never complete theory of the type indicated, lies in its double function. One would be to provide richer materials for the successive needs of what might be called policy theorizing, defined as theoretical attempts to produce relatively complete systems that can yield determinate policy answers. The distinction between empirical and policy theorizing is not meant to be invidious; the former is never quite complete, whereas the latter must always be definitive, if only by dint of heroic assumptions. But the distinction does seem useful, since in its absence an impossible burden is placed both on the empirically minded theorist who is blamed for not completing his structure and on the policy-minded theorist who is blamed for making his oversimplifying assumptions and not taking sufficient account of the empirical data. If the distinction is accepted, a most important practical contribution of the theory suggested is that it will provide policy analysis with data and findings more relevant to policy concern than has heretofore been the case. It may also lead to less than universal claims for validity for the policy-oriented notions or hypotheses. It may eventually bring about realization by the general public that decisions must be made on the basis of incomplete evidence and that economists and other experts should not be asked to give hard and fast answers to social problems.

The second valuable function of work toward a comprehensive, empirical theory is in its contribution to the destruction or qualification of the more ambitious (in their claims) theories. Cultural lag has become a familiar concept and need not be elaborated upon. Much of this cultural lag consists in reliance on notions that have been retained too long as "general laws." Granted, the resistance of popularly held ideas to rapid change is an important positive element in the continuity of social life and in the transmission of accumulated knowledge from one generation to the next. But the persistence of many of these notions is the result of the difficulty with which new data and findings of empirical social research can be obtained and woven into more than just a new detail. Insofar as this difficulty is reduced by work aimed at a comprehensive theory of the type outlined above, the latter should have great practical value as a solvent of obsolete notions and as a distiller of whatever validity remains in them.

The immediate relevance here of the free pursuit and communication of knowledge is obvious enough. For if any of the older theories concerning economic growth or social life in general are congealed into a doctrine and given the official blessing of immutability and perennial validity; if they become the basis, no matter how violated in practice, of a policy gospel that is above criticism; and if means of communication are barred to anyone who dares to review the doctrines in the light of new evidence, the consequences can easily be foreseen. The wider view of the theory of economic growth advocated here forces recognition of the mutability of many partial doctrines that claim allegiance because they glorify, consciously or unconsciously, their conclusions. For this reason, an indispensable prerequisite for work toward such a theory is the fullest freedom in pursuit of testable findings, in continuous reformulation of interrelations in the light of additional evidence, and in the spread of accumulated results to ever-wider circles. In turn, this work might serve to reduce the obstacles stemming from the dogmatism that attaches to theories which claim eternal and universal validity.

Reflections on
the Economic Growth
of Modern Nations

THE FOLLOWING pages deal with some wider aspects of economic growth, which must be treated rather summarily—indeed, largely as speculations. Although reference to specific research findings will be made at several points, the major purpose here is to raise broad questions whose implications may illuminate the field of economic growth from new angles and suggest new interpretation and new directions for research.[1]

[1] Some of the empirical material and related analytical hypotheses is included in this volume in "Toward a Theory of Economic Growth," pp. 1–81; "Regional Economic Trends and Levels of Living," pp. 142–175; and "Economic Growth and Income Inequality," pp. 257–287. Other relevant papers are: "Population, Income, and Capital" in Leon H. Dupriez, ed., *Economic Progress* (Louvain, 1955), pp. 27–46; "International Differences in Capital Formation and Financing" in Moses Abramovitz, ed., *Capital Formation and Economic Growth* (Princeton, N.J.: Princeton University Press for the National Bureau of Economic Research, 1956), pp. 19–106; "Underdeveloped Countries and the Pre-industrial Phase of Advanced Countries" in United Nations, *Proceedings of the World Population Conference, 1954* (New York, 1955), Vol. V, pp. 947–968; and "Quantitative Aspects of the Economic Growth of Nations," a series of papers, the first two of which have been published in *Economic Development and Cultural Change,* V, 1 (October 1956), and as a supplement to V, 4 (July 1957).

A translation of "Sur la Croissance Économique des Nations Modernes," published in Économie Appliquée, X, 2–3 *(April–September 1957), pp. 211–259.*

Since these speculations reflect an empirically delimited record of economic growth, the limits are indicated so that the reader can judge their relevance. The empirical background is constituted by the economic growth of nations during the last two hundred years—from the mid-eighteenth to the mid-twentieth century. Our records of world-wide economic growth during this period are far from complete, and my knowledge of them is even more limited. The reflections therefore rest upon a partial and, in many ways, woefully incomplete record of a short stretch of historical experience. Yet the growth process so observed is sufficiently varied to raise broad questions which may provide an effective base for reorganizing the observations—for that period and perhaps for some other stretches of historical experience.

The reflections fall under three broad heads: the transnational potential of economic growth; the national exploitation of the growth potential which constitutes the process of economic growth of a nation; and international cooperation and conflict in the process of economic growth.

The Transnational Potential of Economic Growth

We measure the economic growth of nations by the rate of sustained, long-term rise in total product, or still better, in product per capita. One outstanding characteristic of economic growth during the last two centuries, when measured in this rough fashion, has been the high rate of increase in population, total product, and product per capita, at least for what we call the developed countries. Western, Central, and Northern Europe, North America, and selected countries elsewhere—the Soviet Union, Japan, Australia, the Union of South Africa, and in recent decades some countries in Latin America—have all witnessed a rise in population and in economic product per capita which in percentage terms was far greater than in the preceding centuries. This exceptionally high rate of secular rise can be easily documented. An average rate of rise of 15 percent per decade in population and per capita income for long periods was not unusual. Yet this rate means that population and per capita product doubled in less than 50 years and more than quadrupled in a century, and total product doubled in less than 25 years.

This sustained growth of population and product was made possible by the increasing stock of tested knowledge. Knowledge of means of preserving life effected a reduction in death rates, knowledge of natural processes and conditions permitted an increase in economic production, knowledge of social institutions and devices yielded new forms of economic organization, and these were all indispensable for the secular upsurge in population and national product, that is, for the high rate of economic growth. In this accumulation of knowledge modern science played a strategic role. Indeed, one might define modern economic growth as the spread of a system of production, in the widest sense of the term, based upon the increased application of science, that is, an organized system of tested knowledge. If any proof of this proposition is needed, a glance at the products of economically developed nations will suffice: from tractors, chemical fertilizers, and hybridization in modern agriculture, to the steel, steam, and electricity framework of modern industry, to the internal combustion and other engines of modern transportation, the overwhelming proportion of modern production employs tools, materials, and processes that rest upon principles discovered by modern science relatively recently. The current developments in atomic energy and its potential uses are further proof, but there is no point in stressing the obvious.

However, some broader implications have not been sufficiently emphasized, if we can judge by the tenacity of some notions that seem to be inconsistent with them. We attempt to summarize and point up these implications under several broad heads.

1. There is a direct connection between the most abstract and "useless" analyses at the theoretical level of scientific work and the most "practical" consequences which take the form of inventions and improvements that spread through and transform economic life. Numerous illustrations can be provided: from Hertz's discovery of shortwaves believed by him to be of little practical value to modern electronic devices and industries; from Darwin's experiments on responses of plant growth to light to modern weed-killers; from Pasteur's work on the crystal structure of chemical compounds to microbiology and its contribution to longevity; and from Einstein's theory of relativity to nuclear reactors.

The reason for this connection is fairly simple. All science is controlled observation of the world around us, and even such disciplines as logic and mathematics provide the mental tools for handling empirical observations. Economic production is manipulation of part of observable reality for the special purpose of providing commodities and services desired by human beings. It is

therefore inevitable that anything that can be learned in a controlled and testable fashion about the observable world can and
probably will become a tool for some desirable modification in the
processes of economic production, that is, the processes of purpose-
ful tampering with the world in which we live.

An important corollary follows. If we wish to take stock of all
the tested knowledge that is potentially useful in economic production, which in fact constitutes one dimension of the transnational
potential of economic growth now being discussed, the view must
be wide indeed. We must include the variety of known technological
practices of proven value, the millions of inventions and patents
that have not yet been introduced, the uncounted items of important
factual information (boiling and melting points; atomic and valence
structures of chemical compounds; maps of the heavens, oceans,
and land), and above all the vast and abstruse theoretical structures
in all the sciences that deal with the many aspects of the natural,
let alone the social, world. The abstract theory or "idle" experiment
of today may in fifty years be the basis of an imposing industry
and the source of a major shift in the productive structure of at
least the advanced economies. No such inventory is possible with
the tools generally available, and much of the difficulty in gauging
the changing role of this knowledge potential of economic growth
lies in the failure to learn enough about this potential.

2. In view of this remark, it seems illogical to discuss the rate
of increase in the stock of knowledge within the historical period
under review. Yet some trends are defined so sharply and seem so
important that it would be foolhardy not to consider them at least
as tentative hypotheses.

A first hypothesis is that the rate of addition to the stock of
knowledge, at least that which bears most directly upon economic
productivity, has been higher in the last century than in the
previous one. Certainly the emergence by the second half of the
nineteenth century of such new scientific disciplines as chemistry,
biology, geology, and microbiology provided a firm theoretical
foundation in economically important fields, where improvements
had previously been achieved almost entirely by trial and error.
Furthermore, there is a marked contrast in the relation of technological discoveries to actual changes between the period of the
Industrial Revolution in England and, say, the twentieth century.
The revolutions in cotton textiles and in pig iron and bar iron
production, and the introduction of steam in the second half

of the eighteenth century were in response to long-felt needs, followed a long search, and were based in at least one case—the introduction of coke in the smelting of iron ore—upon trial and error, with little knowledge of the underlying chemical processes. Here then necessity was the mother of invention, and the period of gestation was long. In contrast, many economically important inventions of the late nineteenth and the twentieth centuries were the results of attempts to apply new scientific discoveries, attempts by people like Edison and Marconi who were not scientists but who understood the scientific advances and were impelled to look for practical applications. Here, the addition to the stock of knowledge came first, and one might say that invention fostered need.

The above remarks may be an oversimplification, but while the hypothesis cannot be fully demonstrated, it does seem plausible and can be explained. To begin with, the stock of knowledge never diminishes: it may be revised because better tools and more cogent theories necessitate modification of some findings, but even this is an addition. Constant accumulation of improved information, accompanied by constant improvement in scientific tools, is likely in and of itself to accelerate the pace of new additions to knowledge. The universe is wide, the variety of its aspects is enormous, and the amount to be learned is great. And it is always easier to learn more from a wide base of existing knowledge than from a base of relative ignorance in which it is difficult to perceive the relation between the "new" and the known.

The point can be restated in terms of the relations among the scientific disciplines. The emergence of modern chemistry redounded to the benefit not only of the "applied" disciplines like medicine, but even of physics, a scientific discipline that had emerged before chemistry. Since they are studying different aspects of one world, the several disciplines are closely related. So long as there are major gaps in the system, even the progress of the older disciplines is often delayed until their sister disciplines are sufficiently mature. This is true even of general theory; and when "practical" application is considered, the availability of knowledge of physics, chemistry, and biology on relatively high levels, makes applications easier.

One important corollary follows. Assume that the rate of additions to the stock of useful knowledge has accelerated, that it was distinctly higher in 1850–1950 than in 1750–1850, or even that the rate was higher in 1900–1950 than in 1850–1900. Has the *utilization* of this increasing stock of knowledge, that is, of the potential of economic growth, kept pace with the additions to the stock? There is always a lag in the translation of existing knowledge into economic and social practices, particularly if knowledge is at different distances, as it were, from wide-scale application. But has this lag, measured as a proportion of the total stock of knowledge not yet utilized, been increasing apace?

The problem has many tenuous aspects largely because it is difficult to gauge the stock of useful knowledge. Since this vagueness affects the denominator and it is not easy to define large-scale application, the ratio, the rate of utilization of the existing stock of knowledge, cannot be estimated; and discussion of its trends is a matter of impressions. Still, if there has been a shift from necessity as the mother of invention, to invention as the mother of new needs and impulses, it is reasonable to assume that the backlog of unutilized knowledge has become proportionately greater.

This conclusion, if true, would have some major economic consequences. For it suggests that *all* countries have become increasingly "underdeveloped," in the sense that none is fully exploiting the growth potential available to it. It suggests that the economically advanced nations have the advantage of a large growth potential and that the *economic* rationale does not always favor capital exports to the underdeveloped areas. If the demand for capital is represented by a curve in which the vertical axis is the yield of the application of the yet unused knowledge and the horizontal axis is the cost in terms of material investment, entrepreneurship, and the elimination of social resistance, it may well be that in the advanced countries the availability of a large growth potential at low social costs means *domestic* capital demand that leaves little for capital exports. The traditional theory, which argues an economic case for the flow of capital from the more to the less developed countries, may thus be negated, partly because it disregards the possibility of this large growth potential even for the most advanced countries and partly because it minimizes the *social* obstacles to foreign capital investment in underdeveloped areas.

3. If the unused potential of economic growth has increased proportionately, another hypothesis can be assumed: as far as potential technological change is concerned, there is no proximate limit to economic growth.

That a social process, like the economic growth of a nation, has no finite limit would seem, on the face of it, an absurdity. Obviously no society can grow infinitely large. But our hypothesis makes no such claim. We do not argue that the population of a nation can increase indefinitely; it may well reach some nearly stable limit because the birth rate may decline to so low a level as to produce a slight rate of natural increase. Or other factors, such as preference for more leisure or low long-term elasticity of demand for economic goods, may permit and warrant only minor increases in per capita product once it has reached certain high levels. Or international relations may be characterized by conflicts which necessitate the expenditure of increasingly larger proportions of national resources on items that are not part of final product. None of these factors which may set a finite limit to the economic growth of a nation is denied by the hypothesis. But it emphasizes the point that the growth potential that follows from progress in science and technology has no upper limit.

Two distinct reasons can be advanced in support of this hypothesis. First, additions to knowledge are largely the product of the free inquiring mind. If there is no effective restriction—either prohibition or complete lack of support—on the curiosity-motivated explorations of the mind, the search for new theories, new data, and new applications will continue. In other words, since the search is continuously self-propelled and aimed at no fixed goal, there is no *internal* source of a limit. This assumption of the *free* mind is both a qualification of the hypothesis and a partial explanation of the impressive development of tested knowledge during the last two centuries.

Given this continuous play of the free mind, the second reason for an unlimited economic growth potential becomes relevant. And that reason is simply the vastness of the observable universe; or, which is the same thing, the quantitative insignificance of mankind in that universe. The stock of tested knowledge therefore concerns a much wider realm than has yet been exploited by mankind, and theoretically the *application* of knowledge can tap an area that extends far beyond our planet. Not only has the exploitation of our oceans barely begun, not only are many new land areas likely to be more productive because of recent discoveries of new sources of energy, but in these days of interplanetary travel discussions we cannot dismiss the possibility of extending processes of economic production beyond the confines of the earth. Under such circumstances, it is difficult to set an effective limit to the potential growth contribution of the increasing stock of knowledge in the foreseeable future.

This argument, which smacks of science-fiction, would perhaps be unnecessary if the contrary notion were not still being stressed in economic theorizing. The writings of the Classical School emphasize the proximate limits on growth imposed by the diminishing fertility of the soil. Those of the Marxian School imply the same assumption in their analysis of the long-term trends in the rate of surplus value. The reasoning in both instances rests upon the assumed inability of scientific progress to cope with the exhaustion of natural resources. Much of the recent Malthusian discussion argues from the premise of a *natural*, rather than social, limitation upon the capacity of mankind to sustain itself. Granted that an imbalance between population and natural resources at a given (usually backward) level of technology poses major problems, one wonders how, in the light of the advance in science and technology during the last two centuries, the premise of a technological limit upon productive capacity in the long run can be retained.

One may add parenthetically that judgments of "experts" on these matters are likely to be at fault. Experts are usually specialists skilled in, and hence bound to, traditional views; and they are, because of their knowledge of one field, likely to be cautious and unduly conservative. Hertz, a great physicist, denied the practical importance of shortwaves, and others at the end of the nineteenth century reached the conclusion that little more could be done on the structure of matter. Malthus, Ricardo, and Marx, great economists, made incorrect prognoses of technological changes at the very time that the scientific bases for these changes were evolving. On the other hand, imaginative tyros like Jules Verne and H. G. Wells seemed to sense the potentialities of technological change. It is well to take cognizance of this consistently conservative bias of experts in evaluating the hypothesis of an unlimited effective increase in the stock of knowledge and in the corresponding potential of economic growth.

4. The preceding discussion does not touch upon two major problems. The first relates to the factors that determine the rate of addition to the stock of useful knowledge. Granted that no fixed limit can be set to the economic growth potential provided by it, we would obviously want to know which conditions favor a high rate and which do not.

This raises a number of complex questions to which I cannot offer clear answers and on which there is not much organized evidence. Presumably conditions would be different for distinct types of scientific discovery, invention, and improvement. And any systematic consideration of the problem would require some classification of types of knowledge, with distinctions drawn eventually, if not in the first instance, upon some hypotheses concerning the differences in the determining conditions involved.

Consider, as an illustration, research in natural science theory and the kind of question that arises. The political and social organization of Tsarist Russia did not bar the emergence of a Lobatschevsky, a Mendeleyev, or a Metschnikov. Would the Stalinist regime have allowed enough free play of the mind and hence discovery in, say, the field of biology? Why under the free conditions of the United States was relatively little original work done in the natural sciences at the theoretical level, and so much in the applied disciplines and practical invention? What are the *optimal* conditions for the "production" of basic scientific discoveries? How much valid argument can be distilled from the many propositions advanced recently in the controversy between the advocates of socially directed group efforts in scientific work (Joseph Needham, J. B. S. Haldane, and others) and the defenders of the untrammeled, unfettered, individual scientists?

These questions are illustrative and may not even be the proper ones. They have been posed merely to suggest the problem. Yet, although they may not help to formulate it properly, they do illustrate its long-term bearing. Clearly any developments in the system of values which society imposes upon its individual members, in the conditions under which the men and women who are the living carriers of intellectual progress operate, may, through their effect on the whole climate of opinion, influence the rate at which additions are made to the stock of knowledge. The problem becomes all the more complicated when one realizes that the scientific and technological efforts are not the only important ones. The insights of artists often foreshadow the configurations that touch off the work of scientists and inventors. The Renaissance in Italy, in freeing the eye of the artist in painting and sculpture, was the prelude to the scientific study of man and the universe. The imaginative rather than scientific intuition of Malthus touched off Darwin's theory of evolution. And the incisive insights of the masters of modern art may well pave the way to some scientific movements. To that extent the values and conditions that affect the whole realm of the human spirit and its operation are important.

This may seem like a far cry from the economic growth of nations; yet it is here that the major steps are taken that provide the basis for modern technology and economics. In my own ignorance of this field, I can only indicate the relation and the gap in our discussion.

5. The other major lacuna in our discussion can perhaps be suggested effectively by considering the meaning of transnational in reference to the potential of economic growth provided by the stock of knowledge.

This term is used because the knowledge is presumably accessible to all mankind. There is no national physics, chemistry, or biology, and there should be no national economics or sociology. The law of gravitation and the periodic table of elements hold for all nations, and the laws of economics and sociology, although limited to specific types of social organization and technology, should hold for all societies that reach the relevant state and level of development. Theoretically, knowledge embodied in overt and objective terms is accessible to anyone, regardless of nation, race, or habitat, who has the necessary vocabulary and has acquired the necessary intellectual tools.

Is this transnational quality true also of applied knowledge, the necessary link between generally formulated tenets of scientific theory and large-scale economic production? Granted that the laws of chemistry and even those for the production of pig iron or steel are world-wide, the discovery of the use of coke for smelting iron ore was directly beneficial only to those nations that had good coking coal and adequate supplies of iron ore. One may argue that this discovery originated in England partly because a technological-economic problem peculiar to England in the eighteenth century had to be solved. Neither Holland, which did not have the raw materials, nor Sweden, which had both wood and iron ore in relative abundance, was under pressure to make such a discovery.

Insofar as there is a strong element of need in the process of adding to applied knowledge, there may well be national *biases* in the stock of useful knowledge. The weight of new inventions and improvements will probably be concentrated in those types that seem most useful to the few advanced societies with the greater supply of intellectual resources. In other words, over and above the core of the general transnational type of knowledge, there may be others of vast direct practical importance that are of more value to some nations than to others.

We are here approaching the variety of factors which explain the underutilization of the economic growth potential contained in the stock of knowledge. Most of these reside in the social and economic structure of nations and will be discussed in the next section. But while dealing with the stock of knowledge, we should note the possible skewness in its supply. This immediately suggests limits on the growth potential not noted so far, limits that can be found in the past concentration of work on many of the applications —inventions, improvements, and the like—in certain areas. Such concentration has been due to the uneven spread of economic and social progress throughout the world: those nations that advanced first were also among the first able to spare a greater proportion of human resources for work on promotion of knowledge, a good part of which was naturally directed to their own technological problems. There is of course an element of generality, some transfer value, even in the most specific discovery or invention; but when technological effort is concentrated on specific problems, a substantial proportion of the addition to the stock of knowledge must be more directly useful to some nations than to others. To cite an obvious example: modern technology in agriculture is far more advanced in economizing labor than in economizing land, yet for many underdeveloped countries a technique by which the dependence of agriculture on land could be reduced would be far more valuable.

This implies that at least for certain categories of our stock of useful knowledge, the growth potential is limited by the supply of human effort applied to them. It also suggests that one major requirement for underdeveloped countries is the skilled human resources that would be directed to the task of adapting and adjusting the existing stock of knowledge to the particular conditions and problems of these countries. This kind of adaptation and adjustment is only one of several involved in exploiting the potential of economic growth provided by the transnational stock of knowledge. We can now turn to a more direct consideration of the full range of this process.

Internal Conditions of Economic Growth

It is clear from the preceding discussion that no nation, even the most advanced, has fully utilized the transnational growth potential.

The reasons must obviously be in the lack of some essential pre-requisites. We can perhaps secure a preliminary view of these prerequisites by noting the social and economic changes in those countries with the largest economic growth. If we find some general corollaries of economic growth, regardless of country and regardless of political and social conditions, we can reasonably argue that these are indispensable concomitants and prerequisites. And this assumption would be even more plausible if we could detect some direct connection between these concomitants and the satisfactory utilization of growth potentials. Having established these con-comitants, we should then be in a position at least to surmise why these prerequisites were lacking in so many areas of the world and resulted in economic backwardness, and why in no country the growth potential can be fully utilized. Here we are concerned only with *internal* conditions and the account will be complete only after we have considered the international relations.

Among the concomitants of modern economic growth are new patterns of population growth, industrialization, urbanization, new patterns of use of national product, an increase in the nonpersonal forms of economic organization, and a rise in the relative importance of economic achievement in the scale of social values. This list, manifestly incomplete, can serve as the focus in our discussion, and although the discussion must be sketchy, a broad view of the process may be secured.

NEW PATTERNS OF POPULATION GROWTH · Modern economic growth has been accompanied by a substantial decline in death rates fol-lowed by a decline in birth rates, and resulting in a long-term rise in the rate of natural increase. The impact of the decline in death rates was unequal; it was absolutely greater in the young, par-ticularly the infant, age groups; and it was greater in the cities, thus removing the excess of urban over rural mortality rates typical of premodern times. The decline in death rates was accompanied by a significant decline in morbidity rates, and the lesser incidence of epidemics and other health catastrophes, which thus made for a temporal stability in the rate of population growth that was previously unknown. The decline in birth rates, when it came, also had unequal impact: associated with voluntary control of family size, it affected the upper economic and social groups first and then spread downward. Finally, during much of the recent period there was a large volume of voluntary migration—a process by which population in some parts of the world could be and was distributed in better adjustment to economic opportunities.

This statement describes the demographic trends which, with different initial dates in different areas of the world, could be observed between the second half of the eighteenth and the mid-twentieth centuries. The trends are well known, but some of their implications for economic growth need to be stressed. The decline in infant and child mortality which, in and of itself, was bound to lower birth rates, eliminated enormous waste. Under premodern, preindustrial conditions, many children were born and raised but never reached productive ages, and the time and resources devoted to the bearing and rearing of these children were a tremendous economic loss. The reduction in the excessively high death rates associated in older times with population density—in cities, armies, or jails—was indispensable since modern economic growth rests upon concentration of population, in plants, cities, or elsewhere. The increasing resistance to epidemics and other mortality catastrophes and the attainment of a temporally *stable* population growth must have had a marked influence by extending the time horizon of individuals, by freeing them from uncertainty, and by encouraging the long-range planning that is characteristic of modern economic activity. The secular decline in birth rates is in a sense a corollary of the movement in death rates and of the changed view of the power of the individual to control his life span and the number of his descendants.

The indispensability of this modern demographic-growth pattern as a base for modern economic growth must be stressed, because the shift to lower death rates and higher rates of natural increase makes for temporary difficulties during the transition process, which often lead to doubts as to its desirability. Yet clearly this modern population-growth pattern cannot be avoided. As will be argued below, a high valuation of material achievement is essential to modern economic growth. Reducing sickness and death is surely the first goal in material attainment, and minimizing health catastrophes is another. If the population must share this view in order to participate effectively in economic growth, how can it be compelled to delay the measures that increase longevity? How, without shifting to a modern pattern of population growth, can the change be made from the joint, large family, with its patriarchal or matriarchal and nepotic tendencies that stifle individual initiative, to the small, individualistic family that is the appropriate unit for modern societies? Without these changes in social valuation and in family organization, the modern economy cannot operate effectively. It is important to emphasize that this shift in the population-growth pattern and in family structure occurred not only in developed countries of Western civilization, which grew under the aegis of business enterprise, but also in Japan and in the USSR, where antecedent historical and recent political conditions were far different. The limitations on material welfare imposed in these countries assumed, and had to assume, a form and rationale different from those involved in a refusal to adopt the contributions of science and technology to the reduction of the death rate and the contributions of the modern way of life to the reduction of the birth rate.

INDUSTRIALIZATION · The long-term increase in product per capita has generally been accompanied by a decline in the proportion of agriculture and related primary industries. This shift in favor of the nonagricultural sectors, or industrialization, is evident in shares in the labor force, capital stock, and national product. Furthermore, there have been shifts among the nonagricultural activities. In many countries, but not in all, the share of manufacturing and construction, including or excluding mining, has become stabilized after a while; but the share of the service industries—transportation and communication, trade, finance, professional and personal services, and governments—has continued to rise. (To deal here with the many other trends, particularly in the relative income per worker in these sectors, would take us too far afield.)

These trends in the industrial structure of national product, capital, and the labor force can be associated with technological necessities, on both the production or supply and consumption or demand sides. The decline in the share of agriculture in the labor force was due to the combination of a marked secular rise in labor productivity in agriculture, indispensable if part of the labor force was to be released for other uses, with the low long-term elasticity of demand for agricultural products—a reflection of the structure of human wants. On the other hand, the marked secular rise in the share of the service industries was due partly to a rather small rise in at least the measurable productivity of labor in several branches of service but perhaps more to the great secular increase in demand. This increase in turn was due partly to the structure of wants of ultimate consumers, in which the proportion of income spent on health, education, recreation, and the like increases with a secular rise in income per capita; partly to the changed conditions of life, noted below under urbanization, which increased the need for services; and partly to the demands of the developing productive organization of commodity output for more transportation, communication, trade, finance, and, not least, government services.

We stress these technological necessities to indicate the indispensability of the shifts in industrial structure in the process of economic growth. For example, if in order to increase per worker productivity in automobile production larger-scale plants were needed, the concentration of production combined with the dispersion of sources of raw materials and of ultimate buyers would mean more transportation, communication, trade, and finance, and hence a greater share of these service industries in the labor force and national product. If, as will be indicated below, industrialization meant urbanization and the growth of cities required more municipal government, the share of government in product and in the labor force also had to rise. In other words, given the structure of human wants and the technological requirements of greater productivity, the shifts in industrial structure are part and parcel of economic growth. This is so even for a single country, since there are secular limits to the concentration of a country's production on a few branches with reliance on the outside world for the rest, particularly at high levels of per capita product.

The secular change in industrial structure involves shifts in the relative weights and positions of various economic, occupational, and other groups within society. A decline in the share of agriculture in the labor force means a decline in the relative weight of farmers and farm workers in society and the movement of a substantial proportion of their descendants into other pursuits. And this process is usually accompanied by differential trends in income per worker in the several industrial sectors, which means that some groups gain, on a per capita basis, relatively to others. Furthermore, the high rate of rise in per capita product that characterized modern economic growth was accompanied by relatively rapid shifts in industrial structure: in only a hundred years the share of agriculture in the labor force in the United States dropped from over 70 percent to less than 20 percent. Obviously, one of the major requirements of economic growth is the capacity of society to undergo these rapid internal shifts, to make feasible this continuous mobility and redistribution of the labor force and population among the various sectors of the country's economy.

URBANIZATION · By urbanization we mean an increase in the proportion of a country's population living in communities above a specific size, the term community implying a concentration of people within a small area. Whether we draw the line between city and countryside at 2,000, 8,000, or higher, urbanization has been a concomitant of economic growth during the past two centuries.

Urbanization is largely a product of industrialization, although the former may occur without the latter and the latter does not fully account for the former. Theoretically, industrialization is possible without urbanization. An authority, determined to prevent urbanization regardless of costs, could prohibit agglomeration of plants and firms within a small area, could require construction of housing for the workers of a single large plant that would assure low density per square mile, to mention only two techniques. However, the costs would be prohibitive. If the technological criteria set the optimum scale of a plant at several thousand workers, forcing them to live far apart would be expensive in transportation to work, in the supply of services to them and their families, and in the cost of land that could be used for more productive purposes. Similarly, locating related plants at a distance from each other just to prevent urbanization would also multiply costs. The fact is that contiguity of related economic units whenever permitted by the productive process (not in agriculture and other extractive industries depending upon extension of the area) is economical, and the cost of dispensing with it is high. In this sense, urbanization is the economic product of industrialization.

But urbanization goes beyond the necessities dictated by optimum scale and location of commodity-producing plants, in the development of highly specialized functions that are feasible only in large cities. And as the economy grows, the need for these functions will itself generate metropolitan areas as centers of activities like wholesale trade, finance, education, legal services, and government. Whereas these functions are in a sense further aspects of industrialization, they are beyond the mere shift from agricultural and related activities and deserve explicit mention. Their location in proximity to other sources of urban concentration—manufacturing, retail trade, etc.—makes urbanization a necessary corollary of economic growth. It is interesting to note that the considered attempt to avoid urbanization while attaining industrialization in the economic planning of the USSR was signally unsuccessful. Although it may have been a wishful slogan rather than a vigorous program, the fact is that urbanization could not be avoided even in this almost completely planned industrialization process.

But the more important point is the effect of urbanization on other trends and concomitants. It sets the conditions for the decline in the birth rate and the shift toward the small family; it requires a vast amount of internal migration, since the cities, particularly in the early days, grew largely by influx from the countryside and this migration meant detachment from roots and easier adaptation to changing economic opportunities; it throws people together so that they can imitate and learn from each other much faster; it facilitates the development of the impersonal relations of modern life, and at the same time teaches cooperation on this impersonal basis. Above all it creates the conditions for the intense intellectual activity associated with modern civilization and thereby creates more favorable conditions for the increase in useful knowledge. In short, urbanization is not only the sole *economical* way to effect industrialization, but in the deeper and perhaps more important sense, it also provides the conditions under which the new way of life can grow and the creative pursuits in art, science, and technology can flourish. These pursuits provide the driving force of the increasing growth potential in the stock of knowledge, and urban life, by spreading them among sufficiently large groups of the population, provides them with a broad base.

NEW PATTERNS OF NATIONAL PRODUCT · The three trends listed above required not only absolutely larger volumes of capital but higher shares of capital formation in national product. A greater rate of increase of population means usually a greater rate of growth of the labor force and, other conditions being equal, a greater rate of additions to capital stock to provide for the increased number of people and workers. Insofar as the rate of growth of total product is raised by the acceleration in the rate of population growth, and the capital coefficients (i.e., ratios of capital to output) remain constant, the proportion of capital formation to national product will rise. Furthermore, the shift in industrial structure meant the setting up of new industries. Many of those, based on the new technology, required large amounts of fixed capital, if only to contain and channel the new powerful sources of energy. And being planned for the long run, the new plants were built before their full capacity could be utilized, which tended to raise the capital-output ratios and to make for higher proportions of capital formation to national product. Finally, urbanization also meant large investments in costly provisions for streets, sanitation, water supply, lighting, transportation, and housing.

It follows that a significant rise in capital formation proportions was requisite for modern economic growth. The statistical records for the early periods of some developed countries, for example Sweden and Denmark, show marked rises in the proportion that net (or gross) additions to capital located within the country formed of net (or gross) domestic or national product. International comparisons at a recent date show that, by and large, these domestic capital formation proportions are much lower in the underdeveloped countries than in the developed countries. For *national* capital formation proportions, which represent the national rate of savings (i.e., domestic adjusted for capital imports or exports), the shift from the low levels of preindustrial times to the higher levels required by modern technology emerges even more sharply.

It may seem at first that the modifications in patterns of use of national product implied by this essential rise in capital formation proportions are moderate and do not involve major changes in economic and social life. After all, the suggested rise is from net capital formation proportions of less than 5 percent to at most about 15 percent, and from gross capital formation proportions of less than 10 percent to about 25 percent. If per capita income rises 10 to 15 percent per decade, as it has in many countries in modern times, keeping per capita consumption unchanged for one decade and adding all of the gain to capital formation would raise the proportions of the latter from 5 to 15 percent. Surely the allocation of a decade's addition to per capita product to capital formation, with no benefit to consumption, does not seem to involve a major social transformation.

But this impression is false for two reasons. The first relates to the timing sequence. If growth of income per capita requires some *antecedent* growth of capital, the rise in the capital formation proportions is needed in advance of the rise in per capita income. To put it more precisely: if a capital formation proportion of 3 percent permitted growth of population at 0.3 percent per year combined with growth in per capita product at 0.1 percent per year, a much larger capital formation proportion will be required just to maintain the per capita product at the same level if population growth is accelerated to 1.0 percent per year. And under such conditions, greater capital accumulation would have to be financed either from abroad or from domestic savings. Financing from abroad, on any sizable scale, might mean some changes at home to permit capital imports on nononerous terms, or special concessions to the foreign creditor that may have distorting or damping effects on economic growth within the country. Financing from domestic savings would mean *reducing* per capita consumption. In other words, the rise in capital formation proportions that must precede any rise in per capita product necessitates substantial changes in the patterns of spending and saving within the country or changes that would induce capital imports from abroad or both.

The second and weightier reason is suggested by the fact that the capital formation proportions are less important than the conditions that give them meaning. In the percentages quoted above, capital formation in the numerator comprised only investments represented by changes in stock of construction, equipment, and inventories (including or excluding net changes in claims against foreign countries as we speak of national or of domestic capital formation). Such capital is effective only if it can be combined with sufficiently skilled labor and management, and developed and underdeveloped countries differ not only in the capital formation proportions but also in the availability of human resources. In this connection, expenditures on some products customarily included under consumer outlay, such as education, recreation, health, and transportation, are capital formation in that they raise the health and skills of labor necessary for combination with material capital. Hence, in emphasizing the rise in capital formation proportions requisite for economic growth, a wider concept of capital is far more relevant, one that would at least include investment in the health and training of the population and in the facilities for social organization that permit increases in productivity. The rises in the capital formation proportions so defined would be far larger than from 5 to 15 percent net, or from 10 to 25 percent gross, and the corresponding international differences between developed and underdeveloped countries would be far wider than those in the ratios currently used. Changes in such proportions would surely mean major shifts in the structure of use of the product and in the patterns of life, and would make the problem of initial capital accumulation all the more complex.

CHANGES IN ECONOMIC ORGANIZATION · Changes in the scale and character of the organizations by which economic activity is carried on are a necessary concomitant of modern technology. The large fixed-capital investments in canals, railroads, steel plants, power stations, and the like could not be entrusted to firms managed by individuals, families, or partnerships. The economic horizon involved far exceeds the life span of an individual or a generation; the mobilization of the necessary savings could not be accomplished without an articulate, nonpersonal structure associated with the limited-liability modern corporation; and the increasing complexity of management requires an organizational form free of the personal limitations of an individual owner or partnership group. Thus the scale of the plant units and the size and life of capital investment required by the technology of modern economic growth, in and of itself, forced a shift from personal ownership-management units to the large-scale corporation. And when the inevitable monopolistic tendencies of the latter, in public utilities, for example, required regulation by the government, regulation in turn contributed to fixing the nonpersonal organization in these industries and at the same time widened the economic role of government, itself a nonpersonal organizational unit.

Empirical data indicate the decline in the shares of capital, product, and labor force engaged under the auspices of individual firms or partnerships, and the increase in the shares controlled by private corporations, and public and governmental bodies, or a mixture of both. The trends are due partly to the rise in relative weight of whole new sectors—railroads, communication, electric light and power, and large-scale manufacturing—which from their beginning had to be nonpersonal organizations, and partly to the increasing share of nonpersonal organizations in sectors where the individual firm or partnership had originally been dominant, such as most manufacturing, construction, trade, and some service industries, and even agriculture. Since both governmental and private corporations are classified as nonpersonal, the suggested trends have only been accelerated by the emergence of the state organization of economic activity exemplified by the USSR.

Three aspects of these trends deserve explicit note. First, the shift required a far-reaching adjustment by members of society. As experience has shown, it is not sufficient to pass a law permitting easy chartering of general purpose, limited-liability corporations.

The people involved, however they are associated with these non-personal organizational units, must act accordingly. A unit that is a publicly chartered, limited-liability corporation in name but is managed as a family firm and so treated by its owners, employees, and the public, is still an individual firm, not a corporation. Governments run by a few families and shot through with nepotism and other forms of corruption are not public agencies but family businesses. Clearly, the growth of genuine nonpersonal organizational units requires a corresponding change in the attitudes of would-be owners, managers, and workers, away from any idea of personal control and relations to rather different and strictly defined roles in these almost statutorily structured units. The owners must learn that their proprietary rights are limited; the managers must learn that they can operate only within specified rules of responsibility and efficiency; and the workers must be ready to accept the purely nonpersonal connection through the labor market.

Second, there is continuous change in the evolution of these non-personal organizational units which, when they first emerge, induce these changes in attitudes. Their continued existence strengthens the change and permits further depersonalization of the whole organizational structure. The very increase in the scale of the productive plant and firm forces an increasing distance, as it were, from the direct and personal type of organization: in a plant with only one hundred workers and a few supervisors, personal relations can persist and decisions can be made in a manner that would be dangerous if not impossible in a corporation with thousands of workers and millions of capital investment. On the other hand, the experience gained by people in dealing *via* these nonpersonal organizational units results in a capacity to cooperate that could hardly have been expected of their elders and ancestors, accustomed to entirely different economic relations. The cumulative character of this process and its close interrelation with urbanization and associated changes in patterns of life are particularly to be noted.

Third, the changing relations among owners, managers, workers, and society as a whole play havoc with the older economic theorizing on the subject, much of which survives even today. Perhaps the notable example is the Marxian theory of classes, in which class is related to ownership of means of production, and the class struggle combined with the labor theory of value is used to derive a number of trends in the breakdown of industrial capitalism. In the modern business corporation, the locus of ownership of means of production is vague. Are the owners the thousands of small stockholders, the banks and insurance companies that hold large blocks of stock, on trust as it were, or the managers, who legally are only employees? Is the modern proletariat devoid of control over means of production if a strong union organization can enforce the right to work? What is the role of government in the modern economy? Is it really, as some vulgarized notions of Marxian theory associated with Lenin and his followers claim, a "lackey" of the capitalists, and if so, who are the latter? And is the bureaucracy in the state-controlled economy of the USSR the servant or the master of the people? Why has the "middle" class failed to disappear, and indeed flourished, particularly in countries like the United States where capitalism was most developed? These questions indicate the gap between the oversimplified terminology of the Marxian theory of class struggle and secular transformation of capitalist society and the changes in the structure of economic organization that in fact occurred, partly in connection with the development of the nonpersonal organizational units in modern economic growth.

CHANGES IN SOCIAL VALUES · The trends in population growth, industrialization, urbanization, spending and saving, and nonpersonal organizational units all imply and must be accompanied by major shifts in the structure of social values. The interplay between social values and the overt processes described by these trends is so close that it is difficult to establish its separate existence. Values are expressed through the behavior of individuals; I cannot point to proofs of the existence of values that are independent of action. Yet it may be argued that modern economic development was partly preceded by and partly accompanied by these shifts in the structure of social values, which had an independent existence in the sense that at critical junctures they constituted the major factor that produced certain social decisions.

The general process of secularization, which placed a high value on the individual and his material welfare in this world instead of his spiritual welfare and the next world, was obviously a foundation without which many trends related to economic growth would have been impossible. This point can be amplified by a few illustrations. The revolution in medicine and public health in England toward the end of the eighteenth century and in the early nineteenth century was not based upon any major scientific discovery. It resulted from a combination of the victory, if only partial, of the empirical frame of mind which refused to accept traditional notions, with a zeal to improve man's lot in this world, a direct rejection of the doctrine of original sin and the view of human suffering as the unavoidable act of a just deity. It is not farfetched to say that this major change in public health practices was largely the result of a change in point of view, in the scale of values. Or to take another example: the theories of human equality, liberty, and fraternity and the denial of the sacredness of status positions not only were instrumental in removing many legal and political obstacles to economic growth but in fact provided the basis upon which the modern view of economic welfare could be developed. And the utilitarian doctrines of the greatest good for the greatest number, which were in a direct line of succession from them, shaped the modern view of social organization and led to the increasing importance of material welfare and economic activity.

This is hardly the place for even a condensed summary of the changes in the view of the world and of mankind that have occurred since the Reformation, the birth of modern science, and the spread of the rationalistic approach. All that need be said here is that, at least as far as Western civilization is concerned—and it is rapidly spreading to the rest of the world—the loss of an overriding religious faith and of the sanctified traditions connected with it not only freed the human mind and effort for the cultivation of science and the arts but also reoriented a vast corpus of human activities. This reorientation was a major prerequisite for modern economic growth. One may regret for esthetic reasons that large proportions of the national product are no longer devoted to pyramids, cathedrals, and castles, but one must admit that power dams, steel furnaces, and skyscrapers are more directly productive of economic growth. One may deplore the decline of those status groups in society that provided for the cultivation of fine traditions, but one must admit that the atomistic, individualistic equality and easy social mobility of modern times are far more conducive to competition and intensive growth. One may deplore the lessening of direct contact between man and nature and the desiccation of some values associated with this contact, but one must grant that the complex and abstract system of modern relations is far more efficient, even though it may require acceptance of some tenuous and apparently empty symbols.

Whether we call these views philosophy, theory, mythology, or religion, the point is that they have changed either in advance of, concurrently with, or after the initiation of modern economic growth.

And they *had* to change if such growth was to take place and continue, since the older views were geared to the type of economic and social life that then prevailed. Economic growth, like all processes of social change, is the result of decisions in response to conditions under which some choices exist. And these decisions must be made within the broader framework of theory, mythology, or religion. In the sixteenth and seventeenth centuries an inventor was considered a public nuisance, to be suppressed as a subverter of established order, whereas in our time and country he is considered the motive force of beneficent progress. These different appraisals can only be the expression of different underlying views of the roles of technical progress and business enterprise in attaining desirable goals, and even of the goals themselves. Obviously, such views and appraisals have far-reaching influence on economic growth since they determine decisions by society that set the conditions for economic activity and progress.

THE COST OF TRANSITION · The list of antecedents, concomitants, and consequences of modern economic growth given above could be expanded further. But it is sufficient to suggest the magnitude of the transformation of economic and social life that accompanied modern economic growth and actually formed its substance. We can now appreciate the difficulties and the costs of transition from premodern, preindustrial modes of economic activity and understand why actual economic performance falls short of the potential provided by the increasing stock of useful knowledge.

In considering the problems just suggested, it is useful to distinguish the transition period from the one that follows. The distinction is in a sense artificial: it would be difficult in any specific country's record of economic development to establish the terminal date of the transition period. The process of growth is continuous and at any time in any economy premodern conditions can be found alongside marked changes from old to new. Yet such a distinction helps to separate the period when the bases of modern economic growth were being established and the resistance of the old order was being overcome, from the later period when the self-sustaining and cumulative trends that carry modern economic growth forward emerge.

The historical records provide us with data for several such transition periods: in England from the last quarter of the eighteenth century through the second quarter of the nineteenth century; in the

United States from the 1840's to the 1880's or 1890's with the interruption of the Civil War; in Germany and France from about the middle to the end of the nineteenth century; in Japan from about the late 1870's to about the end of World War I; and finally in Russia from the abortive attempt begun in the 1890's and interrupted by World War I and the Revolution, through the five-year plans of the Soviet regime from the late 1920's to the 1950's. There are also data for the Scandinavian countries, some dominions of the British Empire, and Italy. Each is a case *sui generis,* conditioned by the country's historical heritage and natural endowments, as well as by the particular time and constellation of international conditions associated with it. Yet comparative analysis, which has only been begun, reveals some general features. During the specified periods all these countries show an acceleration in population growth (except in "empty" areas in the New World); a rise in capital formation proportions; a redistribution of population and the labor force, with shifts from agriculture and the countryside to nonagricultural sectors and the cities; changes in the organizational units; and a transformation of values, with high priority given to economic attainment.

These changes do not occur in a vacuum; they are made in societies that usually have a long tradition of the premodern economic organization and social structure, and they must be directed by agents with the power to overcome resistance and incur necessary costs. If agriculture must be changed to permit greater productivity and release labor for other pursuits, the immediate task is to break through the old organizational patterns, to change the relations of man to land, which means in fact dislodging substantial proportions of the population from their accustomed pursuits without disrupting the whole structure of the country's organization and making economic progress impossible. This task was more formidable in the older countries of Western civilization than in its offshoots in the younger and emptier countries. And history is full of the troubles and turmoils when the revolutionary changes took place in the organization and economics of agriculture in England, France, Germany, let alone the USSR during the years of collectivization. The new economics had equally disruptive effects on handicrafts, on small-scale industry and trade, on a variety of established and entrenched sectors of the old economic order, and on the position of the interest groups associated with them.

It is this dislocation and break with the old order that constitutes the major cost of the transition to modern economic growth. Moreover, the benefits of the innovations are not immediate, since it is during this period that the shift to higher proportions of capital formation may occur; and the rise in consumption per capita, if any, must be smaller than the rise in total product per capita. It is during this period also that one mechanism for attaining these results is a wide, perhaps a widening, inequality in the distribution of income—a characteristic not only of the societies that developed under the aegis of the business enterprise but also of those that used the authoritarian power of the state to manage economic processes. Inequality of income in the USSR during the five-year plans was just as great as, if not greater than, in England in the late eighteenth and early nineteenth centuries, and in the United States in the last quarter of the nineteenth century; and such wide inequality puts an extra strain upon the integral framework of any society and requires a special effort to avoid a breakdown that would imperil the whole process.

In short, the transition periods can be described as periods of controlled social and economic revolution. They are revolutions because they involve rapid changes in long-standing economic, social, and often political institutions; they are controlled in that the integrity of the societies is maintained despite prolonged internal conflicts and permits continued cooperation in the rapidly changing economic tasks. Not every society can muster the necessary ingredients: a minority that can assume leadership and an organizational framework and set of values that can hold the population together and make it accept the costs and cooperate with the minority.

The emphasis on the minority is deliberate: it must be a minority since the changes are directed toward the future and cannot represent the immediate interests of the majority which are lodged in the old premodern order. This minority may be the emerging groups of industrialists and modern agriculturists, the intellectual propagandists of the new order recruited from the educated groups, or some political party that craves power and is willing to force an industrialization program through in order to consolidate its leadership and raise the economic power of the state under its control. But this innovating minority must have minimum cooperation from the population, and it may secure it by different means, ranging from authoritarian compulsion backed by powerful propaganda to instill allegiance to the "wave of the future," to a laissez-faire attitude with government setting the permissive conditions by removing obstacles and providing encouragement on the theory that the activities of the private entrepreneurial groups will redound to the benefit of society as a whole.

The interplay between private groups and the state machinery in this transition process is at the core of much recent controversy. I am not competent to deal with it, nor can we treat it with sufficient detail here. But the interpretation of the historical record has been vulgarized by propagandistic mythology, and two resulting errors should be rejected. The first is the notion that the state played only a passive minimal role in the transition periods of capitalist societies. The most cursory reference to the record dispels this illusion. Even in the United States, which was perhaps as free as any country from the binding historical heritage that requires forcible removal by state power, the record is full of decisions by the state on matters that were vital to economic growth, where a different set of decisions would have meant a different course of economic growth. Every decade marked some decision by the state —on currency, on tariffs, on internal improvements, on land, on labor, on immigration—and each one was reached after explicit discussion in which its importance for the country's economic growth was recognized. This active role of the state was even more patent in the older countries, where the state had to decide about the abolition of old rights and the introduction of new. And this is inevitable: insofar as economic growth necessitates shifts in position, it is a source of internal conflict which can be resolved only by the power of the sovereign state. This is essentially what the state organization is for.

The second error is the opposite of the first: that since the government represents a single organized entity, the state can, by planning and managing, attain a speedier and more effective transition to the new economic order than if the major role were left to private enterprise. Given the past historical record of transition during which private enterprise did play an important part, with much turmoil and suffering, this preference for the orderly and planned performance by the state seems attractive. But it is an illusion. For economic development, and the transition to the new order, is a costly process no matter who guides it, and there is no assurance that the costs will be smaller if the guide is an authoritarian state, essentially an entrenched minority, rather than a democratic state responsive to the pressures of organized groups that represent different interests. The contrast is not between a guided and unguided period of transition or between a planned and unplanned process of economic development. It is rather between guidance by a democratically organized government and guidance by a dictatorship of some minority party; between a plan that reflects some broad theory of economic development subject to change and is put into action *via* some broad secular decisions by government, and a plan that is a compendium of specific priorities and targets compiled by the minority that runs the state machinery in accordance with policy decisions that have not benefited from free discussion.

There are obviously various combinations of democracy and authoritarianism in the use of governmental machinery and private enterprise in the transition process. The relative advantages and disadvantages have to be weighed in terms of the specific character of the combination, the specific conditions, and priorities to be assigned to the short run versus the long run. But on the face of it, one could reasonably argue that if economic growth and development are essentially for the benefit of the members of society, and if they also have to sustain the costs, the broadest participation in decisions by governments that bear upon economic growth is probably the best assurance of maximizing returns and minimizing costs. Granted that continued education of the majority to help it adjust to changing conditions and to make for more farsighted and intelligent decisions is needed, it still seems wiser to require that the minorities, with their articulate views of possible and desirable courses of economic growth, secure approval of their programs from the majorities within a democratic framework, rather than give them the right and power to force the programs on the population. And one need not go too far into the historical records of the authoritarian states to conclude that the cost of the economic transition that they accomplished was extremely high in terms of human lives, while considerable doubt remains whether the results warrant optimism for further economic growth. This naturally is an impression, but whether or not one accepts it, the point to be stressed is that the very nature of the transition period involves a major role of government and state machinery.

These are surely sparse comments on a large problem. But although much more could have been said, the comparative analysis of the transition periods in the twelve to eighteen countries is still to be made, and further discussion of this topic depends upon the results of this analysis.

SUSTAINING GROWTH AFTER THE TRANSITION · How is the pace of economic growth sustained after the transition period? Two points might give this question more substance. First, there have been notable differences in the rates of growth among all the countries that have shifted from the preindustrial to the modern economic basis. Second, even apparently minor differences in the rates of growth sustained over a long period cumulate into large differences. A per capita income that rises 1 percent per year reaches about 164 percent of its original level in 50 years; one that rises 1.5 percent per year is 211 percent of its initial level in 50 years.

The reasons for sustained growth after the transition period are clear enough: the accumulation of capital, both material and invested in the skills and health of the population; the transformation of economic and social institutions; the changed patterns of population growth; and the changed scale of values all permit continued and increasing exploitation of the stock of useful knowledge, and the latter is continuously growing. If some rates of economic growth are appreciably below others, or if some diminish rapidly from the high levels reached at the end of the transition period, the transformation to modern economic processes must have been incomplete or the adaptation of economic and social institutions must have encountered increasingly formidable difficulties.

In this connection the heritage of the transition period may be important, for the ways in which some problems are resolved will determine the capacity of the economy to adapt itself further to the increasing potential of economic growth. The historical record is full of instances where the adjustments in the transition process have been a source of difficulty in generating and sustaining a high rate of growth. In the United States, the resolution of difficulties by the Civil War set a basis for the vigorous economic growth that followed, but the effects of slavery in the South were never fully removed and because of persisting race discrimination policies, the South remained backward and in a way acted as a brake upon the rate of economic growth of the country as a whole. In Germany, the privileged position granted to some land-owning groups, particularly in East Prussia, in order to lower their resistance to the new economic order, remained an element of distortion in the economic and social structure that was productive of later troubles, internal and external. Such evidence of incomplete transition can be identified in almost every country, even if its effects on the rate of economic growth cannot be measured.

These elements of the old economic and social order that may persist during the process of transition are not the only obstacles to the maintenance of a high rate of economic growth. The very changes made in transition may set up entrenched interests and positions which, with changing conditions, become foci of resistance to further changes and hence to further growth. A notable example is the evolution of large-scale firms to monopolistic or near-monopolistic dimensions, with the power to limit competition and perhaps to retard the rate of growth. And we are witnessing right now in the USSR an attempt to reduce the consequences of restrictive elements in the dictatorial organization of the country, to minimize the prestige of the Stalinist regime in its authoritarian and ruthless aspects. No hard and fast generalizations can be drawn, except that high rates of growth mean rapid changes in structure, and any factors that make for the entrenchment of those interests which may be displaced in the process of structural change will thereby set up obstacles to a high rate of economic progress.

It is this circumstance that heightens the importance of the impulses to growth that result from additions to the stock of useful knowledge and from the capacity of society for social invention and innovation. The strategic property of technological changes is that they provide avenues for further growth in new areas of supply and demand not directly limited by the old entrenched interests. Competition and progress within the railroad sector may be stifled by its monopolistic character. But it will be vigorous in the general field of transportation services if technological changes create new opportunities, for example in air and truck transportation. And such interindustry competition may revitalize the railroads themselves. The possibilities of growth in the cotton-textile industry may be limited because only slight further reductions of costs are feasible regardless of technological changes. But if invention yields a new product with comparable uses, such as rayon or nylon, the growth potential increases and may sustain the rate of increase in all the textile industries as a whole. In other words, although at any given time the existing stock of knowledge is not fully utilized, the additions to it open up new areas in which the obstacles are less formidable than in the old. In that sense a continuous flow of inventions and innovations is indispensable if a high rate of economic growth is to be sustained.

Equally indispensable is the capacity of society to devise and accept the institutional changes that may be necessary for these changes in technology and substance of economic production. The introduction of the automobile was surely a major element in sustaining economic growth in the United States after World War I, but the integration of this vast new industry and its subsidiaries needed more than the new plants and new skills. It required institutional adjustments, for example the development of financial institutions to make installment selling possible and economical and thus overcome the difficulties involved in financing this high-cost, durable commodity out of current consumer income. It also required a network of roads that had to be built, managed, and financed— functions new to the existing governmental institutions.

A study of the social, political, and economic institutions of a country and of the methods by which they adjust to the changing opportunities for economic growth provided by new products, new tools, new materials, and new industries would be a difficult but highly rewarding task. The process goes far beyond the simple conception of a Schumpeterian entrepreneur developing an innovation despite the resistance of the mass of the population. The capacity for change is widespread, as is resistance to it. There are elements of both in the functioning of social institutions and in the activities of the human beings who are the carriers of economic and social life. The willingness to experiment with change differs from country to country and period to period. But it is beyond my competence to suggest more precisely how institutional patterns in the organization of society could be analyzed in order to test this capacity for change which is clearly an indispensable prerequisite of a sustained high rate of economic growth.

International Relations and Economic Growth

The economic growth of a country is affected by its coexistence with many other countries, and we supplement our reflections on the *internal* adjustment of a nation to the economic-growth potential by comments on the bearing of *international* relations. Much of modern economic growth is incomprehensible unless it is seen as a reflection of strains and pressures imposed upon a nation by membership in the worldwide concert of nation-states. Hence, although our comments will again be necessarily sketchy, they should serve to emphasize some broad points.

We begin with the following characteristics of nations, as we use the term here: the presence of sovereign state power, which is indispensable for making overriding decisions that set the conditions of economic growth (the function that makes the nation the necessary unit in the study of economic growth); the exercise of this power over a social group located in a specified area, which gives meaning to the terms "territory" and "territorial boundaries"; and possession by that group of a common history, in the sense that its members have a feeling of cohesion and as a group have experienced events that are their particular heritage. Their past may have stretched over centuries or over decades, but the sharing of this common historical past is indispensable to the feeling of cohesion which is the basis upon which the internal power of the sovereign state rests.

On the meaning of these characteristics there have been long and voluminous disputes. The sovereign power of the state vis-à-vis other organizations within the country has been the subject of much discussion, and the internal limits of sovereignty have been a topic of cautious speculation in political theory. Territory has also been a matter of disputatious definition, not only in specific controversies over boundaries but also in connection with problems that emerge whenever man reaches out into another aspect of the universe. Air travel has led to new questions of sovereignty over the air, and the prospective development of satellites may upset many current legal notions concerning national boundaries. History is written and rewritten, and the common history of a group in the viewpoint of some members of a nation may be considered the record of an oppressive and "foreign" majority by some dissident splinter group. But we need not be concerned with the finer points if the three characteristics are taken in their broader meaning as necessary and sufficient to distinguish the nation-state as a unit for which economic growth is studied and among several of which there exist what we call international relations.

From these characteristics we can derive the general nature of international relations, particularly those with economic substance. Nations necessarily differ with respect to territory, since sovereignty is overriding and impenetrable and only one power, in the modern political structure of nations, can reign over one territory. The several segments of the earth, with their different locations, will have different climatic and topographical characteristics and different supplies of natural resources. The possession of a common history means, *ipso facto,* possession of a past different from that of any other group, even if the two groups are close to each other and participate in many common occurrences. A distinctive history ordinarily means also a distinctive constellation of economic and social resources, as a reflection of different scales of values and traditions. Hence not only natural but historical conditions make for differences among nations in economic performance, thus allowing for comparative advantages in international trade, for various pushes and pulls in international migration, and for differences in the attraction of capital in its international movement. Furthermore, since a major purpose of the sovereign state is to secure the country's "place in the sun," there is considerable opportunity for conflicts, for the exercise of political power may run from a mild negotiated arrangement like securing trading rights with other countries to a major intervention like assuming sovereignty over another area and its inhabitants as a colony. The network of international relations is thus partly a web of peaceful, economically motivated flows of goods, men, and capital and partly a web of pressures and tensions that alternate between periods of warless equilibrium and displacement and periods of overt conflicts.

Although the source of economic growth in the stock of useful knowledge is largely transnational, its application—the actual process of economic growth—is most unequal. The transition to the modern level of economic performance occurred in some nations before it did in others, and consequently at any given time some nations were at higher economic levels than others and some nations were growing more rapidly than others.

The unequal impact of economic growth upon nations was due largely to differences in historical background and antecedents. Thus when modern science developed and knowledge reached a point where an industrial revolution could take place, some nations were ready for it but others were not. Were one to ask in what country in the second half of the eighteenth century one could have expected the Industrial Revolution—in the sense of a complex of new methods of agricultural production, new industrial materials in the form of iron and steel (or an approximation to the latter like bar iron), and a new source of power in the form of steam—the answer is that only a few countries felt the need for these new methods of production, and only a few countries could muster the capacity to adapt their economic and social institutions to a wide-scale application of these inventions and discoveries. It was no accident that the Industrial Revolution occurred in England in the second half of the eighteenth century. It was no accident that the countries on the western and northern periphery of Europe—Spain, Portugal, France, the Netherlands, and England—were most active and in fact pioneered in the geographical revolution that led to the discovery of the New World and ushered in the long period of economic growth associated with merchant capitalism.

The major innovation, if one can call it that, which is the base and substance of a distinct epoch in economic growth, does not occur simultaneously in all the nations that comprise mankind, but unfolds itself in a long sequence, beginning in one or two nations which are the pioneering units and spreading to others. This spread of the industrial system, which is the essential substance of economic growth of nations during the period under discussion, points immediately to the significance of international relations. They helped to spread the impetus and basis of economic growth from their point of origin in the pioneering country to the followers, early or late, and thus to domination of economic activity the world over.

No specific attention will be paid in this paper to the long-term movements in peace-type international flows of goods and services in the current transactions accounts, of men in international migration, and of short- or long-term capital funds. These are fairly well-known, and their influence in spreading economic growth can be easily perceived. The increasing extent to which the countries that were earliest to adopt the industrial system of economic production exported the new products and thus the new tastes and techniques—aided by revolutionary changes in means of transportation and communication and by the provision for capital credits—needs no emphasis. It is also clear that the expanding international migration, in the nineteenth and early twentieth centuries, which was voluntary and not politically compulsory, often meant the importation of advanced technological skills and, in any case, helped to man the most promising opportunities for economic growth. The intriguing aspect of these peace-type international flows is the political or power element implicit in them, which grew in importance to a point of forcing a sharp reversal in trend about the time of World War I. This brings us immediately to the political or power element of international relations, which, at its height, results in the use of overt force in armed conflict.

By political or power element I mean simply the threat, implicit or explicit, of the use of physical sanctions. Any action backed by such a threat, whether in offense or defense, is a political or power action. In this meaning, the element is indispensable to the whole concept of a sovereign nation-state. If several million Ruritanians set up their own government and declare their right to govern themselves, they are telling the Lusitanians, Aquitanians, and other inhabitants of the world that they are ready to defend by physical force the right to pass their own laws and enforce these laws upon their fellow Ruritanians. And the sovereign state must retain the monopoly of major physical sanctions within the country no matter how many other rights and privileges it is willing to share with other organizations.

We stress this point because there must be an inescapable power element in all international relations, insofar as they are relations among sovereign states or citizens of states, and if there is, trends in the extent to which it affects international relations are important in their bearing upon economic growth of nations. Thus trading in commodities between the members of two sovereign states, under the prevalent theory and practice of sovereign states, *may* be a matter of easily enforceable agreement; but it may be impossible unless one of the states exercises power pressure to force the other to permit trading—as has happened repeatedly in the last century between some Western power and some country in Asia or Africa. And what is true of commodity trade is true of international migration and of international movements of capital.

The threat of force in international relations is so widespread, particularly in relations between countries at widely different levels of economic development and with different historical heritage and traditions, that it is not easy to measure its use or effects on international relations within the last two centuries. It can range from what may seem to be enforcement of the most elementary requirement of decent intercourse to ruthless subjugation of another state. Overt conflicts are only part of the story. A threat of force that does not result in war because one party yields is still use of force and represents a political or power element in the relation established. Nevertheless, two fairly broad conclusions can be suggested as tentative hypotheses. First, this use of force, this political or power element in international relations, is an important mechanism in the spread of economic growth. Second, its relative weight in international relations, and *pari passu* in spreading economic growth, has increased in the recent half to three quarters of a century.

The first hypothesis can be reduced to a simple paradigm. There will be no continuous economic relations between two countries at different stages of economic and social development unless the more advanced country forces upon the less advanced some conditions that permit stable trade and other relations. The plausibility of this thesis is apparent when one considers that the legal and social framework of any society is closely interrelated with its economic activity and conditions. Differences in economic and social levels therefore make agreement upon conditions of intercourse difficult, and the difficulty is likely to be overcome by the pressure of the economically advanced and hence more powerful nation. Without continuous economic relations between the "laggard" and the more advanced countries, the drive toward modern economic growth is not likely to be generated in the former. It follows that the "opening up" of the laggard countries by the threat of force on the part of the advanced countries is a prerequisite for the spread of economic growth to the former.

This pattern seems simple enough, but it is true only for countries at widely different levels of economic and social development and hence of power. It finds classic corroboration in the "opening up" of Japan and the spread of modern economic growth to that country. It is also an apt description of the effects of Western aggression in many other countries of Asia and Africa. But what about the spread of the industrial system within Europe proper or to the United States? Was any power element instrumental in spreading modern economic growth to these areas from its original locus in Great Britain? The answer is obvious since the power or force element can be used defensively as well as offensively. The sovereign power in the United States and in many European countries was exercised to limit the economic activities of a more advanced country and thus provide more favorable conditions for domestic industrialization. It was no accident that the theory of protection originated in the United States and spread to Germany, and that the United States utilized its sovereign power in its war for independence late in the eighteenth century to set up conditions for rapid economic growth in the nineteenth century.

The heart of the matter is that the political power of the sovereign state is almost indispensable. It is used to mobilize energies within a country for the purpose of economic growth despite the risks and burdens, or to extend the sway of sovereignty into other areas. In either case, it helps spread the new system of economic production as it did in earlier eras. The dominant power organization of society must be involved in the extension of any new methods of economic production, particularly if they necessitate rapid and thoroughgoing transformations such as those associated with the modern industrial system.

I do not mean to argue that the power element in the organization of the sovereign state is always favorable to the spread of economic growth. It sometimes is used to retard it, to isolate a society from the virus of economic change. But on balance the contribution of the power element in international relations is positive simply because it is also a function of economic growth. Despite the disruption, exploitation, and harm that aggression by Western powers brought to preindustrial Asia, Africa, and Latin America, the record of economic growth already achieved in these areas and foreseeable in the future is probably far richer than if they had remained in complete isolation. Despite the costs and wastes of tariffs, protection, and the like, the industrialization and economic growth of countries like the United States and Germany probably exceed the levels that could have been reached with completely free international trade. This does not mean automatic justification of possible excesses in the use of political power, internally or externally, but only recognition of the indispensability of some political power for economic growth. One may well deplore the use of force by a sovereign state for external compulsion or for artificial isolation in international relations, but if the primary concern is with the rise of over-all product, total or per capita, without considering cost and welfare implications, the use of force in international relations does in the long run accelerate the spread of modern economic growth to increasing numbers of nations.

The conclusion that the use of force in international relations has grown in recent decades is an impression, but there are many straws pointing in this direction. The last four decades have witnessed two widespread and relatively costly world wars. What might be called the "politicization" of the peace-type flows—commodity trade, international migration, capital imports and exports—has become more pronounced since World War I; that is, the elements in these flows motivated by political interests of state have become proportionately greater. In several countries, which account for a substantial proportion of world population, the control of the dictatorial state apparatus over international relations is so tight that relations with other national units are essentially a monopoly of the government.

All these changes constitute the substance of the long-term trend suggested. But more important are the reasons behind them since they throw some light on the nature of economic growth of nations in the modern or even earlier epochs. Insofar as one can see, and it is only a speculative suggestion, the increased tension and force in international relations were due to the spread of the new system of economic production, to the emergence of several advanced countries, and to the pressures and struggles that resulted therefrom. The revival of imperialism came only in the last quarter of the nineteenth century, when the United States and Germany emerged as industrial powers threatening the supreme position of Great Britain. The addition of Japan and later of Russia to the roll only increased the possibilities of friction in the struggle for position.

Three features of this spread of economic growth to several major nations deserve note. First, the later a country enters the transition phase from the preindustrial to the industrial system, the greater its lag—for more time has elapsed and the leaders have had a greater opportunity to enjoy the cumulative advantage of greater growth. Given the existing power relations, this sets up increasing tension in the laggard countries and makes the leaders of their industrialization process anxious for quick results to assure them of the minimum economic power necessary to preserve internal stability and external independence. The elements of haste and pressure in the industrialization of Japan and the USSR can be viewed in part as results of fear, warranted or unwarranted, that any delay in reducing the lag would threaten their security.

Second, the correlation between the time span of the lag and the differences in historical heritage and conditions between the pioneer countries and the followers, while not perfect, is significant. The latest countries in the industrialization process—Japan, the USSR, and most recently China—are less like England than the earlier followers, the United States and Germany. The social and political conditions that had to be adapted to the new industrial system were also different, and although certain changes had to be made in them, there was nevertheless room and need for some other political and social concomitants. It is significant that the element of authoritarianism and direct state intervention increases progressively as the time lag in industrialization grows, a product partly of the increasing strain of backwardness and partly of the political and historical heritage within which the modern economic process has to be fitted.

Third, since the emergence of new economic leaders weakens the power of the old, there tends to be a dissolution of some old international relations and the formation of new sovereign nation-states. This readjustment of the political framework to changed power relations sometimes requires a prolonged armed conflict as a final test, but may often take place without a major war. Since the early twentieth century, several such dissolutions have taken place and new sovereign states have emerged, the heirs of the Turkish, Austro-Hungarian, and recently the British and French empires. The process is continuing and the number of independent nation-states is increasing apace.

One result of the spread of the industrial system to an increasing number of nations, of the intensification of the spirit of nationalism which strengthens the power element of the sovereign state, and of the multiplication of nation-states amid increasing tension has been the proliferation of various types of international relations and of political and social organizations designed for economic growth. It may be that the international flows exemplified by lend-lease, Marshall Plan aid, and Point Four are not new. In the long course of social history there may have been many such subventions and aids, but these forms of international flows have not been usual in the peacetime decades of the last two centuries. International agencies and their economic activities may have had their parallels in an earlier past, but they are certainly a recent development in the history of the last two centuries.

The same can be said of the political and social organizations that have been devised, and apparently are going to be devised, for the purpose of exploiting the economic growth potential of the stock of useful knowledge. Some social concomitants of the industrial system are indispensable. However, they still allow for a variety of combinations of the state and private groups, and the patterns that will emerge in countries still to be industrialized cannot be expected to be replicas of those already established. This variety of growth organization and experience, past and prospective, is to some extent an inevitable consequence of the variety of historical heritages and antecedents that shape the characteristics of the scores of nations which, for reasons indicated, must rely on the powers of their sovereign governments to assist them in the transition to the modern economic system.

The Importance of "Noneconomic" Factors

This discussion has purposely underemphasized the economic aspects of economic growth. Much more could have been said about long-term trends in such phenomena as industrial structure, the proportions of capital formation and ultimate consumption and their components, the distribution of the product among various economic or income-size groups, and the volumes and proportions of flows across boundaries. And such an account of trends could have been supplemented by analytical hypotheses in an attempt to explain the underlying factors and their interrelations. Instead, emphasis was put on conditions of economic growth that are often treated in the economic literature as extraneous and impounded into assumptions: technological change, the political and social organization, and the political element in international relations. But these factors, exogenous or not, are of major importance in shaping the course of modern economic growth, and their neglect results in grave errors of omission and commission. If additions to the stock of useful knowledge are in fact a dominant factor in shaping the course and rate of modern economic growth, merely making assumptions about them is hardly helpful. The apparent plausibility of the assumptions is only likely to increase the danger of erroneous conclusions. If the framework of political and social relations must change in the course of economic growth, it is hardly helpful to assume a given political and social framework in analyzing long-term economic processes. If the power element is present in international relations, theories of international trade based on the assumption that two countries behave, in their relations, as if the power element is nonexistent (or that it is equal in both and can, therefore, be cancelled out) have limited value. Of course, one can always argue that economic analysis must deal with economic processes *per se* and leave the analysis of noneconomic conditions to other disciplines. But this argument assumes an independence of the economic processes. (The definition of "economic" has become progressively narrower. At one time population movements were an integral part of economic theory, but since the latter part of the nineteenth century, demography has been a separate field.) Although such independence may perhaps be assumed in the analysis of short-term changes and relations, it cannot be a premise in the analysis of the long-term changes involved in economic growth. In any case, awareness of the full range of factors—regardless of their classification in the rather uncertain nomenclature of the social sciences—should be useful in an analysis of problems of economic growth.

Finally, consideration of the wide range of factors involved in the economic growth of nations should also draw attention to qualitative aspects of economic growth, which often elude us in quantitative economic analysis. One point stressed in the discussion is that economic growth, the increase in total and per capita product, was attained and can be attained by a variety of combinations of state and private elements under different conditions of freedom and compulsion. Yet the results of economic growth in terms of human welfare, the increase in the stock of knowledge, and the possibilities of peaceful relations among nations may be and are likely to be quite different. If one takes the stock of knowledge, the political and social framework, and the state of international relations for granted—usually in terms that permit economic analysis to proceed with major emphasis on economic attainments proper—there is no impelling urge to ask what economic growth so analyzed means in terms of the further progress of knowledge, freedom, and peace. Yet the significance of the patterns and mechanism of economic growth in these terms may well be greater than in terms of the current product, total and per capita. Perhaps not the least advantage of widening the scope of the problem along the lines that were but barely and inadequately suggested in the speculative reflections above is that it compels the extension of analysis not only to factors important in any *explanatory* hypothesis but also to a review of aspects indispensable in any qualitative *appraisal* from the standpoint of the broad criteria of human welfare.

Population Change
and Aggregate Output

FOR THE MODERN period, that is, since the end of the eighteenth century, the available statistical records reveal no cases in which the prevalent substantial rises in population were accompanied by secular declines in per capita product. To be sure, there were sharp drops in total and per capita output, occasioned in the underdeveloped countries by crop failures and in the developed countries by cyclical recessions. In the underdeveloped countries population increase, occurring under conditions of premodern agriculture and primitive transportation and industry, can be viewed as a factor in the persistence of a low per capita standard of living, and hence in the catastrophic impact of famines. Yet the long-term statistical records, error-prone as they are for such countries as India and Egypt over the first half of the twentieth century, give no clear indication of a long-term decline, although they do show failure of the low per capita income to rise significantly. The evidence thus suggests that in modern times growth in population has been accompanied by growth in aggregate output—for many countries so large that there was also a marked secular rise in per capita product.[1]

[1] See Table 1 in my paper, "Quantitative Aspects of the Economic Growth of Nations: I. Levels and Variability of Rates of Growth," *Economic Develop-*

Reprinted by permission from Demographic and Economic Change in Developed Countries, *the report of a Conference of the Universities–National Bureau Committee for Economic Research (Princeton, N.J.: Princeton University Press, 1960).*

It appears that population growth, despite pressure on the limited stock of natural resources and man-made capital, has permitted substantial rises in product per capita, particularly in countries with a social framework attuned to modern technology. However, the empirical evidence, at least in its present state, is insufficient for a detailed analysis of the impact of population growth on the growth of aggregate output. Although it reveals marked contrasts among countries with respect to growth of income per capita, it does not suggest that differences in the rate of population increase are an important variable in accounting for these contrasts. In the discussion that follows, we must, therefore, resort to speculation.

The theme is a broad one: the impact of secular growth of population on per capita output. I speak of growth rather than decline because it has been, and is likely to be, the more prevalent pattern. I focus on per capita output because any conclusion concerning the contribution of population growth to the rise in per capita output leads to obvious inferences for aggregate output. Finally, a word about the drift of the speculations that follow. My impression is that recent professional (and popular) literature has emphasized the disadvantages and dangers of population growth—the drain upon irreproducible resources, upon capital accumulation, upon the organizing capacity of societies, and so on. Little can be added to these arguments. But as a matter of balance, I propose to dwell upon the positive contributions of population growth, even though they must eventually be weighed against the negative effects.

Population as Producers

An increase in population means, other conditions being equal, an increase in the labor force. The precise contribution to the labor force depends upon whether population growth is caused by a decline in the death rate, by net immigration, or by an increase in the birth rate. The differences are of great importance, since reduction in the death rate of the working population or net immigration (usually of persons in the prime working years of life) minimizes the investment in bringing infants to the age of effective participation in the labor force. We recognize these important differences

---

ment and Cultural Change, V, 1 (October 1956), p. 10. Eighteen countries that show a secular growth of population also show a substantial rise in per capita product. Ireland, in the nineteenth century, shows a decline in population and a rise in per capita income.

but prefer not to complicate the discussion by treating them separately.

Let us assume that the labor force increases at the same rate as total population (or somewhat less if there is an increase in the birth rate). This increased labor force will be able to turn out as much or more product per worker (and hence per capita of total population) if it is equipped with the same amount of capital as, or a greater amount than, was previously available per worker and if the reproducible capital-output ratio remains the same or decreases. The latter "if" takes account of the possible effect of pressure upon the limited supply of irreproducible resources. If such pressure develops, there may be need for more man-made capital per unit of output or for some chain of substitution and technological innovation.

I shall deal with the supply of capital in the following section. Here, the point to be stressed is that capital investment must include not only material goods but the more important input into education and training of the population—a factor of particular relevance if population growth stems from the birth rate rather than from the death and immigration rates. Obviously, the productive contribution of these additional numbers is as dependent upon their education and skills as upon the material capital equipment with which they are provided.

Let us assume further that capital investment, thus broadly conceived to include the raising and training of the new generations, is at least as large per capita for the additions to the labor force (B) as for the already existing labor force (A). What are the reasons for assuming that the per worker productivity of $A + B$ would be greater than that of A and that therefore, under the conditions given (constant proportions of labor force to population), per capita income would also be higher? Three somewhat different reasons can be advanced.

The first is connected with the distinctive assumption that there exists in the country a variety of unexploited natural resources and that additions to the labor force would permit greater utilization of these resources. This utilization, combined with a more specialized division of labor, would in all probability lead to a greater product per worker. The crux of this argument lies in two points. First, an increasing density of population spreading to formerly uninhabited parts of the country brings into use resources previously inaccessible, and the wider base of natural resources warrants the expectation of a higher per worker productivity; second, a larger labor force permits a more intensive division of labor with whatever higher productivity benefits attach thereto. This is certainly a special case, but it should be kept in mind in view of the experience of several countries in the Western Hemisphere. For example, the histories of Brazil and of Canada suggest that diversion of most of the available immigration from Europe to the United States deprived these countries of an influx of immigrants before World War I (and perhaps even after) that could have contributed to a greater rise not only in aggregate output but even in output per capita. There may be countries in which a more intelligent and liberal immigration policy would be an impetus to the growth of both aggregate and per capita product.

Second, there is the argument concerning the greater mobility of a growing than of a stagnant labor force, advanced by J. M. Keynes when the specter of stagnant or declining population haunted the advanced Western economies.[2] It is the younger groups in the labor force who are most mobile—in space and within the productive system—since, unlike older workers, they are not committed to family and housing or to established positions. This greater mobility is particularly true of new entrants into the labor force, who naturally veer toward those sectors that are likely to spearhead the country's economic growth and who are oriented toward these sectors even in their training within the educational system.

There is an important related aspect. Population growth may be due either to immigration or to a substantial rate of natural increase (or to both). In the latter case, there are likely to be sizable differences among various social groups and various parts of the country (for example, between the lower and upper income groups and between the countryside and the cities) in the rates of their natural increase. Such differences are usually negatively correlated with differences in economic growth opportunities: while the transition to industrialization is occurring, the countryside and smaller cities with their lesser economic growth opportunities are likely to have higher rates of natural increase than the larger cities with their greater growth potentials; similarly, the rates of natural increase of low-income groups are likely to be higher than those of high-income groups. It follows that the realization of economic-growth potentials is contingent upon a vast internal migration: the movement of peo-

[2] See his "Some Economic Consequences of a Declining Population," *The Eugenics Review*, XXIX, 1 (April 1937), pp. 13–17.

ple from the country to the cities and within the cities from places of lesser to places of greater economic promise. A substantial rate of population growth means, then, either a greater rate of immigration from abroad or a greater rate of internal migration, or both. This migration may be supplementary to the special mobility propensities of the young entrants into the labor force.

The importance of mobility in the distribution of human resources in response to the differential growth possibilities in the economy can easily be underestimated. Modern economic growth is characterized by rapid structural changes, shifts in importance among industries, and shifts in the location of industries within the country's economy. Stickiness in the response of the labor force to such potential changes can be a serious obstacle to economic growth and greater per capita product. If insufficient labor flows to rising economic opportunities, the relative cost of labor and the relative price of the product remain too high to permit the expansion of output to its full potential. Conversely, if the labor force in relatively deteriorating economic opportunities remains attached to them, the national level of product per worker and per capita is not likely to rise. A young or otherwise mobile group within the labor force is therefore strategically important. Moreover, a migrant who has severed familial and other noneconomic ties is a more adaptable economic agent than a person who, like a stationary stone, is overgrown with the moss of his habitual patterns of life. It follows that population growth, in contrast to population stability, may, because of the greater mobility and adjustability of human resources, be conducive to higher per worker (and hence per capita) levels of output; and this may be true, within limits, of greater vs. lesser population increase.

The third argument is perhaps the most far-reaching. The greatest factor in growth of output per capita is, of course, the increasing stock of tested, useful knowledge. The producers of this stock are the scientists, inventors, engineers, managers, and explorers of various description—all members of that population whose growth we are considering. Assume now that, judged by native capacities (and they do differ), 0.05 percent of a given population are geniuses, another 2.0 percent are possessors of gifts that may be described as talent, and another 10.0 percent have distinctly higher than average capacity for fruitful search for facts, principles, and inventions. (These grades of ability and percentages are purely illustrative and would probably be changed by an expert in this field.) Since we have assumed the education, training, and other capital investment necessary to assure that the additions to the population will be at least as well equipped as the population already existing, the proportion of mute Miltons and unfulfilled Newtons will be no higher than previously. Population growth, under the assumptions stated, would, therefore, produce an absolutely larger number of geniuses, talented men, and generally gifted contributors to new knowledge— whose native ability would be permitted to mature to effective levels when they join the labor force.

We now face the question whether an increase in the absolute number of these contributors to new knowledge is likely to produce increasing, constant, or diminishing returns per head. Returns in this case mean potentially useful knowledge in the form in which it can have major effects on economic production. My answer inclines strongly toward increasing returns for two reasons. The first lies in the interdependence of knowledge of the various parts of the universe in which we human beings operate—in the sense that greater knowledge of chemistry contributes to greater knowledge of physics, and progress in both of these contributes to greater knowledge of physiological and biological functions. In the same sense, discoveries and inventions in the field of tensile strength of metals contribute to discoveries and inventions in the field of electric currents; and even new devices in social engineering in one field (for example, corporate organization) facilitate new organizational devices in other fields (for example, credit instruments). A greater supply of people who can contribute to new knowledge may therefore mean a better coverage of a variety of interrelated fields, and where discoveries so complement one another, economies achieved are likely to make for a higher output per worker than would be possible for a smaller group whose coverage of these different but related fields is, perforce, spotty. Second, creative effort flourishes in a dense intellectual atmosphere, and it is hardly an accident that the locus of intellectual progress (including that of the arts) has been preponderantly in the larger cities, not in the thinly settled countryside. The existence of adequately numerous groups in all fields of creative work is one prerequisite, and the possibility of more intensive intellectual contact, as well as of specialization, afforded by greater numbers may be an important factor in stepping up the rate of additions to useful knowledge. Although, for obvious reasons, no simple measure of the stock or flow of new knowledge is available, the course of development of science, technology, and the useful arts suggests acceleration rather than retardation, with no diminishing returns, even taking account of the large increase in the human resources flowing into this particular area of activity. Compared with the two factors mentioned above as likely to make for greater per capita productivity of larger numbers of creators of new knowledge, the possibility of diminishing returns is remote: the universe is far too vast in relation to the size of our planet and what we know about it. Recent spectacular changes in the means of exploring the universe and the wide possibility of new, and eventually usable, knowledge that they suggest only serve to strengthen this point.

Growth of economic output is a function of the growth of the stock of tested knowledge. Since, on the assumptions stated, population increase adds proportionately to the number of creators of new knowledge, it should result in at least a proportional addition to the stock of tested knowledge, and, therefore, to growth of product per capita at least as large as that in the past. If, for reasons suggested just above, we assume increasing returns on output of new knowledge per head of knowledge-creator and hence per head of population, we may infer that, *ceteris paribus,* population growth will contribute to *greater* growth of per capita product.[3] The argument is clearly venturesome; for example, it implies a theory of production of knowledge such that a smaller number of humans could not be compensated for by more intensive training. And I am sure that other objections could be raised, but for the present let me advance this argument as a plausible hypothesis which merits attention if only because of the far-reaching importance of the issues it poses.

Two final comments in this connection may be relevant. First, the argument stresses the importance of human beings not as producers of commodities and services but as producers of new knowledge— as the only carriers of the learning and creative ability that provide the basis for our economic and social progress. This concept is quite close, of course, to the idea of the divine spark in human beings, which is at the core of much religious resistance to policies aimed at limiting population. Passing over these matters, which are beyond my ken and interest, let me point out that there is an element of sound instinct behind such resistance: insofar as it is possible to give the new generations the education and other requisites of

---

[3] I am indebted to Professor Moses Abramovitz for a comment that led me to restate this argument in a form different from the original.

Homo sapiens, failure to increase means failure to add to the possible carriers of light and knowledge, and the implicit losses may be far larger than the costs avoided.

Second, we should recognize that the creative and educated groups in the developed economies—and they are the central reference point here—serve partly, and should serve more fully, the economic needs of the world, not merely of their own countries. Knowledge is transnational in its application, and the returns on the input of effort into new discoveries, inventions, improvements, and so on should be measured in terms of increased output per worker not only in the country of origin but elsewhere. In that sense, greater population growth that leads to a substantial increase in the cadres of creative workers at various levels—and this is likely to occur in developed economies alone, although there have been striking isolated instances elsewhere—may produce a *greater* rise in product per worker both in those countries *and* elsewhere than would result from lesser or no population growth.

Population as Savers

All the arguments above claiming that a population increase may contribute to a higher per capita product are contingent upon the provision of sufficient capital to educate and train the additional workers, equip them with adequate tools, and implement the inventions and innovations they may introduce. We should now consider whether population growth impedes capital formation. A family with ten children is not likely to be able to spend as much on the education and training of each as a family with two, nor is it likely to contribute as much to the savings that finance material capital formation. Generalizing this case, we could argue that population growth, in and of itself, reduces the resources for investment in training and reproducible capital per head of new additions to population. If this argument were valid it would severely limit all those advanced above because the assumption of adequate capital would be removed.

The contention just set forth may be unchallengeable for underdeveloped countries, but in the advanced economies the situation is not that simple and determinate. There are reasons to assume that any *private* failure to make the proper investment in education and training can easily be corrected (and in many cases has been) by public action, and that the very process of population growth contributes to an increased flow of savings to finance additional material capital formation.

We begin with the case where population growth, stemming from natural increase, may result in inadequate investment in the education and training of the younger generation (I include all expenditures needed to develop an effective member of society, over and above bare sustenance). Such inadequacies may result either from inability of the family unit to cover the necessary costs or, despite such ability, failure to appreciate the need. In either case, the shortfall, relative to the economic output of the advanced economies, is likely to be small, and in the past many countries have instituted free primary education, subsidies for higher education, and so forth. We are positing here limits to the birth rate: naturally, if every family unit attempts to raise twenty children, the problem assumes different dimensions. But we shall deal with this qualification toward the end of the paper, since it is relevant to most of the arguments here.

The effects of population increase on the possible shortage of savings to finance material capital formation pose a more serious problem. Indeed, it is the central problem in this section because we are assuming now that investment in raising and educating the younger generation is adequate. Consequently, the additional drain upon resources represented by population increase affects material capital formation alone. Can we assume that in the very process of population growth some forces emerge that tend to augment savings and capital formation? Several such forces can be suggested.

First, there is little ground for supposing that where population grows by natural increase, the added outlay by either parents or society is all at the expense of otherwise proportionately larger savings. So far as private spending-saving units are concerned, it is not clear that expenditures on children are a substitute for savings (particularly in the advanced economies) rather than for more consumer goods or for more leisure. Although correlations are often deceptive, one may point to the fact that the birth rate is higher where the per capita consumer expenditures are lower; and in the big cities the choice is largely between children and a relatively more costly mode of living. Inasmuch as children provide an incentive to work and to save, it is not certain that the savings per child (or per future member of the labor force) generated in a family unit with a large number of children would not be at least as high as in the same family if it had fewer or no children. Nor is it certain that funds allocated by governments for education mean a reduction in governmental capital formation or in the savings of the economic units who pay for public education in taxes.

Second, some major components of aggregate savings tend to be raised when population is growing. One of these, discussed in some detail in an earlier paper, may be briefly noted here.[4] Assume that part of savings is for retirement, to be completely offset by dissavings of the individual or family during post-retirement years. If the labor force is constant, then, given a fixed age at which withdrawal from the labor force occurs and perfect foresight in estimating the amount of post-retirement expenses, it follows that, all other conditions being equal, positive savings in the process of accumulation for retirement will balance post-retirement dissavings and the net contribution to aggregate savings will be zero. By contrast, if population and the labor force are growing, the number of active members of the labor force who are saving for retirement is that much larger than the number of the retired; and their positive savings are larger than the dissavings of those retired. The resultant positive contribution to aggregate savings will reflect the past rate of growth of the labor force, and hence the past rate of population increase stemming from the birth rate or immigration. (An increase in population resulting from a decline in the death rates of the retired has an opposite effect, serving to diminish savings.)

This argument can be applied to all future-expense-oriented savings. If savings are being accumulated to finance future outlays—for a house, a family, and so forth—the net contribution to the countrywide pool of savings is the excess of their flow into stock over their outflow at the end of the period of accumulation and waiting. For the total body of individuals, the net balance of such future-expense-oriented savings will be zero if the population is constant, assuming no indebtedness to the business or government sector, and assuming also that the calculations are correct. On these assumptions, growth in population will produce an excess of accumulation over disbursements, or positive net savings.

Third, there is an indirect and somewhat elusive effect of population increase on the consumption and savings patterns of the *upper* income groups, which may be worth noting. I argued above that in

[4] See the author's "International Differences in Capital Formation and Financing," in Moses Abramovitz, ed., *Capital Formation and Economic Growth* (National Bureau of Economic Research, Princeton University Press, 1955), particularly Appendix D, pp. 98–103.

a developed country children may be a substitute for higher levels of consumption or for more leisure. Insofar as they are a substitute for the former, greater population growth means for those groups whose birth rate is higher than elsewhere, a lower per capita consumption level than would otherwise be enjoyed. This usually pertains to groups in the bottom rather than the top half of the economic scale. There tends to be a definite gradation of consumption expenditure through the whole structure of economic and social groups. We find no sharp break as we move along the scale: the consumption-savings pattern of the multimillionaires at the top is linked with that of the mere millionaires on the next lower rung, the latter is linked with that of the recipients of a $100,000 annual income, and so on for the entire array. The point is that, all other conditions being equal, particularly the size distribution of income, lower per capita consumption expenditures at the bottom, necessitated by population increase, will make for lower per capita expenditures and hence higher savings proportions for all groups—of *those* savings that are not oriented to future purchases, etc., but are a kind of automatic excess of large incomes over limited consumption expenditures. The argument is not that the greater impact of higher birth rates at lower income levels results in a wider inequality in the size distribution of income (on a per capita basis) and hence, other conditions being equal, in a greater proportion of savings. It is rather that, with a given size distribution of income on a per capita basis, greater population increase due to higher birth rates keeps down the per capita consumption levels of those in the lower and intermediate brackets who are in the childbearing and rearing ages; and that, because of the interconnection of consumption levels in the income pyramid, it also keeps down the consumption levels of those groups high enough in the array to save "automatically" and thus raises the savings of these upper income groups.

Finally, it has been assumed throughout that the reproducible capital-output ratio is constant, an assumption contrary to historical experience. The marginal capital-output ratios, and it is with these that we are particularly concerned, have varied considerably over both the short-run business cycle and longer periods. In the early phases of the development of the advanced economies these ratios showed a secular rise, as in the United States from the 1870's to World War I; in the later phases they showed a marked decline, in the United States since the 1920's. The problem therefore assumes different aspects in the different secular phases of the movement of the capital-output ratios. Particularly in the declining phase, such as that in the United States since the 1920's, the presumed pressure of population increase on the supply of savings to finance capital formation would have been much less than during the period before World War I. Yet the changes in the capital-output ratios are not independent of the supply of savings or of the absolute level of the ratios at any given time. Greater pressure on the supply of savings, other conditions being equal, induces more capital-saving inventions, innovations, and improvements, and a high capital-output ratio provides greater incentive and more room for such capital-saving changes.

The bearing upon the present discussion is obvious: if population increase does create greater pressure upon savings and the available stock of material capital, inventive and managerial ability forced in the appropriate direction may result in a greater emphasis on and success with capital-economizing innovations than would otherwise be the case. While this argument may seem like the resolution of a problem by a *deus ex machina*, it does seem plausible for developed economies with a variety of resources responsive to the task.

Population as Consumers

The arguments advanced in the two preceding sections, if valid, justify the expectation that a population increase would lead to a higher per capita product than would a stable population. They implicitly assume the adequacy of final demand, or, more precisely, a distribution between expenditures and savings that assures full employment of resources and the greatest growth possible with these resources, technological changes, related social innovations, and the demand of ultimate consumers. While consideration of the behavior of the population as consumers is implicit in the discussion of their behavior as savers, some specific aspects of consumption lend additional support to the suggestion that population increase may be a positive factor making for higher per capita product.

The first of these aspects of consumption is related to its impact on the size of the domestic market. I argued above that population growth may be partly at the expense of greater leisure. On that score alone, without considering the other arguments in the preceding sections, the demand of a rapidly growing population for consumer goods would be greater than that of a constant or slowly growing population—since even the larger per capita demand of the latter would not be sufficient to compensate for their smaller numbers. If the other arguments in the preceding sections are granted, the total demand (output), including that for producers' goods, of a rapidly growing population can be expected to exceed that of a constant or slowly growing population. Once this is admitted—and the larger demand would be assured *even* if the per capita product of the rapidly growing population were equal to or less than the per capita product of the slowly growing or constant population—it will affect productivity and product per worker in ways not explicitly considered above. A larger domestic market will permit greater economies of scale; the development of industries that, because of the larger optimum size of their plants, are not feasible in countries with small domestic markets unless unwarranted reliance is placed upon foreign markets; and a more diversified productive structure providing more varied opportunities to the population. A smaller population and a smaller domestic market would make certain industries economically unfeasible, might limit the economies of scale for such industries as are indispensable within the country's boundaries, and would result in a domestic industrial structure which, because of its limited size, would tend to be concentrated in fewer sectors.

It is reasonable, I believe, to argue that since reliance on foreign trade is, perforce, limited, particularly in these times of international strain and strife, a large domestic market is an important prerequisite to the economies of scale of many modern industries and to the diversification of the domestic productive structure that provides varied opportunities for the growing population. A higher per capita product is more likely under such conditions than under conditions where no growth or only slight growth of population limits the size of the domestic market. To be sure, larger size poses other dangers, particularly the possibilities of greater disunity among the various parts of a large and regionally diversified population and the consequent difficulties of making promptly and without great cost the secular decisions essential in setting and adjusting conditions for a country's economic growth.[5] But let me limit myself at this point to the positive aspects of population increase.

Second, it is not only the size of the domestic market but its responsiveness to new products that is important. The technological

[5] See discussion of this topic in my paper, "Economic Growth of Small Nations," in Alfred Bonné, ed., *Challenge of Development* (Jerusalem: The Hebrew University, 1958), pp. 9–23.

changes that constitute the basis of modern economic growth affect consumer goods as much as they do the productive processes, and in a free market economy, lack of responsiveness by individuals and families to such new products would be a major obstacle to the growth of total and per capita output. It may be argued that the younger individuals and families are more responsive to new products than the older ones. The latter have more firmly established habits, which are largely a carryover from the past, and they have many more commitments, for example, most of their durable consumer goods have already been acquired and they may find it more difficult to incorporate many new products. Comparable differences in responsiveness to new products may exist, at a given age and income level, between the migrant and the settled unit. The migrant, uprooted from his customary surroundings, may be freer in his choice of the new products and may perhaps be psychologically more disposed toward them. It follows that population increase, accompanied as it usually is by a higher proportion of young and migrating units, may also be associated with greater responsiveness of the body of ultimate consumers to new goods—which in turn facilitates modern economic growth and may contribute to a higher product per capita.

Population Increase: Faith in the Future

We have dealt with the direct effects of population increase on productivity, savings, and consumption, and with the effects of the latter two on productivity. There are some indirect effects of population increase, or rather effects of the general atmosphere accompanying it. Allowing substantial immigration reflects a faith in the country's power to absorb the immigrants and put them to productive use, a faith in the country's future. Having children is also evidence of faith in the future, not in the underdeveloped countries where the motivation may be a desire for support in old age but in the developed countries where children are not expected to support their parents, where family planning is an accepted pattern, and where the social level of the majority of parents warrants the assumption of deliberate choice in the matter. Granted, in recent decades this faith has an apocalyptic tinge, colored by visions of atomic holocausts and Armageddons. It is a faith, nevertheless, in the country's future, unless or until terminated by such calamities as transcend the limits of planning of a household, a firm, or even a country. Contrariwise, a constant or slowly growing population is implicit evidence of lack of faith in the future.

This being the case, it can be argued that the climate of belief in the future within which population increase occurs is itself conducive to greater economic growth and greater growth of product per capita. For it presumably encourages forward-looking ventures by individuals planning their careers and by entrepreneurs planning their investments. The expectation of a future in which larger markets and wider opportunities will prevail encourages extension of capacity, both personal and material, and it discourages the stagnation which results when individuals cling to unsatisfactory but "safe" routine jobs or when entrepreneurs, bankers, the labor force, and other important agents of economic enterprise hesitate to commit themselves to ventures that depart from the "tried and true." It is naturally difficult to assign weights to this factor of buoyancy accompanying population increase, when the latter is a matter of choice rather than of obsolescent patterns of individual behavior under changed conditions. But the effect of the implicit view of the future on decisions by entrepreneurs and households can hardly be denied—particularly for entrepreneurs, for whom there is an economic rationale in being more venturesome, more forward-looking, under such conditions than when the view of the future is pessimistic. Greater venturesomeness, greater willingness to build for the future, is likely to contribute to more vigorous growth of total and per capita product.

Concluding Comments

The preceding discussion has dwelt, by design, on the positive contributions that population growth may make to the increase in per capita product, and it has been pursued largely against the background of developed countries. The concluding remarks are addressed primarily to qualifications, to avoid dismissal of this discussion as an expression of exuberant but unfounded optimism.

First, few if any of the points made are relevant to the underdeveloped countries. By definition, the latter suffer from an acute shortage of capital, not only for material investment but also for the adequate raising and education of their younger generations, and the whole structure of their society is unfavorable to the adoption of many potentials of modern technology, since it necessitates major changes that no living society can absorb within a short period. It is, therefore, unrealistic to assume that population increase in an underdeveloped country is followed by the adequate investment in human beings and material capital, by the advantages of greater mobility, and by the stimulus of a wider and more responsive market associated with population increase in developed countries and which contribute to greater product per capita. This is particularly true in view of the actual (or threatening) acceleration of rates of natural increase in the underdeveloped countries resulting from the maintenance of, or even slight rise in, the already high birth rates combined with the remarkably rapid reduction in death rates made possible by recent revolutionary changes in public health and control of diseases.

Second, even in the advanced and developed economies, population increase means further pressure upon limited natural resources, upon the supply of material capital, and above all, upon the capacity of the social and economic structure to adapt itself to it. All the factors cited in the current (and past) literature that make for the increased burden of larger populations—if higher per capita product is to be attained—are relevant here. In particular, an acceleration of population increase from a previously lower rate (like a marked retardation from a previously high rate), may mean a lag in the adjustment of economic and social institutions, with painful consequences resulting from delaying the kind of response that maximizes the advantages of a growing (or retarding) population and minimizes its disadvantages. The recent delay in this country, particularly on the part of the public sector, in responding to the obviously increasing educational needs of our growing population is a clear case in point, as are some of the lags in response to the reduction of immigration and to the retardation of population growth in the 1920's.

Third, for a single developed country, the impact of growth of its population, compared with the growth of the population of its partners in the concert of nations, should be considered. The contribution to new knowledge and technological change that its increased population may make would most likely become common property, after a short period of initial, pioneering advantage; but if a country's population grows proportionately more than that of its partners in international trade, it runs the risk of greater disadvantages—pressure for more imports, without a fully compensating reduction in cost of export goods and hence of exports. This problem of external balance has not been considered in the previous discussion, and yet it may impose limits upon the contribution of population growth to the economic performance in any single country.[6]

Hence, even in the advanced economies, there is the question whether the positive advantages of population increase outweigh its cost in terms of greater pressure upon limited resources, slowly changing organizational facilities, and external balance. It is at this point that the major qualification of our discussion, and indeed of most of the analysis in the field of relations between demographic and economic processes, becomes patent. Obviously, there can be in any country, no matter how advanced, too much population growth in that its contribution to increased productivity per head is outweighed by the costs. But how much is too much we cannot tell in general terms and often cannot fully ascertain in specific instances. Conversely, there can be too little growth of population in that the various undesirable corollaries in the way of increasing rigidities, the lag in shifting from extensive to intensive investment opportunities, the failure to add to numbers of creators of new knowledge, and the general pessimism about the future are likely to outweigh the advantages of lesser pressure upon limited resources. But, again, we do not know how little is too little. To put it somewhat differently, we have no tested, or even approximate, empirical coefficients with which to weight the positive and negative aspects of population growth. Although we may be able to distinguish the advantages and disadvantages, we rarely know the function that relates them to different magnitudes of population growth.

This is, of course, no excuse for not trying to secure a complete and balanced view, and provide, if policy needs compel it, the most considered answer to a specific problem. In particular, it is no excuse for the consistent bias in the literature in the field, in which the clearly observable limits of *existing* resources tend to overshadow completely the dimly discernible potentials of the new discoveries, inventions, and innovations of the future. Perhaps only those who are alarmed rush into print, whereas those who are less concerned with the possible dangers are likely to be mute. And, to be sure, what exists can be observed; what is yet to come can only be surmised. And scholars naturally tend to dwell on the observable and tangible and are wary of pies in the skies. Yet we are concerned here with processes which have been vitally affected by

---

[6] I am indebted to Dr. Hans Singer for calling my attention to this point.

additions to knowledge, unforeseen and undreamed of (except by Jules Verne, H. G. Wells, and others of their ilk), and scientific caution should not extend to the exclusion of a dominant factor because it is difficult to grasp and fit into a model with a determinate and hence limited outcome.

Finally, increase in per capita product has been a central reference point because it permitted me to handle conveniently the assigned topic of the relation between population change and aggregate product. It is not necessarily a superior desirable criterion for guidance in population policy, nor is it a dominant criterion in population policy as currently practiced (implicitly or explicitly). For example, in an authoritarian society managed by a power-hungry political elite, no real concern is shown for per capita product. The aim there is to accumulate the maximum surplus of resources, material and human, compatible with internal stability of the party elite, for the purpose, however ideologically motivated, of extending its power elsewhere. Assume that of the labor force in such a country 5 percent are the political elite; 15 percent are its policemen, administrators, propagandists, and favored professionals; and the remaining 80 percent are its workers, exploited to yield the surplus, either in labor camps or by propaganda concerning the coming millennium and the threats of the rest of the world. Now, if X of these exploited workers yields Y of power-orientable surplus, $X + a$ might yield $Y + b$; and the underlying population increase would be desired by the political elite even if b/a were a lower ratio than Y/X, that is, even if, with constant consumption per head of the exploited workers, product per head declined as population increased.

But even in free societies, where the consumer is sovereign, maximization of per capita income may not be the paramount or even an important aim, and population change will not be judged in these terms. A society may prefer a smaller population, even if it means smaller aggregate and per capita product; or, what is more likely, it may prefer a larger population, even if it means a lower per capita product than would smaller numbers—if the population feels itself to be in danger and considers that there is greater safety in greater numbers. Many other criteria than per capita income can be used for evaluating population change and formulating population policy in the free countries, but they are outside the scope of this discussion. The only reason for raising this question is that any discussion, even if it is only an attempt to interpret the past or speculate upon the possible relations, inevitably carries policy connotations. And it is well to emphasize that concentration of the discussion here on the relation between population growth and per capita product does not mean that maximizing the latter is a dominant, or even important, criterion in policy evaluation of population change.

Regional Economic Trends
and Levels of Living

THIS PAPER surveys the levels and trends of economic performance and living in different regions of the world during recent decades. For proper perspective, one should go back to the beginning of the century at least. What with the scarcity of adequate data, the difficulties in measuring economic product and levels of living for diverse societies, and the limitations of one man's knowledge, this task cannot be adequately discharged. But we can select from limited and often suspect data information that can be easily summarized, and we can present it so that at least the broader differences in economic performance and living can be seen and some of the more conspicuous trends will become apparent. This is therefore a preliminary sketch rather than a complete picture.

We must rely on statistical estimates of varying quality and reliability, yet it is pointless to dwell upon their limitations or repeat cautionary remarks *ad nauseam*. Let me then offer at the outset an apology for the statistical crimes that will be perpetrated; confess that a strong element of judgment had to be exercised in the use of the available figures; and warn that both the figures and the results must be taken with strong doses of critical salt. Unfortunately, the supply of testable knowledge relating to the economic universe

This paper was presented at the Thirtieth Institute of the Norman Wait Harris Foundation at the University of Chicago, November 24–28, 1954. It is re-printed from Philip M. Hauser, ed., Population and World Politics *(New York: The Free Press of Glencoe, 1958), with the permission of The Free Press.*

leaves much room for individual judgment in accepting and deploying the data, and the public can be protected only if the subject is treated critically by other equally or more knowledgeable students.

Differences in Per Capita Income and Production

We begin with a glance at the available data on per capita income in the different parts of the world. Measures of national income for each country are useful if they record what they are intended to record, that is, the aggregate net product of economic activity, the sum total of the results of production upon which consumption and capital formation can draw. Reduction of this over-all total to a per capita basis is a crude device; nevertheless it helps adjust the differences among countries in the number of people to be supported by the annual output.

We have fairly complete coverage of the world for two years— 1938 and 1949—although only by accepting many suspect estimates. Yet even these rough estimates represent informed and honest judgments backed in part by empirical evidence, and they at least indicate broad differences or similarities, if not precise magnitudes.

The estimates for 1938 and 1949 differ in two respects. The coverage is more complete for the former than for the latter (the omission in the latter, however, is no more than about 2 or 3 percent of world population and does not affect significantly the percentage distributions), and the bases for reducing all estimates to one denominator also differ between the two years (being unmodified exchange rates on the dollar in 1938, and a somewhat more complex procedure in 1949). Not much attention should be paid, therefore, to differences in percentage distributions or in per capita income differentials between the two years, although the *widening* of such differentials from 1938 to 1949 may represent a genuine shift, if not necessarily of the magnitude suggested.

The grouping of countries into regions shown in Table 1 is the most convenient for our purposes; it reflects the conspicuous economic differences, relies heavily upon geographical contiguity, and reduces the world to a few regions to permit easy summary. "Western Europe," including central and northern countries, extends through Germany, Czechoslovakia, and Austria in the East. "Other Europe" comprises the countries of the Balkan, Appenine, and Iberian peninsulas and the Eastern group. The "overseas descendants" of Western Europe include the United States, Canada, Aus-

Table 1. DISTRIBUTION OF WORLD POPULATION AND INCOME, 1938 and 1949

Region	1938 Percent of world population	1938 Percent of world income	1938 Relative income per capita (world = 100)	1949 Percent of world population	1949 Percent of world income	1949 Relative income per capita (world = 100)
1. Overseas descendants of Western Europe	7.1	29.6	419	7.5	44.4	590
United States	6.1	25.9	429	6.5	40.9	626
2. Western Europe	10.1	27.7	275	10.0	21.5	214
3. USSR	7.9	8.1	102	8.4	11.2	133
4. Other Europe	8.4	10.8	129	6.4	6.0	94
5. Latin America	6.0	4.2	71	6.6	4.4	66
6. Asia	53.2	17.3	33	52.4	10.5	20
7 Africa	7.3	2.3	32	8.6	2.0	24
Grouping A						
8. Developed (1–2)	17.2	57.3	335	17.5	65.9	375
9. Semideveloped (3–4)	16.3	18.9	116	14.8	17.2	116
10. Underdeveloped (5–7)	66.5	23.8	36	67.6	16.9	25
Grouping B						
11. Advanced (1–2)	17.2	57.3	335	17.5	65.9	375
12. USSR (3)	7.9	8.1	102	8.4	11.2	133
13. Intermediate (4–5)	14.4	15.0	104	13.0	10.4	79
14. Poor (6–7)	60.5	19.6	32	61.0	12.5	21

The calculations for 1938 are based upon the totals given in W.S. and E.S. Woytinsky, *World Population and Production* (New York: The Twentieth Century Fund, 1953), Table 187, p. 395. The breakdown between Western Europe and Other Europe is based upon the more detailed data for 1938 in Table 185, pp. 389–90.

The calculations for 1949 are based upon the estimates in United Nations, *National and Per Capita Incomes, Seventy Countries, 1949*, Statistical Papers, Series E, No. 1 (New York, October 1950). However, we have added estimates for Eastern Germany, Spain, and Bulgaria, and replaced the estimates for the few countries in Africa by a total for that continent. These additions were made on the basis of the estimates for 1948 given by Woytinsky.

tralia, and New Zealand. "Latin America" includes all countries and regions south of the United States borders, including the Caribbean. Each of these regions except the USSR comprises several countries which may differ fairly widely in per capita income or other characteristics: within Western Europe are Sweden, Great Britain, and Austria; within Other Europe, Greece, Italy, and Spain; within Asia, Japan and China; within Africa, the Union of South Africa and Nyasaland; within Latin America, Argentina and Ecuador. But short of studying the individual countries, each with its peculiar historical heritage and economic characteristics, we must deal in larger regions. These regions, unless we make errors in the groupings, are not entirely artificial entities. There is a community of historical heritage and economic structure among countries in Western Europe which differentiates them from the countries in Other Europe; there is some community among the countries of Latin America.

The broad results of these regional divisions and of their grouping into somewhat wider categories may be summarized as follows.

1. The group with the highest per capita income, the overseas descendants of Western Europe, accounts for over 7 percent of world population and for perhaps one third of world income. Its per capita income is 4 to 6 times the world average.

2. At the other extreme are Asia and Africa. Asia alone accounts for over half of world population. The two continents account for more than six tenths of world population, but for only about one seventh of world income. Their per capita income is only one fifth to one third of the world average, and about one twentieth to one fourteenth of the income of the top group.

3. The other regions lie in between: the per capita income of Western Europe, high on the scale, is more than double the world average; those of the USSR and Other Europe are close to or slightly exceed it; and that of Latin America is about two thirds of it.

4. Among the wider groupings, the developed part of the world (Western Europe and its overseas descendants) accounts for about one sixth of world population and well over one half of world income; it has a per capita income about 3.5 times that of the world. The underdeveloped sector (Asia, Africa, and Latin America) accounts for two thirds of world population and has a per capita income between one quarter and one third of the world average. The range in per capita income between the developed and underdeveloped regions, both conceived broadly, is from about 3.5 to about 0.3, about 12 to 1.

Income figures are money values and necessarily an amalgamation of estimates that should be checked by measures with a somewhat different foundation. We can use for this purpose an interesting study of world production in agriculture, mining, and manufacturing prepared by the Polish Institute of Social Economy and published in 1939 (Table 2). The figures refer to 1929 and are based largely on international production data published by such agencies as the International Institute of Agriculture in Rome and the League of Nations, with output weighted by prices in international trade. For manufacturing, value-added figures were used,

Table 2. World Production (Agriculture, Mining, Manufacturing), 1929

Region	Percent of world population	Percent of world production	Per capita production (world = 100)	Percent of total production		
				Agriculture	Mining	Manufacturing
1. Overseas descendants of Western Europe	7.2	35.8	495	33	7	60
United States	6.3	31.7	501	31	7	62
2. Western Europe	10.8	25.8	238	27	5	68
3. USSR	7.7	7.8	101	59	3	38
4. Other Europe	8.3	7.9	95	59	3	38
5. Latin America	6.0	4.7	79	66	9	25
6. Asia	53.0	16.2	31	79	2	19
7. Africa	6.9	1.8	26	65	18	16
Grouping A						
8. Developed (1–2)	18.0	61.6	342	31	6	63
9. Semideveloped (3–4)	16.0	15.7	98	59	3	38
10. Underdeveloped (5–7)	65.9	22.7	34	76	5	19
Grouping B						
11. Advanced (1–2)	18.0	61.6	342	31	6	63
12. USSR (3)	7.7	7.8	101	59	3	38
13. Intermediate (4–5)	14.3	12.6	88	62	5	33
14. Poor (6–7)	59.9	18.0	30	78	4	18

Based on Ludwik Landau, *Gospodarka Światowa* (The World Economy) (Warsaw: Instytut Gospodarstwa Społeçnego [Institute of Social Economy], 1939), French summary.

and for many countries the estimates had to be based upon the number of workers engaged and a somewhat arbitrary allocation of value added per worker.

The estimates summarized in Table 2 involve much approximation, although perhaps less relatively than the national income estimates. (In the preface, the author justifies the study as a better record of international differences in economic performance than a study of national income estimates which, particularly at the time, were lacking for a large proportion of the world's population.) Be that as it may, the results can serve as a rough check upon the findings of Table 1. However, Table 2 omits the products of handicraft and hand trades and the output of the service industries, ranging from transportation to trade to personal services, except as embodied in agricultural, mining, or manufacturing output. The omission of handicrafts and hand trades reduces the relative position of the less developed regions; that of services reduces the relative position of the more developed regions.

Despite differences in scope, in the year of reference, and in the sources of basic data, the results are quite close to those in Table 1, particularly for 1938. Here again, the range in per capita production between the top group and the lowest is in the ratio of 16 to 1; the order of the several regions is the same, and the differences in per capita production are almost identical with those in per capita income in 1938.

Of some interest is the information in Table 2 on the distribution of output among the three covered sectors. As expected, the less developed areas are characterized by a high proportion for agriculture and, in some cases (Africa and Latin America), for mining; the more developed regions, by a high proportion for manufacturing output. It follows that the contrasts among the regions in agricultural production per capita are much less marked than those in manufacturing output per capita. Thus, agricultural output per capita in the developed group (Western Europe and the overseas group) is 106 (31 percent of 342), compared with 26 (76 percent of 34) in the underdeveloped group (Latin America, Asia, Africa), or about 4 to 1. Manufacturing output, on the other hand, is 216 (63 percent of 342) in the former and 6.5 (19 percent of 34) in the latter, or about 33 to 1, and 8 times as large as the ratio for agriculture.

Differences in Per Capita Consumption Levels

The disparities in per capita income or economic product among the several regions may be viewed as reflections of differences in the capacity to produce, in which case further analysis is directed toward the industrial structure, the relations among population, labor force, natural resources, accumulated reproducible capital, and the like. This view leads ultimately to an analysis of the whole economic and social structure in an attempt to discern the basic forces that limit, in such varying degree, the capacity of different regions to tap the wide technological potential currently available to all mankind. Or regional income disparities may be viewed as differences in capacity to consume; in which case further analysis is directed toward the uses of income, as between consumption and capital formation, and the structure of consumer expenditures, and ultimately leads to an evaluation of consumer expenditures in terms of basic requirements of welfare. The distinction between the two approaches is to some extent artificial: what and how we produce determines to a considerable degree how we live, and thus affects the patterns of consumption and saving; and how we live, consume, and save clearly has a far-reaching effect upon what we can and do produce. Since subsequent discussion is limited to consideration of consumption levels, the broad picture of the production side—of the type of industrial structure associated with high or low income levels—must be kept in mind if we are to understand differences in consumption levels.

As we turn to the latter, it is relevant to point out that from about 85 to close to 100 percent of national income is ordinarily devoted to consumer expenditures; net capital formation, the other share in our classification, ranges from close to 0 to about 15 percent. We refer here to secular levels, since in the short run of a cycle or a war the shares can vary more widely, and to conditions in which the government sector does not bulk large in the country total. This creates a major problem in the analysis of the experience of the USSR, but even here savings proportions of over 20 percent are not a secular characteristic. Without going into this problem further, we assume here that consumer expenditures among the different regions vary over the long run within the limits of 82 to 98 percent of national income.[1] Moreover, the highest savings or capital formation rates are not necessarily associated with the highest per capita income. But if we accept the extreme possibility —that consumer expenditures are 98 percent of national income in the underdeveloped regions and 82 percent in the most highly developed region—per capita income of the former, that is about a seventeenth of per capita income of the latter, is translated into per capita consumer expenditures that are about one thirteenth of those in the most developed region. The relative disparity narrows somewhat as we pass from income to consumption per capita; but disregarding possible errors of estimates, the differences in per capita consumption, in money terms, among the various regions of the world must still be quite wide, exceeding the ratio of 10 to 1.

Into what combinations of categories were these wide disparities in consumption levels per capita translated so that the poor did not die from famine and malnutrition-caused diseases and the rich from sheer surfeit? To answer this question let us look first at the per capita consumption of food (Table 3).

The most telling indexes are those for years immediately before

---

[1] For an attempt to assemble data for international comparisons of capital formation proportions see "International Differences in Capital Formation and Financing," in Moses Abramovitz, ed., *Capital Formation and Economic Growth* (Princeton University Press for the National Bureau of Economic Research, 1956), pp. 19–106.

	Europe Overseas Western Europe Other (1)	Europe USSR (2)	Wes- tern (3)	descen- dants of (4)	Latin America (5)	Asia (6)	Africa (7)
A. Black-Kiefer indexes of food consumption, 1934–38							
1. Cost at U.S. prices	100	83	62	59	69	36	46
2. Calories	100	90	82	87	76	66	71
3. Composition	100	93	76	68	88	55	66
4. Per capita income, 1938 (see Table 1)	100	66	31	24	17	7.9	7.6
B. FAO, Second World Food Survey							
1. Food consumption, in calories, prewar	100	95	86	n.d.	68	67	68
2. Same, postwar (about 1949)	100	91	79	96	75	62	68
3. Per capita income, 1949 (see Table 1)	100	36	16	23	11	3.4	4.1
4. Percent of calories from nonstarches and sugar (postwar, selected countries)	57	43	32	n.d.	33	24	24

Lines A1–3 are based on John D. Black and Maxine E. Kiefer, *Future Food and Agriculture Policy* (New York: McGraw-Hill, 1948), Table 6, pp. 44–45. The three series of indexes, given for 54 countries, were grouped into regions, and then combined with 1938 population totals as weights. Line A1 reflects the different per capita cost of food consumed when the latter is valued at United States prices of the period; line A2 reflects the caloric content of per capita food consumption; line A3 is, for each country, the ratio of the cost to the calorie index (the higher cost per calorie represents better food composition).

Lines B1 and B2 are based on FAO, *Second World Food Survey* (Rome, November 1952), Appendix V (calorie supplies at retail level), p. 53; the averages for regions were derived with population for 1936 and 1949, given in the FAO Appendix V, as weights. Line B4 is from *ibid.*, Table 11, p. 14. Here the list of countries was too limited to permit calculation of weighted means by regions. Instead the following countries were used to represent the regions (listed by column numbers; unweighted means of percentages when more than one country was used): (1) United States; (2) United Kingdom and France; (3) Italy and Greece; (4) USSR; (5) Brazil and Mexico; (6) China and India; (7) Union of South Africa and French North Africa.

World War II. When valued in United States prices, food consumption per capita in the most underdeveloped regions of the world (cols. 6 and 7) was in 1938 about 40 percent of that in the most developed region (col. 1). Income per capita in the former was, however, only about 8 percent of that in the latter. In the United States, which dominates region 1, expenditures on food in 1938 amounted to about 28 percent of total personal income and a slightly higher percentage of national income.[2] The ratio cannot be much more than 2.5 times in the underdeveloped regions, roughly about 70 percent. This means that, given a ratio of incomes between region 1 and 6 or 7 of about 12.5 to 1 (see line A4 of Table 3), the money value of food consumption per capita should be, in comparable terms, 28 (28 percent of 100) and 5.6 (70 percent of 8). The ratio of per capita expenditures on food thus derived is 5 to 1, not about 2.5 to 1, as shown in line A1. The discrepancy may be due partly to differences in the years of coverage and partly to the food consumption data (e.g., the indexes in line A1 probably do not take full account of the cost of services, packaging, etc., covered in United States outlays on food), in which case the range between columns 1 and 6 or 7 should be much wider than that shown in line A1. But it may also be due to the bias in national income estimates toward exaggerating the contrast in per capita economic levels between developed and underdeveloped countries, even when the totals are reduced to common denominators. The exaggeration is probably greater in the 1949 comparison, when the income range is described by a ratio of almost 30 to 1 (line B3).

Yet, the wide differentials in per capita income and consumption would remain even if we adjusted for the biases. Consumers spend a much greater proportion on necessities, such as food, in the underdeveloped, poorer regions than in the developed and richer regions. This is a case, on an international scale, of Engel's law, established and confirmed by intracountry studies of consumption structures at different income levels.

But not only is a larger proportion of limited income spent on such necessities as food in the poorer regions; the food consumption is also adjusted in that more calories are bought per money unit in the less developed than in the more developed countries. The range in per capita consumption of calories (line A2, or B1 and B2) is appreciably narrower than that in the cost of food per capita; from region 1 to regions 6 and 7 it is roughly 1.5 to 1, compared with 2.5 to 1. The structure of food consumption of the less developed regions favors the cheapest sources of calories—the grains and the starches and to some extent sugar—rather than meats, dairy products, and vegetables. The food composition indexes (lines A3 and B4) show clearly the regional differentiation in the

[2] See U.S. Department of Commerce, *National Income* (Washington, D.C., 1954), Tables 4 and 30, pp. 164 and 206.

Table 4. REGIONAL DIFFERENCES IN PER CAPITA CONSUMPTION, VARIOUS CATEGORIES, ABOUT 1934–38, SELECTED COUNTRIES

Consumption categories	Overseas descendants of Western Europe (1)	Western Europe (2)	Other Europe (3)	USSR (4)	Latin America (5)	Asia (6)	Africa (7)
1. Food, calories per 100 lbs. of person	100	97	100	104	88	95	86
2. Percent of calories from nonstarches	100	79	48	35	71	40	40
3. Tobacco per capita	100	59	28	39	30	40	7
4. Textile fibers per capita	100	76	26	31	28	16	12
5. Lumber and cement per capita	100	69	25	33	11	1.3	5.5
6. Energy uses per capita in households, public and non industrial buildings	100	52	11	22	6	2.2	2.6
7. Percent of school-age children (under 20) attending school	100	94	56	53	36	13	10
8. Doctors per 1,000 population	100	62	44	55	30	6	5.7
9. Reciprocal of infant mortality rates	100	82	42	31	43	29	31
10. Pieces of mail per capita	100	75	22	21	11	1.6	1.4
11. Autos, trucks, and 0.5 motorcycles per capita	100	21	2.6	0.7	2.0	0.1	0.5
12. Telephones per capita	100	33	6.4	3.6	4.0	0.2	0.9

These figures are based upon data given in M. K. Bennett, "International Disparities in Consumption Levels," *American Economic Review* (September 1951), pp. 632–649, particularly Table II, p. 647.

The following countries were used as representative of the regions (where more than one country was used, an unweighted arithmetic mean was taken): (1) United States; (2) United Kingdom, France, and Germany; (3) Italy, Spain, Poland, and Yugoslavia; (4) USSR; (5) Mexico and Brazil; (6) India and China; (7) Egypt, Nigeria, and French West Africa (except for line 6 where Nigeria was omitted as highly unrepresentative). Each index was converted to 100, with the United States as the base (in most cases the United States was the country at the peak). The indexes for per capita utilization of lumber and cement, given separately in the source, were combined by simple averaging.

structure of food consumption.

The same results are shown in the first two lines of Table 4. Here the calorie consumption is related not to the number of people but to their weight, since calorie requirement is an important function of a person's weight; and with this adjustment, the disparity in calorie consumption dwindles even further. Line 2 shows clearly how a more adequate supply of calories is secured by the poorer regions *via* a marked shift of the food consumption structure toward the starches.

The major interest of Table 4 is, however, in the indexes of consumption other than food. Three categories of consumption can be distinguished with respect to the regional income elasticity of consumption. In one, per capita consumption differs much less among the regions than per capita income; this is true of food consumption, measured in monetary units, and even more so in terms of calories per capita or per pound of humanity. It may be true also of textiles (compare Table 4, line 4, with Table 3, line A4), but neither series is reliable enough for such minor differences to be significant. Demand for food and textile fibers, is then inelastic as far as income is concerned. In the second group disparities in per capita use do not differ much from those in per capita income: this seems to be true of the proportion of children in school (it tends toward the inelastic) and the proportion of doctors per 1,000 population (it tends toward the more elastic). In the third category per capita consumption differs far more than per capita income: this appears to be true of indexes relating to housing (lines 5 and 6), mail, automobiles, and telephones. But within this group there are some indexes (mail and housing) in which this greater disparity of consumption is true only of the extremes, that is, region 1 in contrast with regions 6 and 7, but not in the intermediate range, that is, between the most developed region 1 and regions 2 to 4. In the others (automobiles and telephones), however, the greater differences in consumption than in income are apparent throughout the range.

Mortality rates, in many ways the most important measure, have not yet been mentioned. The index of infant mortality is most sensitive to physical well-being and economic advancement. Its range, from about 3 to 1, is much narrower than that in per capita income but significantly wider than that in calories per pound of humanity. The crude death rate would show somewhat narrower disparity. For 1934–38, the average level was about 11 per 1,000 in the United States, about 23 in India, and about 27 in Egypt.[3] The range would, therefore, be at most about 2.5 to 1, not too different from that of calorie consumption per capita.

Differences in Internal Income Inequality

We have dealt so far with large and comprehensive aggregates. But these tend to conceal differences: had we distinguished individual

[3] See United Nations, *Demographic Yearbook, 1951*, Table 14, pp. 198 ff.

countries, the contrasts in per capita production and consumption would have been sharper. Even more important for the impact on world politics are the possible differences in the extent of inequality in the distributions of income and of consumption expenditures among the population groups within each country. Two countries with the same per capita income and consumption will present quite different pictures if in one earnings and consumption are distributed with relative equality among all, and in the other, large groups of the population receive small shares of total income.

Unfortunately, information on this topic is scanty, particularly in the form needed for a study of the interrelations between income distribution and economic growth or social trends in general. Data for almost all purposes should be specific in their definition of scope of income and character of the receiving unit, and we prefer comprehensive income concepts and a consuming rather than an income recipient unit. For many purposes, including the present, we want data for all groups in the economy, not for a few. Furthermore, for our purposes we should have distributions in terms of *secular* income levels, free from distortions by business cycles and other transient changes, and for an entire community in which the units in their training and retiring stages (when the secular levels of income tend to be low) are distinguished. Those acquainted with the field know that such information is not available, even for countries most richly supplied with economic statistics. The data that we do have reflect income for single years and thus contain a strong mixture of transient effects, and when they are comprehensive, they include the learners and the retired, together with what might be called the full-time mature economic groups.

But even imperfect data are preferable to unwarranted speculation about a most important aspect of economic life, even if we cannot derive conclusive indications about magnitudes, or the differences among the magnitudes in which we are interested.

With this emphatic warning, we turn to a summary of data on distribution of income by size, mostly among family units, available for a few countries in post-World War II years: the United States and United Kingdom among the developed; Italy, a semi-developed country; and India, Ceylon, and Puerto Rico, underdeveloped. For purposes of comparison suggested by the conclusions emerging for the postwar period, I have added some data on the size distributions of income for the developed countries in earlier years (Table 5).

Table 5. PERCENTAGE SHARES OF AGGREGATE INCOME RECEIPTS, SUCCESSIVE QUINTILES AND OTHER ORDINAL BANDS

A. Post-World War II Distributions

	U.S. families 1944–46, 1950	United Kingdom 1947	Italy 1948	India 1949–50	Ceylon 1950	Puerto Rico 1948
1. Lowest quintile	6 ⎫		6	8	5 ⎫	
2. Second quintile	12 ⎬ 36		11	9	11 ⎬	11
3. Third quintile	16 ⎭		15	11	14	13
4. Fourth quintile	22	19	20	16	21	20
5. Top quintile	44	45	48	55	50	56
6. Top 80–95 percent	24	21	24	22	28	28
7. Top 95–100 percent	20	24	24	33	22	29
8. Sum of deviations from equality, (1+5)	52	50	56	72	60	72
9. Range, lower 60 percent (per decile) to topmost 5 percent (per decile)	34	42	43	61	39	54

B. Pre-World War II Distributions, Developed Countries

	U.S. families 1929	1934–35	United Kingdom 1929	1938	Prussia av. 1907 & 1911	Saxony av. 1907 & 1911
10. Lowest quintile	⎫ 14	4 ⎫	⎫ 31	⎫ 33	⎫ 33	⎫ 26
11. Second quintile	⎬	9 ⎬	⎬	⎬	⎬	⎬
12. Third quintile	13	14 ⎭	⎭	⎭	⎭	⎭
13. Fourth quintile	19	21	15	16	17	17
14. Top quintile	55	52	54	51	50	57
15. Top 80–95 percent	24	25	21	20	20	22
16. Top 95–100 percent	31	27	33	31	30	35
17. Sum of deviations (10+14)	69	65	68	62	60	74
18. Range, lower 60 percent (per decile) to topmost 5 percent (per decile)	58	50	61	57	55	66

All distributions refer to income before taxes and include income in kind. Capital gains and undistributed incomes of corporations are excluded.

All distributions in Panel A are of families, except that for the United Kingdom, which is of taxpayers. All distributions in Panel B are of taxpayers, except that for the United States which is of families.

When shares of given ordinal groups had to be estimated, we interpolated logarithmically (i.e., in terms of logarithms of percentage shares of units and percentage shares of income). See also notes on India.

The specific sources are:

United States: Income Distribution in the United States by Size, 1944–1950, (Washington, D.C., 1953), and Selma Goldsmith, George Jaszi, Hyman Kaitz, and Maurice Liebenberg, "Size Distribution of Income Since the Mid-Thirties," The Review of Economics and Statistics (February 1954), pp. 1–32. Averages of shares for 1944–46 and 1950 were taken. For 1929 the Brookings distribution was used, as adjusted in Simon Kuznets, Shares of Upper Income Groups in Income and Savings (National Bureau of Economic Research, 1953), Table 55, p. 220.

United Kingdom: for 1938 and 1947 from Dudley Seers, The Levelling of Income since 1938 (Oxford, 1951), Table VIII, p. 39; for 1929 from Colin Clark, National Income and Outlay (London, 1937), Table 47, p. 109.

1. By and large, the size distribution of income is more unequal in the underdeveloped than in the developed countries. The total area of deviation from inequality is wider in the former than in the latter. For two of the three underdeveloped countries, the relative range between income levels in the lower brackets and those in the topmost brackets is also wider.

The six countries in Panel A of Table 5 constitute, of course, a highly restricted sample. If the coverage were broader, the conclusion that inequality in the size distribution in the underdeveloped countries is wider might not be valid. But in those underdeveloped countries in which a small privileged minority of Europeans or other non-natives live side-by-side with a large native majority, the income inequality is probably even sharper than that shown for India, Ceylon, and Puerto Rico. Thus in one post-World War II year, the non-African group in Southern Rhodesia, which accounted for only 5 percent of total population, received 57 percent of total income; in Kenya, a minority of only 2.9 percent of total population received 51 percent of total income; and in Northern Rhodesia, a minority of 1.4 percent of total population received 45 percent of total income.[4] Similar situations are likely to be found in other areas in Africa and in some countries in Latin America. For lack of data no definite conclusions can be drawn, but there are no grounds for inferring that the difference shown between developed and underdeveloped countries in Table 5 would disappear if more countries were covered.

Italy: United Nations, *National Income and Its Distribution in Underdeveloped Countries,* Statistical Papers, Series E, No. 3 (New York, 1951), p. 29, and P. Luzzatto Fegiz, "La Distribuzione del Reddito Nazionale," *Giornale degli Economisti e Annali di Economia* (July-August 1950), particularly Table 4, p. 14.

India: from M. Mukherjee and A. K. Ghosh, "The Pattern of Income and Expenditures in the Indian Union: A Tentative Study," *International Statistical Conferences* (India, December 1951), Part III, pp. 49–68. The shares were calculated from an equation for the Lorenz curve given by the authors (p. 56).

Ceylon: from Theodore Morgan, "Distribution of Income in Ceylon, Puerto Rico, the United States and the United Kingdom," *The Economic Journal* (December 1953), pp. 821–834, particularly the table on p. 823.

Puerto Rico: United Nations report quoted above for Italy, and H. S. Perloff, *Puerto Rico's Economic Future* (Chicago: University of Chicago Press, 1950).

Prussia and Saxony: based on distributions and total income estimates in "Das deutsche Volkseinkommen vor und nach dem Kriege, *Einzelschriften zur Statistik des Deutschen Reichs,* No. 24 (Berlin, 1932), particularly p. 126.

4 See United Nations, *National Income and Its Distribution in Under-Developed Countries,* Statistical Papers, Series E, No. 3 (New York, 1951), Table 12, p. 15.

Another qualification of the conclusion is that the data relate to annual income, not to secular levels. Would the reduction in inequality, which must occur as we pass from size distributions of annual income to those of income for longer periods, be greater for underdeveloped countries? The incidence of transient changes may well be relatively greater in underdeveloped countries where the bulk of the lower income earners are in agriculture, subject to annual vicissitudes. But this is in the realm of speculation, and we could only guess at the *magnitude* of the reduction in inequality that would occur in shifting to distributions of secular income levels. Since the only tangible finding is that shown in Table 5, we must conclude that in recent years the internal income inequality was wider in underdeveloped than in developed countries.

2. This tentative conclusion has added significance, since it is based on distributions of income gross of direct taxes and exclusive of government benefits not paid for by recipients. In the developed countries the weight of direct taxes is proportionately much greater than in the underdeveloped; the graduation of direct taxes is much steeper; and a much larger proportion of government expenditures is devoted to economic purposes that directly benefit the lower income groups more than the upper. Deduction of direct taxes and addition of direct benefits from governments would have a much greater equalizing effect on the size distributions of income in the developed countries (particularly those with a relatively high per capita income) than in the underdeveloped countries. Consequently, the greater internal income inequality in the underdeveloped countries would loom even larger.

3. The comparisons commented upon above are for income expressed in money or material terms, not in terms of welfare. Clearly, an unequal distribution of income where the average income is low —as it is in underdeveloped countries—means a much greater inequality in welfare equivalents (no matter how vague). This argument is particularly important for unified societies in which all classes consider themselves members of one community and sharp divergences in economic opportunity or welfare are not easily accepted.

4. Panel B of Table 5 suggests that the present contrast in internal income inequality between developed and underdeveloped countries may be a recent phenomenon. In several developed countries, the size distributions of income for earlier years were much more

unequal than they are now, and in fact were not too different from those in the underdeveloped countries today.

Two aspects of this finding are worth stressing. First, these developed countries in the earlier years of reference were already far in advance of the underdeveloped areas of today: their per capita incomes were far higher than the current incomes of Asia, Africa, or Latin America. Hence the welfare equivalents of their income inequality would not differ as markedly as would identical relative inequalities in the underdeveloped countries today; nor would their impact be as sharp. Second, these were countries in the process of growth and structural change: shifts were occurring in the productive and occupational structure, over-all per capita income was rising, and, therefore, the low income groups of the day could reasonably look forward to an improved relative income position for themselves and especially for their children. Under such conditions of growth and internal mobility, wide income differentials within a country are much more acceptable than under the conditions of slow growth or stagnancy characteristic of underdeveloped countries today.

Hence too much significance cannot be assigned to the apparent similarity of the income distributions of underdeveloped countries today to those in developed countries a few decades ago. There are, in general, limits to the quantitative variations of a size distribution of income like the one presented in Table 5. The reasons for such limited variance cannot be dealt with at length but will be suggested briefly below. Moreover, it is important to stress that such invariance or limited variance may conceal, and usually does, different implications with respect to the welfare or power position of the several groups. For the present theme, it is most relevant that the distributions in Table 5 do not reveal any greater internal income equality in the underdeveloped than in the developed countries, and that it is in the latter that the trend toward equality is suggested.

Trends in Regional Differences in Per Capita Income

We can accept the existence of wide differentials in per capita economic product among the regions distinguished in Tables 1 and 2. As the discussion of Table 3 indicated, there are biases in the magnitude of such differences, which would vary in any case from year to year with changes in the economic conjuncture. But there is little doubt that disparities do exist; that they are quite wide, within the range of, say, 6 to 12 to 1 between the developed group (Western Europe and its overseas descendants) and the great underdeveloped continents of Asia and Africa; and that they have persisted for some time and do not represent ephemeral phenomena.

Have there been any perceptible trends in these per capita income disparities among the regions? For an adequate answer we would need estimates for some earlier points of time, say, at least back to the beginning of the century. No such data are available, and the answer to the question must be sought with the help of odd bits of evidence. This task of statistical detection could be carried through here to only a limited extent.

We have for 1894-95 some estimates of national income by Michael Mulhall. His description of the methods indicates that the sources are data on basic production (agriculture, mining, manufacturing); on numbers occupied in various pursuits; and fairly conventional ratios. Yet the methods are similar for the various countries, and the measures for those countries for which more recent and more reliable estimates are available are fairly close to the latter. Without accepting the absolute values involved, it is perhaps permissible to use Mulhall's figures to study the trend in per capita income. Unfortunately, his data omit most of the world's population, that of Asia, Africa, and Latin America.

In Table 6 the relative per capita incomes for the remaining four regions are compared for 1894-95, 1938, and 1949. There are rather striking differences between the results for 1938 and 1949. These are partly the effect of a genuine difference in the economic conjuncture of the two years and partly perhaps the effect of errors in the underlying estimates. If, to simplify the picture, we average 1938 and 1949, the following conclusions may be suggested.

First, the growth in per capita income of the overseas region, largely the United States, is clearly greater than of the two regions of Europe exclusive of Russia. This is particularly true if we give 1949 a greater weight than 1938, a year in which the recovery in the United States from the great depression of the 1930's was still incomplete.

Second, within Europe proper, the per capita income of Western Europe grew at a faster rate than that of Other Europe. Since the latter comprises the Balkan countries, Eastern Europe, Spain, and Portugal, the result accords with our expectations.

Table 6. RELATIVE DISPARITIES IN PER CAPITA INCOME, MORE DEVELOPED REGIONS OF THE WORLD, 1894–95, 1938, 1945 (all figures are relatives of the per capita income for Other Europe)

	1894–95	1938	1949
1. Overseas descendants of Western Europe	301	325	628
2. Western Europe	186	207	228
3. Other Europe	100	100	100
4. Russia or USSR	65	79	142

Data for 1894–95 are from Michael G. Mulhall, *Industries and Wealth of Nations* (London: Longmans, Green & Co., 1896). For sources for 1938 and 1949, see notes to Table 1.

Third, the movement of the relatives for Russia is a puzzle and reflects the usual difficulties of arriving at consistent and acceptable results for that enigma. Mulhall's estimates for Russia are fairly high compared with other evidence: his per capita income for 1894–95 amounts, at the then current rates of exchange, to over 90 rubles, whereas Prokopovich's estimates for 1900 suggest a per capita income of only 77 rubles.[5] But the latter estimates omit most of the service industries, which are included in the 1949 figure. It is possible that between 1894–95 and 1949 the rate of growth in per capita income in Russia exceeded that in Europe, and was quite close to that in the overseas region, that is, largely in the United States.

If these tentative conclusions are accepted for the areas covered in Table 6, the implication as to trends in per capita income differentials is somewhat mixed. Between Europe and the overseas regions, the differential appears to have increased; between Russia and Europe, it appears to have decreased.

A second and perhaps even more important question is concerned with the trends in the per capita income differences between the third of world population represented in Table 6, and the two thirds in the omitted regions of Asia, Africa, and Latin America. Has the disparity between the per capita income of what is essentially the European group and its descendants and the Asia-Africa group increased? There is almost no evidence on Latin America, but the results derived from a comparison between Europe, at home and overseas, and Asia-Africa, would probably apply also to a comparison with Latin America—if with less force.

In general terms, the disparity has probably increased. The most

[5] See quotation and discussion in Colin Clark, *Conditions of Economic Progress*, 2d ed. (London, 1951), pp. 190–191.

telling evidence is provided by the long-term records for a dozen countries (the United States, Australia, New Zealand, the United Kingdom, France, Germany, Switzerland, Netherlands, Denmark, Norway, Sweden, and Canada). National income estimates are available for periods ranging from 50 to 80 years and can be roughly adjusted for changes in prices. These series, most of them relatively recent in origin, are probably among the most carefully prepared and reliable that we have in this treacherous field of economic statistics. They indicate that the rates of growth per decade in income per capita in constant prices in these countries range from about 10 to 20 percent per decade.

These rates are rather high. An increase of 10 percent per decade cumulates in 50 years to a rise of 61 percent and in a hundred years to a rise of 159 percent. An increase of 20 percent per decade means a rise of 149 percent in 50 years and of 519 percent in a hundred years. The question is: Can we reasonably assume that rates of increase averaging over 10 percent per decade (or well over 15 percent for a country like the United States) occurred in the per capita income in constant prices for the populous regions of Asia, Africa, and Latin America during the last 50 to 60 years?

There is little evidence that any such increase in real income occurred in Asia and Africa, if one excepts Japan and perhaps the Union of South Africa and some other enclaves in Africa. Per capita income on these continents is quite low even today. An assumed rise of 10 percent per decade would mean that incomes fifty years ago were about six tenths of the present levels and a century ago, less than 50 percent of the present levels. Little in the history of these continents would warrant assuming that the rise in per capita income was of any such magnitude, comparable with that of the total European population (including or excluding Russia) and of its overseas descendants in North America and Oceania. Indeed, for purely physiological reasons such a rise seems unreasonable. For example, in the year ending June 30, 1950, about 66 percent of consumer expenditures was spent on food in Indian villages.[6] If we set the over-all ratio for all India at about 60 percent of total income (for urban workers it was about 50 percent) [7] and extrapolate back fifty years to a level of income of about six tenths of the present,

[6] See Ministry of Finance, *The National Sample Survey, General Report No. 1 on the First Round* (Delhi, 1952), Table 6, p. vi.

[7] See W. S. and E. S. Woytinsky, *World Population and Production* (New York: Twentieth Century Fund, 1953), p. 275.

food consumption would be 40 percent less than at present if the food-income ratio remained the same. If the upper limit to this ratio is, say, 80 percent, and if we assume regression back to this ratio, the per capita food consumption would still be 20 percent lower than at present. Yet present consumption in India is only 1,700 calories per head compared with estimated requirements of 2,250.[8] India may be an extreme illustration; the population of Asia and Africa may have been able to subsist in the late nineteenth or early twentieth century on six tenths of the present real income, despite a much lower level of the preventive and curative medical arts, but it is rather unlikely.

We may conclude, therefore, that the per capita relative income disparity between the populations of Europe, North America, and Oceania, and the populations of Asia and Africa has probably widened over the last fifty years, and this widening disparity is even more likely to be true if we cover the last century. A longer period would mean a longer cumulation of the high rates of growth, certainly for Europe west of Russia and for the overseas countries, and it is difficult to assume an equally long period of growth in the per capita income of Asia's and Africa's population. Finally, these widening contrasts become even sharper if we compare the selected top groups—the developed group of Tables 1 and 2 (Western Europe and the overseas region)—with the selected low group (Asia and Africa).

As already suggested, the same conclusion applies, but probably with less force, to comparisons with Latin America. The rates of increase in real per capita income in that area during the last fifty years probably fell short of those in North America and in Western Europe. But this is only a guess, and what the comparison with all Europe would yield one cannot tell. As the tables indicate, average per capita income in Latin America is distinctly higher than that in Asia and Africa; there is room, in a sense, for considerable growth to have occurred. However, it would require more data and knowledge than I possess to arrive at plausible conclusions.

Inequality in Distribution of World Income

The discussion so far has been in terms of per capita income levels, regional differences among them, and trends in regional disparities in per capita income. There is another way of approaching the

[8] See FAO, *Second World Food Survey* (Rome, November 1952), p. 49.

same topic, with a subtle and yet rather significant difference.

Conceive of the world as a unit, and its total income as a single pool. The income of any one country or region is then a share in this pool, just as its population is a proportion of the world's total population. We can then group the countries or regions in ascending order of their per capita income and observe how large a share of total world income is produced-received by the lowest group, say, the 30 or 40 percent of world population with the lowest income per capita. This, of course, is the Lorenz curve technique applied to the distribution of world income, and it serves to shed light on other aspects of inequality in the distribution of world income.

We can apply this technique first to the three groups of data discussed in the earlier sections, Mulhall's for 1894–95, Woytinsky's for 1938, and the United Nations' for 1949. Here we use all the countries covered by Mulhall, Argentina and the Union of South Africa in addition to those covered in Table 6. But this addition is so slight, relative to the mass of population already covered, that to all intents and purposes Tables 6 and 7 are identical in coverage.

We are dealing here with the three tenths of the world's population that represent the economically more developed parts—Western Europe and the overseas descendants of Western Europe—and we are interested in changes in the inequality of distribution of income among countries within this more developed part of the world. The answer provided by Table 7 is unmistakable: between 1894–95 and either 1938 or 1949, the sum of deviations, a measure of inequality, definitely increases (about one third) and so does the range in the per-unit share between the lowest group distinguished, the lowest 40 percent, and the top group, above the 80th percentage line.

This conclusion would be only slightly affected by a downward revision of per capita income for Russia in 1894–95 (a reduction of about one fifth increases the sum of deviations in 1894–95 to 48.8 and the range to 1.440); or by the minor substitutions in the identities of the countries included (see the notes to Table 7). Nor is it inconsistent with the evidence in Table 6, which suggested a much more mixed picture concerning trends in relative disparities among per capita incomes of the several regions. First, the analysis in Table 7 is more sensitive since the underlying data distinguish 24 countries rather than four regions, and can therefore reflect changes in per capita income disparities *within* broad regions. Second, inequality as measured here, and in general, can increase

	1894–95	1938	1949
1. Estimated world population (millions)	1,515	2,140	2,385
2. Population covered in measures below (millions)	451	695	712
3. Percent covered	29.8	32.5	29.9
4. Cumulative shares (percent)			
0–40	19.4	11.7	19.0
0–60	37.0	29.4	29.9
0–80	63.2	60.0	52.3
0–100	100.0	100.0	100.0
5. Shares of successive percentage groups			
0–40	19.4	11.7	19.0
40–60	17.6	17.7	10.9
60–80	26.2	30.6	22.4
80–100	36.8	40.0	47.7
6. Sum of deviations, signs disregarded	46.0	61.2	60.2
7. Ratio to maximum sum of deviations (160)	0.29	0.38	0.38
8. Range in per percentile shares	1.355	1.708	1.910
9. Ratio of line 8 to maximum range (5.0)	0.27	0.34	0.38

Line 1: For 1894–95 and 1949 derived from United Nations, *The Determinants and Consequences of Population Trends,* Table 2, p. 11 (using the Willcox figures prior to 1900). Logarithmic interpolation was used; the 1894–95 figure was set at 1895. For 1938, see Woytinsky, Table 187, p. 395.

Line 2: By addition of the figures in the respective sources for the countries included in the array and grouping (all countries given in Mulhall except Uruguay); the same list of countries for 1938, except that Portugal and Rumania were omitted, and Finland and Poland added; the same list for 1949, except that Spain, Bulgaria, and Rumania were omitted and Finland and Poland added. These substitutions are, however, quite minor in the bulk of population covered, accounting for a few percentage points of total population and much smaller percentages of total income.

Line 4: The basic procedure was to array countries by order of increasing income per capita within each year, cumulate their total population and total income, and then interpolate logarithmically the percentage share of total income corresponding to a given cumulative percentage share of population in the array. The number of countries covered in each year was 24 (23 in 1949).

Line 5: Directly derived by subtraction from line 4.

Line 6: Calculated from line 5 by subtracting the actual share from the equality share.

Line 7: The ratio in line 6 to 160, the maximum calculated on the assumption that all income is assigned to the 80–100 percent class.

Lines 8–9: The range is in the per percentile shares, that is, in the shares given in line 5 divided for each class by percentage of population covered.

even though the relative disparities in per capita income of the components remain the same. This can be seen in a simple illustration. Assume two regions *A* and *B*, weighted 0.8 and 0.2 each, with per capita incomes of 100 and 500. The average income is then 180; the share of component *A* in total income is 44.4 percent, the sum of deviations is 71.2, and the range in per percentile shares is 2.23.

Assume now that with per capita income remaining the same for each region, the proportional weight of A decreases to 0.7 and that of B rises to 0.3. Average per capita income becomes 220, the share of component A is 31.8, the sum of deviations rises to 76.4, and the range declines to 1.82. But the range declines because we are now comparing less extreme segments of the distribution. If within the top 30 percent, the top 20 are marked by a distinctly higher per capita income, the range between the lower 80 percent group and the upper 20 percent group might also have risen.

The point is that if the share of a top minority in the income distribution increases, even if its per capita income does not rise relatively to the per capita income of the rest of the population, inequality will widen; with an increased pool of total income and a higher average income per capita, we assume no offsetting *differential* rise in per capita income of those below the top majority. And this is what happened in the developed regions of the world reflected in Tables 6 and 7. The top 20 percent is largely dominated by the United States and includes Canada and Australia. Their populations have increased at much higher rates since 1895 than the other populations covered in Table 7. The population of the United States accounted for about 15 percent of the total in Table 7 in 1894–95, almost 19 percent in 1938, and over 20 percent in 1949. Hence, even if the per capita income of the United States had not grown at a rate higher than that of the other regions, the mere increase in its weight would have increased the share of the upper 20 percent group; and when the share of one group increases, the total share of the other groups *must* decrease. But in fact, per capita income did grow at a higher rate in the United States than in other regions in Table 7.

We can attempt to apply a similar technique to a comparison between recent years and the end of the nineteenth century for the world at large. Since the attempt involves some assumptions, and its results have only suggestive value, we limit the calculations to 1949 and 1894–95 (Table 8).

For 1949, the population covered in Table 1, for which we also have rough estimates of income, is some 2.29 billion out of an estimated world total of 2.38. But for some segments, for example, Africa, no breakdown by countries is available, and we have limited the analysis of the cumulative distributions of population and income of the Lorenz curve type to the seventy countries listed in the United Nations, Statistical Papers, Series E, No. 1, which to-

	1949	1894–95		
		Assumpt. I	Assumpt. II	Assumpt. III
1. Shares of successive percent bands:				
0–70	19.6	19.6	23.7	29.9
70–82	14.5	15.6	14.8	13.6
82–88	8.9	14.2	13.4	12.3
88–94	15.4	21.1	20.0	18.4
94–100	41.6	29.6	28.1	25.8
2. Sum of deviations	100.8	100.8	92.6	80.2
3. Range in per percentile shares between 0–70% and 88–100%	4.47	3.97	3.67	3.09
4. Ratio of line 3 to maximum (8.33)	0.54	0.48	0.44	0.37
5. Range in per percentile shares between 0–70% and 94–100%	6.65	4.65	4.34	3.87
6. Ratio of line 5 to maximum (16.67)	0.40	0.28	0.26	0.23

Calculations for 1949 assume that: the noncovered part of the world, about 300 million or 14.5 percent of the covered, has a per capita income equal to that of the 0–40 percent group in the total of all seventy countries covered in the United Nations report (see note to Table 1). The share in total income of this lowest group is 5.4 percent. They also assume that the regions covered in Table 7 are all at the top and account for the top 30 percent in the distribution of total world population by size of the country's per capita income.

The calculations for 1894–95 all have a common assumption: that the 30 percent of the world population covered in Table 7 are at the top of the worldwide distribution, and that the 70 percent not covered all have a per capita income below the range covered by the countries represented in Table 7.

It was further assumed that the per capita income of the top 30 percent rose 75 percent from 1894–95 to 1949, that is, at a rate of about 11 percent per decade. Under Assumption I, the per capita income of the lower 70 percent was assumed to have increased at the same rate. Under Assumption II, it was assumed to have grown at about half the rate (i.e., 37.5 percent from 1894–95 to 1949). Under Assumption III, it was assumed to have remained constant between 1894–95 and 1949. All assumptions relate to per capita income in constant prices, and it is the assumed differences or absence of differences in rates between the lower 70 percent and the upper 30 percent that are relevant.

gether account for 2.08 billion. For the remainder we assume that per capita income equals that of the lowest 40 percent group in the cumulative distribution of the seventy countries. Since the omitted sectors are dominated by Africa and Asia, this assumption may yield too high an income and tend to damp the distribution. But the error can have only a slight effect on the inequality analysis.

Having thus pieced out the total world distribution for 1949, we can combine the results with the analysis of the upper 30 percent (in Table 7) to produce a rough distribution for 1949 (Table 8, col. 1). Naturally, the world distribution is much more unequal than that for the more developed part shown in Table 7. The share of the lowest 70 percent in Table 8 is less than 20 percent; in Table 7 it would run close to 40 percent. But our interest is mainly in the comparisons with the situation in 1894–95.

For 1894–95 we know only the distribution of the top 30 percent in the world's population. But we can make some assumptions concerning the relative income of the lower 70 percent (see notes to Table 8). These assumptions relate partly to the rate of growth between 1894–95, and 1949 in per capita income of the upper 30 percent of the world population, and partly to the movements in per capita income of the lower 70 percent. The former, set at about 75 percent, can be supported by available data on the rate of growth of a dozen countries included in the upper 30 percent group. The latter assumptions are illustrative, although assumption II, or some value between assumptions II and III may be plausible, that is, a rate of growth in the per capita income of the lower 70 percent of less than half that in the per capita income of the upper 30 percent.

The conclusions suggested by Table 8 are obvious. Even under assumption I, there is stability in inequality as measured by total deviations from the equality line, although the range in the disparity in per capita income between the lower and the topmost groups is perceptibly wider in the later year. Under either assumption II or III, both the range and the sum of deviations are appreciably greater in 1949 than in 1894–95, indicating that inequality in the distribution of world income has widened during the last half century.

Trends in Differences in Internal Income Inequality

The evidence in the preceding two sections indicates that the relative differences in per capita income between the developed and the underdeveloped countries have increased since the end of the nineteenth century, that the inequality in the distribution of world income has become greater. This does not mean that the per capita income in underdeveloped countries failed to rise: it may well have risen over the last half century, although there is no evidence that it increased substantially. The growth in per capita income of the developed countries, however, has been much greater.

Have there been increasing differences between these two groups of countries in the inequalities in their internal income distributions?

Although no conclusive statement can be made, the present weight of evidence does suggest that the *wider* internal inequality in the income distribution of underdeveloped countries is a recent phenomenon and that this excess may be greater now than a few decades ago.

Table 5 suggests that the size distribution of income in the developed countries has become less unequal during recent decades, and more evidence for the period that goes back to the end of the nineteenth century could be assembled to support this conclusion. It is possible, of course, that in some earlier periods there may have been a tendency toward greater income inequality. In some phases of industrialization and economic growth, with rapid displacement of agricultural population and flow of lower income groups into the cities, income inequality may have been accentuated. Furthermore, graduated income taxes and government benefits emerge only in the later phases of growth of developed countries. A plausible case can be made for a long swing in internal inequality in the size distribution of income, rising in the earlier phases of growth and declining when these turbulent phases have been passed. A considerable amount of evidence could be assembled to support this case, but it would be out of place here. We merely note that over the period that we are considering, the last fifty years, internal income inequality in the developed countries has probably declined.[9]

If we accept this conclusion, the difference in internal income inequality between the developed and underdeveloped countries could have remained the same, or become smaller, only if a similar or greater reduction in internal inequality in income distribution also occurred in the underdeveloped countries. There is no evidence to support such a conclusion; indeed there is no information to reveal any trend. But some general considerations suggest that in the underdeveloped countries, internal inequality in income distribution has not been reduced over the last half century and may perhaps have widened.

The first consideration is that in countries in which per capita income and hence savings proportions are low, income inequality produces greater concentration of savings and of asset holdings than in countries in which per capita income is high. In the former, only the groups at high relative income levels can save at all; in the latter the 0 savings line may well be further down in the rela-

---

[9] A more detailed discussion may be found in "Economic Growth and Income Inequality," pp. 257–287 in this volume.

tive array. For example, if only the top 5 percent of population in the underdeveloped and the top 20 percent in the developed countries save, the process—if continued over time—would, all other conditions being equal, result in greater internal concentration of assets in the underdeveloped countries, and hence in greater inequality in income distribution. The effect on trends over any period would depend upon the inequality in the distribution of savings compared with that in the distribution of property incomes at the start of the period: if the former is wider than the latter, holdings of property income-yielding assets would tend to become *more* concentrated, and, *ceteris paribus*, this would mean widening inequality in the distribution of property and hence of total income. For example, if the top 5 percent of population in the underdeveloped countries has been accounting for 100 percent of savings, and if distribution of assets and of property income was not that sharply concentrated fifty years ago, the greater concentration of savings would, unless offset by other factors, lead to an increasing concentration of wealth and greater income inequality.

This trend, tentatively inferred, would be confirmed by the slower social and economic mobility in the underdeveloped countries, associated with their lower over-all rate of growth. This mobility, this shift in identity of newly emerging successful entrepreneurs and other economic groups, constitutes a powerful factor that tends to prevent or mitigate increasing concentration of wealth in rapidly developing countries. Its almost complete absence from or limited role in the underdeveloped countries permits the cumulation of income-yielding wealth in the same hands over a substantial period of time.

The second relevant consideration is suggested by the wide extent of inequality indicated by Table 5 for the underdeveloped countries in current years. If it is wide now, how much wider could it have been several decades ago to allow for a downward trend over the period? The question is relevant because there are limits to the spread of proportional shares. If the average income of a country is low, the *secular* level of its lower income groups cannot be very much lower or these groups could not survive. Let us assume that such a minimum income level for the lowest decile in underdeveloped countries is, say, 5 percent, that is, an income that is half the average for the country as a whole. Then if all the higher deciles through the ninth receive only slightly more than 5 percent of total income, the share of the top decile should be, at most, somewhat less than 55 percent, that is, $100 - (5 \times 9)$. The measures in the upper panel of Table 5 for the current distributions, although in terms of annual income, indicate that the shares of the top decile in the underdeveloped countries are well over 40 percent. Although the analysis is impeded by the absence of distributions of *secular* incomes, the general argument remains valid: since the current size distribution of income reveals sharp inequality, inequality several decades ago—when per capita income was probably somewhat lower than today—could hardly have been significantly wider. There was no room for any sizable decline in internal inequality of income in the underdeveloped countries, and because of the arguments adduced earlier, there may well have been a rise.

Only one qualification to this conclusion can be suggested. Many of the underdeveloped countries that are sovereign entities today were colonies in the past, and may have contained substantial groups of privileged minorities from the metropolitan countries (as may have been true of countries formally independent but restricted by treaty agreements, for instance). In other words, in these earlier days there may have existed in India, Ceylon, and other independent countries of today minorities who, because of privileged status, enjoyed an income position similar to that observed and commented upon above in some of the present colonial areas in Africa. To the extent that this source of inequality in the internal distribution of income no longer exists, there may have been a reduction in inequality. But this qualification only suggests that the conclusion applies to the indigenous population of the underdeveloped areas, exclusive of foreign enclaves, past or present. Nor is its significance reduced thereby: the lessening internal inequality of income distribution in the richer developed countries still contrasts with the absence of such reduction and, in fact, with the probable increase in inequality in the poorer underdeveloped countries.

Some Implications

What are the implications of the wide contrasts among the world regions in per capita income and the possibly increased disparity since the end of the nineteenth century? What are the implications of the greater internal inequality in the size distribution of income in the underdeveloped countries, and the possibly increased difference between it and the internal inequality of the developed countries? Neither question can be answered fully and the answers to the two are interrelated, but by dealing briefly and separately with them, we may at least point the way to further probing.

1. Differences in per capita income among various regions of the world are, in a sense, similar to differences among various groups within a country. When a question like the first is asked with respect to one country, the problems usually raised are the power of the rich, the misery of the poor, and the integrity and future progress of the whole society. The power of the rich is a problem insofar as abuses are possible: such power can be used to the advantage of specific groups without improving the welfare of society at large or in contravention, in democratic societies, of a proper distribution of weight among its members. The misery of the poor is a more obvious problem in that we expect an economic system to provide a minimum of material welfare to all groups. The problem of integrity and progress of the society as a whole is obviously a question of the extent to which the excessive power of the rich combined with the misery of the poor is likely to snap the integrative ties and cause a breakdown of the minimum social agreement necessary for the functioning of the economy as a productive system of interdependent and cooperating parts, with the possibility of internal warfare spelling the end of the society as a viable unit.

Similar implications can be associated with differences in economic product per capita among regions of the world. In our world of independent sovereign units, it is easy to see the possibility of abuses of power by the rich, the misery of the poor, and the deepening divisive tendencies culminating in a series of conflicts. But it is difficult to translate these implications into consequences that can be measured and diagnosed reliably. In dealing with the two questions posed at the beginning of this final section, I propose to touch upon only one aspect, the misery of the poor, with which much of the current discussion of the problem of underdeveloped regions is concerned.

We may begin with food, the category of consumption that bulks largest, is closest to a basic necessity, and one for which it seems easiest to formulate minimum requirements scientifically. Indeed, the *Second World Food Survey* (Table 10, p. 13) compares the calorie requirements with the recent (1949–50) level of supplies in many countries and regions. According to this table, the supplies exceed requirements in all countries of Europe listed, except Italy, where the shortage is only 4 percent; in North America; in the USSR; and in Australia and New Zealand. Significant shortages, over 10 percent, are recorded for some Latin American countries (Chile, Colombia, Mexico, Peru, and Venezuela) and for most of the countries listed in the Far East. These seemingly conclusive data must, however, be scrutinized in the light of such critical discussion as that recently presented by M. K. Bennett.[10] Mr. Bennett notes that the estimates of calorie supplies are subject to fairly wide margins of error, as revealed by the revisions that the FAO made in its own estimates; that there have been fairly wide changes, usually downward, in the estimates of calorie requirements; that if the requirements are scaled to body weight and cognizance given to genetic in addition to nutritional factors, requirements for some of the lower-calorie per capita countries would be scaled down further; and that there is little evidence that, on a *secular* basis, major shortages of calorie supplies existed in recent decades in the underdeveloped countries or that any significant ill effect could be assigned to the composition of the diet.

A mere economist and statistician cannot pass judgment on the difficulties that arise in any attempt to formulate and quantify minimum *requirements*, and from Mr. Bennett's discussion there appear to be major difficulties in differentiating effects of body weight, degree of physical activity, and the needs for chemical and other constituents in addition to calories proper. But it does seem clear that if such difficulties arise in connection with food, the difficulties with respect to clothing, shelter, and the like must be greater. If by misery is meant hunger and physical deprivation that threaten to shorten existence or impose physical pain—and not a position of inferiority measured either by standards of consumption elsewhere or by standards desired—then, insofar as *aggregate* figures go, it is not easy to demonstrate that the secular differences in economic product per capita unmistakably indicate the existence of such misery for a large proportion of mankind.

In the same connection attention must be paid to the possibly wide differences between food available at retail—the usual measure of food consumption—and actual food ingestion. In commenting upon the differences in per capita food consumption in 1934–38 (see the figures quoted in Table 3), Black and Kiefer observe:

> There is not, of course, this much difference in the foods actually consumed. Perhaps a third of the calory differences represent food

[10] See M. K. Bennett, *The World's Food* (New York: Harper & Row, 1954), particularly Ch. 12.

wastes and losses and possible omissions. Another part represent wastes from overeating in the wealthy countries. On the other hand, part of the wastes and losses in the better fed countries arise from selecting the better portions of foods and discarding the rest; in general, the degree of care that is exercised in saving food is part of the food standard of living. Half, perhaps, of the calory differences between countries measure actual differences in efficient food consumption. (*op. cit.*, p. 45)

The purpose of these comments is not to deny that there are fairly wide differences among regions of the world in per capita economic product and consumption levels, or that these differences are associated with shorter life and more sickness and material misery in the regions at the lower levels. After all, the death rates in the underdeveloped countries are, in many cases, double those in the developed, and the ratio of sickness rates may be even greater. But the point is that it cannot readily be shown, in terms of *aggregates*, that the consumption levels are significantly short of some basic minimum. Subject to further reference to internal income distribution, any statements about the ill-fed, ill-clad, or ill-housed portions of mankind should, therefore, be accompanied by the following qualification: "ill" in these terms means inferior to what has proved possible and desirable by the more fortunate groups in mankind and inferior also to what may be desired by the less fortunate.

This point seems to me particularly important in connection with any discussion of population and world politics, with emphasis on *politics*. There are two reasons for this opinion. First, although the relative disparity in per capita income between the top developed groups and perhaps all developed groups, on the one hand, and the underdeveloped regions on the other, may have increased since the late nineteenth century, the differences in consumption levels as a measure of physical comfort may have diminished. It is impossible to test this hypothesis in the present paper, and it might not be feasible even with a great expenditure of time and effort. For one needs for this purpose reliable long-term measures of income or consumption levels in the underdeveloped countries. But some considerations can be noted briefly in support of this hypothesis. If there was any significant increase in real per capita income in the underdeveloped regions, consumption levels in these areas were brought closer to certain basic minima, regardless of the increase in income in the developed areas. Furthermore, recent changes in nutritional, medical, and public-health technology have made it possible to reduce the incidence of sickness and disease at relatively low economic cost, and it is theoretically possible to attain declining death and sickness rates with a shrinking per capita economic product, provided that social factors favor it. The same effect could be exercised by changes in transportation and communication which would minimize the effects of local shortages unrelieved by local gluts. Indeed, one does find, although the data are far from conclusive, that the death rates among the developed and underdeveloped countries since the early twentieth century tend to converge. Thus, in 1905–09 the crude death rate was 15.4 per 1,000 for the United States; 21.7 for Italy; 32.5 for Chile; 35.4 for India; 20.9 for Japan.[11] In general the range was from 15 (it was lower in Australia and New Zealand) to 35 or over, or a ratio of more than 2 to 1. In 1948–50, the rate was 9.7 for the United States; 10.2 for Italy; 17.1 for Chile; and 16.6 for India. The range in 1948–50 was significantly less than 2 to 1. These are, naturally, selected examples and crude rates, not standardized for sex and age composition. Yet there is no widening here of the relative range, and it may well be that in this connection, the absolute rates and absolute disparities are far more important than the relative.

The second reason for emphasizing that the failure to meet some scientifically established minimum requirements may not be politically the most important aspect of international differences in income and consumption levels is that the possible narrowing of the purely physiological consequences of income or consumption differentials may have actually increased political tension. The plausibility of this apparently paradoxical statement can be illustrated by assuming that the millions of inhabitants of the underdeveloped regions were living in more primitive economic conditions than they are today or were at the end of the nineteenth century—living, say, like the Amazon Indians. The gulf between them and the more developed countries, the low state of their physical health, and the lack of surplus on which to sustain any social leadership would be such that only the barest contact between them and the developed regions would be possible. Since it is only by contact that recognition and tension are created, one could argue that the reduction of physical misery associated with low income and consumption levels, the convergence between developed and

[11] All figures are from United Nations, *Demographic Yearbook, 1951*, Tables 12 and 14.

underdeveloped regions with respect to the consequences of differences in their per capita income to their purely physiological requirements permitted an increase rather than a diminution of political tensions. There are numerous illustrations of this association; the USSR is a recent example.

The tentative answer to the first question is then that the augmented relative difference in *average* per capita income between the developed and underdeveloped countries need not have increased the *material* misery of the poor; indeed, the latter may have been reduced because of some increase in per capita income of the poorer countries and because of the greater skill available for reducing the worst human consequences of low material resources. But the *political* misery of the poor, the tension created by the observation of the much greater growth of other communities, the failure to utilize the patently increasing potential of economic production and welfare, may only have increased.

2. A consideration of the second question, of the implications of the constant or growing internal inequality in the size distribution of income in the underdeveloped countries contrasted with the definitely lessening inequality of income in the developed countries, tends to reenforce the possibility of increasing political tension. For the potential that is being revealed is economic prosperity and a high level of living not merely for a fortunate few in the richer countries but for the broad masses of the total population. If this is contrasted with the persistence in the underdeveloped countries of income levels far below an already low over-all average, with the existence within these countries of striking contrasts between the relatively high levels of a minority and the miserably low levels of the majority, there is a clear probability of internal tensions that provide drives directed simultaneously at some higher level of over-all economic performance and, perhaps contradictory, at a rapid equalization of income and opportunities. It takes little imagination to spell out the consequences of such a situation in terms of tension in political relations *among* countries and in terms of internal tensions which in turn may generate specific types of external policies.

Other questions present themselves. To what extent have the increasing differences in per capita levels and in internal distributions among various groups of countries contributed to growing misunderstanding of the problems of one country or group by another country or group? To what extent have different population patterns, that is, different configurations of levels and trends in birth rates and death rates affected population growth in the underdeveloped countries differently from those that characterized population growth in the now developed countries in the early phases of their industrialization, and to what extent has this produced differences in the problem of raising per capita economic performance? What is the bearing upon the issues suggested by this paper of the recent trend in many underdeveloped countries toward an acceleration in population growth, a result of the rapid fall in death rates due to economically inexpensive innovations in medicine and public health and of the continuation of traditionally high birth rates? What is the relation between the time sequence in the date of entering the phase of modern growth and industrialization and the peculiar political features of state organization that accompany it? There is no intention here to multiply questions as an intellectual exercise. The purpose in suggesting them is to emphasize that differences in levels and trends of economic performance of the several human societies are part and parcel of differences in their demographic movements, in their political organization, indeed in the whole complex of their historical heritage, and in turn affect all of these. Any attempt to deal conclusively with the purely economic aspects of the field is inhibited not only by scarcity of information, but also by the extreme difficulty of dealing with them within an established framework of the social institutions and demographic processes in which they find their full meaning and through which their effects are translated in the living historical process.

Present
Underdeveloped Countries
and Past Growth Patterns

Underdeveloped Countries Identified

BY UNDERDEVELOPED countries we mean those with a per capita product so low that material deprivation is widespread and reserves for emergency and growth are small. The number and identity of such countries depends, of course, upon the level at which marginal per capita income is drawn. For present purposes I prefer to set the dividing line low in order to bring the problem into sharp focus. Specifically, using the per capita national product estimates for 1952–54 (and some earlier years) prepared by the United Nations, I have placed the maximum income for underdeveloped countries at roughly $100 (in purchasing power of 1952–54).[1] By this criterion, most of the populous countries of Asia (China, India, Pakistan, Indonesia, Burma, South Korea) and many in Africa would fall within this group. It is significant that not a single reported Latin

[1] See United Nations, *Per Capita National Product of Fifty-five Countries: 1952–54*, Statistical Papers, Series E, No. 4 (New York, 1957), and *National and Per Capita Incomes of Seventy Countries: 1949*, Statistical Papers, Series E, No. 1 (New York, October 1950). The countries listed in the text are from both publications, with some allowance for maximum growth in countries covered for 1949 but not for 1952–54.

This paper was presented at a conference on economic development held at the University of Texas in April 1958. It is reprinted by permission from Easton Nelson, ed., Economic Growth: Rationale, Problems, Cases (Austin: University of Texas Press, 1960).

American country falls below $100 per capita. Close to half of the world population is in this group and would be even if other criteria were used, not only today, but in the 1930's and for some time back in the past.

That we have come to designate these countries as "underdeveloped" implies that their current low rates of economic performance are far short of the potential. This, as distinct from actual rates of per capita production (no matter how crude), is a presumption rather than a statement of fact. However, it seems plausible to us because in many other countries rates of economic production are at much higher per capita levels; because strikingly high rates of growth have been attained over varying long periods within the last two centuries; and because the stock of tested useful knowledge at the disposal of mankind is large and has been increasing apace. But it is, nevertheless, a presumption and we should be wary of applying patterns of economic growth observed in a few countries, accounting for at most a fifth of mankind, to the large population masses included in the underdeveloped countries as defined above. Indeed, our main purpose in stressing certain basic characteristics of these underdeveloped countries is to point up the differences between them and comparable characteristics of the presently developed countries in the decades preceding their industrialization and growth.

In such an attempt, statistical evidence, even if available, has to be treated summarily, and the choice of characteristics necessarily reflects implicit notions of factors important in economic growth, without providing explicit exposition, analysis, and defense. Nevertheless, the attempt seems worth while. Much of the writing and thinking on problems of economic growth in underdeveloped countries is unconsciously steeped in the social and economic background of the developed Western nations, and there is a temptation to extrapolate from the past growth patterns of these nations to the growth problems and potentials of the underdeveloped areas. An emphasis on the differences, viewed as obstacles to such extrapolation, may contribute to a more realistic appraisal of the magnitude and recalcitrance of the problems.

Summary Results of Comparisons

1. The present levels of per capita product in the underdeveloped countries are much lower than were those in the developed countries in their preindustrialization phase.

This statement can be supported by a variety of evidence and appears to be true, except in reference to Japan, where per capita income before industrialization was as low as in most of Asia today. The preindustrialization phase may be defined either as the decade when the share of the labor force in agriculture was at least six tenths of the total and was just ready to begin its downward movement, or as the decade just before those which Professor W. W. Rostow characterizes as the "take-off into self-sustained growth." [2] In either case, the evidence that we have on the presently developed countries—in Western and Central Europe, in North America, and in Oceania—shows that the per capita incomes in their preindustrial phases were already much higher than those now prevailing in the underdeveloped countries. They ranged well above $200 (in 1952–54 prices) compared with the present well below $100 for the populous underdeveloped countries of Asia and Africa. Even in Russia, per capita income around 1885 was probably more than $150 (in 1952–54 prices), on the assumption that the present level is about $500.[3]

2. The supply of agricultural land per capita is much lower in most underdeveloped countries today than in most presently developed countries even today, let alone their preindustrial phase. Comparison of the supply of agricultural land per agricultural worker would yield similar findings.

This statement conforms to our general knowledge of the higher density of population settlement and the greater pressure of population on land in such countries as China, India, Pakistan, and Indonesia than in the older Western European countries now or even more before their industrialization, not to mention the vast empty spaces of Canada, the United States, and other Western European offshoots overseas or for that matter of the USSR. Statistical evidence assembled by Colin Clark relates agricultural land (reduced to standard units) to male workers in agriculture, and yields ratios of 1.2 workers per land unit for the United States, slightly more than 3 in the USSR, about 10 in Germany and France, and as many as 31 in India and Pakistan, 25 in China, and 73 in Egypt (post-

---

[2] See *The Economic Journal*, LXVI, 261 (March 1956), pp. 25–83, particularly the table of dates on p. 31.

[3] This statement is based on the long-term rates of growth shown for Russia in my paper, "Quantitative Aspects of the Economic Growth of Nations: I. Levels and Variability of Rates of Growth," *Economic Development and Cultural Change*, V, 1 (October 1956), Appendix Table 13, p. 81.

World War II).[4] More directly relevant are the data provided by Professor Bert F. Hoselitz on the density of agricultural settlement in countries with more than half of the active labor force in agriculture, which show that in England and Wales in 1688 and in many European countries in the mid-nineteenth century the number of hectares per male worker (or household) ranged mostly between 5 and 10, whereas similar calculations for Asian countries and Egypt today show a range from well below 1 to at most 2.5 hectares.[5]

3. The lower per capita (and per worker) income in the underdeveloped countries—relative to that in the preindustrialization phase of the presently developed countries—is probably due largely to the lower productivity of the agricultural sector.

We have no direct confirmation at hand, but several items of indirect evidence strongly support this statement. First, and most telling, is the lower supply of agricultural land per worker noted above. Second, cross-section comparisons for recent years indicate that the shortage of per worker income in the agricultural sector relative to that in the nonagricultural sector is negatively associated with real national product per capita or per worker. This association suggests that the shortage of per worker income in the agricultural sector relative to that in the nonagricultural sector in the underdeveloped countries today is greater than it was in the preindustrial phase of presently developed countries. Third, the nonagricultural sector in even the underdeveloped countries includes some modern industries that were nonexistent in the mid-nineteenth century or earlier. It may well be that the per worker income in the nonagricultural sector of the underdeveloped countries is today as high as per worker income in the nonagricultural sector in the preindustrialization phase of currently developed countries. On this possibly extreme assumption, per worker income in the agricultural sector in the underdeveloped countries must be one fourth or one third of per worker income in agriculture in the currently developed countries in their preindustrialization phase (much lower than the one third to one half for *total* income per worker).

4. Inequality in the size distribution of income in the underdeveloped countries today is as wide as, if not wider than, it was in the presently developed countries in their preindustrialization

[4] See his *Conditions of Economic Progress*, 3d ed. (London, 1957), Table XXXIII, following p. 308.

[5] See his "Population Pressure, Industrialization and Social Mobility," *Population Studies*, XI, 2 (November 1957), Table I, p. 126.

phase.

Here again we have only indirect evidence. First, limited statistical data suggest that today the inequality in income distribution in the underdeveloped countries is distinctly wider than in the developed countries.[6] Although this may be due in part to the reduction in income inequality in the process of growth of the developed countries, there is some indication that with industrialization, inequality first widened and then contracted, so that inequality in the phases *preceding* industrialization may not have been as wide as that during the early phases of industrial growth. Second, the very wide difference suggested under point 3 between per worker income in the agricultural and nonagricultural sectors in the underdeveloped countries, a difference wider than that in the preindustrialization phase of currently developed countries, also suggests wider inequality in the size distribution of total income.

Even if relative inequality in the size distribution of income in the underdeveloped countries today were no wider than it was in the preindustrialization phase of the currently developed countries, or even if it were slightly narrower, the appreciably lower income per capita in the underdeveloped countries would aggravate the economic and social implications. For if average income per capita is so low, the majority of the population with incomes significantly below the countrywide average must exist at distressingly low standards of living, and the contrast must be striking between, on the one hand, these large masses of agricultural cultivators and of low-paid *lumpen* proletariat in the few cities and, on the other, the small groups that, either by control of property rights or by attachment to a few economically favorable sectors, manage to secure relatively high per capita incomes.

5. Social and political concomitants of the low-income structure of the underdeveloped countries today appear to constitute more formidable obstacles to economic growth than they did in the preindustrialization phase of presently developed countries.

The vast array of diverse evidence on the point can hardly be summarized here, nor do we claim that these social and political patterns are necessarily consequences of the low-income structure and attributable to it alone. But at the risk of "economocentricity,"

[6] See Theodore Morgan, "Distribution of Income in Ceylon, Puerto Rico, the United States and the United Kingdom," *Economic Journal*, XVIII (December 1953), pp. 821–834, and subsequent discussion by Harry Oshima and Theodore Morgan in *ibid.*, LXVI (March 1956), pp. 156–164. See also "Economic Growth and Income Inequality," pp. 257–287 in this volume.

it can be argued that the low economic base was a factor in producing the social and political results, and a few illustrations will elucidate the point.

First, the crude birth rates in underdeveloped countries even in recent years, are at least 40 per 1,000, and in many cases well above.[7] Rates as high as these or even higher apparently characterized the United States in the early decades of the nineteenth century, possibly Canada, and other "empty" lands overseas. But in the older countries in Western, Central, and Northern Europe, the birth rates in the preindustrialization phase were already down to the middle 30's, and in some cases close to 30 per 1,000. In other words, part of the process of demographic transition had already taken place; birth rates were as high as those in underdeveloped countries today only when the ratio of population to resources was extremely favorable. Obviously, rapid population growth under the conditions prevailing in underdeveloped countries today is an obstacle to accumulation of capital and to economic growth, as it was in the older European countries in their preindustrialization phase.

Second, let us disregard for the moment literacy rates, which are distressingly low in the underdeveloped countries today, and probably well below those in the currently developed countries in their preindustrialization phase. An even more important problem for many is linguistic and cultural disunity, a problem particularly acute for both the large population units like India and China and for the smaller ones in which groups with different antecedents have been brought together. Without claiming that economic factors predominate, one can argue that the persistingly low level of economic performance and, as part and parcel of it, of communication and transportation, has played an important role. No such major problem of linguistic and cultural unity or literacy appears to have plagued the currently developed countries during their preindustrial phase.

Third, a weak political structure is in large measure predetermined by low and unequal incomes, backwardness of transportation and communication, and linguistic and cultural disunity, if by a strong political structure one means a complex of associations culminating in an efficient sovereign government, checked and guided by underlying voluntary organizations. The cleavage between the

---

[7] See, for example, United Nations, *Report on the World Social Situation* (New York, 1957), particularly pp. 6–10.

masses of population struggling for a meager subsistence and the small groups at the top—precluding a widely graded bridge of "middle" classes—certainly militates against a strong political structure and easily leads to dictatorial or oligarchical regimes, which are often unstable and unresponsive to basic economic problems. In all these respects, the situation in the preindustrial phase of the currently developed countries, again with the possible exception of Japan, was far different in the effective interplay between the government and the interests of the population, and in the much greater influence of the various groups in the population upon the basic decisions made by the state in order to facilitate economic growth.

6. Most underdeveloped countries have attained political independence only recently, after decades of colonial status or political inferiority to the advanced countries that limited their independence. This was not true of the currently developed countries in their preindustrial phase; industrialization followed a long period of political independence.

This statement is a partial explanation of the weaknesses in the social and political structure of underdeveloped countries today and to that extent is a corroboration of point 5. But there is an important additional element in it. Insofar as their political independence has recently been won only after a prolonged struggle—and is thus an outcome of decades of opposition to the advanced countries, viewed as imperialists and aggressors—not only were economic problems neglected but the native leadership was trained in political conflict rather than in economic statesmanship. There was also a negative association between the forms of advanced economic operation, as practiced by the invaders and aggressors, and its products as reflected in a higher material standard of living: the higher standard was favored, but the forms of organization which made it possible were hated. A similar condition may have existed in the development of some of the presently developed countries: for example, a distinctive minority may have been associated with a revolutionary economic process that necessitated disruptive changes and adversely affected established interests. But such an association could not have been so widely and distinctly felt as are those in the underdeveloped countries, which have had a long history as colonies or inferior political units. Neither could the disruptive effects of the advanced elements in the economy have been as great, nor in some respects as painful, as those resulting from the introduction of Western methods and practices into a social and political framework whose historical roots were radically different from those of the West.

7. The populations in underdeveloped countries today are inheritors of civilizations quite distinctive from and independent of European civilization. Yet it is European civilization that through centuries of geographical, political, and intellectual expansion has provided the matrix of modern economic growth. All presently developed countries, with the exception of Japan, are either old members of the European civilization, its offshoots overseas, or its offshoots on land toward the East.

This statement is again part of the explanation of the weaknesses in the social and political structure of underdeveloped countries today. But it is useful to recall that the European community went through a series of revolutions from the fifteenth century (to set the initial date as late as possible) to the eighteenth, antedating the agricultural and industrial revolutions in eighteenth-century England which ushered in the industrial system, the vehicle of modern economic growth. The intellectual revolution with the introduction of science, the moral revolution with the secularization of Christo-Judaic religions, the geographical revolution with expansion to the East and the West, the political revolution with the formation of national states, all occurred within the context of European civilization, not in Asia, Africa, or the Americas; and they occurred long before the modern industrial system was born. Whether or not these antecedents were indispensable is unimportant here since we are not concerned with a general theory of the causes of modern economic growth. Our point is simply that participation in this long process of change before the emergence of the industrial system meant *gradual* adaptation, an opportunity to develop within the existing social and political framework the new institutions necessary to exploit the potentials provided by these intellectual, moral, geographical, and political revolutions. Thus when the presently developed countries within the European orbit reached their preindustrialization phase, they already possessed a variety of social, political, and economic institutions, and particularly a prevailing set of views and scale of values that permitted them to make the further adjustments which industrialization brought in its wake or that were essential concomitants.

The present situation in the underdeveloped countries is in sharp contrast. They are the inheritors of different civilizations, the possessors of social, economic, and political institutions with roots that go far back and represent a heritage of adjustment to a different series of historical events, lacking the same kind of geographical, intellectual, and political revolutions, yet possibly containing a wide variety of other marked changes. These changes, however, are *not* the matrix out of which modern economic growth emerges. Consequently, there is no continuity between the adjustments that may have occurred in these underdeveloped areas before their invasion by the aggressive and expanding European civilization and the adjustments that are needed to take advantage of the potentials of modern economic growth. Some of these other civilizations did indeed reach highly impressive levels: after all, China in the seventeenth or early eighteenth century was a political unit that, in size of population and efficiency of administration, dwarfed even the largest European unit of the day; and some of the accomplishments of the native Indian civilizations were far in advance of anything that the European civilization could produce at the time. But this very success, the specific adaptation of the social and cultural patterns to the potential (e.g., the development in China of the nonphonetic written language to overcome the problem of diversities of spoken languages, or in India of the caste system) becomes a serious obstacle in their response to an entirely different range of technological potentials, calling for a markedly different set of social and cultural behavior patterns.

These brief comments hardly exhaust the important *economic* characteristics of the underdeveloped economies today in comparison with the developed countries in their preindustrial phase. We have made no reference to the division between participation incomes (of employees and self-employed) and property incomes; the savings and capital investment proportions; the spread of the market economy and the availability of credit and financial institutions; the fiscal and tax systems; the dependence upon foreign trade. These aspects are to some degree implicit in the comparisons already made, and for some of them the evidence is yet to be assembled. And our comments on the social and political framework and the differences in historical antecedents are no more than a few broad strokes on a vast canvas, only the barest preliminary sketch.

Yet they should suffice to convey the far-reaching and striking differences between the underdeveloped countries today and the presently developed countries before their industrialization. Furthermore, many of these contrasts would persist even if the dividing line between underdeveloped and developed countries were

set at an appreciably higher level of per capita income. Political
weaknesses and heritages radically different from the European
characterize many Latin American countries—even if their ratios
of population to land or population to resources are relatively favorable—and some in the Middle East and Africa.

The Experience of Japan

Before we consider further the significance of the observations just
made, a brief aside on Japan is in order. In almost all respects,
except perhaps political weakness, Japan before its industrialization
appeared to be similar to the populous underdeveloped countries
of Asia. Yet it managed to utilize the potentials of modern economic growth and to forge ahead to higher levels of economic performance. Does this mean that the characteristics of underdeveloped countries indicated in the preceding section are not the
formidable obstacles to satisfactory economic growth that we have
suggested?

The analysis of the growth of Japan in the light of this question
can hardly be presented here; and despite much valuable work in
the field,[8] the lack of basic data precludes a firm answer. But one
point must be stressed: the per capita income of Japan today, about
eight decades after the beginning of the industrialization process,
is still far lower than that in any other developed country within
the orbit of European civilization. According to the United Nations,
Japan's per capita income for 1952–54 was somewhat below $200—
lower than that in any European country covered (even Greece and
Portugal) or in most of the Latin American countries. True, the
comparison cannot be pushed too far, and these postwar estimates
may still reflect transient reductions below the secular level. But
in 1938, when economic levels elsewhere were drastically reduced
after the great depression, Japan's per capita income was $86,
between one third and one fifth of the per capita income in Western developed countries.[9] These low levels may be due to the
limited natural resources of Japan, and cannot be extrapolated
directly elsewhere. But unfavorable ratios of population to resources
also characterize the populous underdeveloped countries of Asia

[8] See particularly W. W. Lockwood, *The Economic Development of Japan*
(Princeton, N.J.: Princeton University Press, 1954).

[9] See W. S. and E. S. Woytinsky, *World Population and Production* (New
York: The Twentieth Century Fund, 1953), Table 185, p. 389.

and the Middle East, and the point to be emphasized is that despite long participation in modern economic growth, Japan does not enjoy adequately high per capita income and still suffers from the pressure of population on limited resources.

Advantages for the Underdeveloped Countries Today

But granted that the characteristics of underdeveloped countries today do constitute obstacles to economic growth that are more formidable than may have been the case in the presently developed countries in their preindustrial phase, are there not, on the other hand, substantial advantages in the very fact that these countries face the task of growth later in history? To state definitively what these advantages are calls for more knowledge than I possess. But clearly there are two major complexes: (1) the increased stock of knowledge and experience in the fields of technological and social invention and innovation, and (2) the extension in the number of developed countries and in their economic attainment.

THE INCREASED STOCK OF KNOWLEDGE · It is hardly necessary to emphasize the striking additions that have been made over the last century, and are being made today, to the stock of basic and applied knowledge of natural processes, and of techniques of production that are the substance of much economic activity. Perhaps less obvious but equally important is the wide diversity of social techniques that have evolved. The known potential of technological and social innovations available to the underdeveloped countries today is, therefore, far greater than was that at the disposal of the presently developed countries at the middle or end of the nineteenth century, let alone earlier.

There seems to be no way to gauge the direct value of this greater potential in terms of feasible economic growth, on the one hand, and to compare it with the obstacles to such growth, on the other. But at the risk of playing the role of Devil's Advocate, I would like to stress certain aspects of this increase in the stock of technological and social knowledge that limit its possible value as a tool in the economic growth of the underdeveloped countries of today.

In the first place, most, if not all, such additions to production and social technology originated in the developed countries and were advanced in response to the needs of these economies or were adapted to the patterns of social and economic life peculiar to them. For example, the remarkable technological changes in agriculture seem to emphasize labor- rather than land-saving innovations; but land is the more limiting factor of production in the large under-developed countries. Likewise, many social inventions, ranging from the more limited types in the field of financial structure or business organization to such major complexes as the planned authoritarian framework of the USSR, were evolved within the contexts of the specific economies, reflecting their distinctive social setting and historical heritage. Some of these technological and social innovations could, of course, be transferred to the underde-veloped economies of today with relatively minor modifications. But others would require major readaptation, for which the material and human resources may not be available; and still others may be so divergent from the historically determined, deep-seated factors in the structure of the underdeveloped economies that their avail-ability in any meaningful sense of the term is questionable.

In the second place, translating any potential of technological and social innovations into reality requires an investment before returns can be expected. This investment can be defined as the input of material resources and social change required for the adoption of the technological or social innovation in more or less the form in which it is known in the developed countries. With costs so defined, this argument becomes a *supplement* to that stated just above as to the "specificity" of much of the invention and innova-tion that emerged during the last century. If costs are defined more widely, to include also those of readaptation and change necessary to overcome the specificity limitations, the argument would, of course, include much of what has already been said in the pre-ceding paragraph.

If we hold to the narrower definition of costs (which is still wider than the usual one in economic analysis), the argument can be stated simply. From a review of the history of technological and economic changes since the mid-nineteenth century, one gets the impression that the stock of potential technological innovations is large, so large in fact that much of it has not been utilized because of limited supplies of capital and of entrepreneurial ability, and because of the resistance of the existing social institutions, even in the most advanced countries of the day. The time span between major innovations—from the stationary steam engine to steam rail-roads; from steam power to electric power; from electric power to internal-combustion engines and subsequently to nuclear power (to mention only one line of change)—can be understood as largely due to the fact that even the most advanced nations of the day had neither sufficient stocks of skills needed for the adaptations involved in secondary and tertiary inventions, nor sufficient stocks of capital and economic entrepreneurship to be able to handle all these major innovations within a short time after the underlying scientific discoveries had been made. This means that most of the presently developed economies, indeed all but the pioneer in its early phases, had, in their preindustrial phase, a much larger potential of technological (and correspondingly social) changes than of the means needed to apply them. If so, the *larger* potential of technological and social innovations of the underdeveloped countries today may be of little importance in any comparison with the presently developed countries in their preindustrial phase. Such a potential, that is, a stock of tested knowledge, is a permissive necessary condition, but in itself is not *sufficient*. Material resources for capital input and readiness for social change are also essential. And as we mentioned in our comments on the characteristics of the underdeveloped economies today, material resources for capital inputs are exceedingly scarce, and the cost of social change, given the historical heritage, is unusually heavy.

Third, some of the additions to the stock of technological and social inventions during the last century may render the task of economic growth in the underdeveloped countries more rather than less difficult, if growth means simply a sustained rise in per capita product. Two illustrations come readily to mind. The first is the effect that recent discoveries and innovations in medical and public-health technology have made on the death rates. These changes have made possible in the underdeveloped countries of today far more rapid declines in mortality than occurred in the past in the currently developed countries of the West, and at extremely low cost.[10] With these rapid reductions in mortality, which require no substantial rises in economic product per capita, and with birth rates remaining high or rising, the rates of natural increase have risen rapidly to levels far higher than those observed in the preindustrial phase of the older European countries. And the resulting rapid growth of population only complicates the task of attaining higher

[10] See, for example, the incisive summary discussion by George J. Stolnitz in *Trends and Differentials in Mortality*, Proceedings of a Round Table at the 1955 Annual Conference, Milbank Memorial Fund (New York, 1956), pp. 1–9.

levels of income per capita. The second illustration is suggested by what has become known in economic discussion as the "demonstration" effect. The impact of technological change during the last century on communication among various parts of the world has been perhaps as great as on any sector of economic and social activity. It brought in its wake a greater awareness in the underdeveloped countries of the higher standards of living in the developed areas, and produced a pressure for higher consumption levels that may have restricted savings and capital accumulation and added to tensions of backwardness, thus making the task of orderly economic growth only more difficult. Both these complexes of technological and social innovations are major contributions to economic product and welfare in the long run, but in the short run they aggravate the economic growth problems in the underdeveloped areas.

THE EXTENSION OF THE DEVELOPED COUNTRIES · The existence of many developed and advanced economic areas today, which was not the case a century ago or earlier, may be an advantage to underdeveloped countries, and not only because they are the originators and repositories of the stock of technological and social knowledge. More directly, these advanced areas can contribute to the growth of the underdeveloped countries by demand for their products, by capital investment, by grants, and in many other ways by which the resources of one area can be placed at the disposal of another.

There is little question that over the last century, population, per capita income, and total income of the developed areas of the world have grown proportionately more than the corresponding aggregates for the underdeveloped areas, particularly if we confine the underdeveloped areas to the lowest income units in Asia and Africa. If the demand by developed areas for the products of underdeveloped countries could be assumed to be a constant proportion of the total income of the former, the increase in the number of developed areas would provide markets for the underdeveloped units that have increased *relative* to their domestic output. Likewise, if capital flow from advanced to underdeveloped areas were a constant fraction of the total income of the advanced areas, or still better of the disparity between the two groups in per capita income, one could state firmly that such a flow should have increased proportionately to the domestic income of the recipient underdeveloped countries. But no such constant proportions can be assumed, as can clearly be seen from the marked trends in the ratios of imports to domestic output in the developed countries, or from the well-known facts that the United States was a net capital importer during most of the nineteenth century when its per capita income was among the highest in the world, and that today many of the erstwhile international creditor countries in Europe are exporting proportionately less capital than they did before World War I, despite the fact that their per capita incomes are much higher.

A vast literature deals with import and export propensities, largely of developed countries and covering all too short a time span, and with past and current trends in capital movements among developed and underdeveloped countries. It is hardly possible, or necessary, to discuss that question now. No extensive documentation is needed to support the major point here, namely, that the mere rise in number and economic magnitude of developed countries relative to the underdeveloped ones does not necessarily mean greater relative availability of markets or capital supply from abroad. The political conditions in the underdeveloped areas may be unfavorable to foreign capital imports and to the assistance by foreign enterprises in developing and stimulating export potentials. In the large underdeveloped countries, like all large countries, capital imports can contribute only a small fraction of total capital needs. The very increase in technological potentials may have created in the developed countries themselves a backlog of investment opportunities attractive enough to absorb their savings despite the presumably greater marginal yields abroad (except in the restricted cases of capital exports needed to assure the supply of raw materials indispensable in the domestic economy). And finally, the larger number of advanced countries, emerging out of somewhat different historical antecedents and with different complexes of social institutions, has resulted in the intensified international friction and conflict which constitute a major drain upon the surplus resources of the developed areas and lead to a greater dominance of political than of economic considerations in trade and capital flows to the underdeveloped areas.

Conclusions

Two conclusions have been suggested in the preceding discussion. The first points to the major differences between underdeveloped countries today and the presently developed countries in their preindustrial phase, and the much greater obstacles to economic growth in underdeveloped areas that these differences imply. The second questions the advantages of a late start, in the way of a greater potential of new knowledge and a larger group of developed countries to draw upon. Both conclusions are only suggested: they can hardly be demonstrated with the evidence now available. And their bearing is wide, but cannot be sharply defined: discussion has been in terms of the very low income countries of Asia and Africa, but much applies to other underdeveloped countries.

If these conclusions can be accepted, at least as working hypotheses, some implications for economic analysis and policy can be drawn. These will become apparent if we envisage the process of modern economic growth as the spread of the industrial system from its origin in pioneering Great Britain to the United States and other overseas offshoots of England, Western, Central, and Northern Europe, Japan, and most recently Russia. Since this spreading productive system has a common core, both with respect to technology and the structure of human wants, some features of economic growth will be common to all countries in which it may be taking place. An agricultural revolution—a substantial rise in per capita productivity in the agricultural sector at home or an increasing reliance upon such abroad—is one important, and an indispensable, early element. Another is the growth of the nonagricultural commodity-producing and transportation sectors, industrialization in the narrow sense of the term. The growth of cities and all that is implied in modern urban civilization is a third. The shift from small, individually managed, almost family-attached economic units to big, impersonal units, whether big business corporations or state trusts, is a fourth. The number of such trends integral to modern economic growth can be multiplied, even if confined to the purely economic aspects, and there is a host of inevitable concomitants in the demographic and social processes: birth and death rates, internal migration, literacy, skills of the labor force, and so on, ranging to changes in scales of values. These will all be found wherever the industrial system flourishes, whether in the older European countries that still retain large residues of the preindustrial social structure or in the young and initially empty countries overseas; under capitalism or under the state-managed system of the USSR.

Yet this common core of technological and of minimum social changes associated with the industrial system was planted, as it spread from country to country, within units with different antecedents and historical heritage. And some of the social forms in which the system was clothed were quite different. They were different partly because the one central complex was combined with diverse initial conditions in the various countries of adoption; partly because the very fact that one country was the pioneer, others the immediate followers, and others came still later, in itself affected the measures by which growth or "catching up" was attempted, and the very spirit in which they were undertaken. Differences were also imposed by the size of the countries, economic growth in small and large countries being quite different in method, if not in the common aim of using the potential of modern technology to attain higher levels of economic performance.

This general model suggests that the aim of research on economic growth is to establish and measure the common and variant characteristics of the process; to "explain" the interrelations of the common and variant characteristics, that is, to integrate them into a theory of the growth of a country's economy viewed as a system of interdependent parts combined with a theory of the spread and modification of the process of economic growth as it occurs among pioneer and follower nations; large and small units; and so on. Such an attempt has barely begun, partly because interest in economic growth has been revived only in recent decades, after a long lapse since the mid-nineteenth century and partly because the available data are hard to come by, and have not yet been properly organized and examined. Economic analysis alone may not be sufficient for the explanation and elucidation of economic growth and the provision thereby of a sound basis for growth policy. It is clear, however, that the empirical findings that we now have, being based largely on data for a few developed countries for insufficiently long periods, cover too narrow a range; that the functional relations established from them cannot be extrapolated too far in time and in space; that the very conceptual structure of economic analysis, having been geared to the Western economies and to the short-run problems, may need substantial revision before it can effectively explain the past economic growth of the presently developed countries—let alone be applied to the growth problems of underdeveloped countries today. The comments above on some of the distinctive characteristics of these underdeveloped countries only point up how far removed these countries are from the observable and measurable economic experience, which is the raw material of almost all our empirical research and theoretical analysis.

This bears also upon discussions of policy related to growth problems in the underdeveloped countries, whether by professional economists or by laymen who either eventually make the decisions or determine them by their attitudes. Such economic-policy decisions should presumably be based upon tested knowledge of the possible impact of various factors or measures in relation to clearly formulated objectives. That little of such tested knowledge exists can hardly be denied; nor is it surprising that much of the technical discussion of growth policy is based on mechanical analogies, no matter how elaborate; and much of the discussion by laymen, particularly in the developed countries, follows along similar lines expressed in the cruder terms of what was good for us should be good for them.

These remarks are not meant to advocate abandoning all attempts to formulate bases for analysis and for intelligent discussion of policy. Failure to analyze and recommend is in itself a decision to do nothing, a policy that can hardly be defended. The plea here is for greater realization of how little is known and how much there is to be learned, and hence for greater caution in building models and writing prescriptions; for a clearer perception, particularly on the part of policy-makers, that the problems facing the under-developed countries are far more difficult than they appear at first sight, and that these countries cannot be expected to follow the patterns of presently developed areas which had entirely different beginnings.

The Economic Requirements
of Modern Industrialization

A COUNTRY's or region's industrialization may be defined as a sustained rise in the share of total product originating or of total labor force and material capital employed in industry. And industry is a complex of commodity-producing activities primarily engaged in fabrication, in changing commodities rather than in growing them or extracting them from water or ground. The industry sector is not a standard group in a comprehensive classification, but usually includes power production, manufacturing, and construction, although in some countries it also includes fisheries, forestry, and mining; and for some purposes commodity transportation may be added.

In the purely formal sense of an increase in the share of industry in product, labor force, and capital, industrialization is a process going back to the urban revolution that preceded recorded history. But we are concerned here with the economic requirements of *modern* industrialization—that observed since the late eighteenth century, most clearly in countries that are now considered economically developed, but also in varying degree in all but the few countries in the world still untouched by modern technology. It is, therefore, important to point out some distinctive features of modern industrialization for they affect the magnitude, if not the nature, of the relevant economic requirements.

Reprinted by permission from Transactions of the Fifth World Congress of Sociology, *Vol. II (Geneva: International Sociological Association, 1962), pp. 73–90.*

Modern industrialization is the product of modern technology and science, a reflection of the marked additions to the stock of useful knowledge, useful because it relates to properties of the universe in which we live and hence to possible controls over these properties designed for a richer and easier life. Modern industrialization is thus largely the rise in the share of the new industries, the first of which were ushered in by the Industrial Revolution in England in the second half of the eighteenth century with mechanized cotton textiles (perhaps the least important of the three), iron, and steam power. Within a century the latter two transformed the technological basis of developed economies and solved the long-standing problem of land transport that, among other conditions, had limited economic expansion. And the continued growth of science and invention produced a series of other major technological innovations—new sources of power, new industrial materials, new devices for both producers and consumers—which fed increasingly new content into the process of modern industrialization, and we are still applying growing scientific and empirically tested knowledge to economic production and industrial production as part of it.

Characteristics of Modern Industrialization

As a result of this technological advance, modern industrialization has developed two distinctive characteristics. First, the increasing use of mechanized power, the greater control over materials, and the greater articulation of the underlying basic knowledge, made for greater economies of scale, and for an optimum size of industrial plants far larger than that of premodern times. Of course, there have been large-scale economic undertakings in the past, for example, the pyramids in Egypt; the irrigation works, aqueducts, roads, etc. in some of the ancient empires; and the cathedrals and drainage works in Europe in the Middle Ages. But as far as manufacturing industries, the major component of the industrial sector, are concerned, modern technology has made possible a scale of plant operation far greater than that prevailing in the past. And the economic requirement of such large-scale industrial production —for labor force and capital, not only for itself but for the necessary "infrastructure" (the supplementary complex of transportation, communication, and other facilities)—is different from that of small-scale industry. Moreover, the increased scale of manufacturing industries, combined with the high rate of population growth, hastened the urbanization of both industry and population.

Second, the growing control over natural processes that the expanding use of science and science-based technology permitted, accelerated economic growth, as is evident from rates of increase in population and per capita product far higher than those which prevailed in the past. Thus with modern industrialization, industry represented increasing shares in rapidly rising total product, labor force, and capital and the rates of growth of *industrial* output, labor, and capital were high indeed. Furthermore, to achieve this rapid growth the industrial sector had to adjust to a per capita income that was climbing rapidly and that produced changes in the structure of ultimate use and consumption. In other words, a second distinctive characteristic of modern industrialization is the combination of a high over-all rate of growth of industry with rapid structural shifts, that is, changes in relative importance and hence different rates of growth of its component industries. These rapid structural shifts were in response not only to the differential impact of technical progress but also to the changing structure of ultimate consumption reflecting the over-all rise in product per capita.

In the light of the preceding comments, the economic requirements of modern industrialization are seen as changes that permit and induce a substantial rise in the relative share of modern industry in the country's product, labor, and capital—where the latter grow at high rates; where modern industry tends toward increasingly large-scale plants and thus requires a countrywide and urban infrastructure; and where, under the impact of technological changes on the supply side and shifts in composition on the demand side, the high over-all rate of growth of industry must be accompanied by marked structural shifts within it. We shall emphasize the economic requirements as they appear in the early stages of modern industrialization of a given country, but it must be remembered that some of them may persist if sustained industrialization is to continue. Moreover, the requirements are not universal. Those of a small country closely tied in international trade with other countries may differ from those of a large country committed to a much lower proportion of foreign trade; those of a freely organized country that depends upon private markets may differ from those of an authoritarian state which rigidly controls the economic processes. But these distinctions can best be indicated in the discussion of the various requirements.

Economic Requirements

The following complex of economic requirements of modern industrialization may be singled out for consideration: (1) a minimum level of efficiency in some major sectors of the economy, *other* than industry; (2) a supply of labor and capital suitable for modern industry; (3) adequate demand for the products of industry; (4) a supply of entrepreneurial talent capable of decisions on labor and capital involved both in modern industry and in the other requirements for it, and of innovations necessary within the changing framework of an industrializing country.

EFFICIENCY IN OTHER SECTORS · Unless other major sectors of the economy attain some minimum level of productivity per worker (or per unit of input), resources for modern industry itself might prove fatally scarce. This applies particularly to agriculture and to transport in the early phases of a country's industrialization, for partly similar but somewhat different reasons.

Agriculture (excluding or including related industries such as fisheries and forestry) provides goods of prime necessity; and in premodern societies by far the larger portion of the labor force (up to 80 percent) and of tangible capital resources are employed in agriculture. For a closed economy this means that most of the labor force is committed to providing the foods and raw materials necessary not only for themselves and their families but also for the remaining small percentage of labor force and population. Unless a smaller proportion of the total labor force (and of capital) can produce the same amount of food and raw materials, and thus release a larger share for other uses, industry among them, industrialization, in the sense of a significant rise in the share of labor force and capital devoted to industry, cannot take place. The only alternative to this required rise in productivity of agriculture within the given country is its attainment elsewhere, and reliance of the given country on exchange of its nonagricultural products for these foreign agricultural goods. That this is a feasible alternative is suggested by the experience of England in the nineteenth century; but even England had to rely heavily on its domestic agriculture in the early phases of its industrialization, that is, from the mid-eighteenth to the second quarter of the nineteenth century. And this alternative cannot be effectively pursued by a large country whose weight is far greater than that of potential suppliers of agricultural products.

Three points with respect to the required rise in the productivity of agriculture as an antecedent and concomitant of modern industrialization, should be stressed. First, although the secular income elasticity of demand for agricultural products is below 1, that is, a rise of 1 percent in per capita income (or per capita product) results in a rise of less than 1 percent in the demand for agricultural products, it is above 0, that is, *some* rise in per capita demand does accompany rising income. Hence, if modern industry is to be introduced and per capita income is to be raised, productivity in agriculture must increase to provide not merely the *same* but a higher per capita supply of agricultural products. Second, since modern industrialization and modern economic growth are accompanied by a substantial rise in population, total domestic demand for products of agriculture grows on that account—and unless foreign supplies are relied upon or unless additional land is brought into use, the domestic demand for agricultural products, increased by growth in population and higher demand per capita, must be supplied by a smaller proportion of countrywide labor and capital (but possibly larger absolute volumes) applied to the *same* amount of land. The technological and other innovations required are more far-reaching than with a constant volume of demand or an increasing supply of land. Third, it may be asked whether the surplus of labor on land, presumably found in many underdeveloped countries today (and much discussed in the current literature), may render it easy to raise agricultural productivity per worker and thus satisfy the requirement. Although the question cannot be discussed thoroughly here, it should be stressed that if the surplus is with reference to some technique *other* than that actually used, the above argument is unchanged; that increasing productivity per worker in agriculture by increasing investment in capital may mean that productivity per unit of capital may not rise, at least for a while, thus creating undesirable pressures on capital supply; and that the problem cannot be resolved by the shift of some presumably idle workers from agricultural to nonagricultural pursuits. The surplus, in fact, is largely potential rather than actual, and a shift to a higher technical level is required to effectuate the substantial release of labor from agriculture that can provide the basis for sustained modern industrialization, the kind of shift that we have been discussing as needed if reliance on domestic agriculture is to continue.

The other sector in the economy whose efficiency is crucial to the development of modern industry is transport and communication, including some related branches (warehousing and the like), closely involved in the *large-scale* character of modern industry. A large-scale plant, such as a steel mill or even a cotton textile mill, cannot operate effectively unless the flows of materials to it and of products from it are continuous and geared to permit operation of the plant at sufficiently high levels of capacity, impeded neither by shortages of raw materials nor by glut of finished products. If these transportation and communication services can be met only at a heavy outlay of labor and capital, much or all of the economy of modern industry to society will be lost. Also within the plant, effective operation may require efficient transportation and communication, and since a large-scale plant often means a sizable urban settlement (even if limited to direct employees plus the people who supply them with service), a structure of urban utilities for effective satisfaction of the demands of the "plant population" is also required. In short, in a variety of ways, modern industry demands *complementary* transportation and other facilities; and unless these can be provided without disproportionate input of labor and capital resources, significant modern industrialization cannot take place.

Here again, as in the case of agriculture, consideration of a given country's possible ties with others introduces some modifications into the requirement—over and above the obvious but highly important point that in meeting such a requirement, the given country can learn from the experience of others. For example, large-scale plants in the less developed countries are often built as close as possible to lines of transportation to the more developed countries so as to exploit the more effective transportation systems of the latter (particularly by water). Also, the first complex of large-scale plants in a less developed country is often built by firms from a foreign, more developed country, interested in exploiting the raw material endowments of the former; and in the process these foreign firms take responsibility for providing efficient transportation and communication. Finally, transportation and public utility facilities are capital-intensive, i.e., have a high ratio of capital investment to net output (and to workers attached); and they are needed early in the economic development of a country, before the rise in total and per capita income permits domestic generation of adequate capital funds. It is thus not unusual for foreign capital to be employed extensively in financing the transportation network of industrializing countries; and it often is accompanied by foreign skills in construction and installation. But except when a given country can, by a happy geographic accident, rely, in developing its large-scale modern industry, on the transportation facilities of foreign and more developed countries, it must still meet the requirement of the infrastructure; and while capital financing and technical aid can be provided from abroad, this does not obviate the need for substantial contributions within the country, in the way of material resources and institutional adjustments.

LABOR AND CAPITAL RESOURCES · If we assume adequate efficiency in agriculture, as the sustaining sector, and in transportation and other complementary sectors, labor and capital resources in the country would presumably be sufficient to raise the share of modern industry in total resources used and in total product turned out. But the *amounts* of labor and capital available for modern industry are not all-important; modern industry requires specific types of labor and capital equipment. In other words, in addition to purely *aggregative* requirements for labor and capital, modern industry has qualitative or *structural* requirements. In considering these for modern industry, we shall implicitly be discussing the qualitative requirements for modern transportation and even modern agriculture already touched upon above, for clearly many of the specific characteristics of labor and capital are common to modern industry, transportation, agriculture, and other sustaining and complementary sectors.

To begin with labor, modern industry, with its increased reliance on science-oriented technology, requires a group of trained professional people capable of understanding and controlling the complicated bases of modern technology. In particular, it should be emphasized that even in the countries that *follow* the industrialization patterns of the pioneer, and most countries are followers after one pioneer, the professional industrial personnel is needed not merely for simple application of the techniques established elsewhere. The existing technology usually must be adapted to the specific conditions and resource endowments of the borrowing, less developed country and needs to be supplemented by new inventions and devices, designed to optimize its contribution to modern industry within the given country. The professional and highly skilled groups are, to be sure, relatively small; but the training and education of such technically qualified personnel are demanding of time and resources. Moreover, the "production" of this selected group is partly contingent on a system of *widespread* education and training that serves as a means of selecting those best fitted for the more difficult tasks of modern technology.

If only for this reason, the specific requirement for qualified top industrial personnel affects a much wider group of people. But, furthermore, requirements of modern industry affect directly also the masses of workers employed in it. They all participate in an activity that involves cooperation with large and diverse groups of co-workers and the use of elaborate equipment that must be properly controlled; and most of these workers are required to be regular and prompt in attendance, capable of understanding and following specific instructions, and willing to cooperate. It is a discipline for which life in the countryside or in family shops does not prepare people; and whatever one may think of its consonance with human nature, if suitable labor cadres are to be provided for modern industry, a substantial economic and social investment must be made in developing such a labor force.

Similarly specific requirements apply to the capital resources for modern industry. Such capital is not merely so many units of resources withdrawn from current consumption. It is rather specific kinds of machinery and construction embodying the ever-growing technological knowledge and power. Although there may be some choice of technology, modern industry needs more than hand tools, and the necessity to borrow and learn from other advanced countries of the day limits the choice within any given industry.

The emphasis on the specific characteristics of labor and capital required for modern industry suggests three important implications. First, the capital investment extends beyond material capital to investment in human beings, a point which only recently has been given increasing consideration in the literature on economic growth. The amounts of such investment in education and training are far from negligible, in comparison either with material capital investment or with national product. Obviously this investment in human beings is necessary not only for modern industry but extends to other modern sectors in the economy, further evidence of the large amounts involved.

Second, the acquisition by the labor force of education, skills, and behavior patterns necessary for and appropriate to modern industry, or, better, all modern sectors of the economy, is far from an easy process. There must be some continuity in human attitudes and behavior; otherwise the introduction of the new elements required by modern industry and economic growth within a framework of beliefs and attitudes retained from a preindustrial society, may produce strain and maladjustment that would greatly reduce the benefits of the new investment. Consider, as a minor but revealing illustration, the difficulties encountered in some underdeveloped countries in applying technical training to productive ends: it is often used as a badge of superior status entitling the possessor to a white-collar job and tending to make him less rather than more cooperative with his manual fellow-workers.

Third, the specific forms of capital investment required may not be producible, for various technical reasons, within the less developed follower country, except at a prohibitive cost. This applies to investment in both human beings and material capital. It is difficult for an underdeveloped country to provide its young professional groups with training, *within* the country, in advanced electronic engineering, atomic technology, or other experimental natural sciences, let alone some of the techniques of social science research or social administration. It is also difficult to produce at the outset, within an underdeveloped country, advanced electrical and electronic machinery, internal combustion engines, atomic reactors, and even steel mills. It is far easier to import such tools and education from more advanced countries, which have a marked comparative advantage with respect to these products of advanced education and technology, in exchange for other goods with respect to which the comparative advantage may lie with the less developed country. The difficulties of domestic production, by the less developed countries, of such advanced commodities have increased, with the continuing progress of modern technology and with the ever-widening gap in the latter between the most and the least developed countries, so that reliance on foreign trade (or unrequited imports) has become greater, and the cost of abstaining from it has become heavier.

As indicated above, a less developed industrializing country can import labor and capital for modern industry (and other modern sectors in the economy), if it enjoys a capacity to export. This means that its savings must assume the form in which existing export demand permits conversion into the capital goods (material or education) that must be imported. Although to some extent the burden of securing an export surplus and export markets may be eased by unrequited capital imports, the relief can be only partial. Another alternative is to select types of capital investment, and thus the type of industry, that can be more easily produced at home. But this may mean foregoing the more advanced and more productive types of modern industry. Another alternative and the most costly is to build within the country as quickly as possible as much as possible of the necessary capital equipment (to produce other capital goods, material or education). This last alternative was, in fact, followed by the USSR, athough even it relied extensively on importing and borrowing in the early years (particularly between 1928 and 1931–32). And it can be achieved only at the expense of consumption, the resources released thereby being devoted to capital formation. Needless to say, the cost is far greater than that of the first alternative. In short, given the desire for modern industry, the choice is between adequate participation through foreign trade in the network and benefits of international division of labor, with the freedom of consumers made inevitable by unrestricted relations with the rest of the world; and the autarkic policy, which facilitates authoritative control by the state over the economy, and, isolating the consumers from the rest of the world, permits a rapid build-up of capital in new equipment and new technical education at the expense of consumer needs.

DEMAND FOR GOODS · If the specific labor and capital resources needed for modern industry can be secured, the next requirement, in logical order, is the assurance of demand for the products of modern industry. This demand may be from abroad, although if we deal with the less developed, follower, countries, a modern industry can hardly be built on the expectation of gaining a firm foothold in foreign markets that have already been developed and occupied by the earlier pioneer countries. The question then is primarily of domestic markets, although the foreign market potentials were an important factor in the expansion of modern industry in the first pioneer countries.

With respect to domestic demand, we should distinguish the scale of preference from the capacity to effectuate it. Demand for the products of modern industry is effective only if it is backed by purchasing power, present or to be secured in the future. But in a sense we have already dealt with the question of effective purchasing power in our discussion of the efficiency of agriculture: a high level of productivity in agriculture was assumed because it meant that resources could be spared for industry, to be paid for from the surplus of agriculture, and this meant also the power to pay for the modern industry's products. Insofar as the value of these products roughly equals the value of the resources put into industry, the power to sustain the latter within the country is *ipso facto* power to purchase the products. The question then really is one of the scale of preference—whether the people in the country would use their economic power to purchase the products of modern industry, thus justifying a continued and sustained input of resources into the latter.

Despite the extensive discussion of the eagerness of the less developed countries for modern industry, international demonstration effect, and the like, we raise this question of the scale of preference. The eagerness referred to above is the result of a penetration that modern economic life has already made into the less developed areas, for it is manifested largely by those members of these societies who have been exposed to the economically advanced countries, often for long periods, and who have thus acquired the new scale of preference. Many of the preferences for modern goods are a result of continuous importation of these products from abroad, of gradual penetration. On the other hand, numerous areas, possessing a surplus from their agricultural and related activities, did not place high priority on the products of modern industry when first exposed to them; they continued to spend their surplus in other ways, for example, on ceremonial food consumption, status-oriented cattle accumulation, and the like. This is natural since the scale of preference has been set within a long-standing production and use context. To repeat, when the less developed countries exhibit a strong demand for modern products, it is the result of prolonged exposure; and the desire to build modern industry within the country is thus in the nature of import substitution rather than new product introduction.

If the demand for modern *consumer* goods is built up only by dint of prolonged contact with more advanced economies, that for modern capital goods is further contingent upon the time horizon of the would-be purchaser or user. Modern capital goods most often represent large bundles of resources with relatively long life and are economical only when continuous use over a long period can be assured. In many less developed countries the very onset of industrialization introduces changes and uncertainties that make commitments to long-term investments far from easy, given the variety of shorter-term opportunities for profits. It is therefore not unusual for the essential demand for capital goods products of modern industry to be satisfied by government intervention. Even in those less developed countries that are anxious to protect the freedom of individuals from encroachment by an economically powerful government, the latter assumes control over the domestic production of basic capital goods (including basic industrial materials), accepting the risk of inadequate demand that is not shouldered by the private sector, and assuring the domestic availability of modern capital goods even if private internal resources may be sufficient for the purpose.

One final aspect of the demand problem should be noted. The size of the domestic market for the products of industry may limit the scale of plant that can be maintained. If the country is small, some modern industries with large-scale optimum plants may not be economically feasible, unless the country possesses such distinct comparative advantage as to be assured of substantial foreign markets. For reasons of national security and pride, plants and industries may be established within a country despite an insufficient market for them, but these are noneconomic. By and large, the smaller countries do not possess the large-scale industries which require large markets for support—unless, again, they have some specific comparative advantage (in the way of raw materials, labor, or location). Thus, in the requirement of adequate demand for products of modern industry, the size of a country is an important selective and limiting factor; and as the number of modern industries with large-scale optimum plants increases, the range of modern industries that are not economically feasible for most small countries widens. This may have been one factor that accelerated the trend among the advanced countries of Europe toward common market alliances.

ENTREPRENEURIAL TALENT · Given the resources for modern industry, afforded by a minimum level of efficiency in agriculture, transportation, and other sectors of the economy; the possibility of converting them to the specific forms of labor and capital suitable for modern industry; and the existence of adequate domestic and foreign markets for the products of such industry, there is need for a group of entrepreneurs to assemble the productive factors and organize them into relatively efficient enterprises. We cite entre-

preneurial capacity as a distinct requirement of modern industry because the availability of resources, the technological feasibility of
modern industry, and the market for its products, all in a given
country, exist only *in potentia* unless a group of entrepreneurs is
available with the capacity to resolve the specific problems that
arise in converting that potential into concrete reality. Someone must
assemble the resources for an efficient modern plant, develop the
plant to levels of adequate performance, and tap the markets that
provide the final proof of the economic viability of the enterprise.

Whether by its existence, the potential of modern industry described in the three groups of requirements above would automatically bring forth the necessary entrepreneurial talent is a question to which I can give no firm answer. It may well be that in
every society there is a pool of such talent waiting to be tapped.
But to accept this thesis may mean an unwarranted simplification
of the problem. Even if one assumes that able entrepreneurship is
genetically widespread through the population and a sizable
amount of such talent is assured, will it be channeled into the
economic rather than the political or military field? And even if it
is directed to the economic field, will it be employed in modern
industry (or in the other modern sectors needed to sustain and
complement modern industry) or in real estate speculation or exploitation of small-scale peasantry? Unless we envisage the per-
sonality characteristics as specifically geared to the demands of
modern industry alone, and so strong as to ensure the development
of modern industry on the base provided by the other requirements,
we still must face the question whether the country's social and
economic institutions will permit channeling into modern industry
(and other modern sectors) a sufficient amount of entrepreneurship.
The requirement of entrepreneurship is thus translated into a requirement of conditions which can effectively channel human resources and talent into a specific economic activity.

These conditions are separate and distinct from the three groups of
requirements already discussed. As an economist, I do not feel
competent to deal with them. However, I do feel that the scale of
values of a society and the priority it assigns to economic achievement obviously determine whether the human talent that is capable of innovational decisions would flow into economic endeavor,
and whether it would apply the rules of rational economic behavior
if so engaged. On this point the discussion in earlier years of Prot-
estant ethics and capitalism and the more recent discussion of the

substitution in Communist countries of the religion of economic growth (or rather of growth in economic power) for other religions and views are clearly relevant. The institutional structure and the beliefs that govern it control the relation between economic success and entrepreneurship applied to modern industry rather than to speculation in currency or socially undesirable money-lending. Much of the literature on policies aimed at stimulating economic growth deals with modifications in institutional arrangements to direct flows of resources and entrepreneurship into channels that would maximize economic growth. And there is the obvious interplay between the requirement of entrepreneurship and the degree to which the other requirements have been satisfied: with limited surplus in other sectors, an inadequately trained labor force, complex capital equipment, and the risk of poorly developed markets, the obstacles that the entrepreneur has to overcome are greater and the human talent capable of doing so, scarcer. But all this is obvious; and the judgment of the importance of entrepreneurial capacity depends essentially upon our view of the role of the individual in economic growth, a view that does not lend itself easily to quantitative tests. If we believe, with Schumpeter, in the key importance of the innovating entrepreneur, and of the supply of entrepreneurial capacity as affecting the application of technological knowledge to problems of economic production, we would attach great weight to the need for an adequate supply of entrepreneurial talent that can be channeled into modern industry. If we are more impressed, as I am, by the way changes in conditions are effected by changes in the technological potential of economic growth and by the changing patterns of behavior of large groups of men engaged in the economy, we would formulate the requirement not in terms of supply of entrepreneurial talent but in terms of changes in social institutions that permit the channeling of usually available talent into the proper directions. The emphasis would then be not on limitations imposed by the exogenously determined supply of entrepreneurial talent, but on those imposed by social institutions on the flow of talent into proper uses.

But whatever the position, whether the genetic or the institutional, the kernel of the requirement is that there be a group of people deeply concerned with modern industry and so placed within society that they have the power to act on their concern. Not only recent developments but a longer history of modern economic growth demonstrate that such functions have been performed not only by private entrepreneurs in search of profit but also by the public governmental entrepreneur, in search of economic growth for the country at large. In the free economies this means a complementary relation between the two groups of entrepreneurs, the public undertaking the more difficult tasks which the private entrepreneur alone cannot shoulder. In the authoritarian economies it means the substitution of the public entrepreneur for the private, a highly centralized operation whose success is measured largely by the consonance of its results with the planned goals of a political minority controlling the state apparatus. In the free economies, subject to constraints imposed by the state under pressure of different groups in the society, the decentralized activity of the private entrepreneurs is tested largely through the decisions of the thousands of units who express their preferences in the markets. Modern industry developed under these different types of entrepreneurship has some common characteristics because modern technology is the same the world over and because, for example, steel mills are essential, to produce other steel mills, or heavy machinery, or consumer goods. However, the structure of industry differs under the two types—in its distribution between producer and consumer goods, in its relation to other sectors in the economy (e.g., to lagging agriculture in the authoritarian countries), and in the very scale of its organization. But adequate discussion of this subject transcends the limited scope of this paper.

Conclusions

The economic requirements of modern industrialization can be summarized as (1) the availability of effective resources in other sectors of a country's economy and abroad; (2) the capacity to convert the surplus resources into forms required by modern industry; (3) a scale of preference at home (and possibly a comparative advantage relative to abroad) that assures markets for the products of modern industry; and (4) institutional conditions that channel available entrepreneurial talent into modern industry. All these are also requirements for other sectors in the economy needed to sustain and supplement modern industry.

On the general level of the discussion here, the conclusions are hardly surprising; and indeed they are essentially a truism. Any economic process is feasible if the resources to conduct it, including the entrepreneurial talent to set it in motion, and the demand for its products are at hand. A large technical literature dealing with the problems of modern industrialization has grown up in an attempt to go beyond such general propositions. There is first the search for the specific links in the cause and effect relations among the various sectors and aspects of the economic system, some of which we distinguished above as requirements and others as the product attained by satisfying these requirements. Here questions arise as to the sequence in the relation between the rise in productivity in other sectors and in modern industry; the varying contribution of labor and capital to the increase of product; the interplay between technological change and changes in demand; the institutional conditions governing the entrepreneurial activity; and so on.

Second, there is the need to attach empirically measured weights to the sectors and links involved, to determine the level and range of the quantitative coefficients, and to distinguish the relatively similar or invariant parameters from those subject to wide differences in space or in time. Much of the theoretical analysis of sequential relations depends upon the quantitative framework within which these relations assume specific values; and when these are approximated for a number of countries and periods, the variety of structures and trends stimulates revision and further work in the qualitative analysis. Finally, a wide variety of policy devices, relating to modern economic growth and industrialization, is generated in the adjustment of various societies to ever-changing problems. Not only do these devices need to be examined systematically but new policy approaches that the changing course of performance of the economy may suggest need to be considered. Hence, much of the literature is directly concerned with policy questions in the fields of money and credit, taxation, industrial organization, international trade, and labor relations, in their bearing upon problems of economic growth and stability.

It would have been extremely difficult to distill from this extensive literature a set of specific formulations of economic requirements of modern industrialization, to substitute for the general discussion above; and the latter approach obviated the use of extensive references for notions that are rather common in the literature. Firmly established findings, both empirical and analytical, are still far too few relative to the variety of modern economic growth already experienced, let alone the possible variants in the proximate future. For this reason any attempt to specify precisely the economic requirements, to assign to them some quantitative coefficients, and to spell out their most important corollaries, would mean a wide range of alternative answers, the explanation of which would far transcend the limits of this paper. In particular, such an approach would reveal some problematical aspects of economic requirements. It is perhaps fitting to conclude by commenting briefly on these aspects.

First, as already suggested, these requirements cannot be conceived as a unique combination which, if present, will assure a sustained process of modern industrialization. At the same early phase of industrialization in two countries, the requirements might assume different quantitative dimensions and ranges, depending upon conditions not only in the countries themselves but also in the rest of the world and depending also upon the time of occurrence, since it would be related to the stage in development of science and technology. One and the same set of domestic conditions may mean different levels of satisfaction of requirements, depending upon the historical time and the level of development in the rest of the world. At a later phase of modern industrialization in the two countries, requirements for further industrialization would again be different—with respect to the volumes and even the structural characteristics of labor, capital, and entrepreneurial ability involved. In this connection our earlier reference to the rapid changes in the structure of modern industry must be recalled, for such structural changes are likely to mean corresponding changes in requirements for further growth. In short, the economic requirements of modern industrialization change over time, with the phase of growth of modern industry in a given country, with differing conditions in the rest of the world, and with the changing worldwide potential of modern technology. Thus any further attempt at specificity in formulating economic requirements would show that they differ in magnitude and in structure from country to country, from phase to phase, and from time to time.

Second, the distinct economic requirements are partly substitutable for each other at a given point of time, in the sense that the stimulus provided by one might bring another into being after some limited period. Thus we have already suggested that a wealth of resources, convertible into productive factors for modern industry, may substitute for that scarce entrepreneurial talent which would be needed to cope with a smaller amount of resources. Also, if resources and entrepreneurial ability for modern industry are at hand, and modern plants are set up despite uncertain demand,

that demand might develop as ultimate consumers become acquainted with the products and change their scale of preference
for them. Thus, given this "creative" interrelation among requirements, all of them do not have to be satisfied at the same time, but
only enough of some to form the basis for an entrepreneurial venture that might eventually call forth the latent but missing requirements. Indeed, this interplay between requirements and actual
growth, in which growth strengthens some of the bases of its own
progress, is one of the mechanisms of economic growth. Thus, a
surplus of resources in a tolerably efficient agriculture, if used in
modern industry, would improve the efficiency of agriculture and
provide additional resources for further expansion of industry. But
modern industrialization is also partly self-defeating, since the
process may cause blocks that would make further growth more
rather than less difficult.

Third, given the changeability and dynamic character of economic
requirements, we must emphasize that modern industrialization can
be assigned different magnitudes; and requirements would differ
for different levels of modern industrialization. The potential of
modern industrialization, in the sense of economic growth permitted by the progress of modern technology under the most favorable economic and social conditions, is always large, and probably
no country exploits it fully. On the other hand, few if any countries
are so completely bereft of domestic resources convertible to modern
industrialization and have a scale of preference so opposed to
modern products that they lack completely the economic requirements for, and cannot effect, *some* industrialization. But *some*
modern industrialization may not be sufficient to raise per capita
income and increase the diversity of economic product, two prerequisites of minimum economic levels. It is the magnitude of industrialization that lends importance to much of the work on
empirical coefficients and policy problems. The latter broadens our
understanding and analysis of the links between specific magnitudes of economic growth and economic requirements and the characteristics of the policy steps relating to them.

Finally, economic requirements are never purely economic; they
are always formulated within a wider social framework, just as the
very potential of modern industrialization rests on the growing stock
of useful knowledge that is the product of the humanistic search
for knowledge. Such notions as minimum efficiency in agriculture,
or demand for products of industry, or channeling of entrepreneurial

talent into modern industry, are full of implications concerning the political and social aspects of the economy. The economic aspect of human activities emerges when men deal with scarce resources for the satisfaction of wants, largely *via* the market place. But their pattern of behavior even in this sphere and the process by which that pattern is formed depend upon other social institutions as well as upon the play of the human mind in science and invention. The "economic rationality" of economic agents lies within a broader context which limits it to some specified means, and prescribes some specified ends. If there is a hard core of meaning in the economic requirements of modern industrialization, it is there because we assume some broader social framework within which such requirements are formulated and from which many contingencies are excluded (e.g., slavery or genocide as ways of securing resources, or religious asceticism as a way of curbing ultimate consumption). Only by the direct consideration of the noneconomic requirements of modern industrialization can the framework within which the economic requirements are formulated be elucidated.

Notes on the Take-off

Requirements for a Theory of Stages

THE SEQUENCE OF stages, of which the take-off is one, is offered by Professor W. W. Rostow as a scheme for viewing and interpreting modern economic development. It is, therefore, a gloss on the major distinction between modern and nonmodern (traditional) types of growth; I regret that in offering his scheme, Professor Rostow does not spell out the characteristics inherent in modern economic growth that distinguish it from the traditional and other types. Many come easily to mind: a high and sustained rate of increase in real product per capita, accompanied usually by a high and sustained rate of increase in population; major shifts in the industrial structure of product and labor force, and in the location of the population, commonly referred to as industrialization and urbanization; changes in the organizational units under whose auspices and guidance economic activity takes place; a rise in the proportion of capital formation to national product; shifts in the structure of consumer expenditures, accompanying urbanization and higher income per capita; changes in the character and magnitudes of international economic flows; and others could be added. Underlying all this are the increasing stock of useful knowledge derived from modern science and the capacity of society, under the spur of modern ideology, to evolve institutions which permit the

From W. W. Rostow, ed., The Economics of Take-off into Sustained Growth, Proceedings of the Conference of the International Economic Association (London: Macmillan & Co., 1963). Reprinted by permission of St. Martin's Press.

exploitation of the growth potential provided by that increasing stock of knowledge.

The distinction between modern economic growth and other types, and our concentration on the former, are justified by a basic working assumption that we can study the characteristics of such growth most effectively if it is not merged with the evolution of economies before the eighteenth century or with the growth of those parts of the world that have not yet begun to tap the sources of modern technology. If we assume that modern economic growth is different from other types and affected by new and different factors, we would only confuse matters and face an impossible task in treating the growth of Germany in the second half of the nineteenth century and that of France in the thirteenth century, for example, as members of the same family of economic growth processes. In short, although allowing for historical continuity, we recognize modern economic growth as something quite new; and in order to observe it clearly, perceive its mechanism, and understand its driving forces, we must distinguish it from other types and study it by itself.

Distinguishing stages within modern economic growth is an operation similar to that which distinguishes modern from nonmodern economic growth, and the basic assumption that justifies the former parallels the one that justifies the latter. By claiming that stage A is distinct from stage B, we are saying that the characteristics commonly found in stage A are so distinct from those in stage B that it is methodologically improper to treat the two indiscriminately. Stages within an economic epoch or some such general construct, like the constructs themselves, are a classificatory device, governed by the hypothesis that the generality of observation and invariance of analytical relations secured thereby are maximized.

An adequate test of such a hypothesis comes at the end, not at the beginning, of a long period of study. But this does not mean that we need take seriously every suggestion of stages or other dividing lines within the sequence of modern economic growth, particularly if we recognize the major differences between it and nonmodern growth. For if these differences are recognized, and the cumulative character of growth is a matter of definition, it is all too easy to suggest stages. Since modern economic growth presumably has roots in the past, a nonmodern economy stage and a stage of preparation are readily suggested, and we can divide the latter into several phases: initial preparatory phase, middle preparatory phase, and final preparatory phase. Then, since, again by definition, modern economic growth is not attained in a few years, we can discuss the early or emergence period, the middle stage, maturity (biological analogy), postmaturity, and so on. The very ease with which separate segments can be distinguished in the historical movement from nonmodern to modern economic growth and within the long span of the latter should warn us that any sequence of stages, even if offered only as a suggestive, not a substantive, scheme must meet some minimum requirements.

1. A specific stage must display empirically testable characteristics, common to all or to an important group of units experiencing modern economic growth. This means the specification of modern economic growth, identification of the units that have manifested such growth, and establishment of the empirically testable characteristics claimed to be common to these units at the given stage.

2. The characteristics of a specific stage must be distinctive in that, not necessarily singly but in combination, they are unique to that stage. Mere precedence (or succession) in time does not suffice: given the unidirectional character of growth (by definition) any period is characterized by larger economic magnitudes than earlier ones and by the structural shifts that accompany such larger magnitudes (particularly a rise in per capita income). Stages are presumably something more than successive ordinates in the steadily climbing curve of growth. They are segments of that curve with properties so distinct that separate study of each segment seems warranted.

3. The analytical relation to the preceding stage must be indicated. This involves more than saying that the preceding stage is one of preparation for the given stage. More specifically, we need to identify (again in empirically testable terms) the major processes in the preceding stage that terminate it, and, with the usual qualifications for exogenous factors, make the next (our given) stage highly probable. Optimally, this would permit us to diagnose the preceding stage *before* the given stage is upon us, and thus would impart predictive value to the whole sequence. But even short of this aim, it means specifying the minimum that must happen in the preceding stage to allow the given stage to emerge.

4. The analytical relation to the succeeding stage must be indicated. Here, too, a clear notion (again in empirically testable terms) must be given of the occurrences in the given stage that bring it to a close, aside from mere passage of time. Optimally,

such knowledge would permit us to predict, *before* the given stage is finished, how long it still has to run. But even short of such precision, we should know the essentials that occur during a given stage to bring about its end and clear the ground for the next stage.

5. These four requirements relate to the common and distinctive characteristics of a specific stage in an analytical (and chronological) sequence that links successive stages. However, these common and distinctive characteristics may differ among important groups of units undergoing modern economic growth. Consequently, the fifth requirement is for a delineation of the universe for which the generality of common and distinctive characteristics is claimed, and for which the analytical relations of a given stage with the preceding and succeeding ones are being formulated.

Characteristics of the Take-off

Against the background of the requirements just stated, we may consider Professor Rostow's discussion of the common and distinctive characteristics of the take-off stage and the relations between it and the contiguous stages.

The three common characteristics explicitly listed by Professor Rostow are:

> (1) a rise in the rate of productive investment from (say) 5 percent or less to over 10 percent of national income (or net national product); (2) the development of one or more substantial manufacturing sectors with a high rate of growth; (3) the existence or quick emergence of a political, social and institutional framework which exploits the impulses to expansion in the modern sector and the potential external economy effects of the take-off and gives to growth an ongoing character.[1]

To these we add three more characteristics implicit or explicit in Professor Rostow's discussion.

4. A marked rise in the rate of growth of national income (or net national product) and of per capita income, in constant prices. This follows directly from the rise in the proportion of investment listed under 1, and Professor Rostow's discussion of the "Prima Facie Case" (*ibid.*, p. 34), which assumes no rise in the marginal capital-output ratio. The rate of growth of real income per capita rises from close to zero to about 2 percent per year.

---

[1] W. W. Rostow, "The Take-Off into Self-sustained Growth," *The Economic Journal,* LXVI, 261 (March 1956), p. 32. Referred to henceforth as Rostow I.

5. The leading sectors in the take-off have ranged historically "from cotton textiles, through heavy-industry complexes based on railroads and military end-products, to timber, pulp, dairy products and finally a wide variety of consumer goods" (*ibid.*, p. 46). But these sectors were leading because of the enlarged demand for their products brought about by appropriate transfers of income, capital imports, etc.; because of their new production functions; because of their profitability and inducement to entrepreneurs to plow back profits; and because of the expansion and technical transformation in other parts of the economy effected by their expansion.

6. The take-off is a relatively short period: in many of the countries identified by Professor Rostow it is appreciably less than thirty years and in most of these it is little more than twenty.

How distinctive are these characteristics? Do they occur in combination only in the take-off stage and in no other stage, particularly the preceding transition, or pre-conditions, stage and the succeeding self-sustained growth, or drive to maturity, stage? Professor Rostow is not explicit on this point. Presumably a rise in the investment proportion from 5 to 10 percent or more does not occur in the transition stage. Yet much of what Professor Rostow would attribute to the take-off has already occurred in the pre-conditions stage.[2] Thus, the agricultural revolution assigned to the pre-conditions stage "must supply expanded food, expanded markets, and an expanded supply of loanable funds to the modern sector" (Rostow II, p. 24); much of social overhead capital is already invested in transport and other outlays in the pre-conditions stage (*ibid.*, p. 24); and, in general, "the essence of the transition can be described legitimately as a rise in the rate of investment to a level which regularly, substantially and perceptibly outstrips population growth" (*ibid.*, p. 21). In short, one wonders whether the three specifically stated characteristics of take-off could not be found in the pre-conditions stage unless explicit qualifications are attached: for example, the investment proportion in that earlier stage must stay below 5 percent; the marked agricultural revolution does not immediately call for, and in fact is possible without, a contemporaneous rapid growth in some manufacturing sector; and investment in overhead capital in transport and other areas is not necessarily accompanied by a rapid growth of one or more modern manufacturing sectors.

---

[2] W. W. Rostow, *The Stages of Economic Growth* (Cambridge, Mass.: Harvard University Press, 1960), Ch. 3, pp. 17–35. Referred to henceforth as Rostow II.

Finally, one should note that characteristic 3 of the take-off mentions both the *existence* and the *quick emergence* of the political, social, and institutional framework favorable to exploiting "the impulses to expansion in the modern sector" as admissible alternatives. But if that framework already exists at the beginning of the take-off, its emergence must be assigned to the pre-conditions stage. How then does the latter differ from the take-off in which the framework emerges?

The line of division between the take-off and the following stage of self-sustained growth or drive to maturity is also blurred. Presumably the later stage is marked by the existence of the proper social and institutional framework, which also exists during the take-off. Presumably this later stage also witnesses the rapid growth of one or more modern manufacturing sectors. Indeed, the only characteristics that are distinctly appropriate to the take-off and not to the next stage are the rise in the rate of productive investment to over 10 percent of national income and the implicit rise in the rate of growth of total and per capita income. But are we to assume that both the rate of investment and the rate of growth of product (total and per capita) level off at the high values attained at the end of the take-off stage? And is it this cessation of the rise in the rate of investment and in the rate of growth that terminates the take-off stage? No explicit statement is made by Professor Rostow; Chapter 5 in Rostow II contains a list of dates when "maturity" was reached in a number of countries but there is little discussion of what took place between the end of the take-off stage and the end of the next stage.

Given this fuzziness in delimiting the take-off stage and in formulating its distinctive characteristics, and given the distinctiveness only in the level of the rate of productive investment (and the implicit rate of growth), there is no solid ground upon which to discuss Professor Rostow's view of the analytical relation between the take-off stage and the preceding and succeeding stages. At any rate, the brief comments that can be made within the scope of this paper will follow the review of the empirical evidence.

To what universe do the common characteristics claimed for the take-off period apply? In his most recent presentation, Professor Rostow distinguishes the "general" case of a traditional society from that of the small group of nations (the United States, Australia, New Zealand, Canada, and "perhaps a few others") "born free." (Rostow II, pp. 6 and 17–18). The distinction is particularly important in the analysis of the pre-conditions stage, and Professor Rostow does not indicate whether the characteristics of the take-off stage in the originally traditional societies are different from those in the countries "born free." The distinction made in the discussion of pre-conditions is not repeated in the discussion of the take-off, unless the qualification about the rates of investment higher than 5 percent in some countries (Canada and Argentina) before the take-off stage, necessitated by heavy overhead social capital needs (see Rostow II, p. 8) can be interpreted as such. But this qualification does not stress the distinction between traditional and free-born countries: overhead social capital needs were presumably heavy in Russia and for that matter, on a relative scale, in Switzerland. We may therefore infer that Professor Rostow, who includes the dates of the take-off period for both types of economy in the same list, assumes that the characteristics of the take-off are broadly the same for all countries undergoing modern economic growth.

Empirical Evidence on the Take-off Stage

In dealing with the empirical evidence on the take-off, I am impeded by three difficulties. First, much of the specific evidence on the take-off period will presumably be presented in the individual country papers, and I am neither competent to assemble it nor eager to duplicate it. Second, quantitative evidence, and much of it must be quantitative, is not available for some of the take-off periods suggested by Professor Rostow. Third, as already indicated, Professor Rostow's discussion does not yield a description of take-off characteristics sufficiently specific to define the relevant empirical evidence.

Thus I do not know what "a political, social and institutional framework which exploits the impulses to expansion in the modern sector, etc." is; or how to identify such a framework except by hindsight and conjecture; or how to specify the empirical evidence needed to ascertain whether such a framework is in "existence or in quick emergence." It seems to me that Professor Rostow, in the passage cited, defines these social phenomena as a complex that produces the effect he wishes to explain, and then treats this definition as if it were a meaningful identification.

It is easier to define the characteristic that specifies "the development of one or more substantial manufacturing sectors with a high rate of growth" once high is explained. But a review of empirical evidence on this point holds little interest if I am correct in assuming that the major distinctive characteristic of the take-off is a marked rise in the rate of growth of per capita and hence of total income. If the rate of growth does accelerate, some sectors are bound to grow more rapidly than others, as has been demonstrated in Arthur F. Burns' and my own work on production trends, partly in response to the differential impact of technological opportunities (including raw material supplies) and partly in response to the different income elasticities of the demand for various goods. Under these conditions, one or more manufacturing sectors, and one or more sectors of agriculture, transportation, services, etc. are bound to show high rates of growth. The pertinent question is why manufacturing and not agriculture, transport, or any other rapidly growing industry should be specified as the leading sector.

In considering this question, we must keep in mind the two essentials of a leading sector. First, sector A leads, if it moves independently of sectors B, C, D, etc., within the country but under the impact of factors which for the given national economy may be considered autonomous. These may be technological changes embodying some new inventions; changes in the resource base resulting from new discoveries; changes in foreign demand, which are external to the given economy; and breaks in social structure (political revolution, agrarian reform, and the like), which could be viewed as changes exogenous to economic processes proper. The point to be noted is that the autonomous nature of this characteristic, relative to the given national economy, rests upon the stimulus, not upon the response. The response may reflect many other factors besides the stimulus which are part and parcel of the economy and society.

This brings us to the second essential of a leading sector, the magnitude of its effects, or more specifically, the magnitude of its contribution to a country's economic growth. Sector A may be responding to an autonomous stimulus, but unless its contribution to the country's economic growth is substantial, it does not lead the country's economic growth, no matter how high its own rate of growth. After all, a thousandfold rise in the production of paper napkins over a decade does not make it a leading industry.

The lower limit to a significant contribution can be set only in terms of empirical analysis. We must distinguish the direct contribution to the growth of the economy, total and per capita, of sector A— the product of its weight in the economy and its percentage rate of growth—from its indirect contribution, through its backward and forward linkages with sectors *B, C, D,* etc.; and from its contribution, again indirect, through its effects on social structure and qualities of the population (e.g., urbanization, organizational form of the economic unit, education, and the like), which in turn affect a country's economic growth in a variety of ways. The magnitude and particularly the timing of these direct and indirect effects differ. A sector's direct and indirect contributions in a given period may be quite small, although its own rate of growth is high and the novelty of its technology makes it the cynosure of the eyes of its contemporaries and of latter-day historians; whereas in a later period its contributions may be far greater, although its rate of growth has declined and the bloom of its novelty faded.

To establish these leadership characteristics of sectors—the autonomous character of the impulse and the timing and magnitude of their direct and indirect contributions to a country's economic growth—involves intensive study, not only of the leading sectors but also of those affected by them, extending into the quantitative framework of the whole economy. Leadership of sectors, or any other element in the acceleration of the rate of growth, can be established only by careful analysis of the particular circumstances preceding and during the period of acceleration, country by country, and by the application of statistical, theoretical, and other tools to the historical evidence. This type of analysis is lacking in Professor Rostow's discussion and is beyond my powers here.

I therefore turn to the purely statistical characteristics claimed for the take-off stage; but even here I find it difficult to specify Professor Rostow's meaning. I assume from the context that "rate of productive investment" refers to *net,* rather than *gross,* capital formation, and that the adjective "productive" means the inclusion of all components of the presently accepted definition of capital formation. But does he mean net *domestic* capital formation, that is, all net additions to the stock of reproducible material capital within the country, whether financed by domestic savings or by capital imports (and excluding capital exports, when such occur), or net *national* capital formation (usually referred to as net capital formation without further qualification), that is, only net additions to reproducible stock within the country financed by domestic savings plus capital exports, if any? Professor Rostow emphasizes changes within the country (under characteristic 3 above) that should help mobilize domestic savings, and much of his discussion is in terms of maximizing domestic savings, that is, in terms of the net national capital formation proportion to national income. This emphasis is corroborated by the use of national income as denominator, since the proper denominator for net domestic capital formation is net domestic product (although for most countries the two totals are numerically close). Yet in the analysis of capital-output relations, the appropriate ratio, particularly for a capital importing country, is that of net domestic capital formation to net domestic product. Professor Rostow cites long-term data for Sweden and Canada, and for one he uses the domestic capital formation proportion and for the other the national capital formation proportion. There is the further question whether the ratios of capital formation to national product should be based on totals in current or in constant prices: the former are more appropriate to the view of the proportion as a savings rate, the latter to the view of the proportion as affecting output.

Before presenting the statistical results, I shall attempt to resolve these doubts and define the measures more precisely. For a capital-exporting country we may use the ratio of net national capital formation to net national product; for a capital-importing country we should use both net national and net domestic capital formation, as proportions of net national and net domestic product, respectively. Further, we use ratios based on current price totals, partly because the available price indexes are crude and partly because in most cases the differences in long-term movement between the capital formation proportions based on current and on constant price totals are not appreciable. We can then ask whether in the periods of take-off dated by Professor Rostow the rises in these capital formation proportions are of the magnitude he suggests. I shall deal here with four countries, all included in Professor Rostow's "general" category: Great Britain, Germany, Sweden, and Japan.

FOUR COUNTRIES · For Great Britain, Phyllis Deane and W. A. Cole have recently completed a major study. Their results indicate a net national capital formation proportion of about 6.5 percent for England and Wales in 1770–1800, a period close to Professor Rostow's dates of 1783–1802, compared with about 5 percent indicated by Gregory King at the end of the eighteenth century. The Deane-Cole estimates, which thenceforth apply to the United Kingdom, suggest a climb to about 9 percent for the period from the 1820's to the 1850's, and a further rise to a pre-World War I peak of

14 percent in 1905–14. The picture is thus one of a slow and relatively steady, rather than sudden and rapid, acceleration. The rate of growth of national income (in constant prices) follows the same general pattern. For England and Wales, the annual rate of growth for 1770–1800 is 1.5 percent, compared with 0.9 percent for 1740–70 and 0.3 percent for 1700–40. Then the rate of growth for the United Kingdom rises to well over 2.5 percent per year in the last quarter of the nineteenth century.

For Germany (the territory of the German Reich in 1913) we have the studies by Professor Walther Hoffmann of net capital formation and by Professors Hoffmann and J. Heinz Müller of national income for the period back to 1851. For 1850–73, the period dated by Professor Rostow as the take-off, we have the following proportions of net capital formation to national income (in current market prices): about 8.5 percent for the 1850's, 9.75 percent for the 1860's, 13.5 percent for the 1870's. The rise is appreciable but is due in part to the favorable business cycle of the 1870's, and in the 1880's the net capital formation proportion is still below 14 percent. Then the proportion rises to a peak of 16.5 percent in 1901–13. Here the net capital formation proportion increases only about 60 percent in the twenty-odd years dated as the take-off, and doubles only after a steady and sustained climb for about six decades. This steady rise in the net capital formation proportion is accompanied by a relatively stable rate of growth of net national product: about 2.5 percent per year for the entire period, somewhat more in the decades from 1851 to 1880, and somewhat less in the decades from 1880 to 1913.

For Sweden the most recent estimates, by Dr. Östen Johansson, currently at the University of Stockholm, are a revision of the older series which I used in my earlier paper and which Professor Rostow cites in his discussion. The major correction was for the understatement of construction in the early decades.

The directly available estimates yield a *gross* domestic capital formation proportion (to gross domestic product) of somewhat over 9 percent in 1861–70. On the assumption of a ratio of capital consumption to gross domestic capital formation of about 0.4, the net domestic capital formation proportion is almost 6 percent. The gross domestic capital formation proportion climbs, somewhat unsteadily, to 13.5 percent in 1901–10, and the implied net capital formation proportion to over 8 percent. The rise continues to a peak in 1941–50 of 21 percent gross, and roughly 13 percent net.

In short, the net domestic capital formation proportion rises gradually, and doubles only after almost eight decades, not just two or three.

The *national* capital formation proportions present about the same picture, except that the steady climb begins after the 1880's. From an average of about 9.5 percent in 1861–80, the gross capital formation proportion rises to 11 percent in 1891–1910, to over 14 percent in 1911–20, and to 20.5 percent in 1941–50. The corresponding net national capital formation proportion would be somewhat less than 6 percent in 1861–90, almost 7 percent in 1891–1910, and slightly over 12 percent in 1941–50.

The rate of growth of total product is also gradual. Although it ranges from 1.8 to 5.4 percent per year for decadal periods (the high rate being for 1941–50), the average for 1871–80 (Professor Rostow's take-off dates are 1868–90) is about 2.3 percent per year, compared with 3.2 percent for the 1860's and 3.4 percent for 1891–1910. The averages for the longer periods suggest a perceptible although gradual acceleration in the rate of growth, from 2.6 percent for 1861–90 to 2.9 percent for 1891–1920, to 3.8 percent for 1921–50.

For Japan, the recent and only acceptable estimates of capital formation (by Professor Henry Rosovsky of the University of California) begin in 1888 and therefore include only part of 1878–1900, the take-off period dated by Professor Rostow. The *gross* domestic capital formation proportion excluding military investments (which were large in Japan) was between 10 and 11 percent in 1888–97, and the gross national proportion was slightly higher. On the assumption that capital consumption was about 0.4 of gross domestic capital formation, the corresponding net capital formation proportions were between 6 and 7 percent, and there is no ground for assuming that they were significantly lower in the preceding decade. Subsequently, the domestic capital formation proportion fluctuated around the same level until World War I, and it was only after that war that it rose significantly, to between 16 and 17 percent on a gross basis and to between 10 and 11 percent on a net basis. The *national* capital formation proportion moved somewhat more erratically, with substantial capital imports in 1900–10 and 1920–30, but the broad secular trend was the same. Not until four or five decades later were the capital formation proportions twice their initial size.

There is no evidence of a perceptible acceleration in the rate of growth of either total or per capita income. From 1878 to 1902 the average rate of growth of total income was about 4.9 percent per year; from 1893 to 1917 it was 3.2 percent; from 1908 to 1932, 4.9 percent; from 1918 to 1942, 4.9 percent.[3] The average rate of growth of income per member of the gainfully occupied population for the same four long periods was: 1878–1902, 3.7 percent per year; 1893–1917, 2.6 percent; 1908–32, 4.3 percent; 1918–42, 4.0 percent.

A SUMMARY FOR TWELVE COUNTRIES · Two or three other countries for which Professor Rostow suggests tentative dates for the take-off period could be added. But the presentation of all the statistical evidence, even for a few countries, would far transcend the limits of this paper, and summaries like those above are barely adequate. We now have long-term records on capital formation and national product for twelve countries, excluding those in the Communist bloc, and a detailed discussion of these is now available.[4] Here I only summarize the evidence for the few countries in Professor Rostow's list and consider its bearing on his assumptions concerning the movement of the capital-investment proportions and the implicit movement of total product during what he defines as the take-off period. Unfortunately, I do not now have adequate estimates for France, Belgium, and Russia, additional countries in Professor Rostow's list.

In a number of countries, the net capital formation proportions, particularly domestic, are substantially higher than "5 percent or less" at the beginning of the take-off periods. This is certainly true of Germany; of the United States, where the estimates by Professor Robert Gallman for the 1840's and the 1850's suggest a gross domestic capital formation proportion of between 15 and 20 percent; of Canada where Dr. O. J. Firestone's estimates indicate gross domestic capital formation proportions of 15 percent in 1870, 15.5 percent in 1890, and 13.5 percent in 1900. Also, if net rates of 6 to 7 percent may be considered significantly higher than those of "5 percent or less," this is true of Great Britain, Sweden, and Japan.

[3] These and the following rates are from Kazushi Ohkawa et al., *The Growth Rate of the Japanese Economy since 1878* (Tokyo, 1957), Table 6, p. 21 and Table 7, p. 24.

[4] See "Quantitative Aspects of the Economic Growth of Nations: VI. Long-Term Trends in Capital Formation Proportions," *Economic Development and Cultural Change*, IX, 4, Part II (July 1961). Paper V, dealing with the international comparison of capital formation proportions for recent, post-World War II years, appeared in *ibid.*, VIII, 4, Part II (July 1960). Since the detailed statistical data and sources are cited in these two papers, they will not be repeated here.

In no case does the net domestic capital formation proportion even approach twice its initial size in the two or three decades dated as the take-off; and although the movements of the net *national* capital formation proportions are more erratic, they too fall far short of doubling during the take-off periods.

There is no evidence to support the assumption of a marginal net domestic (or national) capital-output ratio of 3.5 to 1. The ratio is neither the same for different countries nor stable over time. For the United Kingdom, the marginal net national capital-output ratio at the beginning of the nineteenth century was about 3 (it was about 4 for England and Wales in 1770–1800, if the crude data can be trusted). In Germany in the 1850's the net national capital-output ratio was between 3 and 3.5; in Sweden in 1881–90, on a *gross* basis, the ratio was between 3 and 4, but on a net basis it would have been between 2 and 3.5; in Japan in 1888–97, the gross domestic capital-output ratio was about 3, and the net somewhat less than 2. Moreover, in many countries the net capital-output ratios show a marked trend over time. For example, in the United Kingdom, the marginal net national capital-output ratio, which was 3 in the first part of the nineteenth century, rose to almost 6 in the period from 1880–89 to 1910–13; and even the net *domestic* capital-output ratio rose from about 3 before the middle of the nineteenth century to 3.7 in the three decades before World War I. The net national capital-output ratio for Germany rose from between 3 and 3.5 in the 1850's to about 5.5 for the decades from 1891 to 1913.

In no case do we find during the take-off periods the acceleration in the rate of growth of national product implied in Professor Rostow's assumptions of a doubling (or more) in the net capital formation proportion and of a constant marginal capital-output ratio. The capital formation proportions, if they rise, climb at a sustained rate and for a much longer period than the two or three decades of take-off. Rates of growth of total product, if they show any long-term acceleration (and those for only a few countries do within the period beginning with the take-off stage) increase slowly, and certainly over a longer period than the short span of the take-off.

The summary above relates to a few countries, none of which is in the Communist bloc, and is based upon crude estimates. But the data are firm enough to suggest rough orders of magnitude, and they bear directly upon what seem to be the essential statistical characteristics of the take-off period as Professor Rostow identifies them. Unless I have completely misunderstood Professor Rostow's definition of take-off and its statistical characteristics, I can only conclude that the available evidence lends no support to his suggestions.

The Distinctiveness and Generality of the Take-off Stage

The failure of aggregative data to reveal the characteristics claimed by Professor Rostow as typical of the take-off stage, at least in countries that did not experience the drastic and forced transformation associated with Communist revolutions, is disturbing. It casts serious doubt on the validity of the definition of the take-off as a general stage of modern economic growth, distinct from what Professor Rostow calls the pre-conditions, or transition, stage preceding it and the self-sustained-growth stage following it. The doubt is only reinforced by some more general questions concerning Professor Rostow's over-all scheme. These questions can be discussed under three heads: (1) the meaning of pre-conditions; (2) the effects of the widely diverse historical heritages of pre-modern economies on the characteristics of their transition to modern economic growth; (3) the meaning of self-sustained growth.

THE PRE-CONDITIONS STAGE · Professor Rostow treats the pre-conditions stage and much of the sequence as analogous to a mechanical, or more specifically, an aeronautical process, despite his several references to economic growth as essentially "biological." The picture suggested is that of the sequence involved in putting an airplane (or a glider) into flight. First there are the checking and fueling, which provide the pre-conditions, then there is the relatively brief take-off, when the driving force is accelerated to produce the upward movement, and finally there is the levelling-off into self-sustained flight. This analogy, perhaps unfair to Professor Rostow's stage sequence, is useful because it pinpoints the basic question in connection with the whole pre-conditions stage: can such pre-conditions be created without *at the same time* producing changes throughout the economy that, in and of themselves, initiate modern economic growth, that is, a higher rate of increase of total product, a higher rate of capital formation, growth of one or several modern productive sectors, and so on? To put it differently, is it realistic to talk of the pre-conditions created in one time span and of the initiation of modern economic growth in another span chronologically distinct?

The answer to this question depends upon the pre-conditions. Since modern developed economies make effective use of a wide variety of technical and social inventions, many of which date back to a time far earlier than the initiation of modern economic growth, pre-conditions whose creation is chronologically distinct from the early periods of modern economic growth can be found. Thus many current commercial instruments, maritime laws, and monetary practices originated, in much the same form, long before the second half of the eighteenth century, which may be taken as the date of the beginning of modern economic growth. But for the pre-conditions that Professor Rostow emphasizes in his discussion (Rostow II, Ch. 3)—transformation of agriculture and overhead capital investments—the answer is, to my mind, quite different. I do not see how, particularly in the "general" traditional society not "born free," a major change in agricultural productivity that provides more food per capita and more savings can be achieved without a rapid growth of some manufacturing and other sectors not only to provide employment for the displaced agricultural population but also to supply the producer and consumer goods required by the higher agricultural productivity and by the people who share in its benefits. And the production relations associated with increased overhead capital investments should bring about similar concomitant changes. Indeed much of what Professor Rostow says in Chapter 4 about income shifts and income flows in the process of take-off (particularly about agricultural incomes in Rostow II, pp. 46–47) is equally relevant to the discussion of pre-conditions in his Chapter 3.

Perhaps by further specification one could distinguish clearly, and in chronological sequence, some phases of the agricultural revolution and of increased capital investments that precede the distinctive changes that can be established for the take-off stage, but I doubt that this is possible. For any significant transformation of agriculture in the crowded traditional societies and any marked rise in overhead capital investment are, to my mind, already part and parcel of modern economic growth; and, given the technological, economic, and social interrelations within the economy, they can hardly occur unless *accompanied* by the changes that Professor Rostow assigns to the take-off stage. In short, the case for separation between the rather vaguely defined pre-conditions stage and the apparently more sharply defined take-off stage presented by Professor Rostow seems to me extremely weak. And Professor Rostow's casual reference to the duration of the pre-conditions stage—"a long period up to a century or, conceivably, more" (Rostow I, p. 27)—does not make the case stronger.

PAST HISTORY AND THE NATURE OF TRANSITION · In his recent book, Professor Rostow treats traditional economy as a single stage in a sequence of five stages and, as already indicated, draws only one relevant distinction, that between the small group of nations "born free" and all others in the single category of traditional economies. Thus, the latter includes the Western European countries, whose civilization was in many ways the cradle of modern economic society and which, during the epoch of merchant capitalism, were on the "taking" side vis-à-vis the rest of the world. It also includes the old Asian countries with their different history and endowments, the African societies with their specific heritage and culture, and many countries in the Western Hemisphere which are not among the "free-born." The inclusion of all these countries in one group implies that the stages of pre-conditions and take-off in all of them are characterized by basically the same important features. And we disregard for the present a major question of the legitimacy of characterizing all premodern economies as a stage.

To say that this is a heroic oversimplification is not to condemn the scheme out of hand. After all, modern economic growth, when and where it occurs, does have distinctive characteristics, not merely by definition but because it draws upon a transnational stock of useful knowledge and of social invention and is powered by human views and desires that have many similar features the world over. Yet it is fair to argue that the stocks of knowledge and social inventions themselves change over time, and that the modern economic growth of different countries is a process of combining the different complexes of historical heritage with the common requirements of the modern "industrial system." The parameters of the combination are likely, therefore, to differ from country to country, depending upon their specific historical heritages, upon the time when they enter modern economic growth, and upon their relations with other countries, particularly those already developed. The proper analysis of the process of modern economic growth in individual countries requires, therefore, a far more meaningful typology of "traditionalism" (or, to use another term, "underdevelopment") than is provided by Professor Rostow.

Nor can we disregard the timing of the process in relation to other countries, an aspect that plays such an important role in Professor Gerschenkron's intriguing hypothesis of the increasing "strain of backwardness" and the association between the degree of backwardness and the characteristics of the transition to modern economic growth.

The point is that it is in the *early* phases of a country's modern economic growth particularly that these distinct peculiarities of historical heritage, position in the sequence of spread of the industrial system, and relation to other already developed countries put their impress upon a country's growth. After 70 to 100 years of modern economic growth, one developed country would conceivably be similar in its characteristics to others despite differences in initial position. (Even this comment has limited validity: compare Japan today, after eight decades of rapid economic growth, with, say, Germany or France after a century of it.) However, in the early phase the differences in pattern of growth are likely to stand out most clearly, for at that point the diverse historical heritages have not yet been overlaid with the similarities imposed by sustained modern economic growth. And since the take-off stage, which to my mind overlaps with much of the pre-conditions stage, is an early phase of modern economic growth, the differences among countries in the parameters of the take-off are likely to be more notable than those in growth at later stages. An adequate stage theory or any other analytical scheme for studying economic growth, should point out not only the similarities but also the major differences, which reflect observable differences in historical antecedents, timing of entry into the process of modern economic growth, and other relevant factors. Professor Rostow's disregard of the major sources of differences in the early phases of modern economic growth among the developed "traditional" countries imposes severe limits on his claims to generality.

THE MEANING OF SELF-SUSTAINED GROWTH · The self-sustained growth that is supposed to occur in the stage following take-off is somewhat of a puzzle. Is it self-sustained in a sense in which it is *not* during the take-off and/or any earlier phase? If the reference is to the higher per capita income attained at the end of the take-off, which permits higher savings and capital formation proportions, which, in turn, permit higher rates of growth (assuming the marginal capital-output ratio is constant)—then one can argue that the same automatic mechanism operates during the take-off, once a significant increase in per capita income occurs, which presumably happens at the beginning of the take-off stage. If the reference is to the existence of favorable social institutions, these must also have existed through most of the take-off stage. Furthermore, many institutional changes are gradual, and if they have continually improved during take-off or earlier, their effects on the rate of growth should have been continuous. Consequently, since both income increases and institutional improvements abounded, it is difficult to accept the suggestion that growth was not self-sustained before the end of the take-off stage, but acquired that property only during the succeeding stage.

Obviously, the term is an analogy rather than a clearly specified characteristic, and for this reason alone it should be avoided. In one sense any growth is self-sustained: it means an irreversible rise to a higher level of economic performance that may facilitate the accumulation of reserves for further growth, whether these are funds for capital investment, greater efficiency of the labor force supplied with more consumption goods, economies of large scale, or other uses. In another sense any growth is self-limiting: the rise to a higher level may mean a reduction in incentive, pressure upon scarce irreproducible resources, and, perhaps most important, the strengthening of entrenched interests that may resist growth in competing sectors. And, indeed, the analysis of any widely and broadly conceived process of economic growth must reveal these and many more self-sustaining and self-limiting impacts of growth. If then Professor Rostow characterizes one stage of growth as self-sustained and others, by inference, as not, he must mean that in the latter stages the obstacles generated by past and current growth outweigh the self-sustaining impacts, whereas in the former stage the self-sustaining impacts outweigh the self-limiting ones. Obviously, both sets of impacts need documentation, both need to be weighed in terms of empirical evidence, far more than Professor Rostow provides in his casual characterization. Given the two sets of impacts of economic growth, the outcome is uncertain, and the process can never be *purely* self-sustained since it always generates *some* self-limiting effects. In this sense, economic growth is always a struggle; it is misleading to convey an impression of easy automaticity, a kind of soaring euphoria of self-sustained flight to higher economic levels.

Concluding Comments

The gist of our discussion can be given in a few brief propositions.

1. Leadership of a sector depends upon the origin of its growth in an autonomous impulse, not in response to other sectors in the country, and upon the magnitude of its direct and indirect contributions to the country's economic growth. The autonomous impulse and the various types of contribution to growth differ in timing, and the identification and chronology of leading sectors requires specification and evidence lacking in Professor Rostow's discussion.

2. The doubling of capital investment proportions and the implicit sharp acceleration in the rate of growth of national product, claimed by Professor Rostow as characterizing his take-off periods, are not confirmed by the statistical evidence for those countries on his list for which we have data.

3. There is no clear distinction between the pre-conditions and the take-off stages. On the contrary, given the pre-conditions emphasized by Professor Rostow—transformation of agriculture and overhead capital investments—there is a *prima facie* case for expecting the pre-conditions and the take-off stages to overlap.

4. The analysis of the take-off and pre-conditions stages neglects the effect of historical heritage, time of entry into the process of modern economic growth, degree of backwardness, and other relevant factors on the characteristics of the early phases of modern economic growth in the different traditional countries.

5. The concept (and stage) of self-sustained growth is a misleading oversimplification. No growth is purely self-sustaining or purely self-limiting. The characterization of one stage of growth as self-sustained, and of others, by implication, as lacking that property, requires substantive evidence not provided in Professor Rostow's discussion.

A few comments may help to put these conclusions into proper perspective.

First, the evidence used to test Professor Rostow's scheme is not conclusive. Some non-Communist countries for which we have no data may have experienced a period of growth conforming with Professor Rostow's take-off stage. Also, his scheme may fit the Communist "take-offs," but my knowledge of them is inadequate for checking. All that is claimed here is that aggregative data for several countries do not support Professor Rostow's distinction and characterization of the take-off stage. On the other hand, the fact that the evidence is confined to aggregative data does not limit their bearing. Economic growth is an aggregative process; sectoral changes are interrelated with aggregative changes, and can be properly weighed only after they have been incorporated into the aggregative framework; and the absence of required aggregative changes severely limits the likelihood of the implicit strategic sectoral changes.

Second, although we concentrated on the take-off stage, and the two contiguous stages—pre-conditions and self-sustained growth—much of what was said applies by inference to other stages in Professor Rostow's scheme. Moreover, the characterization of the traditional economy as a stage raises numerous questions. But an explicit discussion of the rest of the scheme would take us too far afield.

Third, my disagreement with Professor Rostow is *not* on the value and legitimacy of an attempt to suggest some pattern of order in the modern economic growth experience of different countries. On the contrary, I fully share what I take to be his view on the need to go beyond qualitative and quantitative description to the use of the evidence for a large number of countries and long periods, in combination with analytical tools and imaginative hypotheses, to suggest and explain not only some common patterns but also, I would add, the major deviations from them. However, for reasons indicated above, I disagree with the sequence of stages he suggests.

If we cannot accept Professor Rostow's sequence of stages, and particularly his notion of a distinct and commonly found take-off stage, what are we left with?

Let us begin by agreeing that modern economic growth displays certain observable and measurable characteristics which in combination are distinctive to it, that is, were not evident in earlier economic epochs; and that these characteristics can, in principle, be established with the help of quantitative and other data wherever such growth occurs. What these characteristics are is a matter for discussion; but I believe that agreement could easily be reached on some of them, for example, those relating to rates of growth of national product, total and per capita, and to structural shifts that commonly accompany them. Let us assume for purposes of illustration that such growth requires a minimum rise in per capita income sustained over a period of at least two or three decades, a minimum shift away from agriculture, and any other identifiable indispensable components of modern economic growth that we may specify.

With this specification of modern economic growth, it becomes possible, given the data, to place its beginning in the various countries in which it occurred. The date of inception need not be a year, or even a quinquennium; it may be a band of some width, but still narrow enough to permit us to say that the two or three decades following it are the early phases of modern economic growth and the two or three decades before it are those directly preceding the beginning of modern economic growth—without missing much in between. If, then, we consider it important to study only the early decades of modern economic growth, those immediately preceding it, or both, in the hope of establishing characteristics and relations that would permit us to construct an adequate theoretical scheme, we may want to call the first two or three decades following the initiation of modern economic growth the "early growth phase" and the two or three decades preceding it the "late premodern phase."

Obviously, the two or three decades are only illustrative, and the length of the period may vary from country to country: the phase selected for concentrated study would have to be defined in terms of some reasonably realistic preliminary notions concerning the length of time during which the distinctive characteristics of early growth persist or during which the immediate antecedents must be studied. The firm point in this approach is the feasibility of dating the beginning of modern economic growth by some "hard" data, relating to one or several characteristics inherent in modern economic growth. In doing this, all that we specify is the *early* phase of the segment of the long record of modern economic growth on which we wish to concentrate. The termination of the period is then to be set on the basis of any substantive hypotheses concerning the distinctive characteristics of the early phase, although one would assume that since the span of modern economic growth in most countries is not much over a hundred years, there are narrow limits to the length of the early growth phase that an economist *of today* can set.

The term "early phase" of modern growth is far less appealing than "take-off": it does not carry the suggestive connotation of the latter. And the same is true of "late premodern period" compared with "pre-conditions," and of "middle growth period" compared with "self-sustained growth." But the appealing terms employing mechanical or biological metaphors carry the danger of misleading us into believing that the suggested connotations are relevant to observable reality. It is my conviction that at the present stage of our knowledge (and ignorance), it is the better part of valor to link the constraining influence of phase distinction to the bare lines of observable and measurable growth processes; and to concentrate discussion on the early decades of modern economic growth in those countries for which we can identify its beginning, with excursions into the premodern growth past and the post-early decades of modern growth when they seem warranted.

Economic Growth and the
Contribution of Agriculture

Aspects of Economic Growth

WE DEAL here with the economic growth of nations since the late eighteenth or early nineteenth century. This limitation allows us to specify the distinctive aspects of modern economic growth that should be measured.

The aspect most easily perceived and most commonly measured is the aggregative. In fact, the usual definition of economic growth —a sustained increase in a nation's total and per capita product, most often accompanied by a sustained and significant rise in population—stresses this aspect. "Sustained" means persisting over a long period and not in the nature of a cyclical or otherwise short-term expansion. "Increase" means more than a formal mathematical requirement, in that it could not be satisfied by a rate of one millionth of 1 percent per century. In the eighteen to twenty-four nations that may be said to have experienced modern economic growth, product per capita grew at rates ranging from well above 10 to close to 30 percent per decade, and total product at rates ranging from 15 to over 40 percent per decade, and with some striking exceptions, population grew at rates ranging from 8 to 20

This paper was delivered at the Eleventh International Conference of Agricultural Economists in Mexico in 1961. Reprinted from the Proceedings *of the conference (London: Oxford University Press, 1963).*

percent per decade.[1] A rate of 10 percent per decade means doubling in somewhat over 70 years; of 20 percent in less than 40 years; of 30 percent in less than 30 years; of 40 percent in about 20 years. With modern economic growth extending over a century in many of the developed nations, the rise sustained in total and per capita product was of a magnitude rarely if ever reached in the past.

The second interesting aspect is the structural. The significant characteristics of the rises associated with modern growth are the large and rapid shifts that occur in the structure of an economy—in the relative importance of various industries, regions, classes of economic units distinguished by form of organization, economic classes, commodity groups in final output, and so on. The frequent references to modern economic growth as "industrialization" and to its important constituent elements as "urbanization" and "mechanization," clearly indicate these structural aspects, while even slight acquaintance with the literature reveals that the main burden of the analysis is not on the aggregative but on the structural characteristics. The measures usually provided are the familiar distributions of product, capital, and labor among industrial sectors; among regions; between the private and the public sectors, and by further divisions within each; and among various socio-economic groups.

The third aspect is the international. We distinguish this aspect in order to stress the facts that, except for the pioneer nation, all nations participating in modern economic growth view the prospects initially as the task of adopting (and adapting) potentials already demonstrated elsewhere; that no nation can grow in an international vacuum; and that the process of a nation's growth involves a pattern of sequential interrelations with others that are more developed and less developed. In a sense, then, the modern economic growth of any one nation is a process of shifting from the underdeveloped to the developed group by utilizing the appropriate channels of international trade, finance, and communications. Although this whole process of borrowing the knowledge and resources that are indispensable in a nation's modern economic growth cannot be measured, a wide variety of statistical data on foreign trade, foreign capital movements, and international migrations have been assembled. Hence the view of the changing *domestic* structure of a nation's economy in its process of growth can be supplemented by a view of the sequential pattern of the economic flows between

[1] See my *Six Lectures on Economic Growth* (New York: The Free Press of Glencoe, 1959), pp. 19–28.

it and the rest of the world.[2]

The three aspects are interrelated. The rise in per capita product, essential to the aggregative view of economic growth, in and of itself means a shift in consumption and savings patterns and thus contributes to the shift in the industrial and other structures of the economy. On the other hand, the utilization of the technological potential of modern times through the development of new industries and new methods of production—which means structural shifts —permits a rise in product per capita. And the aggregative growth and certain structural shifts provide the surpluses for international trade and capital movements; whereas the latter, bringing the benefits of international division of labor, are in turn conducive to the greater aggregative growth of the participating nations and thus to greater structural shifts within them. This close association is hardly surprising, since a nation's modern economic growth may be described as the utilization of domestic and international division of labor, under conditions of changing technology, to increase per capita product of a growing population.

Given this interrelation, it is difficult to specify the contribution of a single industrial sector, say agriculture, to each aspect of economic growth, nor is it particularly illuminating to do so. For if a sector contributes directly to the growth of product per worker, it contributes indirectly to structural shifts and greater international division of labor; if a sector contributes directly to foreign trade, it contributes indirectly to growth of product per capita and to structural shifts within the country. It would seem preferable to consider the contribution of agriculture to economic growth jointly in all three aspects of the process, and then examine the various ways in which such a contribution may be rendered. Some of these ways bear more directly on aggregative aspects of growth than on the structural; others bear more directly upon the structural or international than upon the aggregative. But each has some bearing on all three related aspects of economic growth.

[2] The importance of this aspect is not denied by the experience of the Communist countries. Initially they also borrowed extensively and imported considerably from abroad, which is natural since they were follower nations. That these ties with other nations have not continued to grow as they did with the more freely organized societies is but another case of changes in the pattern of economic growth as we move from the pioneer nation to the first and then the more removed (in time and in character of historical antecedents) follower nations.

The Product Contribution

In considering the contribution of agriculture, or for that matter of any sector, to the economic growth of a country, we must first recognize an element of ambiguity. Since any sector is part of an interdependent system represented by the country's economy, what a sector does is not fully attributable or credited to it but is contingent upon what happens in the other sectors (and perhaps also outside the country). Thus, even if we deal with net product originating in, or contributed by, a sector, deducting the purchases or contributions from others and limiting the total to the product of the factors attached to that sector, the magnitude and movement of the net product so measured still depend upon the rest of the economy; and its product may perhaps be more correctly described as the result of the activities of the economy whose particular *locus* is the given sector rather than as a contribution of the given sector fully creditable to it as if it were outside the economy and offering something to the latter. But so long as we keep the semantic caution in mind and remember that the capacity of a sector to "contribute" depends not upon the sector alone, no harm is done by retaining this familiar expression.

The first type of contribution of agriculture to the economic growth of a nation is that constituted by growth of product within the sector itself. An increase in the net output of agriculture represents a rise in the product of the country, since the latter is the sum of the increases in the net products of the several sectors. This type, which we may call the product contribution, can be briefly examined—as a contribution first to the growth of *total* net or gross product, and second to the growth of product per capita.

We begin with a simple algebraic notation and refer to "product," since the formal conclusions are the same for product gross of capital consumption (gross national product, and corresponding gross product originating in the sector) or net of it (net national product, and corresponding net product originating in the sector).

Designate:

P_a = product of agriculture (A sector).
P_b = product of all other sectors (non-A sector).
P = total product = $P_a + P_b$.
δP = increment in total product or aggregate growth.
r_a = rate of growth of P_a so that $P_a{}^1 = P_a{}^0(1 + r_a)$, the superscripts referring to time.

r_b = rate of growth of P_b so that $P_b^1 = P_b^0(1 + r_b)$.

Then,
$$\delta P = P_a r_a + P_b r_b. \tag{1}$$

And the equation for the share of the growth of agricultural product in the growth of total product is

$$\frac{P_a r_a}{\delta P} = \frac{1}{1 + \left(\dfrac{P_b}{P_a} \times \dfrac{r_b}{r_a} \right)}. \tag{2}$$

Thus, if at the initial point of time, the share of agriculture in countrywide product is 60 percent—about the highest for an underdeveloped country [3] —and if over the next decade the rate of growth of the non-A sector (r_b) is four times as high as that of the A sector (r_a), the product contribution of agriculture to the growth of total product will be 1 divided by $[1 + (0.67 \times 4)]$ or about a quarter. At the end of that decade the initial share of agriculture in total product will be less than 60 percent and if r_b/r_a remains four, the following decade will witness a product contribution of agriculture to growth of total product smaller than a quarter.[4]

---

[3] See my "Quantitative Aspects of the Economic Growth of Nations: II. Industrial Distribution of National Product and Labor Force," *Economic Development and Cultural Change*, V, 4, Supplement (July 1957), Table 3, p. 10.

[4] There is a direct relation between the ratio of rates of growth of product in the non-A and A sectors (r_b/r_a) and the movement of the ratio of the product of the A sector to the total. This can be expressed by the following equation:

$$\frac{(1 + r_b)}{(1 + r_a)} = \frac{P_a^0}{P_b^0} \left(\frac{P^1}{P_a^1} - 1 \right). \tag{3}$$

Thus, if at time point 0, the first ratio in the right-hand side of equation (3) is 1.5, meaning that the shares of the A sector and the non-A sector in total product are 60 and 40 percent respectively; and if over the next decade the share of the A sector drops to 55 percent, the value on the right-hand side becomes 1.5 $(1/0.55 - 1)$ or 1.23. Then, if the rate of growth for agriculture is 10 percent per decade, $(1 + r_a)$ becomes 1.10; and $(1 + r_b)$ becomes 1.35; and the rate of growth for the non-A section 35 percent per decade, or 3.5 times as high as that for the A sector. When the share of agriculture drops from 30 to 25 percent, the right-hand side of equation (3) becomes

$$\frac{0.30(4 - 1)}{0.70} \text{ or } 1.29;$$

and if $(1 + r_a)$ is still 1.10, $(1 + r_b)$ becomes 1.42, yielding a rate of growth 4.2 times as high as that for agriculture. Likewise, if we lower the rate of growth in agriculture, and set $(1 + r_a)$, at, say, 1.05, under the conditions illustrated above, $(1 + r_b)$ becomes 1.29 and 1.35 respectively, yielding rates

Several conclusions can be derived from equation (2). First, so long as the rate of growth of the non-A sector is higher than that of agriculture, all other conditions being equal, the proportional contribution of agriculture to the growth of total product will decline. The only component in equation (2) that might prevent such a decline is the ratio r_b/r_a: a decline in *it* might counteract the effect of the rise in P_b/P_a. Second, if r_b/r_a rises, that is, if the rate of growth of the nonagricultural sector is increasingly higher than that of agriculture, the decline in the share of agriculture in the growth of total product will be even greater. Third, if we assume that the rate of growth of countrywide product is *constant* over time (only a few countries showed acceleration in the long-term movement), and if r_b/r_a is over 1, that is, if the rate of growth of the nonagricultural sector is higher than the rate of growth of agriculture, then either r_b or r_a, or both, must decline over time. For if they remain constant, the increasing weight of P_b (enjoying a higher rate of growth) will make for an *acceleration* in the rate of growth of total product.

Let us turn now from the product contribution of agriculture to the growth of countrywide product per capita or rather per worker, a more meaningful unit for sectoral analysis.

Designate (in addition to the notation above):

L_a = workers in the A sector.
L_b = workers in all other sectors.
L = all workers = $L_a + L_b$.
R = rate of growth of product per worker (same in both the A and non-A sectors).

Then we have the following expression for the change in total product per worker:

$$\frac{P^1}{L^1} - \frac{P^0}{L^0} = \left(\frac{P_a^1}{L_a} - \frac{P_a^0}{L_a^0}\right)\left(\frac{L_a^1}{L^1}\right) + \left(\frac{P_b^1}{L_b^1} - \frac{P_b^0}{L_b^0}\right)\left(\frac{L_b^1}{L^1}\right)$$
$$+ \left(\frac{P_b^0}{L_b^0} - \frac{P_a^0}{L_a^0}\right)\left(\frac{L_b^1}{L^1} - \frac{L_b^0}{L^0}\right). \qquad (4)$$

Equation (4) tells us that the increment in a country's aggregate product per worker is the sum of: (*a*) the increment in product per worker in the A sector, weighted by the share of the A sector in labor force *at the end* of the period; (*b*) the increment in product

---

of growth for the non-A sector 6 or 7 times as high as those for the A sector.

per worker in the non-A sector, weighted by the share of the non-A sector in labor force *at the end* of the period; (*c*) the *change* in the share of the non-A sector in the labor force (usually a rise) during the period, weighted by the difference between product per worker in the non-A and A sectors at the beginning of the period.

If we assume that P_b/L_b is larger than P_a/L_a, which is usually the case, and set the ratio for time 0 at 2; and if we assume further that product per worker grows at about the same rate in the A sector and in the non-A sector—not an unreasonable assumption in the light of records for the developed countries—equation (4) can be simplified to

$$\frac{P^1}{L^1} - \frac{P^0}{L^0} = \frac{P_a{}^0}{L_a{}^0} \left[(L_a{}^1/L^1)R + (L_b{}^1/L^1)2R + (L_b{}^1/L^1 - L_b{}^0/L_0) \right].$$

(5)

Thus, if the initial share of the labor force in agriculture is as high as 75 percent, product per worker in agriculture only half that in the nonagricultural sector, the rate of growth in product per worker per decade (for both sectors) 20 percent, and the share of labor force in the nonagricultural sector increases 5 percentage points per decade—a not unreasonable figure—the right-hand side of equation (5) for the first decade becomes

$$\frac{P_a{}^0}{L_a{}^0} \left[(0.70)0.20 + (0.30)0.40 + 0.05 \right].$$

The first component of the right-hand side of both equations (4) and (5) is a measure of the contribution of agriculture to the growth of countrywide product per worker; the second component is a measure of the contribution of the non-A sector. But what about the third component, the effect of the shift in the percentage distribution of the labor force from the A to the non-A sector? It is in this connection that the ambiguity of the term "contribution" emerges. In one sense it is a contribution of the A sector, since the latter provides additional labor force to the non-A sector; and as will be seen below, the internal migration involved in this shift must be quite large in the process of modern economic growth. In another sense the shift is a contribution of the non-A sector, since the latter provides the essential employment opportunities to the labor moving from the A sector. The allocation of this joint contribution to the A and non-A sectors is clearly a matter of judgment. If we divide it equally between the two, the proportional contribution of agriculture to the countrywide growth of per *worker* product becomes in the example above $(0.14 + 0.025)/0.31$, or somewhat over one half.

On the assumptions underlying equation (5), and however we allocate the third component, some general statements can be made about the level and movements of the proportional contribution of agriculture to additions to countrywide product per worker. First, this proportional contribution will be larger, the larger the terminal share of agriculture in the country's labor force and the higher the ratio of product per worker in agriculture to that in the non-A sector. And, if we permit the rate of growth of product per worker in the A and non-A sectors to differ, the proportional contribution of the A sector will be larger, the higher the ratio of the rate of growth of product per worker in the A sector to that in the non-A sector. Second, insofar as in the course of economic growth the share of agriculture in the labor force declines, there will be a continuous decline in the proportional contribution of agriculture to the growth in countrywide product per worker, unless the rate of growth of product per worker in the non-A sector falls behind the rate of growth of product in the A sector, which is unlikely. Third, if we assume that the countrywide product per worker grows at a constant rate, the continuous shift of the labor force from the A sector with its lower product per worker to the non-A sector with its higher product per worker *must* be accompanied by a decline in the rate of growth of product per worker in the A sector, or in the non-A sector, or in both. The slight damping influence of the third component—the absolute rise in the share of the non-A sector in the labor force—may be disregarded, since its weight is likely to be small. The parallelism of these conclusions to those derived for the proportional contribution of agriculture to growth of total product is obvious.

These rather simple schemes could be applied to the empirical long-term records on product, labor force, and product per worker —in total and for the two sectors separately—for a number of countries, and with product valued at constant prices to eliminate the effect of price changes. Such statistical analysis would probably show in countries with a high rate of economic growth, a rapid decline in the proportional contribution of agriculture—from a quarter or more of the growth of total product and a half or more of the growth of per *worker* product, to a few percentage points. It must be remembered that currently the share of agriculture in both product and labor force in many developed countries is well below 20 percent. The analysis of the statistical evidence might also reveal more about the time pattern of the movements. But to present such an analysis would transcend the limits of the paper, and we prefer to devote the rest of the discussion to other somewhat less obvious and perhaps less familiar types of contribution of agriculture to a country's modern economic growth.

The Market Contribution

A given sector makes a contribution to an economy when it provides opportunities for other sectors to emerge, or for the economy as a whole to participate in international trade and other international economic flows. We designate this contribution the market type because the given sector provides such opportunities by offering part of its product on domestic or foreign markets in exchange for goods produced by the other sectors, at home or abroad.

Thus in the case of agriculture, we can envisage two contrasting situations. In one, agriculture engages 100 units of labor force to turn out 1,000 units of product without any purchases from other sectors, and thus is completely independent of the country's production processes. In another, agriculture engages 80 units of labor force and still turns out 1,000 units of product, but does so by purchasing 200 units of fertilizers, etc., provided by 20 units of the country's labor force. In both cases, the net output of the economy, with the same labor force, is the same—1,000 units of final goods. But in the second case we have market transactions and diversification of production.

The example is unrealistic, for the division of labor in the second case would usually result in an appreciably higher product per worker. Indeed, this rise is the very reason for the sacrifice of economic independence by a sector and its engagement in trade with other sectors at home or abroad. But the illustration does emphasize the contribution of changes in a sector to a significant element in economic growth, diversification of structure and the intensification of the internal and international division of labor. These changes are important in and of themselves—apart from the contribution that they make to growth in total or per capita product.

Thus agriculture makes a market contribution to economic growth by (1) purchasing some production items from other sectors at home or abroad; (2) selling some of its product, not only to pay for the purchases listed under (1) but also to purchase consumer goods from other sectors or from abroad, or to dispose of the product in any way other than consumption within the sector. In all these ways, agriculture makes it feasible for other sectors to emerge and grow and for international flows to develop; just as these other sectors and the international flows make it feasible for the agricultural sector to operate more efficiently as a producing unit and use its product more effectively as a consuming unit.

In this connection, some familiar trends in agriculture in countries that have experienced modern economic growth come easily to mind. There is first the spread of modern technology to agriculture proper: chemical fertilizers, machinery, and mechanical power replaced extensively means of production originating within agriculture itself (natural fertilizers, draught animals, and hand-made tools). The need to purchase these new production goods from other sectors meant an increasing "marketization" of the production process within agriculture, and it is reflected in the increasing proportion that purchases from other sectors constitute of the product of agriculture—gross of all production expenses. To cite an easily available example: in the United States the *net* farm income in 1910 amounted to slightly less than 80 percent of *gross* farm income; whereas in 1950 it was less than 70 percent (both totals are in constant prices, and are five-year averages centered on the years cited).[5] Thus the proportion of purchases (including capital consumption) rose over the forty years from about 20 to about 30 percent of the gross product.

The proportion of gross income accounted for by purchases from other sectors is clearly a crude and incomplete measure of the marketization of the production process in agriculture. We treat all agriculture here as one sector, disregarding the network of market transactions within agriculture—transactions which presumably grow in absolute and *proportional* volume as agriculture becomes more specialized and diversified in the course of economic growth. A more complete measure would be based on records of purchases by each farm, making it independent of arbitrary definitions of a sector. But so long as we understand what is involved in the marketization of the production process in agriculture, we need not dwell upon its measurement.

But how to measure the "contribution" to economic growth? The

[5] See Alvin Tostlebe, *Capital in Agriculture: Its Formation and Financing since 1870* (New York: National Bureau of Economic Research, 1957), Table 20, p. 101.

measure just discussed is a gauge of relative importance of purchases to the gross product of a sector, not of their proportional contribution to a country's economic growth. We need here to define the aspect of the latter to which we think marketization contributes over and above its indirect contribution to total and per capita product.

That aspect is clearly development of sectors other than agriculture; and it could be measured by comparing the nonagricultural sectors in the country providing production goods to agriculture with all the nonagricultural sectors. In other words, the percentage of the growth in output of all nonagricultural sectors (including the transportation and other facilities involved) accounted for by the fertilizer, agricultural machinery, and other plants that provide the production goods to agriculture, would measure the proportional contribution which marketization of the production process in agriculture made to the industrialization aspects of economic growth within the country. Unfortunately, we do not have the facts, but a realistic illustration may suggest the order of magnitude. Assume that the proportion of purchases from other sectors to *gross* product of agriculture increased in the process of growth from 10 to 30 percent, which meant a shift from 11 to 43 percent of *net* product. Assume further that at the initial point of time the proportion of net income from agriculture to net national product was 60 percent, and declined to 15 percent at the end. Purchases by agriculture from other sectors (gross) were therefore 6.6 percent of net national product at the initial point of time and less than 6.5 percent at the end point; if we reduce this proportion by a fifth to allow for the difference between gross and net content ("net" representing returns to factors), we have roughly 5.3 percent of net national product represented by industries whose only function is to supply producers' goods to agriculture. The proportion works out to 13 and 6 percent respectively (5.3/40 and 5.3/85) of the net product of all nonagricultural industries. Marketization of the agricultural production process thus accounted for a significant but declining fraction of the "industrialized" sectors and of the structural aspect of economic growth.

We turn now to the increase in the proportion of agricultural *net* product which is not consumed within the producing farm or agriculture proper but is sold on the markets to other sectors of the economy or abroad. This trend is largely due to a rise in net product per worker within agriculture combined with the low secular income elasticity of the demand for agricultural consumer goods, but it may also reflect technical progress that reduces cost and facilitates transportation and trade over wide areas. The contribution to economic growth here is the release of a larger proportion of the *net* product of agriculture as a basis for demand for consumer goods (or, to a more limited extent, for producer goods) from other sectors and from foreign countries.

Some suggestion of the magnitude of such marketization of the net product of agriculture can be made on two alternative assumptions, both disregarding the minor fraction of the net product that may be saved (rather than consumed). On the first assumption, the per worker (or per capita) consumption of agricultural net product is the same in both the A and non-A sectors, despite the large difference in their total income per capita. On this assumption, if we begin with a share of the A sector in net national product of 60 percent and in the labor force of 75 percent, per worker or per capita consumption of agricultural net product throughout the economy will be 0.6 (in percentages of net national product); the consumption by the agricultural population of its own product will be 75 percent multiplied by 0.6, or 45 percent of net national product; and their consumption of other goods will be 15 percent (i.e., 60 percent of total net product minus 45 percent represented by agricultural product). If we also assume that all the nonagricultural final product goes through the market, the total marketed net product is 55 percent of net national product, of which 15 percent is agricultural final product. The contribution of agriculture to total marketed net product is then slightly over a quarter, and it is clear that as the shares of agriculture in national product and in labor force decline, its proportional contribution to the growing marketed net product will decline. Thus when the share of agriculture in the national product is down to 15 percent, and in the labor force correspondingly down to 26.1 percent (to preserve a ratio of product per worker in the non-A sector to that in the A sector of 2 to 1), the marketed proportion of agricultural net product will, on the assumptions stated, be 11.1 percent of national product; the total marketed portion will be 96.1 percent (i.e., 85 percent nonagricultural output plus 11.1 percent agricultural); and the proportional contribution of agricultural marketings to total will be about a ninth rather than over a quarter.

An alternative assumption would be that the distribution of final consumption (which, disregarding savings or capital formation, we equate to net national product) between agricultural and nonagricultural products—for both agricultural and nonagricultural populations—is the same and in fact is shown by the shares of agriculture and of other sectors in the countrywide total of net product. Thus, at the initial point of time, with the share of agriculture in the net national product 60 percent, the agricultural population would consume only 60 percent of its net income in the form of agricultural products; and trade the remainder, that is, 24 percent of net national product, to the people dependent upon the nonagricultural sectors. The total marketed product would be 64 percent of net national product (40 percent represented by nonagricultural output, all marketed; and 24 percent by the marketed, agricultural output); and agriculture's contribution to it will be 24 out of 64, or close to four tenths. On this assumption, when the share of agriculture in national product drops to 50 percent, half of the agricultural output would be traded, that is, 25 percent of total product—a slightly higher percentage than in the first instance, but a lower share of the total marketed output (which will be 75 percent).

Which assumption is the more realistic would have to be determined by empirical study, and the actual behavior of agricultural and nonagricultural producers and consumers may fall within the range suggested by the two assumptions. However, the main points to be noted are suggested under either assumption. First, at the initial point of time, when agriculture accounts for a large share of the net output of the economy, the extent to which its product is traded with the other sectors has a major bearing upon the width of the economic base which these other sectors may enjoy. If, for simplicity's sake, we think of a closed economy, any difficulty in increasing the marketable surplus of agricultural product will restrict the growth base of the other sectors. Second, once growth occurs and is accompanied by a decline in the shares of agriculture in product and labor force, the increased productivity per worker in agriculture reflected in these trends assures an increasing proportion of marketed agricultural net product and at the same time a decreasing proportional contribution of such marketings to the total product of the economy. In short, the market contribution of agriculture to a country's economic growth, strategic in the early periods of growth, must, in the nature of the case, diminish in relative weight once growth has proceeded apace.

The same conclusion is suggested by the third aspect of the market contribution of agriculture: that bearing upon the trading partner with whom market relations are established. The market contribution to economic growth will be the greater the higher the growth-inducing power of the trading partners whose cooperation *via* the market is being secured. The same volume of purchases by agriculture from a host of village carpenters and blacksmiths and from a factory that produces agricultural machinery by advanced methods, will have different impacts on the growth not only of the nonagricultural sectors of the economy but also of agriculture itself.

It is in this connection that the contribution of agriculture to exports assumes strategic importance since in most countries modern economic growth is a matter of following the pattern set by the nations that have already experienced this process; and a follower nation must trade with the more advanced countries which can provide it with the tools of modern technology. Even with allowance for capital imports, a country in the early stages of economic growth that cannot itself produce, even at high cost, the tools of modern technology, must be able to offer the more advanced countries a *quid pro quo*. It can do this only with products in which it has a comparative advantage, and this advantage is likely to lie in natural resources rather than in skills. Since agriculture, after mining, is the sector in which natural endowments have greatest weight, it is hardly a surprise that in the initial stages of growth of many presently developed countries, agriculture was a major source of exports and that the resulting command over the re- sources of the more developed countries played a strategic role in facilitating modern economic growth. It is also apparent that, as economic growth continued, the advantage with respect to products affected by natural resource endowments might recede relative to that resulting from economies of scale and accumulation of skills in other sectors. Consequently, in addition to the reduction in the weight of agriculture in the total output of a country, there may be an even greater reduction in its share of exports. Thus the market contribution of agriculture, this time in specific connection with the capacity of a country through international trade to tap the resources of the more advanced units, is likely to be large in the initial stages of growth (unless the mineral resources are sufficiently great to make agricultural exports less strategic) and bound to decline as economic growth takes hold. While any detailed analysis of the relations touched upon here would raise difficult questions concerning the phasing of this process of building economic growth on trade with the more advanced countries, the substance of the contribution is clear and the measures, in terms of shares of exports and feasible imports of capital goods, are obvious without further discussion.

The Factor Contribution

The third type of contribution by a sector to economic growth occurs when there is a transfer or loan of resources from the given sector to others. Thus if agriculture itself grows, it makes a product contribution; if it trades with others, it renders a market contribution; if it transfers resources to other sectors, these resources being productive factors, it makes a *factor* contribution.

The resources are either capital, that is, funds for financing acquisition of material capital, or labor. In the case of the former, two different types of transfer may occur. In the first there is a compulsory transfer from agriculture for the benefit of other sectors; this is ordinarily done through taxation in which the burden on agriculture is far greater than the services rendered by government to agriculture (including an adequate share of overhead government expenses), the residue being spent by government for the benefit of other sectors. To illustrate, the government may use a tax on agriculture as its only revenue, and expend it all either on a subsidy to some manufacturing industry (thus in fact providing capital funds for the latter), or use it all in the construction of some public utility. To be sure, both the factory and the public utility contribute to growth within agriculture proper, but the direct contribution to economic growth is to the nonagricultural sectors, and this flow, originating in the agricultural sector, is not covered in its product or market contribution.

The measurement of such forced contributions of agriculture to economic growth is not easy; the incidence of some indirect taxes is difficult to ascertain and the allocation of government expenditures in terms of benefits to agriculture and to economic growth elsewhere is far from simple. But this factor contribution by agriculture was clearly quite large in the early phases of economic growth in some countries. Thus in Japan in the last two decades of the nineteenth century the land tax was over 80 percent of central government taxation, and the direct tax ratio to income produced was between 12 and 22 percent in agriculture, compared with from 2 to 3 percent in the nonagricultural sectors.[6] Forced extraction of surplus from agriculture by taxation, confiscation, and other measures also probably financed a considerable part of industrialization in the Soviet Union. Indeed, one of the crucial problems of modern economic growth is how to extract from the product of agriculture a surplus for the financing of capital formation for industrial growth without at the same time blighting the growth of agriculture, under conditions where no easy *quid pro quo* for such surplus is available within the country. It is only the open economy, with access to the markets of the more highly developed countries, both for goods and for capital loans, that can minimize this painful task of initial capital accumulation.

The other form of capital transfer is, of course, lending, or the utilization of savings originating in the agricultural sector in financing the growth of the nonagricultural sectors. If we had data on both savings and capital formation, in agriculture and in other sectors of the economy, there would be no problem in measuring the extent to which savings originating in agriculture contribute to the financing of capital formation elsewhere in the economy. But no such data are at hand and we are forced to speculate on the magnitudes involved.

In such speculation the following general points must be taken into account. In the initial phases of growth the share of agriculture in total national product is large, but the per capita income in the A sector is distinctly lower than that in the non-A sector. Hence the share of domestic savings originating in agriculture is a function of the share of agriculture in total income, the lower level of real income in agriculture than in the other sectors, and the relative propensity to save of the agricultural population and of other groups in the economy. To assay these three variables would necessitate much empirical study. But to make the discussion more meaningful, let us begin with a share of the A sector in income of 60 percent, in labor force of 75 percent; and assume that savings amount to 5 percent of the A sector income, which on a per capita basis is only half of the income in the non-A sector, compared with a 10 percent savings rate for the non-A sector. Total domestic savings would then amount to 7 percent of national income, 4 percent

<hr>

[6] See Kazushi Okhawa and Henry Rosovsky, "The Role of Agriculture in Modern Japanese Economic Development," in *City and Village in Japan*, the October 1960 issue of *Economic Development and Cultural Change*, IX, 1, Tables 14 and 15, pp. 61 and 62.

originating in the non-A sector and 3 percent in the A sector.

The flow of savings out of the A sector to finance capital formation elsewhere would depend largely upon the relative needs of these sectors for capital, as reflected in differential rates of return (all other conditions being abstracted from). Perhaps the incremental capital–output ratios might suggest how much capital is needed to secure additional output. The data for recent years indicate that in all but the most fully developed countries, the incremental capital–output ratios for the A sector, while higher than those for manufacturing, are not too different from the countrywide ratios and hence from those for the non-A sector as a whole.[7] If this situation can be assumed for the early phases of economic growth, the allocation of savings depends largely upon the relative rates of growth of the A and non-A sectors, reflecting differences in long-term demand for additions to their product. Hence, the possible flow of savings from the A sector to finance capital formation in the non-A sector will be revealed by a comparison of two fractions: the first is the ratio of additions to product of the A sector to additions to the total product of the economy—already discussed under the product contribution of agriculture, and expressible as $P_a r_a/(P_a r_a + P_b r_b)$; the other fraction is the ratio of savings originating in agriculture to all savings originating in the economy, which can be written as $s_a/(s_a + s_b)$. Now if we assume, in addition, that the net savings rate is 7 percent, that national product grows at a rate of 3 percent per year (or 34.4 percent per decade), implying an incremental capital–output ratio of 2.3 to 1; and that the rate of growth of the product of the non-A sector is four times that of the product of the A sector, the *needed* capital formation in the A sector will be only 27 percent of total capital formation needed;[8] whereas savings originating in agriculture are 43 percent of total savings. There will therefore be a flow of savings originating in the A sector into capital formation in the non-A sector, accounting for

[7] See "Quantitative Aspects of the Economic Growth of Nations: V. Capital Formation Proportions: International Comparisons for Recent Years," *Economic Development and Cultural Change*, VIII, 4 (July 1960), Table 15, p. 64.

[8] This can be calculated from the equation: $(0.60)r + (0.40)r = 3.0$. The rate of growth for the A sector, r, is then 1.364 percent, that for the non-A sector four times as high, or 5.456 percent. Multiplying the former by 0.60 yields the increment of the product of the A sector, or 0.818; multiplying the latter by 0.40 yields the increment of the product of the non-A sector, or 2.182; and the ratio of the increment in the A sector to increment in total product, and, on the assumption used, of the capital needs of the A sector to total capital needs, is then 0.818/3, or 27 percent.

16 out of 73, or somewhat less than a quarter of the latter.

The example is purely illustrative, and the discussion is designed only to bring out the variables that would have to be measured in empirical study. The rate of growth of the product of the non-A sector might well be more than four times that of the A sector. The incremental capital–output ratio for the A sector might well be distinctly lower than, rather than equal to, the capital–output ratio for the non-A sector—in some countries in some periods agricultural output could be increased significantly with little or no capital investment. If these two contingencies were to materialize, the flow of savings from agriculture to finance capital formation elsewhere would be relatively larger than is suggested in the illustration. On the other hand, we are dealing with domestic savings alone, disregarding capital imports that were quite important in the early phases of growth of several countries, such as Canada, Australia, and Scandinavia.

We now turn to the third factor contribution made by agriculture to the economic growth of a country—the provision of labor. Although this shift of labor from the A to the non-A sectors in the process of modern economic growth has become quite familiar, the magnitude of the migration and of the factor contribution involved may not have been given the attention that it deserves.

To begin with, we must stress the fact that through the periods under discussion and in almost all the countries, the crude (and refined) birth rates of the agricultural populations were distinctly higher than those of the nonagricultural; whereas the death rates were at least equal, if not lower, for the agricultural.[9] This means that the rate of natural increase was very much higher for the agricultural than for the nonagricultural population; and consequently for the agricultural than for the nonagricultural labor force.

The orders of magnitude can now be suggested. At the initial point of time, when the share of the A sector in the labor force was 75 percent, we may set the crude birth rate for the agricultural

[9] See a summary discussion in United Nations, *The Determinants and Consequences of Population Trends* (New York, 1953), p. 62 on urban-rural differentials in mortality and pp. 85–86 on urban-rural differentials in fertility. For more recent discussion of these differentials in fertility see the papers by Gwendolyn Johnson (pp. 36–72) and by Clyde Kiser (pp. 77–113), in Universities-National Bureau Committee on Economic Research, *Demographic and Economic Change in Developed Countries* (Princeton, N.J.: Princeton University Press, 1960), and T. Lynn Smith, "The Reproduction Rate in Latin America: Levels, Differentials and Trends," *Population Studies*, XII, 1 (July 1958), pp. 1–17.

population at about 40 per 1,000, with that for the nonagricultural at about 27 (the ratio of the former to the latter being roughly 1.5). If we set the crude death rates at 20 per 1,000 for both groups, the rate of natural increase for the two sectors, for population and hence for the labor force (with some lag), will be 20 and 7 per 1,000, respectively. Thus the rate of growth of the agricultural labor force, owing to its rate of natural increase, is almost three times that of the nonagricultural. Incidentally, on these assumptions the rate of natural increase for total population, that is, the countrywide rate, works out at 16.75 per 1,000.

Consider now the internal migration of the labor force that would be required over a decade for the share of the A sector in the labor force to decline from 75 to 70 percent, under the assumption of a closed population (i.e., no international migration). Over that decade, the total labor force would rise from 100 to 118.23, the labor force in the A sector would rise from 75 to 91.425, and that in the non-A sector from 25 to 26.805. To secure a 70-30 apportionment, the 91.425 in the A sector would have to be reduced by internal migration to 82.761—a migration out of the A sector of roughly 8.7 percent of the countrywide initial labor force, or over 9 percent of the labor force that *would* have been in the A sector at the end of the decade if not for internal migration.

This transfer of workers from the A to the non-A sector means a sizable capital contribution because each migrant is of working age and represents some investment in past rearing and training to maturity. What is the magnitude of this investment in human beings? Let us assume that every worker migrating from the A sector embodies outlays on rearing, education, and training equal to ten times the current product per worker in the A sector (this is a rough ratio, based on an average prior year's outlay of about six tenths of the current per capita income multiplied by 17, the age assumed at transfer). If, then, in each year of the decade something like 1.01 percent of the labor force in the A sector moves to the non-A sector (the difference between a rate of natural increase of 2 percent and 0.89 percent required by the conditions of the illustrative example), we have a transfer embodying outlays equal to 10.1 percent of the total income of the A sector. This, in the first interval, would be 10.1 percent of 60, or over 6 percent of total national product; but the addition to the factor endowment of the non-A sector is over 25 percent of its current product (10.1 as a percentage of 40).

The figures in the illustration could be modified in the light of empirical data, but they are realistic enough for us to draw some plausible conclusions. First, if we accept the interpretation of internal migration as a transfer of capital invested in human beings, this factor contribution of the A sector to the growth of the non-A sectors must have been quite large in the early and even later phases of modern economic growth—since internal migration of the labor force was from the A to the non-A sectors and sizable. In the illustration, the value of the transfer was estimated at over 6 percent of total current income, and it would have been easier, without violating the rules of plausibility, to raise this percentage significantly than to lower it. Yet under the assumptions of the illustration, total net savings in the economy were not more than 7 percent of national income. And, granting that the "contribution" in question depends upon the employment capacity of the non-A sector, we could still argue that the internal migration of labor from agriculture represents a large transfer of valuable resources to the non-A sectors and a large contribution to the country's economic growth. This conclusion has several implications, not the least of which is that the kind of investment in human beings that is, and can be, made in the A sector determines the quality of an important part of the labor force in, and hence of its contribution to the growth of, the non-A sector.

Second, if the share of the A sector in the labor force and the relative magnitude of labor transfers from it decline, there is bound to be a decline even in the absolute value of the factor transfers thus made, and most certainly in its proportion to the stock of labor already available in the non-A sector. After a while, although it may be fairly late in the course of modern economic development, the absolute numbers of workers in the A sector decline, and transfers that may be a large fraction of the current labor force in agriculture would mean only minor fractional additions to the labor force outside agriculture, and for the country as a whole.

Finally, it need hardly be pointed out that what is true of internal migration applies to the international movement of labor which through the nineteenth and early twentieth centuries assisted a number of rapidly developing countries. This migration was most often from the agricultural sector in one country to the non-A sector in another, and in that sense was similar to what we have been discussing—except that the factor contribution was to the economic growth of another country. At some time this may have had a curious effect on internal migration within the recipient country, impeding internal migration from at least some parts of the domestic A sector. But these aspects of the factor contribution of the A sector, while of great interest, would take us into an analysis of the growth process for different groups of countries that would be too detailed for treatment here.

Economic Growth
and Income Inequality

THE CENTRAL theme of this paper is the character and causes of long-term changes in the personal distribution of income. Does inequality in the distribution of income increase or decrease in the course of a country's economic growth? What factors determine the secular level and trends of income inequalities?

These are broad questions in a field of study that has been plagued by looseness in definitions, unusual scarcity of data, and pressures of strongly held opinions. Although we cannot completely avoid the resulting difficulties, it may help to specify the characteristics of the size-of-income distributions that we want to examine and the movements of which we want to explain.

Five specifications may be listed. First, incomes should be recorded and grouped for family-expenditure units, properly adjusted for the number of persons in each, rather than income recipients for whom the relations between receipt and use of income can be widely diverse. Second, the distribution should cover all units in a country rather than a segment either at the upper or lower tail. Third, if possible we should segregate the units whose main income earners are either still in the learning or already in the retired stage of their life cycle in order to avoid complicating the

This paper was the presidential address delivered at the Sixty-seventh Annual Meeting of the American Economic Association, Detroit, Michigan, December 29, 1954. Reprinted, by permission, from The American Economic Review, XLV, 1 (March 1955).

picture by including incomes *not* associated with full-time, full-fledged participation in economic activity. Fourth, income should be defined as it is now for national income in this country, that is, received by individuals, including income in kind, before and after direct taxes, excluding capital gains. Fifth, the units should be grouped by *secular* levels of income, free of cyclical and other transient disturbances.

For such a distribution of mature expenditure units by secular levels of income per capita, we should measure shares of some fixed ordinal groups—percentiles, deciles, quintiles, etc. In the underlying array the units should be classified by average income levels for a sufficiently long span so that they form income-status groups, say for a generation or about 25 years. Within such a period, even when classified by secular income levels, units may shift from one ordinal group to another. It would, therefore, be necessary and useful to study separately the relative share of units that, throughout the generation period of reference, were continuously within a specific ordinal group, and the share of the units that moved into that specific group, and this should be done for the shares of "residents" and "migrants" within all ordinal groups. Without such a long period of reference and the resulting separation between "resident" and "migrant" units at different relative income levels, the very distinction between "low" and "high" income classes loses its meaning, particularly in a study of long-term changes in shares and in inequalities in the distribution. To say, for example, that the "lower" income classes gained or lost during the last twenty years in that their share of total income increased or decreased has meaning only if the units have been classified as members of the "lower" classes throughout those 20 years; for those who have moved into or out of those classes recently, such a statement has no significance.

Furthermore, if one may add a final touch to what is beginning to look like a statistical economist's pipe dream, we should be able to trace secular income levels not only through a single generation but at least through two, connecting the incomes of a given generation with those of its immediate descendants. We could then distinguish units that, throughout a given generation, remain within one ordinal group and whose children, through *their* generation, are also within that group, from units that remain within a group through their generation but whose children move up or down on the relative economic scale in their time. The number of possible combinations and permutations becomes large, but it should not obscure the main design of the income structure called for—the classification by long-term income status of a given generation and of its immediate descendants. If members of society—as producers, consumers, savers, and decision-makers on secular problems—react to long-term changes in income levels and shares, data on such an income structure are essential. An economic society can then be judged by the secular level of the income share that it provides for a given generation and for its children. The important corollary is that the study of long-term changes in the income distribution must distinguish between changes in the shares of resident groups—resident within either one or two generations—and changes in the income shares of groups that, judged by their secular levels, migrate upward or downward on the income scale.

Even if we had data to approximate the income structure just outlined, the broad question posed at the start—how income inequality changes in the process of a country's economic growth—could be answered only for growth under defined economic and social conditions. And, in fact, we shall deal with this question in terms of the experience of the now developed countries which grew under the aegis of the business enterprise. But even with this limitation, there are no statistics that can be used directly for the purpose of measuring the *secular* income structure. Indeed, I have difficulty in visualizing how such information could practicably be collected—a difficulty that may be due to lack of familiarity with the studies of our colleagues in demography and sociology who have concerned themselves with problems of generation or intergeneration mobility and status. But although we now lack data directly relevant to the secular income structure, the setting up of reasonably clear although difficult specifications is not merely an exercise in perfectionism. For if these specifications do approximate, and I trust that they do, the real core of our interest when we talk about shares of economic classes or long-term changes in these shares, then proper disclosure of our meaning and intentions is vital. It forces us to evaluate critically the data that are available; it prevents us from jumping to conclusions based on these inadequate data; it reduces the loss and waste of time involved in mechanical manipulations of the type represented by Pareto-curve-fitting to groups of data whose meaning, in terms of income concept, unit of observation, and proportion of the total universe covered, remains distressingly vague; and most important of all, it propels us toward a deliberate construction of testable bridges between the available data and the income structure that is the real focus of our interest.

Trends in Income Inequality

Forewarned of the difficulties, we turn to the available data. These data, even when relating to complete populations, invariably classify units by income for a given year. From our standpoint, this is their major limitation. Because the data often do not permit many size-groupings, and because the difference between annual income incidence and longer-term income status has less effect if the number of classes is small and the limits of each class are wide, we use a few wide classes. This does not resolve the difficulty; and there are others due to the scantiness of data for long periods; inadequacy of the unit used, which is, at best, a family and very often a reporting unit; errors in the data; and so on through a long list. Consequently, the trends in the income structure can be only dimly discerned, and the results must be considered preliminary informed guesses.

The data are for the United States, England, and Germany, a scant sample but at least a starting point for some inferences concerning long-term changes in the presently developed countries. The general conclusion is that the relative distribution of income, as measured by annual income incidence in rather broad classes, has been moving toward equality, with these trends particularly noticeable since the 1920's but beginning perhaps in the period before World War I.

Let me cite some figures, all for income before direct taxes, in support of this impression. In the United States, in the distribution of income among families (excluding single individuals), the share of the two lowest quintiles rises from 13.5 percent in 1929 to 18 percent in the years after World War II (average of 1944, 1946, 1947, and 1950); whereas the share of the top quintile declines from 55 to 44 percent, and that of the top 5 percent from 31 to 20 percent. In the United Kingdom, the share of the top 5 percent of units declines from 46 percent in 1880 to 43 percent in 1910 or 1913, to 33 percent in 1929, to 31 percent in 1938, and to 24 percent in 1947; the share of the lower 85 percent remains fairly constant between 1880 and 1913, between 41 and 43 percent, but then rises to 46 percent in 1929 and 55 percent in 1947. In Prussia, income inequality increases slightly between 1875 and 1913, the share of the top quintile rising from 48 to 50 percent, of the top 5 percent from 26 to 30 percent. The share of the lower 60 percent, however, remains about the same. In Saxony, the change between 1880 and 1913 is minor: the share of the two lowest quintiles declines from 15 to 14.5 percent; that of the third quintile rises from 12 to 13 percent, of the fourth quintile from 16.5 to about 18 percent; that of the top quintile declines from 56.5 to 54.5 percent, and of the top 5 percent from 34 to 33 percent. In Germany as a whole, relative income inequality drops fairly sharply from 1913 to the 1920's, apparently due to decimation of large fortunes and property incomes during the war and inflation, but then begins to return to prewar levels during the depression of the 1930's.[1]

Even for what they are meant to represent, let alone as approximations to shares in distributions by secular income levels, the data are such that differences of two or three percentage points cannot be assigned significance. Judged by its general weight and consensus, the evidence—which unfortunately is limited to a few countries —justifies a tentative impression of constancy in the relative distribution of income before taxes, followed by some narrowing of relative income inequality after World War I, or earlier.

Three aspects of this finding should be stressed. First, the data are for income before direct taxes and exclude contributions by government (e.g., relief and free assistance). It is fair to argue that both the proportion and progressivity of direct taxes and the pro-

[1] The following sources were used in calculating the figures cited:

United States. For recent years we used *Income Distribution by Size, 1944–1950* (Washington, 1953) and Selma Goldsmith and others, "Size Distribution of Income Since the Mid-Thirties," *Review of Economic Statistics,* XXXVI (February 1954), pp. 1–32; for 1929, the Brookings Institution data as adjusted in Simon Kuznets, *Shares of Upper Income Groups in Income and Savings* (New York, 1953), p. 220.

United Kingdom. For 1938 and 1947, Dudley Seers, *The Levelling of Income since 1938* (Oxford, 1951), p. 39; for 1929, Colin Clark, *National Income and Outlay* (London, 1937), Table 47, p. 109; for 1880, 1910, and 1913, A. Bowley, *The Change in the Distribution of the National Income, 1880–1913* (Oxford, 1920).

Germany. For the constituent areas (Prussia, Saxony, and others) for years before World War I, based on S. Prokopovich, *National Income of Western European Countries* (published in Moscow in the 1920's). Some summary results are given in Prokopovich, "The Distribution of National Income," *Economic Journal,* XXXVI (March 1926), pp. 69–82. See also "Das Deutsche Volkseinkommen vor und nach dem Kriege," *Einzelschrift zur Statistik des Deutschen Reichs,* No. 24 (Berlin, 1932), and W. S. and E. S. Woytinsky, *World Population and Production* (New York, 1953), Table 192, p. 709.

portion of total income of individuals accounted for by government assistance to the less privileged economic groups have grown during recent decades. This is certainly true of the United States and the United Kingdom, but in the case of Germany is subject to further examination. It follows that the distribution of income after direct taxes and including free contributions by government would show an even greater narrowing of inequality in developed countries than size distributions of pretax, ex-government-benefits income similar to those for the United States and the United Kingdom.

Second, such stability or reduction in the inequality of the percentage shares was accompanied by significant rises in real income per capita. The countries now classified as developed have enjoyed rising per capita incomes except during catastrophic periods such as years of armed conflict. Hence, if the shares of groups classified by annual income position can be viewed as approximations to shares of groups classified by secular income levels, a constant percentage share of a given group means that its per capita real income is rising at the same rate as the average for the country; and a reduction in inequality of the shares means that the per capita income of the lower-income groups is rising at a higher rate than the per capita income of the upper-income groups.

The third point can be put in the form of a question. Do the distributions by annual incomes properly reflect trends in distribution by secular incomes? As technology and economic performance rise to higher levels, incomes are less subject to transient disturbances, not necessarily of the cyclical order that can be recognized and allowed for by reference to business cycle chronology, but of a more irregular type. If in the earlier years the economic fortunes of units were subject to greater vicissitudes—poor crops for some farmers, natural calamity losses for some nonfarm business units, if the overall proportion of individual entrepreneurs whose incomes were subject to such calamities, more yesterday but some even today, was larger in earlier decades, these earlier distributions of income would be more affected by transient disturbances. The temporarily unfortunate might crowd the lower quintiles and depress their shares unduly, and the temporarily fortunate might dominate the top quintile and raise its share unduly—proportionately more than in the distributions for later years. If so, distributions by longer-term average incomes might show less reduction in inequality than do the distributions by annual incomes; they might even show an opposite trend.

Probably this qualification would not upset a narrowing of inequality as marked as that for the United States, and in as short a period as twenty-five years. Nor is it likely to affect the persistent downward drift in the spread of the distributions in the United Kingdom. But I must admit a strong element of judgment in deciding how far this qualification modifies the finding of long-term stability followed by reduction in income inequality in the few developed countries for which it is observed or is likely to be revealed by existing data. The important point is that the qualification is relevant; it suggests need for further study if we are to learn much from the available data concerning the secular income structure, and such study is likely to yield results of interest in themselves in their bearing upon the problem of trends in temporal instability of income flows to individual units or to economically significant groups of units in different sectors of the national economy.

An Attempt at Explanation

If the above summary of trends in the secular income structure of developed countries comes perilously close to pure guesswork, an attempt to explain these dimly discernible trends may surely seem foolhardy. Yet we must make the attempt, if only to bring to the surface some factors that may have been at play; induce a search for data bearing upon these factors; and thus confirm or revise our impressions of the trends themselves. Such preliminary speculations are useful provided it is recognized that we are at a relatively early stage in a long process of interplay among tentative summaries of evidence, preliminary hypotheses, and search for additional evidence that might lead to reformulation and revisions—as bases for new analysis and further search.

The present instalment of initial speculation may be introduced by saying that a long-term constancy, let alone reduction, of inequality in the secular income structure is a puzzle. For at least two groups of forces in the long-term operation of developed countries make for *widening* inequality in the distribution of income before taxes and excluding contributions by governments. The first group relates to the concentration of savings in the upper income brackets. According to all recent studies of the apportionment of income between consumption and savings, only the upper income groups save; the total savings of groups below the top decile are fairly close to zero. For example, the top 5 percent of units in the United States appear to account for almost two thirds of individuals' savings, and the top decile accounts for almost all of it. What is particularly important is that the inequality in distribution of savings is greater than that in the distribution of property incomes, and hence of assets.[2] Granted that this finding is based on distribution of annual income, and that a distribution by secular levels would show less inequality in income and correspondingly less concentration of savings, the inequality in savings would still remain fairly sharp, perhaps more so than in holdings of assets. Other conditions being equal, the cumulative effect of such inequality in savings would be the concentration of an *increasing* proportion of income-yielding assets in the hands of the upper groups—a basis for larger income shares of these groups and their descendants.

The second source of the puzzle lies in the industrial structure of the income distribution. An invariable accompaniment of growth in developed countries is the shift away from agriculture, a process usually referred to as industrialization and urbanization. The income distribution of the total population, in the simplest model, may therefore be viewed as a combination of the income distributions of the rural and of the urban populations. What little we know of the structures of these two components reveals that: (1) the average per capita income of the rural population is usually lower than that of the urban [3]; (2) inequality in the distribution for the rural population is somewhat narrower than in that for the urban population—even when based on annual income; and this difference would probably be greater for distributions by secular income levels.[4] Operating with this simple model, what conclusions do we reach? First, all other conditions being equal, the increasing

[2] See Kuznets, *op. cit.*, particularly Chs. 2 and 6.

[3] The lower per capita income of the agricultural or rural population compared with that of urban is fairly well established for this country by states, and for many other countries (see, e.g., a summary table of closely related measures of product and workers engaged, for various divisions of the productive system, in Colin Clark, *Conditions of Economic Progress*, 2d ed., London, 1951, pp. 316–318). The same table suggests, for the countries with sufficiently long records, a stable or increasing relative difference between per worker product in agriculture and per worker product in other sectors of the economy.

[4] This is true of the U.S. distributions before World War II (see sources cited in footnote 1); in later years the difference seems to have disappeared. It is true of the distributions for Prussia, cited by Prokopovich, and most conspicuous for India today as shown in the rough distributions by M. Mukherjee and A. K. Ghosh in "The Pattern of Income and Expenditures in the Indian Union: A Tentative Study," *International Statistical Conferences* (December 1951), Calcutta, India, Part III, pp. 49–68.

weight of urban population means an increasing share for the more unequal of the two component distributions. Second, the relative difference in per capita income between the rural and urban populations does not necessarily decrease in the process of economic growth: indeed, there is some evidence to suggest that it is stable at best. If this is so, inequality in the total income distribution should increase.

Two questions then arise: First, why does the share of the top income groups show no rise over time if the concentration of savings has a cumulative effect? Second, why does income inequality decline and particularly why does the share of the lower income groups rise if the weight of the more unequal urban income distribution rises and the relative difference between per capita urban and per capita rural incomes increases?

The first question has been discussed elsewhere, although the results are still preliminary hypotheses,[5] and it would be impossible to do more here than summarize them briefly.

FACTORS COUNTERACTING THE CONCENTRATION OF SAVING · One group of factors counteracting the cumulative effect of concentration of savings upon upper-income shares is legislative interference and "political" decisions. These may be aimed at limiting the cumulation of property directly through inheritance taxes and other explicit capital levies. They may produce similar effects indirectly, for example by government-permitted or -induced inflation which reduces the economic value of accumulated wealth stored in fixed-price securities or other properties not fully responsive to price changes; or by legal restriction of the *yield* on accumulated property, as happened recently in the form of rent controls or of artificially low long-term interest rates maintained by the government to protect the market for its own bonds.

To discuss this complex of processes is beyond the scope of this paper, but its existence and possible wide effect should be noted and one point emphasized. All these interventions, even when not directly aimed at limiting the effects of accumulation of past savings

[5] Some elements of the discussion appeared in "Proportion of Capital Formation to National Product," *American Economic Review*, 1951 Proceedings, XLII (May 1952), pp. 507–526. A more elaborate statement is presented in "International Differences in Capital Formation and Financing" (particularly Appendix C, "Levels and Trends in Income Shares of Upper Income Groups"), in Moses Abramovitz, ed., *Capital Formation and Economic Growth* (Princeton, N.J.: Princeton University Press, 1955).

in the hands of the few, do reflect the view of society on the long-term utility of wide income inequalities. This view is a vital force that would operate in democratic societies even if there were no other counteracting factors. This should be borne in mind in connection with *changes* in this view even in developed countries, which result from the process of growth and constitute a re-evaluation of the need for income inequalities as a source of savings for economic growth. The result of such changes would be an increasing pressure of legal and political decisions on upper-income shares —increasing as a country moves to higher economic levels.

We turn to three other, less obvious groups of factors countervailing the cumulative effects of concentration of savings. The first is demographic. In the presently developed countries there have been differential rates of increase between the rich and the poor— family control having begun in the former. Hence, even disregarding migration, one can argue that the top 5 percent of 1870 and its descendants would account for a significantly smaller percentage of the population in 1920. This is even more likely in a country like the United States with its substantial immigration—usually entering the income distribution at the lower income levels, and may be less likely in a country from which the poor have emigrated. The top 5 percent of population in 1920 is, therefore, comprised only partly of the descendants of the top 5 percent of 1870; perhaps half or a larger fraction must have originated in the lower income brackets of 1870. This means that the period during which effects of concentration of savings can be assumed to have cumulated to raise the income share of any fixed ordinal group (whether it be the top 1, 5, or 10 percent of the population) is much shorter than the fifty years in the span; and hence these effects are much weaker than they would have been if the top 5 percent of 1870 had, through their descendants, filled completely the ranks of the top 5 percent of the population of 1920. Although the cumulative effect of savings may be to raise the relative income of a *progressively diminishing* top proportion of total population, their effect on the relative share of a *fixed* top proportion of the population is much reduced.

The second group of forces resides in the very nature of a dynamic economy with relative freedom of individual opportunity. In such a society technological change is rampant and property assets that originated in older industries almost inevitably have a diminishing proportional weight in the total because of the more rapid growth of younger industries. Unless the descendants of a high income group manage to shift their accumulating assets into new fields and participate with new entrepreneurs in the growing share of the new and more profitable industries, the long-range returns on their property holdings are likely to be significantly lower than those of the more recent entrants into the class of substantial asset holders. "From shirt-sleeves to shirt-sleeves in three generations" probably exaggerates the effects of this dynamism of a growing economy: there are, among the upper-income groups of today, many descendants of the upper-income groups of more than three or even four generations ago. But the adage is realistic in the sense that a *long unbroken* sequence of connection with rising industries and hence with major sources of continued large property incomes is exceedingly rare; that the successful great entrepreneurs of today are rarely sons of the great and successful entrepreneurs of yesterday.

The third group of factors is suggested by the importance, even in the upper-income brackets, of service income. At any given time, only a limited part of the income differential of a top group is accounted for by the concentration of property yields: much of it comes from the high level of service income (professional and entrepreneurial earnings and the like). The secular rise in the upper incomes due to this source is likely to be less marked than in the service incomes of lower brackets, and for two somewhat different reasons. First, insofar as high levels of service incomes of given upper units are due to individual excellence (as is true of many professional and entrepreneurial pursuits), there is much less incentive for and possibility of keeping such incomes at continued high relative levels. Hence, the service incomes of the descendants of an *initially high* level unit are not likely to show as strong an upward trend as the incomes for the large body of population at lower-income levels. Second, a substantial part of the rising trend in per capita income is due to interindustry shift, that is, a shift of workers from lower-income to higher-income industries. The possibilities of rise due to such interindustry shifts in the service incomes of the initially high-income groups are much more limited than for the population as a whole: they are already in high-income occupations and industries and the range for them toward higher paid occupations is more narrowly circumscribed.

These three groups of factors, even disregarding legislative and political intervention, are all characteristics of a dynamic growing economy. The differentials in rate of natural increase between the upper- and the lower-income groups are true only of a rapidly growing population—with or without immigration—but accompanied by declining death and birth rates, a demographic pattern associated in the past only with the growing Western economies. The impact of new industries on obsolescence of already established wealth as a source of property income is clearly a function of rapid growth, and the more rapid the growth the greater the impact will be. The effect of interindustry shifts on the rise of per capita income, particularly of lower-income groups, is also a function of growth since only in a growing economy is there much shift in the relative importance of the several industrial sectors. One can then say, in general, that the basic factor militating against the rise in upper-income shares that would be produced by the cumulative effects of concentration of savings, is the dynamism of a growing and free economic society.

Yet although the discussion answers the original question, it yields no determinate answer as to whether the trend in income shares of upper groups is upward, downward, or constant. Even for the specific question discussed, a determinate answer depends upon the relative balance of factors—continuous concentration of savings making for an increasing share, and the offsetting forces tending to cancel this effect. To tell what the trend of upper-income shares is likely to be, we need to know much more about the weights of these conflicting pressures. Moreover, the discussion has brought to the surface factors that, in and of themselves, may cause either an upward or a downward trend in the share of upper-income groups and hence in income inequality—in distributions of annual or of secular income. For example, the new entrants into the upper groups—the upward "migrants"—who rise either because of exceptional ability or attachment to new industries or for a variety of other reasons—may be entering the fixed upper group of say the top 5 percent with an income differential—either annual or long-term—that may be relatively *greater* than that of entrants in the preceding generation. Nothing in the argument so far excludes this possibility, which would mean a rise in the share of upper-income groups, even if the share of the old "resident" part remains constant or declines. Even disregarding other factors that will be noted in the next section, no firm conclusion about trends of upper-income shares can be derived from the bare model discussed. Search for further data might yield evidence that would permit a reasonably rough but determinate conclusion, but I have no such evidence at hand.

THE SHIFT FROM AGRICULTURAL TO NONAGRICULTURAL SECTORS ·
What about the trend toward greater inequality due to the shift from the agricultural to the nonagricultural sectors? In view of the importance of industrialization and urbanization in the process of economic growth, their implications for trends in the income distribution should be explored, even though we have neither the necessary data nor a reasonably complete theoretical model.

The implications can be brought out most clearly with the help of a numerical illustration. This table deals with two sectors: agriculture (A) and all others (B). For each sector we assume two percentage distributions of total sector income among sector deciles: one (E) is of moderate inequality, with the shares starting at 5.5 percent for the lowest decile and rising one percentage point from decile to decile to reach 14.5 percent for the top decile; the other (U) is much more unequal, the shares starting at one percent for the lowest decile, and rising two percentage points from decile to decile to reach 19 percent for the top decile. We assign per capita incomes to each sector: 50 units to A and 100 units to B in case I (lines 1–10 in the illustration); 50 to A and 200 to B in case II (lines 11–20). Finally, we allow the proportion of the number in sector A to the total number to decline from 0.8 to 0.2.

The numerical illustration is only a partial summary of the calculations, showing the shares of the lowest and highest quintiles in the income distribution for the total population under different assumptions.[6] The basic assumptions used throughout are that the per capita income of sector B (nonagricultural) is always higher than that of sector A; that the proportion of sector A in the total number declines; and that the inequality of the income distribution within sector A may be as wide as that within sector B but not

[6] The underlying calculations are quite simple. For each case we distinguish 20 cells within the total distribution—sets of ten deciles for each sector. For each cell we compute the percentage shares of both number and income in the number and income of total population, and hence also the relative per capita income of each cell. The cells are then arrayed in increasing order of their relative per capita income and cumulated. In the resulting cumulative distributions of number and countrywide income we establish, by arithmetic interpolation, if interpolation is needed, the percentage shares in total income of the successive quintiles of the country's population.

	Proportion of number in sector A to total number						
	0.8 (1)	0.7 (2)	0.6 (3)	0.5 (4)	0.4 (5)	0.3 (6)	0.2 (7)
I. Per capita income of sector A = 50; of sector B = 100							
1. Per capita income of total population	60	65	70	75	80	85	90
Distribution (E) for both sectors							
2. Share of 1st quintile	10.5	9.9	9.6	9.3	9.4	9.8	10.2
3. Share of 5th quintile	34.2	35.8	35.7	34.7	33.2	31.9	30.4
4. Range (3–2)	23.7	25.9	26.1	25.3	23.9	22.1	20.2
Distribution (U) for both sectors							
5. Share of 1st quintile	3.8	3.8	3.7	3.7	3.8	3.8	3.9
6. Share of 5th quintile	40.7	41.9	42.9	42.7	41.5	40.2	38.7
7. Range (6–5)	36.8	38.1	39.1	39.0	37.8	36.4	34.8
Distribution (E) for sector A, (U) for sector B							
8. Share of 1st quintile	9.3	8.3	7.4	6.7	6.0	5.4	4.9
9. Share of 5th quintile	37.7	41.0	42.9	42.7	41.5	40.2	38.7
10. Range (9–8)	28.3	32.7	35.4	36.0	35.5	34.8	33.8
II. Per capita income of sector A = 50; of sector B = 200							
11. Per capita income of total population	80	95	110	125	140	155	170
Distribution (E) for both sectors							
12. Share of 1st quintile	7.9	6.8	6.1	5.6	5.4	5.4	5.9
13. Share of 5th quintile	50.0	49.1	45.5	41.6	38.0	35.0	32.2
14. Range (13–12)	42.1	42.3	39.4	36.0	32.6	29.6	26.3
Distribution (U) for both sectors							
15. Share of 1st quintile	3.1	2.9	2.7	2.6	2.6	2.7	3.1
16. Share of 5th quintile	52.7	56.0	54.5	51.2	47.4	44.1	40.9
17. Range (16–15)	49.6	53.1	51.8	48.6	44.8	41.4	37.9
Distribution (E) for sector A, (U) for sector B							
18. Share of 1st quintile	7.4	6.2	5.4	4.7	4.2	3.9	3.8
19. Share of 5th quintile	51.6	56.0	54.6	51.2	47.4	44.1	40.9
20. Range (19–18)	44.2	49.8	49.2	46.5	43.2	40.2	37.2

For methods of calculating the shares of quintiles, see text above and footnote 6. Some differences will not check because of rounding.

wider. With the assumptions concerning three sets of factors—intersector differences in per capita income, intrasector distributions, and sector weights—varying within the limitations just indicated, the following conclusions are suggested:

First, if the per capita income differential increases, or if the income distribution is more unequal for sector B than for sector A, or if both conditions are present, the rise over time in the relative weight of sector B causes a marked increase in inequality in the countrywide income distribution. We have here a demonstration of the effects upon trends in income inequality of interindustry shifts away from agriculture discussed above (pp. 264–265).

Second, if the intrasector income distribution is the same for both sectors, and the widening inequality in the countrywide income distribution is due only to the increasing per capita income differential in favor of sector B, such widening is greater when the intrasector income distributions are characterized by moderate rather than wide inequality. Thus, if the intrasector distributions are of the E type, the range in the countrywide distribution widens from 23.7 to 26.3 as the proportion of A drops from 0.8 to 0.2 and as the ratio of per capita income of sector B to that of sector A changes from 2 to 4 (see line 4, col. 1, and line 14, col. 7). For the U distributions, the range, under identical conditions, widens only from 36.8 to 37.9 (see line 7, col. 1, and line 17, col. 7). This difference is revealed more clearly by the change in the share of the first quintile, which bears the brunt of widening inequality: for the E distribution, the share drops from 10.5 (line 2, col. 1) to 5.9 (line 12, col. 7); for the U distribution, from 3.8 (line 5, col. 1) to 3.1 (line 15, col. 7).

Third, if the per capita income differential between sectors is constant, but the intrasector distribution of B is more unequal than that of A, the widening inequality in the countrywide distribution is the greater, the lower the assumed per capita income differential. Thus for a differential of 2 to 1, the range widens from 28.3 when the proportion of A is 0.8 (line 10, col. 1) to 36.0 at the peak when the proportion of A is 0.5 (line 10, col. 4) and is still 33.8 when the proportion of A drops to 0.2 (line 10, col. 7). For a per capita income differential of 4 to 1, the widening of the range at the maximum is only from 44.2 (line 20, col. 1) to 49.8 (line 20, col. 2) and then the range declines to 37.2 (line 20, col. 7), well below the initial level.

Fourth, the assumptions utilized in the numerical illustration—of a rise in proportions of total number in sector B, of greater inequality in the distribution within sector B, and of the growing excess of per capita income in B over that in A—yield a decline in the share of the first quintile that is much more conspicuous than the rise in the share of the fifth quintile. Thus the share of the first quintile, with the proportion of A at 0.8, distribution in B more unequal than in A, and a per capita income differential of 2 to 1, is 9.3 (line 8, col. 1). As we shift to a proportion of A of 0.2, and a per capita income differential of 4 to 1, the share of the first quintile drops to 3.8 (line 18, col. 7). Under the same conditions, the share of the fifth quintile changes from 37.7 (line 9, col. 1) to 40.9 (line 19, col. 7).

Fifth, even if the differential in per capita income between the two sectors remains constant and the intrasector distributions are identical for the two sectors, the mere shift in the proportions of numbers produces slight but significant changes in the distribution for the country as a whole. In general, as the proportion of A drifts from 0.8 downward, the range tends first to widen and then to diminish. When the per capita income differential is low (2 to 1), the widening of the range reaches a peak close to the middle of the series, that is, at a proportion of A equal to 0.6 (lines 4 and 7); and the movements in the range tend to be rather limited. When the per capita income differential is large (4 to 1), the range contracts as soon as the proportion of A passes the level of 0.7, and the decline in the range is quite substantial (lines 14 and 17).

Sixth, of particular bearing upon the shares of upper income groups is the finding that the share of the top quintile declines as the proportion of A falls below a certain, rather high fraction of total numbers. There is not a single case in the illustration in which the share of the fifth quintile fails to decline, either throughout or through a substantial segment of the sequence in the downward movement of the proportion of A from 0.8 to 0.2. In lines 6 and 9, the share of the fifth quintile declines beyond the point at which the proportion of A is 0.6; and in all other relevant lines the downward trend in the share of the fifth quintile sets in earlier. The reason lies, of course, in the fact that with increasing industrialization, the growing weight of the nonagricultural sector, with its higher per capita income, raises the per capita income for the whole economy, and yet per capita income within each sector and the intrasector distributions are kept constant. Under such conditions, the upper shares would fail to decline only if there were either a greater rise in per capita income of sector B than in that of sector A, or increasing inequality in the intrasector distribution of sector B.

Several other conjectural conclusions could be drawn with additional variations in assumptions, and multiplication of sectors beyond the two distinguished in the illustration. But even in this simple model the variety of possible patterns is impressive, and one is forced to the view that much more empirical information is needed to permit a proper choice of specific assumptions and constants. Granted that several of the conclusions could be generalized in formal mathematical terms, useful inferences would be within our reach only if we knew more about the specific sector distributions and the levels and trends in per capita income differentials among the sectors.

If then we limit ourselves to what is known or can be plausibly assumed, the following inferences can be suggested. We know that per capita income is greater in sector B than in sector A; that, at best, the per capita income differential between sectors A and B has been fairly constant (e.g., in the United States) and has perhaps more often increased; that the proportion of sector A in total numbers has diminished. Then, if we start with an intrasector distribution of B more unequal than for A, we would expect results suggested by either lines 8–10 or 18–20. In the former case the range widens as the proportion of A drops from 0.8 to 0.5, and then narrows. In the latter case, the range declines beyond the point at which the proportion of A is 0.7. But in both cases, the share of the first quintile declines, and fairly appreciably and continuously (see lines 8 and 18). The magnitude and continuity of the decline are partly the result of the specific assumptions made, but one would be justified in arguing that within the broad limits suggested by the illustration, the assumption of greater inequality in the intrasector distribution for sector B than for sector A, yields a downward trend in the share of the lower income groups. Yet we find no such trend in the empirical evidence that we have. Can we assume that in the earlier periods the internal distribution for sector B was not more unequal than for sector A, despite the more recent indications that urban income distribution is more unequal than the rural?

There is, obviously, room for conjecture. It seems most plausible to assume that in earlier periods of industrialization, even when the nonagricultural population was still relatively small in the total, its income distribution was more unequal than that of the agricultural population. This would be particularly so during the periods when industrialization and urbanization were proceeding apace and the urban population was being swelled, and fairly rapidly, by immigrants—either from the country's agricultural areas or from abroad. Under these conditions, the urban population would run the full gamut from low-income positions of recent entrants to the economic peaks of the established top income groups. The urban income inequalities might be assumed to be far wider than those for the agricultural population which was organized in relatively small individual enterprises (large-scale units were rarer then than now).

If we grant the assumption of wider inequality of distribution in sector B, the shares of the lower-income brackets should have shown a downward trend. Yet the earlier summary of empirical evidence indicates that during the last 50 to 75 years there has been no widening in income inequality in the developed countries but, on the contrary, some narrowing within the last two to four decades. It follows that the intrasector distribution—either for sector A or for sector B—must have shown sufficient narrowing of inequality to offset the increase called for by the factors discussed. Specifically, the shares of the *lower* income groups in sector A or B or both must have increased sufficiently to offset the decline that would otherwise have been produced by a combination of the elements shown in the numerical illustration.

This narrowing in inequality, the offsetting rise in the shares of the lower brackets, most likely occurred in the income distribution for the urban groups, in sector B. Although it may also have been present in sector A, it would have had a more limited effect on the inequality in the countrywide income distribution because of the rapidly diminishing weight of sector A in the total. Nor was such a narrowing of income inequality in agriculture likely: with industrialization, a higher level of technology permitted larger-scale units and, in the United States for example, sharpened the contrast between the large and successful business farmers and the subsistence sharecroppers of the South. Furthermore, since we accept the assumption of *initially* narrower inequality in the internal distribution of income in sector A than in sector B, any significant reduction in inequality in the former is less likely than in the latter.

Hence we may conclude that the major offset to the widening of income inequality associated with the shift from agriculture and the countryside to industry and the city must have been a rise in the income share of the lower groups within the nonagricultural sector of the population. This provides a lead for exploration in what seems to me a most promising direction: consideration of the pace and character of the economic growth of the urban population, with particular reference to the relative position of lower income groups. Much is to be said for the notion that once the early turbulent phases of industrialization and urbanization had passed, a variety of forces converged to bolster the economic position of the lower-income groups within the urban population. The very fact that after a while an increasing proportion of the urban population was "native"—born in cities rather than in the rural areas and hence more able to take advantage of the possibilities of city life in preparation for the economic struggle—meant a better chance for organization and adaptation, a better basis for securing greater income shares than was possible for the newly "immigrant" population coming from the countryside or from abroad. The increasing efficiency of the older, established urban population should also be taken into account. Furthermore, in democratic societies the growing political power of the urban lower-income groups led to a variety of protective and supporting legislation, much of it aimed to counteract the worst effects of rapid industrialization and urbanization and to support the claims of the broad masses for more adequate shares of the growing income of the country. Space does not permit the discussion of demographic, political, and social considerations that could explain the offsets to the declines in the shares of the lower groups, declines otherwise deducible from the trends suggested in the numerical illustration.

Other Trends Related to Those in Income Inequality

One aspect of the conjectural conclusion just reached deserves emphasis because of its possible interrelation with other important elements in the process and theory of economic growth. The scanty empirical evidence suggests that the narrowing of income inequality in the developed countries is relatively recent and probably did not characterize the earlier stages of their growth. Likewise, the various factors that have been suggested above would explain stability and narrowing in income inequality in the later rather than in the earlier phases of industrialization and urbanization. Indeed, they would suggest widening inequality in these early phases, especially in the older countries where the emergence of the new industrial system had shattering effects on long-established preindustrial economic and social institutions. This timing characteristic is particularly applicable to factors bearing upon the lower income groups: the dislocating effects of the agricultural and industrial revolutions, combined with the "swarming" of population incident upon a rapid decline in death rates and the maintenance or even rise of birth rates, would be unfavorable to the relative economic position of lower-income groups. Furthermore, there may also have been a preponderance in the earlier periods of factors favoring maintenance or increase in the shares of top income groups: insofar as their position was bolstered by gains arising out of new industries, by an unusually rapid rate of creation of new fortunes, we would expect these forces to be relatively stronger in the early phases of industrialization than in the later when the pace of industrial growth slackens.

One might thus assume a long swing in the inequality characterizing the secular income structure: widening in the early phases of economic growth when the transition from the preindustrial civilization was most rapid; becoming stabilized for a while; and then narrowing in the later phases. This long secular swing would be most pronounced for older countries where the dislocation effects of the earlier phases of modern economic growth were most conspicuous; but it might be found also in the "younger" countries like the United States, if the period preceding marked industrialization could be compared with the early phases of industrialization, and if the latter could be compared with the subsequent phases of greater maturity.

If there is some evidence for assuming this long swing in relative inequality in the distribution of income before direct taxes and excluding free benefits from government, there is surely a stronger case for assuming a long swing in inequality of income net of direct taxes and including government benefits. Progressivity of income taxes and, indeed, their very importance characterize only the more recent phases of development of the presently developed countries; in narrowing income inequality they must have accentuated the downward phase of the long swing, contributing to the reversal of trend in the secular widening and narrowing of income inequality.

No empirical evidence is available for checking this conjecture of a long secular swing in income inequality;[7] nor can the phases be dated precisely. However, to make it more specific, I would place the early phase in which income inequality might have been widening, from about 1780 to 1850 in England; from about 1840 to 1890, and particularly from 1870 on in the United States; and from the 1840's to the 1890's in Germany. I would put the phase of narrowing income inequality somewhat later in the United States and

---

[7] Prokopovich's data on Prussia, from the source cited in footnote 1, indicate a substantial widening in income inequality in the early period. The share of the lower 90 percent of the population declines from 73 percent in 1854 to 65 percent in 1875; the share of the top 5 percent rises from 21 to 25 percent. But I do not know enough about the data for the early years to evaluate the reliability of the finding.

Germany than in England—perhaps beginning with World War I in the former and in the last quarter of the nineteenth century in the latter.

Is there a possible relation between this secular swing in income inequality and the long swing in other important components of the growth process? For the older countries a long swing is observed in the rate of growth of population—the upward phase represented by acceleration in the rate of growth reflecting the early reduction in the death rate which was not offset by a decline in the birth rate (and in some cases was accompanied by a rise in the birth rate); and the downward phase represented by a shrinking in the rate of growth reflecting the more pronounced downward trend in the birth rate. Again, in the older countries, and also perhaps in the younger, there may have been a secular swing in the rate of urbanization, in the sense that the proportional additions to urban population and the measures of internal migration that produced this shift of population probably increased for a while from the earlier, much lower levels; but then tended to diminish as urban population came to dominate the country and as the rural reservoirs of migration became proportionally much smaller. For old, and perhaps for young countries also, there must have been a secular swing in the proportions of savings or capital formation to total economic product. Per capita product in preindustrial times was not large enough to permit as high a nationwide rate of saving or capital formation as was attained in the course of industrial development: this is suggested by comparisons between current net capital formation rates of 3 to 5 percent of national product in underdeveloped countries and of 10 to 15 percent in developed countries. If then, at least in the older countries, and perhaps even in the younger ones—before initiation of the process of modern development—we begin with low secular levels in the savings proportions, there would be a rise in the early phases to appreciably higher levels. We also know that during recent periods the net capital formation proportion, and even the gross, failed to rise and perhaps even declined.

Other trends might be suggested that would possibly trace long swings similar to those for inequality in income structure, rate of growth of population, rate of urbanization and internal migration, and the proportion of savings or capital formation to national product. For example, such swings might be found in the ratio of foreign trade to domestic activities; in the aspects, if we could measure them properly, of government activity that bear upon market forces (there must have been a phase of increasing freedom of market forces, giving way to greater intervention by government). But the suggestions already made suffice to indicate that the long swing in income inequality is part of a wider process of economic growth, and interrelated with similar movements in other elements. The long alternation in the rate of growth of population can be seen partly as a cause, partly as an effect of the long swing in income inequality which was associated with a secular rise in real per capita income. The long swing in income inequality is also probably closely associated with the swing in capital formation proportions: wider inequality making for higher, and narrower inequality for lower, countrywide savings proportions.

Comparison of Developed and Underdeveloped Countries

What is the bearing of the experience of the developed countries upon the economic growth of underdeveloped countries? Let us examine briefly the data on income distribution in the latter, and speculate upon some of the implications.

As might have been expected, the data are scanty. For the present purpose distributions of family income for India in 1949–50, for Ceylon in 1950, and for Puerto Rico in 1948 were used. Although the coverage is narrow and the margin of error wide, the data show that income distribution in these underdeveloped countries is somewhat *more* unequal than in the developed countries during the period after World War II. Thus the shares of the lower 3 quintiles are 28 percent in India, 30 percent in Ceylon, and 24 percent in Puerto Rico—compared with 34 percent in the United States and 36 percent in the United Kingdom. The shares of the top quintile are 55 percent in India, 50 percent in Ceylon, and 56 percent in Puerto Rico, compared with 44 percent in the United States and 45 percent in the United Kingdom.[8]

This comparison is for income before direct taxes and excluding free benefits from governments. Since the burden and progressivity of direct taxes are much greater in developed countries, and since

[8] For sources of these data see "Regional Economic Trends and Levels of Living," pp. 142–175 in this volume. This paper, and an earlier one, "Underdeveloped Countries and the Pre-industrial Phases in the Advanced Countries: An Attempt at Comparison," in *Proceedings of the World's Population Conference 1954* (New York: United Nations, 1955), Vol. 5, pp. 947–970, discuss issues raised in this section.

it is in the latter than substantial volumes of free economic assistance are extended to the lower income groups, a comparison in terms of income net of direct taxes and including government benefits would only accentuate the wider inequality of income distributions in the underdeveloped countries. Is this difference a reliable reflection of wider inequality also in the distribution of *secular* income levels in underdeveloped countries? Even disregarding the margins of error in the data, the possibility raised earlier in this paper that transient disturbances in income levels may be more conspicuous under conditions of primitive material and economic technology would affect the comparison just made. Since the distributions cited reflect the annual income levels, a greater allowance should perhaps be made for transient disturbances in the distributions for the underdeveloped than in those for the developed countries. Whether such a correction would obliterate the difference is a matter on which I have no relevant evidence.

Another consideration might tend to support this qualification. Underdeveloped countries are characterized by low average income per capita, low enough to raise the question how the populations manage to survive. Let us assume that these countries represent fairly unified population groups, and exclude, for the moment, areas that combine large native populations with small enclaves of non-native, privileged minorities, for example, Kenya and Rhodesia, where income inequality, because of the excessively high income shares of the privileged minority, is appreciably wider than even in the underdeveloped countries cited above.[9] On this assumption, one may infer that in countries with low average income, the secular level of income in the lower brackets could not be below a fairly sizable proportion of average income—otherwise, the groups could not survive. This means, to use a purely hypothetical figure, that the secular level of the share of the lowest decile could not fall far short of 6 or 7 percent, that is, the lowest decile could not have a per capita income less than six or seven tenths of the countrywide average. In more advanced countries, with higher average per

[9] In one year since World War II, the non-African group in Southern Rhodesia, which accounted for only 5 percent of total population, received 57 percent of total income; in Kenya, the minority of only 2.9 percent of total population, received 51 percent of total income; in Northern Rhodesia, the minority of only 1.4 percent of total population, received 45 percent of total income. See United Nations, *National Income and Its Distribution in Underdeveloped Countries*, Statistical Papers, Series E, No. 3 (New York, 1951), Table 12, p. 19.

capita incomes, even the *secular* share of the lowest bracket could easily be a smaller fraction of the countrywide average, say as small as 2 or 3 percent for the lowest decile, that is, from a fifth to a third of the countrywide average, without implying a materially impossible economic position for that group. To be sure, there is in all countries continuous pressure to raise the relative position of the bottom income groups, but the fact remains that the lower limit of the proportional share in the secular income structure is higher when the real countrywide per capita income is low than when it is high.

If the long-term share of the lower income groups is larger in the underdeveloped than in the average countries, income inequality in the former should be narrower, not wider as we have found. However, if the lower brackets receive larger shares, and at the same time the very top brackets also receive larger shares—which would mean that the intermediate income classes would not show as great a progression from the bottom—the net effect may well be wider inequality. To illustrate, let us compare the distributions for India and the United States. The first quintile in India receives 8 percent of total income, more than the 6 percent share of the first quintile in the United States. But the second quintile in India receives only 9 percent, the third 11, and the fourth 16; whereas in the United States, the shares of these quintiles are 12, 16, and 22, respectively. This is a rough statistical reflection of a fairly common observation relating to income distributions in underdeveloped compared with developed countries. The former have no "middle" classes: there is a sharp contrast between the preponderant proportion of population whose average income is well below the generally low countrywide average, and a small top group with a very large relative income excess. The developed countries, on the other hand, are characterized by a much more gradual rise from low to high shares, with substantial groups receiving more than the high countrywide income average, and the top groups securing smaller shares than the comparable ordinal groups in underdeveloped countries.

It is, therefore, possible that even the distributions of secular income levels would be more unequal in underdeveloped than in developed countries, not in the sense that the shares of the lower brackets would be lower in the former than in the latter, but in the sense that the shares of the very top groups would be higher and that those of the groups below the top would all be significantly lower than a low countrywide income average. This is even more likely to be true of the distribution of income net of direct taxes and inclusive of free government benefits. But whether a high probability weight can be attached to this conjecture is a matter for further study.

In the absence of evidence to the contrary, I assume that it is true: that the secular income structure is somewhat more unequal in underdeveloped countries than in the more advanced—particularly in those of Western and Northern Europe and their economically developed descendants in the New World (the United States, Canada, Australia, and New Zealand). This conclusion has a variety of important implications and leads to some pregnant questions, of which only a few can be stated here.

In the first place, the wider inequality in the secular income structure of underdeveloped countries is associated with a much lower average income per capita. Two corollaries follow, and they would follow even if the income inequalities were of the same relative range in the two groups of countries. First, the impact is far sharper in the underdeveloped countries, where the failure to reach an already low countrywide average spells much greater material and psychological misery than similar proportional deviations from the average in the richer, more advanced countries. Second, positive savings are obviously possible only at much higher relative income levels in the underdeveloped countries: if in the more advanced countries some savings are possible in the fourth quintile, in the underdeveloped countries savings could be realized only at the very peak of the income pyramid, say by the top 5 or 3 percent. If so, the concentration of savings and of assets is even more pronounced than in the developed countries, and the effects of such concentration in the past may serve to explain the peculiar characteristics of the secular income structure in underdeveloped countries today.

The second implication is that this unequal income structure presumably coexisted with a low rate of growth of income per capita. The underdeveloped countries today have not always lagged behind the presently developed areas in level of economic performance; indeed, some of the former may have been the economic leaders of the world in the centuries preceding the last two. The countries of Latin America, Africa, and particularly those of Asia, are underdeveloped today because in the last two centuries, and even in recent decades, their rate of economic growth has been far lower than that in the Western World—and low indeed, if any growth there was, on a per capita basis. The underlying shifts in industrial structure, the opportunities for internal mobility and for economic improvement, were far more limited than in the more rapidly growing countries now in the developed category. There was no hope, within the lifetime of a generation, of a significantly perceptible rise in the level of real income, or even that the next generation might fare much better. It was this hope that served as an important and realistic compensation for the wide inequality in income distribution of the presently developed countries during the earlier phases of their growth.

The third implication follows from the preceding two. Income inequality probably has not narrowed in the underdeveloped countries within recent decades. There is no empirical evidence to check this conjectural implication, but it is suggested by the absence, in these areas, of the dynamic forces associated with rapid growth that in the developed countries checked the upward trend of the upper income shares that was due to the cumulative effect of continuous concentration of past savings; and it is also indicated by the failure of the political and social systems of underdeveloped countries to initiate the governmental or political practices that effectively bolster the weak positions of the lower income classes. Indeed, inequality in the secular income structure of underdeveloped countries may well have widened in recent decades—the only qualification being that where there has been a recent shift from colonial to independent status, a privileged, *nonnative* minority may have been eliminated. But the implication, in terms of the income distribution among the *native* population, still remains plausible.

The somber picture just presented may be an oversimplified one. But I believe that it is sufficiently realistic to lend weight to the questions it poses—questions as to the bearing of the recent levels and trends in income inequality, and the factors that determine them, upon the future prospect of underdeveloped countries within the orbit of the free world.

The questions are difficult, but they must be faced unless we are willing completely to disregard past experience or to extrapolate mechanically oversimplified impressions of past development. The first question is: Is the pattern of the older developed countries likely to be repeated in the sense that in the early phases of industrialization in the underdeveloped countries income inequalities will tend to widen before the levelling forces become strong enough first to stabilize and then reduce income inequalities? While the future cannot be an exact repetition of the past, there are already certain elements in the present conditions of underdeveloped societies, for example, "swarming" of population due to sharp cuts in death rates unaccompanied by declines in birth rates, that threaten to widen inequality by depressing the relative position of lower-income groups even further. Furthermore, if and when industrialization begins, the dislocating effects on these societies, in which there is often an old hardened crust of economic and social institutions, are likely to be so sharp as to destroy the positions of some of the lower groups more rapidly than opportunities elsewhere in the economy may be created for them.

The next question follows from an affirmative answer to the first. Can the political framework of the underdeveloped societies withstand the strain which further widening of income inequality is likely to generate? This query is pertinent if it is realized that the real per capita income level of many underdeveloped societies today is lower than the per capita income level of the presently developed societies before *their* initial phases of industrialization. And yet the stresses of the dislocations incident to early phases of industrialization in the developed countries were sufficiently acute to strain the political and social fabric of society, force major political reforms, and sometimes result in civil war.

The answer to the second question may be negative, even granted that industrialization may be accompanied by a rise in real per capita product. If, for many groups in society, the rise is even partly offset by a decline in their proportional share in total product; if, consequently, it is accompanied by widening of income inequality, the resulting pressures and conflicts may necessitate drastic changes in social and political organization. This gives rise to the next and crucial question: How can either the institutional and political framework of the underdeveloped societies or the processes of economic growth and industrialization be modified to favor a sustained rise in economic performance and yet avoid the simple remedy of an authoritarian regime that would use the population as cannon fodder in the fight for economic achievement? How to minimize the cost of transition and avoid paying the heavy price— in internal tensions, in long-run inefficiency in providing means for satisfying wants of human beings as individuals—which the inflation of political power represented by authoritarian regimes requires?

Facing these acute problems, one is cognizant of the dangers of taking an extreme position. One extreme—particularly tempting to us—is to favor repetition of past patterns of the now developed countries, patterns that, under the markedly different conditions of the presently underdeveloped countries, are almost bound to put a strain on the existing social and economic institutions and eventuate in revolutionary explosions and authoritarian regimes. There is danger in simple analogies; in arguing that because an unequal income distribution in Western Europe in the past led to accumulation of savings and financing of basic capital formation, the preservation or accentuation of present income inequalities in the underdeveloped countries is necessary to secure the same result. Even disregarding the implications for the lower-income groups, we may find that in at least some of these countries today the consumption propensities of upper-income groups are far higher and savings propensities far lower than were those of the more puritanical upper-income groups of the presently developed countries. It is dangerous to argue that because they may have proved favorable in the past, completely free markets, lack of penalties implicit in progressive taxation, and the like are indispensable for the economic growth of the now underdeveloped countries. Under present conditions the results may be quite the opposite—withdrawal of accumulated assets to relatively "safe" channels, either by flight abroad or into real estate; and the inability of governments to serve as basic agents in the kind of capital formation that is indispensable to economic growth. It is dangerous to argue that, because in the past foreign investment provided capital resources to spark satisfactory economic growth in some of the smaller European countries or in Europe's descendants across the seas, similar effects can be expected today if only the underdeveloped countries can be convinced of the need of a "favorable climate." Yet, it is equally dangerous to take the opposite position and claim that the present problems are entirely new and that we must devise solutions that are the product of imagination unrestrained by knowledge of the past, and therefore full of romantic violence. What we need, and I am afraid it is but a truism, is a clear perception of past trends and of conditions under which they occurred, as well as knowledge of the conditions that characterize the underdeveloped countries today. With this as a beginning, we can attempt to translate the elements of a properly understood past into the conditions of an adequately understood present.

Concluding Remarks

In concluding this paper, I am acutely conscious of the meagerness of reliable information presented. The paper is perhaps 5 percent empirical information and 95 percent speculation, some of it possibly tainted by wishful thinking. The excuse for building an elaborate structure on such a shaky foundation is a deep interest in the subject and a wish to share it. The formal and no less genuine excuse is that the subject is central to much of economic analysis and thinking; that our knowledge of it is inadequate; that a more cogent view of the whole field may help channel our interests and work in intellectually profitable directions; that speculation is an effective way of presenting a broad view of the field; and that so long as it is recognized as a collection of hunches calling for further investigation rather than a set of fully tested conclusions, little harm and much good may result.

Let me add two final comments. The first bears upon the importance of additional knowledge and a better view of the secular structure of personal income distribution. Since this distribution is a focal point at which the functioning of the economic system impinges upon the human beings who are the living members of society and for whom and through whom the society operates, it is an important datum for understanding the reactions and behavior patterns of human beings as producers, consumers, and savers. It follows that better knowledge and comprehension of the subject are indispensable, as a step in learning more about the functioning of society—in both the long and short run. Without better knowledge of the trends in secular income structure and of the factors that determine them, our understanding of the whole process of economic growth is limited; and any insight we may derive from observing changes in countrywide aggregates over time will be defective if these changes are not translated into movements of shares of the various income groups.

But more than that, such knowledge will contribute to a better evaluation of past and present theorizing on the subject of economic growth. It was pointed out in the opening lines of this paper that the field is distinguished by looseness of concepts, extreme scarcity of relevant data, and, particularly, pressures of strongly held opinions. The distribution of national product among the various groups is a subject of acute interest to many and is discussed at length in any half-articulate society. When empirical data are scanty, as they are in this field, the natural tendency in such discussion is to generalize from what little experience is available—most often the short stretch of historical experience within the horizon of the interested scholar, which is brought to bear upon the particular policy problems in the forefront. It has repeatedly been observed that the grand dynamic economics of the Classical School of the late eighteenth and early nineteenth centuries was a generalization, the main empirical contents of which were the observed developments during half to three quarters of a century in England, the mother country of that school; and that it bore many of the limitations which the brevity and exceptional character of that period and that place naturally imposed upon the theoretical structure. It is also possible that much of Marxian economics may be an overgeneralization of imperfectly understood trends in England during the first half of the nineteenth century when income inequality may have widened, and that extrapolations of these trends (e.g., increasing misery of the working classes, polarization of society, etc.) proved wrong because due regard was not given to the possible effects upon the economic and social structure of technological changes, extension of the economic system to much of the then unoccupied world, and the very structure of human wants. Wider empirical foundations, observation of a greater variety of historical experience, and a recognition that any body of generalizations tends to reflect a limited stretch of historical experience must force us to evaluate any theory—past or present—in terms of its empirical contents and the consequent limits of its applicability—a precept which should also be applied to the oversimplified generalizations contained in the present paper.

My final comment relates to the directions in which further exploration of the subject is likely to lead us. Even in this simple initial sketch, findings in the field of demography were used and references to political aspects of social life were made. Uncomfortable as are such ventures into unfamiliar and perhaps treacherous fields, they cannot and should not be avoided. If we are to deal adequately with processes of economic growth, processes of long-term change in which the technological, demographic, and social frameworks are also changing—and in ways that decidedly affect the operation of economic forces proper—it is inevitable that we venture into fields beyond those recognized in recent decades as the province of economics proper. For the study of the economic growth of nations, it is imperative that we become more familiar with findings in those related social disciplines that can help us understand population growth patterns, the nature and forces in technological change, the factors that determine the characteristics and trends in political institutions, and generally patterns of behavior of human beings—partly as a biological species, partly as social animals. Effective work in this field necessarily calls for a shift from market economics to political and social economy.

Inequalities in the
Size Distribution of Income

IN THIS article we assume an awareness on the part of the reader of
the technical aspects of the size distribution of income, particularly
the dependence of its parameters on the definition of the income
receiving unit, the limits of the universe of recipients covered, the
scope of the income total classified by size, the time period over
which income is cumulated, and the stability or mobility of units
within the distribution. We also assume knowledge of the broad
findings of empirical studies relating to the size distribution of
income, particularly on the differences between those in developed
and underdeveloped countries and on trends over time in the
developed countries.[1] Here we confine discussion to a few questions
and implications suggested largely by the differences between the
size distributions in developed and underdeveloped countries.

Characteristics of the Size Distribution

Let us assume that the distributions—among family or consuming
units, for income before direct taxes and excluding government serv-

[1] For a convenient summary of the technical aspects and the empirical findings see Simon Kuznets, "Quantitative Aspects of the Economic Growth of
Nations: VIII. Distribution of Income by Size," *Economic Development and
Cultural Change*, XI, 2, Part II (January 1963), and the monographs referred
to in that paper.

English text of a paper published in Économie Appliquée, *1964.*

Successive ordinal groups increasing income (percent)	Developed countries		Underdeveloped countries	
	Percent share in total income (1)	Multiple of average income (2)	Percent share in total income (3)	Multiple of average income (4)
1. 0–20	4	0.2	8	0.4
2. 21–40	11	0.55	11	0.55
3. 41–60	16	0.8	13	0.65
4. 61–80	22	1.1	16	0.8
5. 81–90	16	1.6	12	1.2
6. 91–95	11	2.2	10	2.0
7. 96–100	20	4.0	30	6.0

ices in kind—indicated in the illustrative table are typical of the two sets of countries. The shares shown are based on observations for recent years for a number of countries in both the developed and underdeveloped groups, although those for the underdeveloped countries are less firmly grounded because of the scarcity of reliable data. Communist countries are excluded, because of the almost complete absence of data and adequate studies; as indicated in the article cited in footnote 1, inequality of income in these countries is probably fairly wide.

The only modification of available figures on underdeveloped countries made in preparing the table was to limit the share of the top 5 percent group to 30 percent of total income; for several countries the share is well above that figure.[2] Were we to raise this share, the shares of the other groups, particularly in the middle brackets, would be reduced.

Several significant differences between the developed and underdeveloped countries are clearly indicated. First, the share of the top 5 percent group is larger in the underdeveloped than in the developed countries (line 7), and the difference would be even greater for income net of direct taxes and including direct services by governments. Second, the share of the lowest ordinal group—the lowest quintile (line 1)—is also distinctly larger in the underdeveloped than in the developed countries, although I may have exaggerated the former share slightly. The share of the next quintile (line 2) is the same in the two distributions. Third, the shares of the middle groups, indeed all extending from 40 to 95 percent (lines 3–6), are lower for the underdeveloped than for the developed

[2] *Ibid.*, Table 3, p. 13.

countries (particularly of the middle 50 percent, lines 3–5). Fourth, the distribution among the lower 95 percent, excluding the share of the top 5 percent group, is distinctly less unequal in the underdeveloped than in the developed countries.

For a proper interpretation of these differences in the size distributions of income for the two groups of countries, we need to recognize the differences between the real per capita incomes of the two groups. The measures we use are *relative* to average income per consuming unit, and to per capita income, on the assumption that there is no significant association between per consuming unit income and the size of the unit; hence, one and the same income multiple represents quite different per unit or per capita incomes in the two groups of countries. Here we face the difficult task of converting the income totals involved, expressed in domestic currencies, to some equality in purchasing power. In the United States, personal income (including the minor item of income of nonprofit institutions) amounted in 1958 to about 90 percent of gross domestic product at factor costs. In India, while the ratio was probably somewhat higher, it could not have been much above 95 percent. If then we apply these ratios to per capita gross domestic product at factor cost for 1958, expressed in United States dollars, per capita personal income is $2,092 for the United States and $64 for India, a ratio of over 32 to 1.[3] The conversion rates used in the United Nations publication clearly understate differences in purchasing power of the currencies. But suppose we reduce the ratio sharply, from over 32 to 1 to 6 to 1. If we disregard possible differences in size of family units associated with per unit income, assume that the shares shown in the illustrative table are for original groups in numbers of people rather than in numbers of consuming units, and use the 6 to 1 ratio for per capita income (setting the latter at $349, i.e., $2,092/6, for the underdeveloped countries), only the per capita income of the top 5 percent group in the underdeveloped countries equals the *average* per capita income of the developed countries. The application of the 6 to 1 ratio to the income multiples in column 4 yields strikingly low absolute per capita incomes in even the highest income brackets in the underdeveloped countries, and correspondingly relatively high absolute per capita incomes in the low income brackets in the developed

[3] The data are from United Nations, *Yearbook of National Accounts Statistics, 1962* (New York, 1963), the tables for the United States and International Table 3, pp. 314 ff.

countries. The result has been exaggerated by the use of extremes: the United States, a high-income country even within the developed group, on the one hand and India, a rather low-income country, on the other. But our hypothetical ratio of 6 to 1 may be too low for some purposes, and furthermore it is well to sharpen the questions by dealing with extremes.

IMPLICATIONS IN THE UNDERDEVELOPED COUNTRIES · Several significant questions and implications are suggested by this comparison. (1) How do the upper income groups in the underdeveloped countries manage to save, if their real per-capita income is no higher than the countrywide average income in the developed countries manage to save, if their real per capita income is no income generate no savings? Two answers come to mind. First, it may well be that at the same real income per capita, the proportions saved are higher and those consumed are lower in the underdeveloped than in the developed countries, even after we make allowance for the effect of direct taxes on total personal income. The whole structure of consumption in the underdeveloped countries is geared to a low per capita income, so that even the upper income groups may be partly inclined, partly compelled (not legally but by a prevalent social pattern) to spend a smaller proportion of their income than groups with equal per capita income in the developed countries. To put it differently, a family in an underdeveloped country with, say, the equivalent of the United States average of over $2,000 per capita ($8,000 plus for a family of four) might find it difficult to spend as high a proportion of its income as the average family in the United States—unless that unit became so "Americanized" in its pattern of life as to be a major deviant.

Second, it may also be that of the top 5 percent group in the underdeveloped countries, only the very peak of the group generates savings, while the rest in that group manage to get along without incurring dissavings. In the United States, the top 1 percent of population received about half of the total income of the top 5 percent.[4] If this allocation is applied to the share of the top 5 percent in underdeveloped countries in the illustrative table, the top 1 percent would account for 15 percent of total income, have an income multiple of 15, a per capita income about 2.5 times the average of the developed countries (on the assumption of a 6 to 1 ratio), and thus a high enough absolute income to warrant a fairly

[4] Kuznets, *op. cit.*, p. 61.

high savings proportion. If, to extend the illustration, we assume a 40 percent savings ratio, the savings of the top 1 percent group would be about 6 percent of personal income; but these would have to be offset by personal dissavings in other brackets. Whether or not these answers have any validity, and whether other answers should be suggested, the above comment stresses the need for more detailed and reliable data on the upper income shares in underdeveloped countries, directed in particular at establishing the loci within the size distribution of income at which personal savings originate.

The second question is: How have the low-income groups in the underdeveloped countries managed to survive, and indeed to grow at increasing rates in recent years, on absolute incomes that are such low multiples of the average income of the developed countries? Several answers may be noted, although the weight of the factors they suggest is still to be measured. (1) The prices of the products purchased by these groups may be far lower relatively than those implied in the conversion rates, even after the shift from a 32 to 1 to a 6 to 1 ratio, for clearly the low-income groups must obtain their necessities at the lowest possible cost, as indicated by their food-consumption patterns, chiefly carbohydrates and starches, and few proteins. (2) In underdeveloped countries the proportion of these low-income groups living in rural areas must be much higher than for the total population, or than for low-income groups in the developed countries. Residence in the country eliminates many of the needs of urban living that require substantial resources even at a minimum level of satisfaction. This is a matter not of differences in prices or costs but of differences in needs. (3) And, finally, even with all these adjustments, the low-income groups in the underdeveloped countries do suffer from inadequate incomes, even though this inadequacy has not resulted, as in the past, in high over-all death rates and a low rate of natural increase. In particular, these groups are deprived of goods other than necessities that represent a valuable, and essential, investment in the quality of life not only of the current but also of succeeding generations. Here again, as for the upper-income groups, we need better data, with particular attention to the locus of *dissavings,* and, even more, to the impact of low incomes on the consumption patterns and efficiency of the large population groups affected. The data on consumption expenditures are more plentiful here than for the upper-income groups; but coverage is still inadequate, and has not yet been fully evaluated in terms of the impact on efficiency.

IMPLICATIONS IN THE DEVELOPED COUNTRIES · These questions concerning the implications of income inequalities in the underdeveloped countries for the *use* of incomes by upper- and lower-income groups in their effect on savings and efficiency can be paralleled by two similar questions regarding the developed countries. (1) Why, despite high real per capita income even after direct taxes, are the proportions of savings to income so moderate, even among groups with incomes above the average? In other words, what is there about the pattern of life that makes for high per capita expenditures? If the answer to this question emphasizes the urbanized pattern of life with its extra costs, the requirements for greater investment in training, education, recreation, and health (usually included with consumer expenditures, not savings), the attractions of new consumer goods that result from technical progress, and the general expansibility of human wants by learning and imitation, the second question can be raised. (2) If the pattern of life imposes high per capita expenditures, how do the low-income groups adjust to this pattern? What effects do their low incomes have on the structure of their expenditures and on efficiency and quality, their own and those of their offspring?

An extended discussion of these questions would involve too lengthy an analysis of the structure of consumption and savings at different income levels within the developed countries, particularly of the distinction between consumption expenditures that are essential for the production activities of the persons involved (investment for higher personal productivity) and those that are dispensable.[5] Two brief comments may, however, be appropriate.

First, undoubtedly the much higher per capita consumption expenditures in the developed countries are largely due to the urban pattern of life and to the implicit costs of participation in the country's productive performance. Such participation may demand extra costs of residence, transportation, recreation, and the style of life in general, over and above the requirements relating to education and training, that are unnecessary in many rural, and even

---

[5] For some discussion of this aspect of consumption on an aggregative basis see Simon Kuznets, "Quantitative Aspects of the Economic Growth of Nations: VII. The Share and Structure of Consumption," *Economic Development and Cultural Change*, X, 2, Part II (January 1962).

urbanized, productive activities in the less developed countries. One component of consumption expenditures, investment in training and education, that is far larger relatively in the developed than in the underdeveloped countries, is a major factor underlying the higher quality and greater productivity of the labor force in the developed countries. The magnitude of this component of the higher per capita expenditures in the developed countries could be ascertained only by an intensive analysis and classification of consumer expenditures, but even a brief survey of the data in the *Yearbook of National Accounts Statistics* indicates that it is absolutely and proportionately quite large.

Second, it is in the light of the factors just mentioned and others that contribute to the high per capita consumer expenditures in developed countries that the effects of and problems connected with the low-income groups in these countries must be considered. The recent concern in the United States with the large, economically "deprived" groups may seem ironical, in view of the fact that such groups are identified as families with annual incomes up to $3,000. At the top, for a family of four, this means an income of $750 per capita per year, much higher than the average per capita income for most countries in the world and significantly higher than the per capita income in the upper-income groups among most of the world's population. Nevertheless, the "deprivation," the loss of efficiency, and the major source of dissatisfaction are all genuine. For a substantial proportion of these groups, although obviously not for all, low income is a result of inadequate investment in education and training, and hence means a substantial loss of potential productivity. For others low income is the result of maladjustments to rapidly changing employment opportunities. While these maladjustments are no fault of the individuals involved, they nonetheless induce in them a feeling of genuine deprivation, of inadequate opportunity to participate fully in the country's economy and society. If one adds the consequences of discrimination and of persistent inequalities of initial opportunities, as well as those of the established patterns of life and consumption, the problem is a real one in terms of the prevailing standards of a developed economy—no matter how high the absolute levels of even low incomes in these countries may be, compared with per capita income among the large population masses of the economically underdeveloped parts of the world.

The Size Distribution as an Effect: Sources of Inequalities

In the preceding section we considered some of the implications of income inequalities for the *use* of income, treating the size distribution as the cause and the consequences for consumption, savings, and efficiency as the effects. We now turn to the sources of income inequalities in the economic system, viewing the size distribution as an effect. Here, as in the preceding section, we must be selective, and will deal, in particular, with: (1) factors that may have contributed to the higher share of the top income groups in the underdeveloped than in the developed countries; (2) factors that may account for the lower share of the low income groups in the developed than in the underdeveloped countries.

THE SHARES OF TOP INCOME GROUPS · Two different but nonconflicting reasons may be advanced to explain the higher share of income received by top income groups in the underdeveloped than in the developed countries. One lies in the existence of occupational groups that, because of their high level of training and responsibility, need a substantial minimum income to enable the participant to pursue his activity effectively and to attract an adequate supply of new entrants. A highly qualified engineer, research scientist, business or government executive, or medical practitioner cannot operate efficiently on an income that might be sufficient for an unskilled manual laborer, an individual farmer, or a shopkeeper running a small store. The income must provide compensation for his past investment in education, without which an adequate flow into his occupation would not be assured, unless government paid fully for such an investment in other ways. It must also be large enough to free the professional or highly skilled practitioner to pursue his task intensively and to keep abreast of new developments, while living at a level of minimum comfort. It should also be adequate for a family milieu that would yield a supply of new and well-trained members of these highly skilled occupations, for the latter are trained and motivated not only in schools but also within the home (since only the exceptional child in a family in which the economic status of the head is low and other conditions are unfavorable can rise into such occupations). The substantial minima of real income for such occupations are set by the patterns of modern skill occupations like those listed above (we did not include an authority on Brahmin lore, or even an expert in handicrafts), and in terms of income of equivalent purchasing power are likely to be much the same the world over, if they are truly minima. It follows that these minima are higher multiples of the low per capita income of the underdeveloped countries than of the high per capita income of the developed countries. Let us assume that, in the purchasing power of United States dollars within the United States, the minimum for a high-level professional occupation in 1958 is $8,000 for a family of four, or $2,000 per head. This is a multiple of 0.96 of the per capita personal income of the United States ($2,092), but six times as high in India if we assume that its per capita income is one sixth of that of the United States. The restriction in the USSR and Israel, for example, of the egalitarian tendencies that were dominant during the early phases of development—to allow sufficiently large incomes for the high skill and responsibility occupations and assure their availability and efficiency—is proof of the relevance of this argument.

To be sure, the incomes of individuals with these occupations may be above the minima because of a monopoly element in their supply, caused by the scarcity of family units economically able to provide the training and investment necessary to produce recruits (assuming, as is the case in all but the Communist countries and to a great extent even there, that the government does not provide the total investment). This brings us to the second explanation of the higher share of the top income groups in the underdeveloped countries: a greater element of monopoly and a possibly greater concentration of wealth in these groups. Since upward mobility and the rate of displacement within the upper-income brackets are slower in the underdeveloped economies, greater concentration of wealth is more likely. Such concentration of wealth combined with a share of property income in total income of households that is no lower in underdeveloped than in developed countries, would make for a larger share of the upper-income groups. In the developed countries, the larger absolute stock of income-yielding wealth per capita tends to be more equally distributed, as indicated by the widespread ownership of claims. This is particularly true in recent years—since the 1920's in many European countries and since the late 1930's in the United States, when the share of property incomes in the total declined significantly.[6]

[6] See Simon Kuznets, "Quantitative Aspects of the Economic Growth of Nations: IV. Distribution of National Income by Factor Shares," *Economic Development and Cultural Change*, VII, 3, Part II (April 1959), pp. 44–49.

One other contributing factor should be noted. Most of the high income occupations and groups in both the underdeveloped and developed countries are concentrated among urban residents. As already indicated, the dominant proportion of the low income groups lives in the countryside in the underdeveloped countries, but not in the developed countries. Consequently the contrast between the income of the top group and that of the rest of the population is much more in the nature of a contrast between the city and the country in the underdeveloped than in the developed countries. Furthermore, the differentials in productivity and per worker income between the countryside and the city are significantly wider in the underdeveloped than in the developed countries, reflecting their far greater economic backwardness in the agricultural than in nonagricultural sectors, which do include some modern industries (factory manufacturing, railroad transportation, communications, and the like). Thus the larger share of income of the top groups in the underdeveloped countries reflects in part the greater contrast between rural and urban incomes. Of course, insofar as this contrast also reflects wider differences in prices and costs between country and city in the underdeveloped countries, an adjustment for these cost differentials would reduce the shares of the upper groups more in the underdeveloped than in the developed countries. But as the measures now stand, uncorrected for internal price differences, the wider discrepancy in product and income between country and city in the underdeveloped countries may be a factor, in addition to the others mentioned, in raising the shares of the top groups in these countries above those in the developed countries.

THE SHARES OF LOW-INCOME GROUPS · As for the lower shares of the bottom groups in the developed than in the underdeveloped countries, the simple explanation may be that with high average per capita incomes in the former, low multiples are feasible; whereas survival would be almost impossible with such low multiples in the underdeveloped countries. This basic argument is valid, but the specific forms that it assumes are important and should be explicitly indicated.

Given the general income differentials, reflecting different skills of the occupations and differences in the distribution of income-yielding assets, and disregarding transient, short-term income components, it would help to distinguish some major groups among the low-income units in developed countries. The first group includes family units whose head is either at the beginning of his occupational life cycle, at the learning or journeyman stage so to speak, or is in an occupation that will lead to a later increase of income (e.g., farm workers before they become independent farmers, unskilled laborers before they develop skills). The second group includes family units whose head is at the other end of the occupational life cycle—past the peak and semi-retired or fully retired—and often receiving a low income because he is unable to participate fully. Of the bottom quintile among family units in the United States in 1959 (grouped by money income), 33 percent had family heads 65 years old or over, compared with an average of less than 9 percent of such units in the remaining four quintiles.[7] The third group comprises family units that have been "broken" by death, separation, or otherwise, or are greatly affected by some basic maladjustments that influence their response to economic opportunities. To cite one group, the proportion within the lowest quintile in the United States in 1959 of family units with female heads was about a quarter, while the average share in the four other quintiles was about 6 percent. A fourth group which partly overlaps this group comprises units whose heads are in islands of backwardness and obsolescence, such as subsistence farmers who had no other occupation and victims of prolonged structural unemployment who failed to retrain. The proportion of this group—with the head of the family not in the labor force or in the armed services, or unemployed—was over 50 percent in the lowest quintile in 1959, while in the other quintiles it averaged about 14 percent. This list is far from complete and makes no specific mention of the group whose low income is the result of discrimination.

Independent separate family units whose head has some income-limiting characteristic are much less important in the underdeveloped than in the developed countries. The occupations which require high skill, call for long training periods, and pay poorly at the learning stage in the expectation of much higher incomes eventually are also far less important in the underdeveloped than in the developed countries. Perhaps more to the point, in the underdeveloped countries these learners, even if married, are likely to be members of a large extended family rather than independent,

[7] The data in this paragraph are from Simon Kuznets, "Income Distribution and Changes in Consumption," in Hoke S. Simpson, ed., *The Changing American Population* (New York, 1962), Table 5, pp. 34–35.

separate family units. The extended family encompasses as well the retired group, widows and other members of broken families, the chronically ill or disabled, and even the structurally unemployed. Since the extended family is more prevalent in underdeveloped countries, these low-income groups are likely to be parts of a large extended unit comprising other and more productive members of the labor force, and their low incomes are pooled with the larger incomes of other members. Only in the developed countries, with their higher per capita incomes, broader provisions for social security, greater opportunity to accumulate savings for retirement, and a pattern of life that encourages the small nucleated family, is it feasible for many of these low-income family units to exist separately; and the size distribution can have a much wider range at its lower end than in the underdeveloped countries. Moreover, this trend has been relatively recent: even in the United States, this movement toward greater separation of family units whose heads are in the learning, retired, or other stage, with depressed income possibilities, has evolved with the lowering of the age of marriage, reduction of competitive pressures among the young, expansion of social security, and a general rise in per capita income. The tendency of income inequalities in the United States to remain stable since 1950 or 1951 may well be due to this trend, which reflects changes that create a new group of low income family units previously nonexistent and are changes in family structure concealing possible changes in size distribution of income.

Three Criteria for Analyzing Size Distribution

A given size distribution of income can be analyzed in terms of three criteria: adequacy, equity, and efficiency. The problem of *adequacy* arises from the consideration that whatever the system of economic rewards of a given society, members who, for reasons often beyond their control, fail to earn adequate shares are nevertheless to be provided a minimum consonant with the general economic level of the society. Whether this policy is implemented by the pooling of resources within an extended family, by programs of voluntary charity, by the institutionalization of a beggar class, or by systematic public programs of relief and social security, the prevalence of such arrangements to provide minimum needs indicates that no society can completely neglect its unsuccessful members. Neglect of the poor would create a disruptive element in the society which can be ill afforded. My knowledge is quite limited; there may be societies in which economic scarcity is so great that they are forced to abandon their unsuccessful members to starvation and death. Unless this situation exists, however, the society goes at least part way to meet the criterion of adequacy, while, at the same time, it may be pursuing efforts to minimize the incidence of failures that make the need large.

By *equity* we mean two things: (1) the absence of systematic discrimination in rates of return for economically similar goods and services: and (2) the restraint of inequalities in opportunities to members of the society for more productive and greater income-yielding economic roles, if they have the required capacities. Whether the criterion of equity is applied only within and not among distinct groups, as has been the case in slave, caste, and generally rigid status-structured societies, or whether it is applied within the society as a whole, its general meaning is imparted by the basic views on the proper organization of society by which it is governed. To my mind, an indispensable requirement of modern economic growth, the basic philosophy upon which it rests and which is the source of its great dynamism, is the belief that equality of both political and economic opportunity is to be extended to all groups within the society; consequently any differences in opportunities *realized* should be based largely upon differences in human capacity (governed by age, sex, genetic endowment, and the like) tested in action rather than on preconceived notions of inequality. Even these differences in the economic results of different human capacities are subject to the criterion of minimum adequacy, to be applied to the poorly equipped and unsuccessful members of the community.

The criterion of *efficiency* implies a relation to some desirable goal, in the light of which the size distribution is to be appraised. For our purposes it may help to define this goal as economic growth: a sustained and significant rise in product per capita. The application of this criterion would require us to examine the distribution of income and gauge its contribution to or restriction of the rise in product per capita, either through its effects on consumption and savings or through the growth-promoting and growth-inhibiting activities that are sources of income.

Other criteria for evaluating size distributions of income could probably be suggested, but these three seem to be the ones most widely employed. Their formulation above is vague, but a more effective specification that would remove vagueness and ambiguities would require attempts to apply the criteria to quantitative and qualitative data, a task not feasible here and beyond my competence. Although as an economist I cannot deal adequately with the first two criteria, it is perhaps warranted to suggest that the three are both complementary and conflicting. They are complementary in that *complete* neglect of adequacy and equity is likely to reduce efficiency, because of possible disruption and revolt by the depressed affected groups and because of the possible waste in the denial of opportunity to all members of the society, which may mean failure to exploit a sizable stock of human endowments. The criteria are also complementary in that complete neglect of efficiency would lessen the value of the criteria of adequacy and equity since it would make returns from them so much lower than otherwise. On the other hand, the three criteria are conflicting because an attempt to apply one to its maximum would reduce the extent to which the others could be applied, unless we established definite interdependent limits for all three. For example, if the criterion of minimum adequacy were pushed beyond limits consonant with equity and efficiency, it would reduce efficiency and consequently the value of equal opportunities within which equity operates. If equity were pushed beyond simply equalizing opportunities to an extreme egalitarianism, it would reduce efficiency and consequently limit the levels of minimum adequacy. Finally, if the efficiency criterion were pushed to the maximum, that is, were closely related to current standards of performance and with reference to the potential of growth, it might endanger equity by denying opportunities to groups previously deprived (on the grounds of unproved efficiency) and minimum adequacy by unduly restricting necessary transfers.

These comments suggest some possible directions of closer examination of the size distributions of income, in combination with data on educational and other opportunities, provisions for relief and social security, transfers, and a host of institutional arrangements through which these criteria operate. But these are still only general comments of uncertain value until they have been applied and reformulated in the empirical study of different countries.

A few comments are perhaps in order on the criterion of efficiency in terms of its contribution to economic growth, since it bears most closely on the aspects of the size distribution of income discussed in the preceding sections. The criterion suggests the possible value of distinguishing between what might be called warranted and unwarranted components in income inequalities: warranted, if, on net balance, their contribution to economic growth is positive and unwarranted if, on net balance, it is negative (perhaps "neutral," when the net balance is zero).

From this standpoint, examination of the extremes in the size distribution—of the groups at the low and high ends of the range—might prove illuminating, although this does not deny the value of examination of the entire range. The specific question could be framed as follows: Since economic growth requires some additional investment (material or in human beings) or some social or institutional change, or both, are the low incomes in the size distribution fully warranted in the sense that raising them would make for less growth (properly discounted for its "futurity") than an alternative use of the additional resources; or are they unwarranted in the sense that raising them would make for greater economic growth (again properly discounted) than the alternative use of capital or of institutional change? The basic assumption is that the supply of capital and the stock of feasible institutional change are both limited over the proximate period under consideration, and any draft upon them to raise incomes in one part of the distribution would reduce the stock of resources available to raise incomes in another part. A similar question could be posed concerning the high-income brackets: Would lowering the high incomes, while possibly depressing the contribution of these groups, be more than offset by the contribution of these released resources to other uses by other income groups; and thus on net balance would the change mean a significant positive contribution to economic growth? If the answer is in the affirmative, then some components of the high-income brackets are unwarranted from the standpoint of economic growth. Obviously, similar questions could be raised about the net effects of raising or lowering any set of incomes in the income distribution, evaluating the net balance of effects on economic growth, and approximating the warranted and unwarranted components in them.

The specific application of such an approach requires known and tested relations between given economic activities and their responsiveness to potential growth in productivity, so that incomes as inducements to participation in such activities could be evaluated; it also requires tested relations between uses of income and potential economic growth, so that income as a factor governing uses can be evaluated. Extreme cases of unwarranted components can be identified. For example, the incomes of the groups at the bottom of the distribution are unwarrantedly low, if minor additional capital investments and relatively easy institutional changes would raise both productivity and income. Also, the incomes of the top income groups that are derived from monopolistic positions, and in fact impede economic growth, and that are used for conspicuous consumption rather than savings, are large unwarranted components on counts of both origin and use. But even in such obvious cases, the cost of institutional change must be taken into account. In other cases the net balance is not easily struck, for there may be both growth-promoting and growth-opportunity costs not only in the source of income but also in its use, and there may also be margins of uncertainty in estimating the probable yield of additional capital investment and additional institutional change for different groups in the size distribution of income.

Nevertheless, the comments above, when added to our discussion of some aspects of the size distribution in the preceding sections, may suggest analytical leads. In particular, they stress the fact that the size distribution of income is the junction at which the production and the use of income meet within the family or consuming unit, the latter acting in two roles, as producer and as consumer. This distribution represents an intersection of the system of rewards for productive activity with the system of allocation of these rewards, or the use of income, and both systems affect the relation between actual and potential economic growth. Granted the major human and political aspects of the size distribution that are prominent in the criteria of adequacy and equity and have a marked influence on efficiency (which must not be overlooked in broader comparisons), even the narrower use of the criterion of efficiency alone involves an analysis of the size distribution as a dual system—of differential rewards for productive activity and of consequences for consumption and savings. It is these two substantive aspects of the size distribution that must be stressed, not the formal measures of inequality, especially since formal measures may be quite misleading: a highly unequal distribution of income may in one case be most conducive to economic growth whereas in another case it may constitute a major obstacle, even if it does not go so far as to threaten political breakdown. The importance of inequality lies in its economic rationale, in its origins in production, and in its consequences in consumption, with due cognizance of the limits of human and political tolerance for such inequality in roles in production and shares in consumption.

Notes on the Pattern of U.S. Economic Growth

ECONOMIC GROWTH is a long-term process whose features can properly be observed only in a historical perspective. Since its quantitative dimensions, in the aggregate and for major components, are of the essence, its measurement is indispensable. In view of the wide discussion of the country's growth (or lack of growth) during recent years, it may be helpful to take a longer look. Some of the distinctive quantitative characteristics of our economic growth over the long stretch may be useful in evaluating recent changes.

A Comparison of Long-term Growth Rates

Crude as the estimates are, we can approximate the rates of growth of the gross national product, population, and labor force in this country back to 1840, the year that may be accepted as dating the entry of this country into the period of modern industrialization. Over the one hundred and twenty years from 1840 to 1960, population grew at an average rate of about 2 percent per year; labor force, at a slightly higher rate of 2.2 percent per year; gross national product, at 3.6 percent per year; per capita product at 1.6 percent per year; and product per worker, at 1.4 percent per year (Table 1). These rates mean that in 1960 population was about

Reprinted from Edgar O. Edwards, ed., The Nation's Economic Objectives, Rice University Semicentennial Publications (Chicago: University of Chicago Press, 1964).

Table 1. RATES OF GROWTH PER YEAR, GROSS NATIONAL PRODUCT,
POPULATION, AND LABOR FORCE IN THE UNITED STATES IN SUCCESSIVE AND
OVERLAPPING DECADES AND LONGER PERIODS, 1840–1960 (percent)

	Product[a] (1)	Popu- lation[b] (2)	Labor force[b] (3)	Product per capita (4)	Product per worker (5)
Successive decades					
1. 1839–49	4.24	3.11	3.57	1.10	0.64
2. 1949–59	4.95	3.09	3.18	1.80	1.71
3. 1959–69	1.99	2.39	2.07	−0.39	−0.08
4. 1869–79	4.95	2.33	3.01	2.56	1.88
Overlapping decades					
5. 1878–82–1888–92	3.73	2.26	2.70	1.44	1.00
6. 1883–87–1893–97	3.10	2.02	2.50	1.05	0.58
7. 1888–92–1898–1902	4.04	1.80	2.50	2.20	1.50
8. 1893–97–1903–07	5.03	1.78	2.60	3.19	2.36
9. 1898–1902–1908–12	3.71	1.95	2.67	1.73	1.01
10. 1903–07–1913–17	2.60	1.87	1.95	0.72	0.63
11. 1908–12–1918–22	2.60	1.50	1.05	1.08	1.53
12. 1913–17–1923–27	3.62	1.40	1.14	2.19	2.45
13. 1918–22–1929	3.99	1.47	1.35	2.49	2.61
14. 1923–27–1933–37	−0.35	0.98	1.16	−1.33	−1.49
15. 1929–1939–41	1.37	0.74	1.21	0.62	0.15
16. 1933–37–1943–47	7.02	0.96	1.84	6.00	5.09
17. 1939–41–1948–52	4.27	1.39	1.40	2.84	2.83
18. 1943–47–1953–57	2.47	1.67	0.80	0.78	1.65
19. 1948–52–1959–61	3.24	1.71	1.19	1.50	2.03
Longer periods					
20. 1840–80	4.03	2.73	2.96	1.26	1.04
21. 1880–1920	3.52	1.88	2.23	1.61	1.26
22. 1920–60	3.15	1.31	1.28	1.81	1.84
23. 1840–1960	3.56	1.97	2.15	1.56	1.38
Absolute values[c]					
24. 1959–61[d]	509.0	179.9	69.9	2,829	7,282
25. 1959–61 as multiple of 1840[e]	66.7	10.4	12.9	6.4	5.2
26. 1840[f]	7.63	17.1	5.42	446	1,408

[a] For 1839–79 we used estimates in 1879 prices of commodity product (value added in agriculture, mining, manufacturing, and construction) by Robert E. Gallman, "Commodity Output, 1839–1899," in *Trends in the American Economy in the Nineteenth Century* (Studies in Income and Wealth, Vol. XXIV) (Princeton, N.J.: Princeton University Press, 1960), Table 1, p. 16. Since the ratio of these estimates adjusted to 1929 prices for 1874–99 (for each fifth year) to those of gross national product (quinquennial averages centered on the same years) is relatively constant—it fluctuates from 0.58 to 0.67, without any trend —we assumed that the rate of growth of commodity product for 1839–79 represents the rate of growth of gross national product.

For 1878–82–1918–22, the estimates in 1929 prices are from Simon Kuznets, *Capital in the American Economy* (Princeton, N.J.: Princeton University Press, 1961), Table R-26, Variant III, pp. 563–564.

For 1918–22–1959–61, the estimates in 1961 prices are those of the Department of Commerce, given in the *Economic Report of the President* (January, 1962), Table B-2, p. 208. For 1929–58 the estimates have been extrapolated from 1958–61 by gross national product in 1954 prices, given in the *Survey of Current Business* (July 1962), Table 5, p. 8; and they have been extrapolated from 1929 to 1918 by the 1954 price estimates in U.S. Department of Com-

10.5 times as large as in 1840; labor force, almost 13 times; per capita product and, presumably, per capita real income, over 6 times; and product per worker, over 5 times.

How does this record compare with the long-term growth of other countries? The countries of most interest to us here are those that we now consider developed: those that have managed to take advantage of the wide potentials of modern economic growth and those that are (or were) fairly large, so that their growth conditions and problems have not been too different from those of the United States.

If then we look at the long-term records of the United Kingdom, France, Germany, Russia (and the USSR), and Japan, allow for changes in boundaries, and observe long periods (ranging from 79 years for Japan to 117 years for the United Kingdom), the results of the comparison may be stated simply (Table 2). First, the annual rate of growth of population in the United States was much higher than in these other large, developed countries: compared with 2

---

merce, U.S. *Income and Output* (Washington, D.C., 1958), Table I-16, pp. 138–139, and Table I-2, pp. 118–119.

The estimates for 1960 and 1961 given in the *Survey* were reduced $1 billion to exclude Alaska and Hawaii. This adjustment was indicated for 1960 in the *Survey*, p. 5, and assumed for 1961, since personal income in the two states in 1961 was less than 5 percent larger than in 1960.

b Before 1880, the values are for the census years, given in the U.S. Bureau of the Census, *Historical Statistics of the United States* (Washington, D.C., 1960), Series A-20, p. 8, and Series D-57, p. 74. For 1878–82–1918–22 they are from Simon Kuznets, *op. cit.*, Table R-37, pp. 624–626, and Table R-39, pp. 630–631, and include armed forces overseas. For 1918–22–1959–61 they are those given in the *Economic Report of the President* (January, 1962), Table B-16, p. 227, and Table B-19, p. 230 (including armed forces for 1929–61), and extrapolated to 1918–22 by the Kuznets series on the basis of the relationship in 1933–37. The population figures for 1960 and 1961 were reduced by population of Alaska and Hawaii, given in the U.S. Bureau of the Census, *Population Reports* (Series P-25, No. 258 [November 21, 1962]); and labor force for 1960, excluding the two states, was extrapolated to 1961 by the movement in labor force, including the two states, from 1960 to 1961.

In lines 5–19 the initial and terminal values are arithmetic means of the five- or three-year period shown in the stub, except for 1929, where we used the single year to exclude the years of the thirties. In lines 20–23, the rates are geometric means of those for the underlying successive decades, and those for 1839–79 are assumed to apply to 1840–80.

c Product is in billions of 1961 dollars; population and labor force, in millions; and product per capita and per worker, in 1961 dollars.

d Cols. 1 and 2 are the absolute values underlying line 19; col. 3 = line 25 × line 26; col. 4 = col. 1 ÷ col. 2; col. 5 = col. 1 ÷ col. 3.

e These figures are based on cumulated growth rates.

f Col. 1 = line 24 ÷ line 25; cols. 2 and 3 are the values underlying line 1; col. 4 = col. 1 ÷ col. 2; col. 5 = col. 1 ÷ col. 3.

Table 2. Rates of Growth per Year, Product, Population, and Per Capita Product for Selected Countries over Long Periods[*] (percent)

	Duration of period[a] (1)	Product (2)	Population (3)	Product per capita (4)
Great Britain and United Kingdom[b]				
Great Britain				
1. 1841–81	40	2.54	1.19	1.33
2. 1881–1921	40	1.77	0.91	0.86
United Kingdom				
3. 1921–1957–59	37	1.88	0.43	1.44
4. Total, 1841–1957–59	117	2.07	0.86	1.20
France[c]				
5. 1841–50–1861–70	20	2.23	0.39	1.84
6. 1871–80–1901–10	30	2.00	0.22	1.77
7. 1901–10–1920–28	18.5	1.46	−0.13	1.60
8. 1920–28–1958–60	35	1.55	0.37	1.18
9. Total, 1841–50–1958–60	103.5	1.80	0.24	1.55
Germany[d]				
1913 boundaries				
10. 1851–55–1871–75	20	1.63	0.74	0.89
11. 1871–75–1913	40	3.09	1.20	1.87
Interwar boundaries				
12. 1913–1935–37	23	0.57	0.53	0.04
Federal Republic				
13. 1936–1958–60	23	3.97	1.40	2.53
14. Total, 1913–1958–60	46	2.25	0.97	1.28
15. Total, 1851–55–1958–60	106	2.45	1.01	1.43
Sweden[e]				
16. 1861–65–1881–85	20	2.88	0.72	2.15
17. 1881–85–1921–25	40	2.69	0.66	2.01
18. 1921–25–1958–60	36	3.77	0.59	3.16
19. Total, 1861–65–1958–60	96	3.13	0.64	2.47
European Russia and USSR[f]				
European Russia				
20. 1860–1913	53	2.67	1.30	1.35
USSR				
21. 1913–28	15	0.54	0.54	0
22. 1928–58	30	4.40	0.67	3.71
23. Total, 1913–58	45	3.10	0.63	2.45
24. Total, 1860–1958	98	2.87	0.99	1.86
Japan[g]				
25. 1878–82–1918–22	40	4.14	1.05	3.05
26. 1918–22–1958–60	39	3.97	1.36	2.57
27. Total, 1878–82–1958–60	79	4.05	1.21	2.81

[*] Unless otherwise indicated, all series were brought up to date by use of various issues of the United Nations, *Yearbook of National Accounts Statistics* and its *Demographic Yearbook.*

[a] For series with initial or terminal periods longer than one year, duration is calculated between midyears.

[b] All the estimates are from Phyllis Deane and W. A. Cole, *British Economic Growth, 1688–1959* (Cambridge: Cambridge University Press, 1962). Population for Great Britain for 1841–1921 is from Table 3, p. 8; that for the United Kingdom (in present boundaries) for 1921 and 1958 is derived from Table 90, pp. 329–331. Per capita income for Great Britain for 1841 and 1881, in average 1865 and 1885 prices, is given in Table 72, p. 282; and we estimate it for 1921

percent in this country, the rates in the other countries ranged from 1.2 percent for Japan to 0.2 for France and, except for Japan, were half or less than half of the rate of growth of U.S. population. Second, the annual rates of growth of per capita product for the United States and for the large European countries were within a

by extrapolating from 1901 on the basis of per capita income in 1913–14 prices for the United Kingdom. The latter is given annually in Table 90. We estimated total national income by multiplying population by per capita income.

c The main series for France are from Simon Kuznets, "Quantitative Aspects of the Economic Growth of Nations: I. Levels and Variability of Rates of Growth," *Economic Development and Cultural Change*, V, 1 (October, 1956), Appendix Table 3, pp. 59–60. The estimates exclude Alsace-Lorraine from 1871–80 to 1901–10 and include it from 1841–60 to 1861–70 and 1901–10 to the present. Net national product is in 1938 prices.

d The estimates refer to national income in 1913 and 1928 prices and are extrapolated forward by gross national product. The basic sources are: W. G. Hoffmann and J. H. Müller, *Das deutsche Volkseinkommen 1851–1957* (Tübingen: J. C. B. Mohr [Paul Siebeck], 1959), Table 2, p. 14, and Table 14, pp. 39–40 (for 1851–1913); and Paul Jostock, "The Long-term Growth of National Income in Germany," in Simon Kuznets, ed., *Income and Wealth, Series V* (Cambridge: Bowes and Bowes, 1955), Table I, p. 82 (for 1913–1950–52).

e Gross domestic product in 1913 prices, 1861–1953, is from Östen Johansson, "Economic Growth and Structure in Sweden, 1861–1953," a mimeographed paper presented at the 1959 meeting of the International Association for Research in Income and Wealth, Table 18, pp. 62–65. Population for 1861–1930 is from Erik Lindahl, Einar Dahlgren, and Karin Kock, *National Income of Sweden, 1881–1930* (London: P. S. King & Son, 1937), Part II, Table 64, pp. 4–5.

f For European Russia the basic estimate of commodity product is from Raymond W. Goldsmith, "The Economic Growth of Tsarist Russia, 1860–1913," *Economic Development and Cultural Change*, IX (April 1961), p. 471. Population for the pre-World War I period through 1928 is from Frank Lorimer, *The Population of the Soviet Union: History and Prospects* (Geneva: League of Nations, 1946), Table A-2, p. 208 (for 1859 and 1897, European Russia only); Table 15, p. 35 (for 1897 and 1914, prewar European Russia); Table 16, p. 36 and Table 54, p. 135 (for 1914 and 1928, post-World War I Soviet area). We assumed that per capita income in 1928 was the same as in 1913, an assumption supported, for example, by the Birmingham Bureau of Research on Russian Economic Conditions, *The National Income of the U.S.S.R.* (Memorandum No. 3 [November 1931]), particularly p. 3.

For 1928–58 the product estimates are of national income in 1937 prices, and they and the population figures are from Simon Kuznets, "A Comparative Appraisal," in Abram Bergson and Simon Kuznets, eds., *Economic Trends in the Soviet Union* (Cambridge, Mass.: Harvard University Press, 1963), Table VIII-2, p. 337.

g The main source for Japan through the early 1950's is Kazushi Ohkawa *et al.*, *The Growth of the Japanese Economy since 1878* (Tokyo: Kinokuniya Bookstore, 1957), Table 1, p. 7; Table 3, p. 19; Table 2, p. 234. The estimates relate to national income in 1928–32 prices and in 1934–36 prices.

fairly narrow range: from 1.9 percent for Russia (for a period reaching back to 1860) to 1.2 percent for the United Kingdom (for a period reaching back to 1841), with 1.5 to 1.6 percent for this country. We cannot place much stress on such differences, and for practical purposes, we can assume that the U.S. rate of growth in per capita product was about the same as in the large, developed European countries. The Japanese rate, estimated for 1880–1960 at 2.8 percent, was distinctly higher. Third, the much higher rate of growth of population in the United States, combined with the same or roughly the same rate of growth of per capita product, means that there was a correspondingly higher rate of growth in aggregate product here than in the European countries. Thus, the rate of rise in gross national product in the United States was from a fifth to almost twice as high as that in the large, developed European countries.

It need hardly be mentioned that these averages are for long periods, covering subperiods that differ markedly in the rates of growth of product and population. Furthermore, for several countries, particularly Japan, the period is significantly shorter than that for the United States; and extension of the period to 1840, the initial date for this country, would only lower the averages for both the European countries and for Japan. Yet the comparison is valid and indicates the exceptional performance in the United States: high rates of growth of population and of total product, if not of per capita product, have existed over the long period 1840–1960.

The conclusions just noted would be modified only slightly if we were to extend the comparison to the smaller, developed European countries like Denmark, Norway, Sweden, and the Netherlands—to list the four for which we have long-term records. In general, the rate of growth of population in the United States was much higher, whereas the rate of growth of per capita product was either about the same or slightly higher or lower, except in comparison with Sweden, which combined a high rate of growth of per capita product, 2.5 percent, with a low rate of population growth, 0.64 percent (see Table 2). Indeed, the rapidity of population growth in this country is matched over the long period only in other overseas offshoots of Europe such as Canada, Australia, and Argentina. As a result of this rapid population growth, the United States forged ahead to a position of dominance. In 1840 the population of the United States was about 17 million; that of Great Britain was 18.6

million, significantly larger; those of France and Germany (1913 boundaries) were well over 30 million each, or almost double; and that of Russia was over 50 million, or almost three times as large. In 1960, the population of the United States, 180 million, was over three times as large as that of the United Kingdom, almost four times as large as that of France, two and a half times the total of East and West Germany, and only about a seventh below that of the USSR, despite the recent expansion in the latter's territory.[1]

One further implication of the conclusions should be noted. We know that at present the per capita product of the United States is the highest in the world and appreciably higher than that in the developed European countries. Such comparisons are treacherous, but this statement is undeniable even if we do not accept at face value the United Nations estimates that indicate that in 1952–54 per capita income of the United States was more than double those of the United Kingdom and France and over three times that of Germany.[2] Nor is it easy to ascribe meaning to a calculation that shows that per capita product in the United States was almost three times that of the USSR in 1958.[3] But let us assume moderately that the advantage in recent years is, say, one and one half to one. Then, if the rate of growth in per capita income in the United States is about the same as for these European countries, the implication is that in 1840 the per capita income of the United States was also at least one and one half times as high, and relatively higher if the rates of growth of per capita income in the large Euro-

---

[1] Population data for other countries for 1840 are from Phyllis Deane and W. A. Cole, *British Economic Growth, 1688–1959* (Cambridge: Cambridge University Press, 1962), p. 8 (statistics for Great Britain, 1841); and R. R. Kuczynski, *The Balance of Births and Deaths* (New York: The Macmillan Co., 1928), Vol. I, pp. 98–99. The estimates for Russia are from W. S. and E. S. Woytinsky, *World Population and Production: Trends and Outlooks* (New York: Twentieth Century Fund, 1953), Table 17, p. 44. The estimates for 1960 are from the United Nations, *Demographic Yearbook, 1961* (New York, 1962).

[2] See United Nations, *Per Capita National Product of Fifty-five Countries, 1952–54*, Statistical Papers, Series E, No. 4 (New York, 1957).

[3] Abram Bergson in *The Real National Product of Soviet Russia since 1928* (Cambridge, Mass.: Harvard University Press, 1961), p. 261, states that "on the eve of the five-year plans the USSR was producing annually an output on the order of $170 per capita [in terms of 1929 prices]." With such output in 1928 and the rate of growth in per capita product of 3.71 percent per year (see Table 2, line 21), per capita product in the USSR in 1958 works out to $507 in 1929 prices, or about $1,020 in 1961 prices, if we use the ratio of 1961 prices to 1929 prices, 2.01, as given in the *Economic Report of the President* (January 1962). The USA gross national product per capita in 1958, in 1961 prices, is close to $2,680, or over 2.6 times as high.

pean countries were greater than that of the United States. A crude but suggestive calculation indicates that from the beginning of our period, the per capita income of the United States—even before its industrialization—was close to that in the most developed country, the United Kingdom, and appreciably higher than in most European countries, let alone the rest of the world (with the exception of a country like Australia in its very early period of growth).[4] In other words, the very high per capita income of the United States compared with those of other developed countries observed today is due largely to the fact that at the beginning of its industrialization its per capita income was already relatively high, and during the 120 years following, it managed to sustain rates of growth in per capita income that were not much lower than those of the developed countries which initially had much lower per capita incomes.

The Characteristics of Long-term U.S. Growth

The high rate of population growth in the United States, higher than in other large, developed countries, was due primarily to the power of this country to attract immigrants. From 1840 to 1930, through

4 Such calculations are necessarily rough and are not fully consistent with comparisons of coterminous estimates in the early years. Thus, from Table 3 and Table 72 of Deane and Cole (op. cit., pp. 8, 282), we can estimate income per capita in Great Britain in 1841 at £24.3, or about $121 at the current rate of exchange. According to Table A-1, Variant A, Gallman, op. cit., p. 43, commodity product per capita in 1839 was $60.6 and assuming a ratio of commodity product to national income of 0.65 (it averages about 0.63 of gross national product between 1874 and 1899), we secure a per capita income of $93, which is about a fourth below that of Great Britain. If we apply to the two per capita incomes the rates of growth for one hundred and twenty years, shown in Tables 1 and 2, the ratio of incomes at the end of the period would be 1.18 for the USA to 1 for Great Britain—an appreciably narrower spread than that between the United States and the United Kingdom as shown by the United Nations figures. While the discrepancy would be reduced by a shift from the per capita income of Great Britain to that of the United Kingdom, most of it would remain. Alternatively, if we estimate gross national product per capita for the United States in 1839 at $96.2 (dividing $60.6 by 0.63) and convert it to 1961 prices by linking the successive price indexes, product per capita for 1839 would be $356 in 1961 prices or, say, $360 for 1840 rather than $446, as shown in Table 1. The discrepancy is due in part to the fact that the Department of Commerce estimate of gross national product in 1918–22, averaging $127.8 billion in 1954 prices and $73.4 billion in 1929 prices, is about 6 percent larger than the National Bureau of Economic Research estimate of $69.4 billion; it is partly due to the fact that the cumulative rate of growth tends to be reduced by the use of price indexes based toward the end of, or beyond the period of, coverage.

three quarters of the long period covered here, the population of native stock grew from 14.2 to 82.7 million, less than six times the initial number; the population of foreign stock (foreign-born and native-born of foreign or mixed parentage) grew from somewhat less than 3 million to over 40 million, or over thirteen times the original number. In 1930, about a third of the country's total population was of foreign stock.[5] Also, the rate of natural increase (the excess of births over deaths) may have been slightly higher here than in the older, developed countries, with the birth rates higher (particularly in the early nineteenth century) and the death rates somewhat lower. But the major source of the difference in the rate of growth of population and still more in that of the labor force was immigration, in ever-increasing streams and from diverse sources in Europe, although not from other continents. The importance of this stream for the economic growth of the United States is still not fully understood or completely analyzed, much of the past literature having concentrated on difficulties of adjustment and assimilation and having been biased by reformers concerned with short-term problems rather than with long-term gains. Nor have we paid sufficient attention to the effect of the decline in this

---

But even allowing for such discrepancies, the rough calculation does suggest orders of magnitude, and it is clear that per capita income in the United States in 1840 was only slightly below that of Great Britain and appreciably higher than those in France and Germany—let alone Russia and Japan.

[5] The estimates for 1840 are extrapolations of (1) the number of foreign-born, first reported in the census for 1850; (2) the number of native-born whites of foreign parentage, first available in 1870; (3) the number of native-born whites of mixed parentage, also first available in 1870. For a convenient summary of these data see E. P. Hutchinson, *Immigrants and Their Children, 1850–1950* (New York: John Wiley & Sons, 1956), Tables 1 and 2, pp. 2–3. Foreign-born were derived by subtracting one half of the cumulated immigration for 1841–50 from the total for 1850; the reduction ratio was derived from comparisons of decennial immigration (given in U.S. Bureau of the Census, *Historical Statistics of the United States,* Series C-88, pp. 56 ff.) with net changes in foreign-born for 1851–60 to 1901–10 (the ratios varied from 31 to 73 percent). Native whites of foreign parentage were estimated on the basis of the ratio of native whites of foreign parentage, at a given census date, to the average of foreign-born whites at the same and the preceding census dates, the latter being derived by the procedure described above. The ratio, calculated for 1870–1910, ranged from 0.9 to 1.1. The ratio used for the 1840 estimate was 1.0. The native whites of mixed parentage were estimated on the basis of the ratio to native-born whites of foreign parentage, which rose from 0.28 in 1870 to 0.46 in 1910. The ratio used for the 1840 estimate was 0.25. The resulting numbers for 1840 were, in millions: foreign-born—1.38; native whites of foreign parentage—1.23; native whites of mixed parentage—0.31.

source of growth in population and labor force—initiated in World War I, furthered by restrictive legislation in the 1920's, and sharply accentuated in the depression of the 1930's, never to be relaxed significantly—on the economic growth and adjustment problems of this country in recent years.

That the rate of growth in per capita product in the United States was no higher than in the large European countries (except moderately, compared with England) and in Japan, despite freedom from destructive impacts of the major wars which affected the latter countries and which are included in the averages cited above, is somewhat of a surprise. As to the comparison with Russia— where the average rate of growth of per capita product was raised largely during the costly three decades under authoritarian rule from 1928 to 1958 and where relative disregard of the more difficult problems of fitting economic growth to the needs and wishes of the population may account in good part for its high rate of measured increase—it is subject to grave doubts, but the results are hardly a puzzle. This is perhaps also true of the comparison with Japan, a country that started from initially very low levels and much later in time and in which a long-lived hierarchical social system was harnessed to the cause of rapid industrialization, while many traditional industries in the fields of consumer goods and housing were preserved. To repeat, the puzzling finding is a rate of growth of per capita product in the United States that was not significantly higher than in France and Germany, only slightly higher than in England, and significantly lower than in Sweden. Could the very rapid rate of growth of population and labor force in this country have restricted the rates of growth in per capita and per worker product? If so, what is the connection? Surely one cannot assume that the supply of natural resources had any limiting effects, insofar as most of the period of growth in the United States is concerned, compared with the conditions in the European countries. Could the limitation stem from difficulties in supplying adequate capital per worker, engendered by a rapidly growing labor force, despite the high long-term capital formation proportions in the United States, compared with the other developed countries? Or did the problems of adjustment and assimilation faced by immigrants lower average productivity, despite the fact that most immigrants were in the prime labor ages and presumably endowed with strong economic incentives? Or, finally, did the very high level of per capita income induce a lower rate of growth by permitting the exchange of work for leisure, since there was no great pressure to "catch up"?

These and other questions come easily to mind. But unless the hypotheses underlying them concerning the connection between the high rate of population growth and the less than record rate of growth in per capita or per worker product, or between the latter and the high per capita product, can be formulated so as to reveal links that can be studied by means of empirical data, the conjectures are not very helpful. Answers to such questions require much additional analysis of a variety of long-term data that will permit a detailed comparison of the United States' rates of growth with those in other countries. This cannot be done here and I am compelled to set the questions aside and turn to other aspects of the long-term rates of growth of product, population, and labor force in the United States. In any case, our observation of these rates should not be limited to averages over as long a period as 120 years. How have they changed *during* that period?

First, has there been a long-term acceleration or retardation in the rates of growth? For population and labor force, the answer is clear: the rate of growth has declined markedly. Thus over the first forty years, from 1840 to 1880, despite the fact that the period includes the Civil War years, the population grew 2.7 percent per year; during the next forty years, the rate dropped to 1.9 percent per year; in the last forty years, from 1920 to 1960, it was only 1.3 percent per year. Likewise, the rates of growth in the labor force, through the successive forty-year periods, declined from 3.0 to 2.2 to 1.3 percent per year. To be sure, population growth has recovered since World War II; the rate of increase over the last decade (1950 to 1960) was 1.7 percent per year, but it still was lower than the rate for 1880 to 1920; and the rate of growth of the labor force in the last decade was among the lowest, less than 1.2 percent per year (reflecting the low birth rate of the 1930's), but it may recover to higher levels in the 1960's.

The retardation in the rate of growth of population and labor force was accompanied by a decline in the rate of growth of aggregate gross national product. It was slightly over 4 percent per year from 1840 to 1880, 3.5 percent per year from 1880 to 1920, and 3.1 percent per year from 1920 to 1960 (over the last decade, it was 3.2 percent per year). It should be noted that except for the earliest period, all product rates are calculated from either five- or three-year averages at terminal points, to reduce the effects of short, cyclical disturbances.

But while the rates of growth of population and labor force declined to less than half of the early levels, the retardation in the rate of growth of gross national product was much less marked—about a quarter. This means, of course, that the rate of growth of per capita or per worker product showed a significant acceleration. The rate of growth of per capita product from 1840 to 1880 was 1.3 percent per year; from 1880 to 1920 it was 1.6 percent per year; from 1920 to 1960 it was 1.8 percent per year; and even in the last decade it was only slightly below 1.6 percent per year. The per worker product rate was slightly above 1 percent per year from 1840 to 1880; 1.3 percent per year from 1880 to 1920; and over 1.8 percent per year from 1920 to 1960. Over the last decade, from 1950 to 1960, the rate of growth of gross national product per worker was 2.0 percent per year, among the highest in the long-term record.[6]

Two important recent monographs, one for the period since the 1880's and the other for the period since 1909, show acceleration in the rate of growth of product per worker.[7] At the danger of over-burdening this paper with statistical detail, I shall give the major conclusions of these studies in a brief listing. The conclusions of the Kendrick study are: (1) Between 1879–1919 and 1919–53, the rate of growth of national product per unit of labor input (man-hours weighted by hourly wage rates in the base year) rose from 1.4 to 1.9 percent per year; the rate of growth of product per unit of capital

---

[6] A study under way by Professor Gallman, who kindly made some partial results available to me, indicates that the rate of growth of gross national product for 1839–79 may be somewhat higher than that shown in Table 1, with the average rise per year for 1839–59 being of the order of 4.9 percent rather than the 4.6 shown. If final calculations confirm this preliminary finding and we extend the relative upward adjustment to the full period, the average percentage rise per year in gross national product for 1839–79 would be 4.29, instead of 4.03; in product per capita, 1.52, instead of 1.26; in product per worker, 1.29, instead of 1.04. The broad trends—retardation in the rate of growth of gross national product and acceleration in the rate of growth of product per capita and per worker—would remain largely as now shown. With the same change for 1840–80, the average percentage rises per year for the full period 1840–1960 would be 3.65 for gross national product, instead of 3.56; 1.65 for product per capita, instead of 1.56; and 1.47 for product per worker, instead of 1.38.

[7] See John W. Kendrick, *Productivity Trends in the United States* (Princeton, N.J.: National Bureau of Economic Research, 1961); and Edward F. Denison, *The Sources of Economic Growth in the United States and the Alternatives before Us*, Supplementary Paper No. 13 (New York: Committee for Economic Development, 1962).

input rose from 0.4 to 1.2 percent per year; and that of product per unit of combined factor input rose from 1.1 to 1.7 percent per year. (2) The measured acceleration in the rate of growth of productivity was kept down by the inclusion of the government sector and the finance and services sector, for both of which measures of productivity are quite tenuous. When these are excluded, the rise in product per unit of labor input accelerates from 0.8 percent per year in 1879–1919 to 2.4 percent in 1919–53. (3) Within the private domestic economy, excluding finance and services, the acceleration in the rate of growth of product per unit of labor input was observed in all sectors except contract construction. (4) Findings for individual sectors and for branches of manufacturing suggest that the divisions of the productive system in which the greatest acceleration in the rate of growth of product per unit of labor (or total factor) input occurred were either those in which such growth was quite low in the past (such as agriculture and woodworking manufactures) or those in which technological changes were particularly conspicuous (such as chemicals, petroleum, and electrical machinery, among manufactures).

The Denison study also shows a rise in the rate of growth of national product per unit of factor input: from 1.2 percent per year for 1909–29 to 2 percent per year for 1929–57 (per man-hour of labor, from 1.9 to 2.5). From the analysis that attempts to allocate productivity to the various components, we can gather that of the increase in the rate of growth of productivity of some 0.8 percent per year (from 1.2 to 2), greater education of the labor force accounts for 0.32 points while the major portion of the remainder is likely to be accounted for by an increased weight credited to the advance of knowledge.[8]

Despite the difficulties of establishing long-term trends in records for the European countries and Japan, affected far more by wars and revolutions than this country, it is clear that no common pattern of marked retardation in the rate of growth of population and total product and of acceleration in the rate of per capita product exists.

[8] With an allowance for the increased education of the labor force of 0.32 and for other sources of increased quality of labor of 0.13, the rate of growth in product per unit of factor input rises from 0.56 in 1909–29 to 0.93 in 1929–57, or 0.37 points (see Denison, *op. cit.*, Table 32, p. 266). Of the 0.56 in 1909–29 and 0.93 in 1929–57, 0.28 and 0.27, respectively, are assigned to economies of scale, which leaves 0.28 and 0.66 as residuals. Of the latter, as much as 0.58 is assigned to advance of knowledge. It is thus defensible to argue that much of the difference between 0.28 and 0.66 must be due to a lower weight for "advance of knowledge" in the earlier period.

To be sure, for Great Britain–United Kingdom, the rate of population growth dropped from 1.2 percent per year in 1841–81 to 0.4 percent in 1921–58, and in Russia, wars and revolution reduced the rate of population growth from 1.3 percent per year for 1860–1913 to 0.6 percent in 1913–58. But in France, Germany, Sweden, and Japan, there was no marked trend in the rate of population growth, or there was, if anything, an acceleration. And one can infer reasonably that if the rate of population growth did not decline, it is unlikely that the rate of growth of the labor force did. Nor is there much indication of a long-term upward trend, like that observed for the United States, in the rate of growth of per capita product in the European countries and in Japan—except for the effects of the revolutionary break in Russia. England, France, Germany (except for the initial acceleration after 1870), and Japan show no increase in the rate of growth of per capita product and that of Sweden emerges only in the last period, largely since the 1940's.

The Variability of the U.S. Growth Rate

Although it is tempting to speculate on the implications of a combination of retardation in the rates of growth of the population and the labor force with acceleration in the rate of growth of product per capita and per worker, a distinctive feature of long-term growth in this country, we must turn now to a third aspect of our experience —the variability of growth. The rates of growth for each decade— calculated wherever possible from five-year averages centered on the initial and terminal years and thus largely eliminating the effects of business cycles of three to nine years in duration—fluctuate widely (Table 1). Even from the 1870's to World War I, a period unaffected by a major war, the rate of growth in per capita product varied between a low of about 1.1 percent per year (from 1883–87 to 1893–97) to a high of 3.2 percent per year (from 1893–97 to 1903–07). Swings of approximately twenty years in the growth rates of aggregate product, population, labor force, and product per capita and per worker are observable even after we cancel out as best we can the short-term business cycles.

These long swings in the rate of growth have been the subject of increasing attention in recent years in this country, and the literature dealing with them has grown markedly.[9] Their relevance to the

[9] The most convenient summary appears in Moses Abramovitz' statement in

interpretation of recent short-term changes is being examined afresh.[10] Consideration of the technical details of the procedures for the isolation and description of these long swings and of the controversial hypotheses advanced in attempts to account for them would be out of place here. A few general comments may, however, point up the significance of these swings for the present discussion.

First, regardless of the procedure employed to eliminate the short-term business cycles or to distinguish the sustained, unidirectional long-term trends, if we limit the cancellation to cycles that are completed within a decade at most and if we stipulate that the underlying long-term trends make no more than one turn in a period of at least forty to fifty years, the resulting smoothed indexes of product, population, and labor force, as well as of per capita and per worker product, would show significant variations around the underlying long-term trend. And if we describe these variations effectively, their amplitude is found to be significantly wide in relation to the average rate of growth in the underlying trend—to the point where, at the peak of a swing, the decadal rate of growth may be over twice as high as in the underlying trend, and at the trough, less than half as high. It is hardly surprising that even if we disregard periods affected by wars and revolutions and cancel out the short-term cycles, the course of economic performance is not a simple curve that can be adequately and fully described by a second-degree equation over a period of five to fifteen decades. The capacity to attain such a smooth and sustained performance would in itself be more surprising than the observed variability and would require as much explanation as the latter.

Second, granted that the long swings in product may be due in part to prolonged underutilization of economic capacity, we must

---

the *Hearings on Employment, Growth and Price Levels* (86th Cong., 1st sess. [1959]), Part II, pp. 411–466, and his "The Nature and Significance of Kuznets Cycles," *Economic Development and Cultural Change*, IX (April 1961), pp. 225–248. See also "Long Swings in the Growth of Population and in Related Economic Variables," pp. 328–378 below, and Simon Kuznets, *Capital in the American Economy* (Princeton, N.J.: Princeton University Press, 1961), Chs. 7 and 8, pp. 316–388.

[10] See the following articles in *American Economic Review, Papers and Proceedings*, LIII, No. 2 (May 1963): Bert G. Hickman, "The Postwar Retardation: Another Long Swing in the Rate of Growth?," pp. 490–507; Burnham O. Campbell, "Long Swings in Residential Construction: The Postwar Experience," pp. 508–518; Jeffrey G. Williamson, "Dollar Scarcity and Surplus in Historical Perspective," pp. 519–529; and the discussion of the three papers, pp. 530–540.

not overlook the long swings in the rates of growth of population and labor force. So long as the latter are present, even the full utilization of labor and capital will not eliminate the long swings in the rate of growth of aggregate product; and if the swings in population and labor differ in timing, as they well may if they originate in processes of natural increase, there will be long swings also in the rate of growth of output per capita, even under full employment. Thus, in the United States, the rate of population growth reached a low of 0.8 percent per year in the 1930's, and while this was due to the depression following the contraction phase of a long swing, it produced a low rate of growth in labor force in the 1950's, about twenty years later. A low growth rate in the labor force leads to a low rate of aggregate growth, even under full empoyment, unless there is an opposite swing in the rate of growth of product per worker.

Finally, as we would expect, long swings can be found in the rates of growth of other developed economies, particularly of those for which we have long records of growth.[11] Even in Sweden, a country for which we have tolerably good continuous estimates for a full century, from 1861 to 1960, and one that sustained a high rate of growth in product per capita, the decadal rates of growth in the latter varied from 0.9 and 1.3 percent per year, to 3.7 and over 4 percent per year, while the rate of growth in total gross domestic product varied from 1.5 to over 5.5 percent per year. More than two long swings can be discerned within the one hundred years. And the rates of growth in the Communist countries would probably show the same variability, if there were a long enough record undisturbed by wars or revolutions. The "echo" effects of downward swings in the rates of growth of population and labor force, even if occasioned by wars, are just as marked for the Communist countries; and in addition, the errors in planning and the struggles for political succession and their associated policy choices cannot help but affect rates of growth for periods long enough to constitute phases of long swings.

Recent Growth in the Context of the Secular Trend

What is the relevance of the findings discussed above to the evalua-

[11] See a preliminary summary in Simon Kuznets, "Quantitative Aspects of the Economic Growth of Nations: I. Levels and Variability of Rates of Growth," *Economic Development and Cultural Change*, V, 1 (October 1956), pp. 44–51.

tion of recent growth in this country? To be sure, one may deny any relevance, either because the underlying estimates are judged to be completely unreliable or because the present is assumed to be separated from the past by a void that prohibits any inference from a long-term perspective. The first argument rests on technical grounds, and all one can say against it is that despite obvious limitations, rough estimates of the longer past are far more useful than more precise data within a short-term span that do not permit comparisons over time. The second argument implies that we are in a completely new era, not only in the sense that conditions are new but that even our inheritance from the past has been dissipated or is irrelevant, an assumption that cannot be accepted because it disregards the many important ways in which the past has shaped this country's observable responses to new problems.

The difficulty is not in a general demonstration that long-term levels, trends, and variability of the rates of growth are relevant to the evaluation of recent growth experience here and abroad, but rather in formulating this evaluation, in establishing the full bearing of the past upon the present and the proximate future. And the difficulty stems from the fact that these quantitative findings on the past are relatively new, that we do not know, in an empirically testable fashion, the factors, particularly the institutional adjustments, that were involved in the growth trends and in their long swings—so that even if we could establish the current and prospective conditions under which the economy would be operating, we have no fully learned lesson of the past to apply to them. The speculations suggested above on the relation between our high rate of growth of population and labor force and our not-so-high rate of growth in product per capita and per worker, similar questions concerning the association between the marked retardation in the rates of growth of our population and labor force and the significant acceleration in the rate of growth of per capita and per worker product, and our inadequate knowledge of the mechanism that produces the long swings—all point to the meagerness of analytical understanding of these basic quantitative aspects of the country's economic growth, which are so directly relevant to the evaluation of our recent or prospective growth rates.

The above may well be an overstatement, for it disregards the significant contribution to our understanding of aggregative growth which is made by consideration of structural and international aspects—neither of which we could treat here except incidentally.

If, in addition to dwelling on the average level, the retardation or acceleration, and the long swings in the rates of aggregate growth, we could deal with the associated changes in the industrial structure of the product and the labor force, in the distribution of incomes between those from labor and those from assets or by size of income among various groups in the population, in the allocation of total output between consumption and capital formation, in the share of the country's output per capita linked with others by foreign trade or capital flows, the significance of long-term trends in these aspects of economic growth on the evaluation of current changes and problems would appear far greater and more directly illuminating than our limited discussion of the aggregative measures suggests; and our knowledge would not seem so limited. But we can only keep in mind these structural and international aspects of economic growth, without being able to deal here with the pattern of their long-term changes.

Under the circumstances, we can only raise a few questions about the evaluation of recent changes, but even these are worthwhile if they expose the danger of easy judgments and too ready answers. The first and most obvious question is in regard to the meaning of the term "growth" when it is applied to changes over short periods, and they have to be short when we deal with current policy problems. If we say that from 1955 to 1960, the United States' gross national product grew x percent per year, and we are concerned over the low rate observed, does growth, whether of total or of per capita gross national product, mean the underlying trend *plus* the long swing around it? If so, how can we distinguish the underlying trend? How can we distinguish the factors that affect our long-term growth from those that cause the long swings and further distinguish these from the factors associated with deviations from full employment in the business cycle, so that in choosing policy actions directed at the short-term movements we do not neglect the possible effects on the rate of growth in the underlying long-term trend?

Whatever the answer to this question, and its vital importance is obvious, one clear implication of our earlier discussion is the need not only for a sharp distinction between the shorter and the longer periods when measuring the rate of economic growth but also for care in comparing these rates. The relevance of this comment can be illustrated by a citation from the January 1962 *Economic Report of the President*. Table 11 of the report contains rates of growth of gross national product per man-year for eleven countries, the United States among them, for the periods 1913–59 and 1950–59. For all the countries the rates are substantially higher for 1950–59 than for 1913–59. The accompanying text reads: "Further evidence that modern industrial economies are not helpless prisoners of past long-term trends is to be found in Table 11, which shows that the major countries of Western Europe, and Japan as well, have recently exceeded their own long-term performance" (p. 114). This statement may have been intended merely to argue against a naïve acceptance of statistically established long-term trends as true descriptions of the paths that economies had to follow and as the bases for projections into the future. But the statement can also be read as suggesting that the 1950–59 rates of change constitute a new long-term trend. Yet comparisons between rates of growth for a nine- and a forty-six-year period do not tell us that the long-term trend in the specific nine-year period was different from that in the forty-six-year period; there may have been other nine-year periods that, as phases of long swings, also greatly exceeded the average trend rate for the long period of half a century, and clearly the short-term elements in a nine-year period must be examined for their effect on the average for that period as a measure of long-term trend.[12] Since at least eight of the eleven countries were adversely affected by World War II, since the subsequent recovery processes have lasted through most of 1950–59, and also since the four countries with the highest rates of growth for 1950–59—Japan, Italy, Germany, and France—were among those most damaged by the war, such an interpretation of the differences between the rates of growth for the recent nine years and for the longer period of forty-six years would seem incautious.

Second, care must also be exercised in comparing rates of growth for short periods among countries, for they may not portray even roughly the differentials in the underlying long-term trends. In the table in the *Economic Report of the President,* already referred to, the United States, whose rate of growth in gross national product per man-year in 1950–59 was 2.2 percent per year, is eighth in rank,

[12] In the original paper that contained the table discussed in the *Economic Report of the President* (January 1962), the authors note that "these rapid rates [i.e., the ones for 1950–59] are not unprecedented" and refer to past periods of growth at rates as fast. See Deborah C. Paige *et al.,* "Economic Growth: The Last Hundred Years," reprinted in Edmund C. Phelps, ed., *The Goal of Economic Growth* (New York: W. W. Norton & Co., 1962), pp. 69–87, especially p. 86.

with six European countries and Japan all showing appreciably higher rates for the same nine-year period. But if, from the same table, we calculate the rates of growth for 1913–50, the preceding thirty-seven years, the rate of growth for the United States, 1.7 percent per year, is only slightly below that for Japan, 1.8 percent, and much above the rates for all the other nine countries, particularly the large European countries. One is tempted to argue, in line with the suggestion already made, that the high rates of growth in Europe and Japan in recent years reflect attempts to "catch up" in two ways: first, to recover from the war and, second, to take advantage of the opportunities for greater growth in productivity that were previously utilized in the United States and not, for various reasons, in these other countries. This does not deny the possibility that the acceleration in the rate of economic growth in Europe contains elements—partly associated with the Common Market and partly caused by a shift in public policy—that may induce persistently higher rates of growth than were attained in the long-term pre-World War II past. But it would require discriminating analysis to establish these secular elements making for high growth, and no easy inferences can be drawn from simple statistical comparisons for recent short periods.

Concluding Remarks

The comments above should not be taken to mean that we need not concern ourselves with short-term changes in the level of the country's performance or that we can trust that even if they indicate a lag, the underlying secular trend will somehow eventually sweep us onward to higher levels. If rates of increase in the country's performance slow down, if persistent unemployment of labor and other resources develops, policy action must be considered— whether or not it has been attempted in the past—for we are continuously expanding our knowledge of methods of stimulating and sustaining an economy's growth. But this granted, the value of relating these short-term changes to the longer run of the economy is undeniable, and it would be enhanced if the application of the longer perspective were based on better knowledge and understanding of our past. Consider, for example, the finding that in the last forty years the rate of growth of product per capita and per worker in this country was distinctly higher than in the past, despite the inclusion of the period of the 1930's, with the greatest depression on record. Was this merely the result of the retardation in the rate of growth of population and labor force? Should we consider an entirely different hypothesis, one which would assume that the course of technological change since the late nineteenth century permitted increasing rates of growth of product per worker or even per man-hour and that this country was able to exploit this potential, unlike the countries in Europe, which suffered devastating wars and faced other obstacles (overcome only recently)? Conversely, how much of the higher rate of growth of product per capita or per worker in recent decades in this country has been associated with World War II and its aftermath? The implications of these different questions, in terms of the different groups of factors that would have to be examined, are obvious enough; and depending upon the answers, different interpretations of the recent past and proximate future would be suggested, and different policies would seem relevant.[13]

It is tempting to conclude this paper with one rather general comment on the implications of our long-term pattern of economic growth. This growth occurred through decades marked by a succession of turbulent changes in this country and in the rest of the world, and these changes have been particularly rapid since World War I, the last third of the long period covered by Table 1. From a

[13] After having observed the acceleration in the rate of growth of productivity in the United States, characterized as a "break in the trend," John W. Kendrick comments briefly as follows:

"It is not possible adequately to analyze the factors that may have been responsible for the change in productivity trend around the time of World War I. . . . A step in this direction can be taken by noting a few changes that occurred about the same time in associated variables. The scientific management movement, based on the ideas of Frederick W. Taylor, spread widely in the 1920's; college and graduate work in business administration expanded rapidly; and it was only after 1919 that organized research and development became a significant feature of the industrial landscape. . . . It has also been suggested [by Professor Milton Friedman] that the drastic change in national immigration policy promoted a more rapid increase in the average education of the labor force. That is, since the immigrants had less schooling, on the average, than the domestic labor force, the mass influx of workers from abroad prior to World War I had tended to retard the increase in average education.

"It is tempting to enumerate specific innovations that became important after 1919, such as mass or 'flow' production techniques in manufacturing. Certainly, there was a remarkable acceleration in manufacturing productivity in the 1920's. But significant innovations were occurring throughout the whole period; short of a thorough study of their cost-reducing impact, it would not be possible to isolate those that contributed most to the speeding-up of productivity advance" (op. cit., pp. 70–71).

relatively small and young country, protected by what were then wide ocean distances as well as by the pax Britannica, open to immigration from the more advanced countries of the time (those in Europe), the United States has emerged to a position of leadership, of dominant size and high per capita and per worker economic performance, but vulnerable and exposed to all the dangers of leadership in a divided world in which technological advance means not only gains in peaceful productivity but also more extreme gains in destructiveness of weapons. And much of the change in the international scene was concentrated in the brief span of thirty years, from the 1930's to date.

These trite observations suggest what may not be so obvious—that the pattern of past growth leaves its impression in the institutions that the country develops to deal with the problems generated by past growth; that these institutions may persist beyond their useful time and constitute obstacles to further growth under changed conditions; and that sustained economic growth requires continuous adjustments of social and political institutions to changed conditions—adjustments that are in good part required because the institutions that proved useful earlier and were, in fact, required in earlier economic growth are now obsolete. The impressive record of economic growth in this country was not accomplished by the repetitive application of invariant rules of economic and social behavior; it had to be a creative adjustment to changed conditions, and the cost of some of the conflicts that had developed between old and new institutions (the most striking and costly example was the Civil War) was quite high. Minimization of such costs of adjustment is as desirable today as it ever was, and the general point that economic growth almost naturally produces obsolescence and thus requires attention and drive to remove the resulting obstacles could, I believe, be illustrated today.

The following illustrations are, unfortunately, *ad hoc* examples rather than the results of thorough study. The whole system of primary and, to some extent, even secondary education in this country in the past has played a profound socializing role as an institution for the assimilation, if not so much of the foreign-born immigrants themselves, of their children. Without it, the unity and consensus so important in making the social decisions necessary to resolve possible conflicts (many of them originating from growth) would not have been secured. Yet, despite the pressure developing for higher educational standards and more advanced levels throughout the system, the tradition of the schools as a way of life rather than a way of learning is not easily overcome.

And again speculating on the influx of immigrants and the increasing proportion of foreign stock in this country, one wonders whether some of the distinctive aspects of political organization in the United States have not been, in part, a consequence. Could the resistance to reapportionment of voting power in response to greater growth of urban population be rationalized, in part, as an attempt to limit the political power of groups among whom the foreign-born and those of foreign stock are far more predominant than in the nonurban areas? Was the attainment of equality in political power by immigrants and their children delayed much beyond their attainment of economic gains and assimilation? If so, whatever elements of strength and stability were lent to the political system by such past attitudes may have been succeeded by a much more obstructive role of political traditions in dealing with current problems generated by economic growth. And, finally, one may ask whether the emphasis on limiting federal power and on the advantages of decentralized political authority, which in the past fostered so many centers of vigorous economic growth across the country, is equally valid today, when the graver problems of the international scene tend to convert economic growth into a competition rather than permit it to remain a self-determining and self-pacing process.

Perhaps the examples cited above are of dubious validity or, less likely, of small weight. But if at all pertinent, they illustrate the general point urged here, that past patterns of long-term growth leave an economic and institutional heritage which may in part be an obstacle to future growth. If so, understanding past experience may not only mean being able to evaluate properly the significance and likely persistence of current short-term changes in the level of the economy's performance. It may also help to identify those institutional obstacles to further growth that have resulted from adaptation to past growth problems. Likewise, a proper analysis of long-term trends in other countries that are sufficiently similar in organization and orientation for comparison (perhaps with some adjustments), should reveal a variety of growth experience and of feasible institutional changes which may be borrowed with some assurance of their tested contribution. Such understanding of the historical origin and of the obsolescence of institutional arrangements is no guarantee that they can, and will be, effectively modified. But one may hope that knowledge of this type contributes to general social intelligence and should at least weaken the traditional reactions that tend to sanctify, because of long usage, patterns that may have become impediments to possible growth under changed historical conditions.

Long Swings in
Population Growth and
Related Economic Variables

BY LONG swings we mean up and down movements extending over periods substantially longer than those associated with business cycles (four to eleven years). But these periods must be sufficiently brief so that the swings can be detected in series extending over secular stretches observable in social data, at most over a century and a half to two centuries. It follows that the duration of the swings so defined is limited to a range from over a decade to not much longer than half a century.[1]

[1] Such swings in economic activity in this country were discussed in Simon Kuznets, *Secular Movements in Production and Prices* (Boston: Houghton Mifflin, 1930), where they were called "secondary secular movements," and in Arthur F. Burns, *Production Trends in the United States since 1870* (New York: National Bureau of Economic Research, 1934), where they were called "trend cycles." For some recent discussions, see Brinley Thomas, *Migration and Economic Growth* (Cambridge, Eng.: Cambridge University Press, 1954); W. Arthur Lewis, "Secular Swings in Production and Trade," *Manchester School of Economic and Social Studies*, XXIII (May 1955); and Kuznets, "Quantitative Aspects of the Economic Growth of Nations: I. Levels and Variability of Rates of Growth," *Economic Development and Cultural Change* (October 1956). Professor Moses Abramovitz is initiating a study of these swings in capital formation in this country (see National Bureau of Economic Research, *37th Annual Report* [May 1957], pp. 72–75).

This article analyzes quinquennial series on population movements back to

Reprinted from Proceedings of the American Philosophical Society, *102, 1 (February 1958), pp. 25–52.*

We study these swings in the changes in population increase and in population movement components (births, deaths, emigration, immigration, etc.). For a stock series, such as total population, the basic form of observation is the second derivative (absolute change in the absolute change, or change in the population increase). For flow series, such as births, deaths, and so on, which are in themselves gross additions to or drafts upon the population stock, the basic form of observation is the first derivative, the absolute change from one time unit to the next. We proceed likewise with the national product and other series.

The changes are taken for decade totals or averages, overlapping by five years. The decade is employed in order to eliminate short-term changes associated with business cycles or other transient disturbances. It would have been more revealing to deal with ten- or eleven-year moving averages and the resulting annual observations. But data on population and its components, except the series on migration and the foreign born, are available by years only for a brief recent period. Even the population estimates at quinquennial intervals necessitated laborious calculations and a fair amount of approximate interpolation.

These second-order changes in stocks or first-order changes in flows, measured for overlapping decade totals and averages, would be constant if the underlying trend for the stock series were describable by a second-degree potential equation on an arithmetic scale, and that for the flow series by a straight line on an arithmetic scale. If the secular trend lines for the stock and flow series were straight lines on a *log* scale, the changes in both, as calculated here, would show a systematic rise or decline. In general, any relatively simple mathematical trend line for either the stock or the flow series would yield changes, as measured here, that would either rise or decline systematically (or be constant) with only gradual acceleration or retardation. Here, however, we shall find that the change in the rate of absolute increase and the change in the flow fluctuate

1870, which have only recently become available as the result of the project on Population Redistribution and Economic Growth at the University of Pennsylvania, directed by Professor Dorothy S. Thomas and myself. The basic tables prepared in this project were published in "Population Redistribution and Economic Growth, United States, 1870–1950," *Memoirs of the American Philosophical Society*, XLV (1957). I am particularly indebted to Dr. Everett S. Lee for assistance in preparing the population series and to Miss Elizabeth Jenks of the National Bureau of Economic Research for assistance in preparing the series on national product and its components.

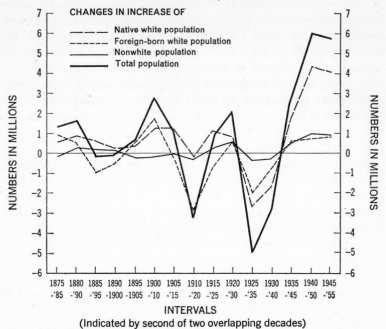

conspicuously, rising and declining fairly markedly from one five-year interval to the next.

The amplitude of the swings is damped by the use of a quinquennial overlap between decades. An annual overlap, mentioned above, would reveal these swings more clearly, and would register their amplitude more accurately since there would be less averaging out at the peaks and at the troughs.

Swings in Population Movements

The net additions to total population fluctuate from one decade to the next, describing over the period since 1870 three long swings from peak to peak, or two complete and two incomplete swings from trough to trough (see Fig. 1, based on Tables 1 and 2; all tables are at the end of this article). The first peak is in the interval from 1875–85 to 1880–90; the trough is in the two following intervals, population increase diminishing to the decade 1890–1900. The next peak is in the interval from 1895–1905 to 1900–10; and the trough in the interval from 1905–15 to 1910–20. The next maximum rise is in the interval from 1915–25 to 1920–30; and the low point is reached in the next interval but with the decline continuing to the 1930–40 decade. There follows the rising phase of a new swing. The average duration of the swings is twenty years, but five-year intervals do not permit precise determination of average duration in terms of years.

The changes in net additions to native white and foreign born population follow a fluctuating pattern similar to that just indicated. There seems to be a tendency for the long swings in additions to the foreign born population to *lead*, but because of the crudity of the units of measurement this finding cannot be accepted with any assurance. Additions to the nonwhite population move differently. They drop fairly continuously from a peak in the intervals during the 1880's and fail to reveal the second of the three swings. It is particularly noteworthy that additions to the nonwhite population do not show a rise from the 1890's to the first decade of the twentieth century similar to that in the additions to other sectors of the population.

The swings observed in changes in net addition to population are also found in changes in births (Fig. 2, based on Table 3). We find in *total* births the same three peak-to-peak swings, and the same combination of complete and incomplete trough-to-trough swings. There is some tendency in the early part of the period for the changes in births to lag somewhat behind those in net increase of population (thus the first peak is shown a quinquennium later in Table 3, col. 6, than in Table 2, col. 8, and the first trough a decade later). But again in view of the crudity of the underlying units not much emphasis can be placed on the timing comparison. More important is the fact that the long swings in the births of nonwhite population also show a markedly different pattern from those in white population—the former missing the second swing during the first decade to decade and a half of the twentieth century.

Immigration to this country has been almost exclusively of the white race and long swings in immigration have played a dominant part in the long swings in total population increase. Since native white births can be either of native, foreign born, or mixed parentage, long swings in immigration should produce, with some lag, similar movements in native white births. It is, therefore, of interest to inquire whether the fluctuations observed in Figure 2 and Table 3 in native white births (and hence total births) can be due exclusively to long swings in net immigration. Table 4 is designed to answer this question by showing for the period from 1885 to 1930

Fig. 2. CHANGES IN BIRTHS BY RACE, OVERLAPPING DECADES, 1870–1955

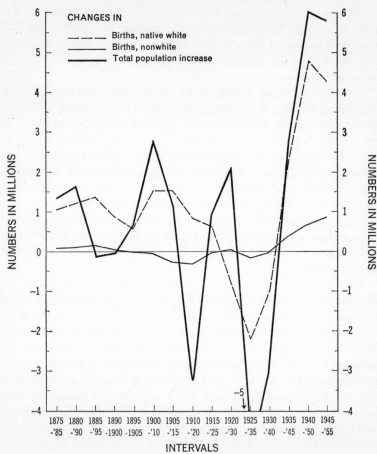

white births of native and of foreign-born or mixed parentage. Since long swings can be observed in changes in births in which both parents are native born, and in which, therefore, no direct contribution of immigrant population is involved, immigration is not the sole factor affecting swings in native white births. A similar conclusion over a longer period, based on a much rougher comparison using decade intervals, was suggested in an earlier study.[2] In short, long swings in births may be associated with the same conditions that produce long swings in immigration, but only in part are they

[2] Simon Kuznets and Ernest Rubin, *Immigration and the Foreign Born*, Occasional Paper No. 46 (New York: National Bureau of Economic Research, 1954), Table 9, pp. 46–48.

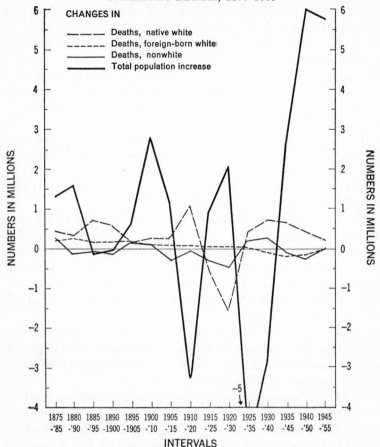

Fig. 3. CHANGES IN DEATHS BY NATIVITY AND RACE,
OVERLAPPING DECADES, 1870–1955

a direct consequence of the latter.

The susceptibility of deaths to long swings is tested in Table 5 and depicted graphically in Figure 3. Fluctuations in deaths may tend to have positive association with those in births, since the age specific death rates of infants are much higher than the total crude death rates. On the other hand, economic conditions favorable to population increase may be unfavorable to deaths. We do find swings in changes in total deaths, but the timing relationship to swings in net increase in population is rather irregular at first. In the former there appears to be a single long swing to a trough in the interval from 1900–10 to 1905–15. Then two events occur: the influenza epidemic of 1918 which raises the deaths substantially in the 1910–20 and 1915–25 decades, and the depression of the 1930's which raises them in the 1930–40 decade. The resulting peaks in the decade totals of deaths, coinciding as they do with troughs in population increase due to other causes (the decline of immigration during the World War I period and the 1930's, and the decline of births in the later period), produce the expected inverse correlation between the long swings in changes in deaths and those in total population increase in the twentieth century.

Here again fluctuations in the deaths of the nonwhite population differ substantially from those of the white, the former declining and the latter rising during the 1890's and the early twentieth century. The difference in the timing pattern is most pronounced after the 1870–80's and until about World War I.

The long swings are most prominent in the inflow of aliens or immigrants and the outflow of aliens or emigrants (Fig. 4, based on Table 6), despite the crude procedures adopted here.[3] Since these long swings are familiar, we note just two aspects. First, the magnitude of the fluctuations in arrivals is large even during recent intervals, after the introduction of restrictive laws that reduced the average volume to a trickle. Second, swings in departures tend to be positively correlated with those in arrivals, particularly before World War I. Departures in the decades of unrestricted migration were primarily from the ranks of recent arrivals who failed to adjust to conditions in this country.

Both the balance of births over deaths, that is, additions resulting from natural increase, and the balance of arrivals over departures, that is, net migration, fluctuate in long swings similar to those revealed in the net increase in total population (see Fig. 5, based on Table 7). Until World War I, changes in the natural increase tended to lag by about a quinquennium behind those in the migration balance; but there is complete synchronism thereafter. The two series relating to changes in net increase in total population (Table 7, columns 4 and 5) differ because one is derived by adding migration balance items that have not been adjusted to the census population totals of foreign born and the other is based directly upon these census totals; but long swings in the two series are identical in timing, and differ but little in magnitude.

Two further aspects of the long swings in population increase

[3] In Kuznets and Rubin, *ibid.*, the swings were studied by observing the succession of short-cycle averages in the annual data; see particularly Table 4 and Chart 3, pp. 28–29.

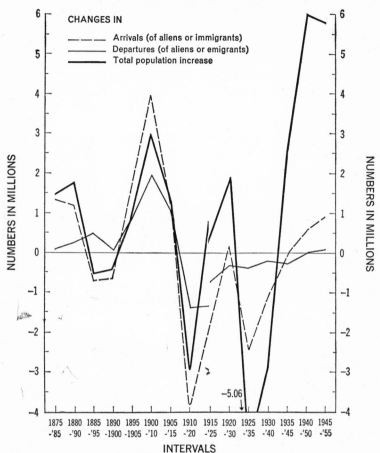

Fig. 4. CHANGES IN IMMIGRATION AND EMIGRATION,
OVERLAPPING DECADES, 1870–1955

and component flows may be noted. The first concerns the magnitude of these swings. The tables presented so far measured them in absolute numbers, in millions of persons. But obviously if the average volume of native white births is many times larger than that of nonwhite, we would expect the absolute fluctuations in the former to be much larger than those in the latter. It is, therefore, of interest to relate the absolute changes recorded so far to some base, expressing them as percentages of the latter. Two somewhat different sets of bases can be suggested. The first is the population that could and did *produce* the changes, the flows whose fluctuations we are studying. The second is the population to which the

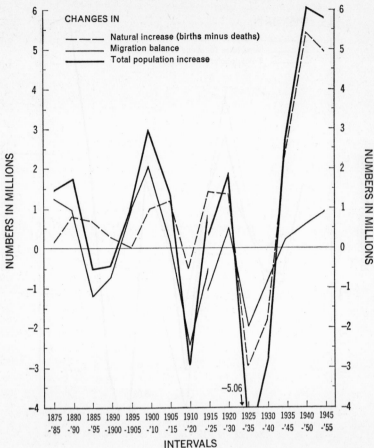

Fig. 5. CHANGES IN THE NATURAL INCREASE OF POPULATION AND IN THE MIGRATION BALANCE, OVERLAPPING DECADES, 1870–1955

changes *accrued*. In the case of a closed, homogeneous population, the two bases are identical: since under these conditions only population can produce population, the originating and the receiving base are the same—as is the case with the nonwhite population in this country, in which migration over the period under question is so small that it can be neglected. But this is true neither of the native white population, nor of the foreign born.

Table 8 summarizes the relevant calculations. Changes in native white births and deaths are related to the native white population, the "receiving" group, but since it is not the complete "producing" group, an alternate line is given in which changes in native white births are related to the sum of native white and foreign-born population. Nonwhite births and deaths are related to total nonwhite population, both the producing and the receiving population. Arrivals, departures, and deaths of the foreign-born are related to the total foreign-born population in the country, whose changing numbers reflect or receive all these streams, but which "produce" only deaths and departures. Arrivals are "produced" (originate) elsewhere. The producing base in this case is the total population in all the areas of the world whose residents can enter freely, under United States law, for purposes of settlement. I have no measure of this "producing" base at hand.

The average percentages which changes in the flows (gross additions such as births or arrivals, gross drafts such as deaths or departures, net additions such as the natural increase or migration balance) constitute of the population base are either wholly or partly a function of the rate of increase of that base. If the average percentages which changes in births or in natural increase constitute of the population base are high, the rate of growth of that population will also be high.

In Table 8 we show the average percentages which changes in births or arrivals, deaths or departures, and natural increase or net balance, constituted of the appropriate population bases for three long periods—the first extending roughly from 1870 to 1900; the second from about 1900 to 1930; the last from the 1920's to date. Each of these long periods includes five intervals and is based upon estimates for six overlapping decades. Figure 6 shows these averages separately for native white, nonwhite, foreign-born, and total population.

In general, changes in births and deaths, taken as a percentage of the base population, for the nonwhite group are exaggerated replicas of those for the native white group—except that the birth percentage for nonwhites is extremely high in the most recent period. Consequently, the percentage level of changes in net additions declines for native white population, but not for the nonwhite. For the foreign-born, the long-term trend movements are clear: the percentages of changes in arrivals, deaths and departures, and net additions all decline.

The results for total population are intriguing. The natural increase percentages rise from the first period to the second, and from the second to the third. Even this does not assure constancy, let alone increase, in the percentage rate of natural increase to total population, since we deal here with *absolute* additions to the

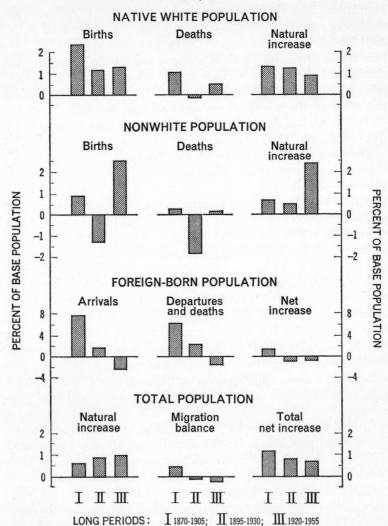

Fig. 6. Changes in Inflows, Drafts, and Net Additions to the Population as Percentages of the Base Population, Averages for Three Long Periods, 1870–1955

NATIVE WHITE POPULATION

Births   Deaths   Natural increase

NONWHITE POPULATION

Births   Deaths   Natural increase

FOREIGN-BORN POPULATION

Arrivals   Departures and deaths   Net increase

TOTAL POPULATION

Natural increase   Migration balance   Total net increase

LONG PERIODS: I 1870-1905; II 1895-1930; III 1920-1955

balance of births over deaths, while the total population base is rising steadily. But the migration balance percentages move in the opposite direction, declining consistently. And it is this decline that produces a decline in the percentages which changes in total additions to population constitute of the population base.

In Table 8 we also show the deviation of the change for each interval in births or arrivals, deaths or departures, and in net addi-

338

tions (expressed as percentages of the population base) from the arithmetic mean percentage for each of three long periods. These deviations, averaged regardless of sign, thus relate to the arithmetic means in Figure 6. They are crude measures of the relative amplitude of long swings (of their amplitude related to population stock at the base). As expected, the swings in net additions to the foreign-born population show the widest relative amplitude. Less expected and hence of more interest is the consistently wider amplitude of the swings in additions to nonwhite population than in those to native white population; apparently, the birth and death volumes are subject to more violent long-term fluctuations for the nonwhite than for the native white population, despite the fact that swings in native white births are magnified by the rather wide fluctuations in the foreign-born.

Of particular importance is the finding that the relative amplitude of the long swings widens with the passage of time. The average deviations in the measures relating to net increase of native white population (line III1d), nonwhite population (line II2c), and total population (line II4c or II4d) all rise. That for the foreign-born population (line II3d) declines because of the restriction of immigration which reduced markedly the amplitude of fluctuations in additions. Apparently, for the other population stocks the decline in the rate of secular growth was accompanied by a widening of the long swings—the result partly of major wars, partly of greater sensitivity of birth and death rates to social conditions, partly of a possibly wider amplitude of swings in other conditioning factors.

How large, then, is the contribution of each component to swings in total population growth? Can we measure the proportional contributions to these swings of movements in births, deaths, or migration of the various sectors of the population? An attempt to answer this question is provided in Table 9. We established the dates of "reference" phases of long swings in the net increase in total population (see headings of columns) and for each phase calculated the shortage or excess in the *actual* population increase by comparing it with a *hypothetical* population increase based on carrying forward the change of the initial interval. Hence for a declining phase in the long swing, the change in the initial interval is a peak positive change; and its extrapolation over the subsequent intervals included in the phase yields a population shortage. The opposite effect is attained during an upward phase of the long swing. Calculating similar shortages or excesses for each component by the same procedure, we derived component figures that should add out to the total population excess or deficiency in line 2 (for which the underlying series of total population is a sum of components).

The results in Table 9, particularly the percentage distribution, confirm what we learned from the preceding tables, and throw the findings into sharper focus. Briefly, the foreign-born segment (largely immigration and emigration) accounts for by far the dominant share of the excesses and deficiencies associated with the swings, at least through World War I. But even beyond that period, despite restriction of immigration and decline in the relative proportion of foreign-born population in the country, this segment still contributes a share appreciably larger than its share in total population (compare lines 34 and 37). On the other hand, the native white population contributes much less than its share in the total population—at least through the 1920's. However, in the last two phases distinguished in Table 9, the share contributed by the native white population becomes dominant—and is much closer to its share in the country's population stock. The nonwhite population's record is most curious: until World War I its swings tend, if anything, to run counter to those in net additions to total population, and only in the last three phases is the contribution of nonwhite population to the swings in total net additions positive—and somewhat in excess of its share in the total population stock.

An even more important distinction is that between the contributions of natural increase and of migration balance (lines 28 and 31). These, expressed as percentages of the base population, are plotted in Figure 7. In the first three phases covered the balance of births over deaths contributes only from about a fiftieth to an eighth of the total population excesses and deficiencies involved in the "reference" long swings. That share jumps in the fourth phase and then rises to eight tenths in the last phase. By contrast, the share of the migration balance, dominating the first three phases at about nine tenths of the total, drops down to about one fifth by the last phase. Finally, total excesses and deficiencies, expressed as percentages of the population base, range from plus to minus 10 percent (in the early phases) and increase proportionately in the last two.

The findings of Table 9 can be summarized as follows. During the early periods and until the 1920's, the long swings in population growth are accounted for largely by the migration balances, with some minor contribution of the natural increase of native white, but not of nonwhite, population. Since the 1920's, these swings are

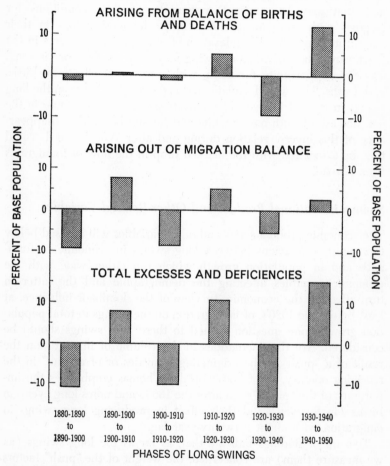

EXCESSES AND DEFICIENCIES IN PERCENT OF TOTAL
POPULATION IN THE MIDDLE OF EACH PHASE:

(Decades shown are the second of two overlapping)

ARISING FROM BALANCE OF BIRTHS
AND DEATHS

ARISING OUT OF MIGRATION BALANCE

TOTAL EXCESSES AND DEFICIENCIES

PERCENT OF BASE POPULATION

PERCENT OF BASE POPULATION

| 1880-1890 to 1890-1900 | 1890-1900 to 1900-1910 | 1900-1910 to 1910-1920 | 1910-1920 to 1920-1930 | 1920-1930 to 1930-1940 | 1930-1940 to 1940-1950 |

PHASES OF LONG SWINGS

accounted for mostly by the natural increase of native population,
both white and nonwhite—although the foreign-born component
still contributes a share appreciably larger than its dwindling share
in total population.

The deviant movement of nonwhite births, deaths, and net increase during most of the period before World War I requires
further exploration. It may well be, as Brinley Thomas argues, that
fluctuations in immigration, most of which went to the industrial

North, limited opportunities for Negroes (the dominant group in the nonwhite population) and inhibited their migration northward.[4] If variations in the flow of immigration meant variations in economic opportunities for Negroes, the upward phase in the long swing in migration may have meant worsening economic conditions for Negroes with consequent effects upon the long swings in their natural increase; and the relaxation of immigration pressures in the downward phase of the long swing may have meant more internal economic opportunity for them, with consequent effects on births and deaths. This would explain an *inverse* relation between the long swings in the net increase of nonwhite population and those in the net increase of both native white and foreign born. The disappearance of this inverse relation during and after World War I would then be associated with the marked drop in the flow of immigrants from abroad.

Swings in National Product and Other Related Variables

The economic-product series and other variables will be used below to suggest connections between long swings in economic performance and in population growth which run either way, with the economic variables affecting the demographic and the latter in turn affecting the economic. In view of the dominant influence, at least before the 1920's, of immigration on the swings in total population growth, one question related to these long swings should be considered. Are the fluctuations in the volume of immigration the result of a "push" in the originating countries or of a "pull" in the receiving country, or of both? Brinley Thomas emphasizes the importance of the "push," even after the 1860's and notes long cycles in births (in Sweden) and their effect in producing long swings in emigration with about a twenty-year lag.[5]

Two major findings indicate that, as far as the long swings (as we measure them) are concerned, the weight of the "push" factors cannot have been very large and that much more weight is to be attached to the "pull" factors in this country. The first is that the long swings observed in *total* immigration are also found fairly uniformly in the several groups by originating areas (Fig. 8, based on Table 10). In Table 10 we distinguish nine European areas, and the Americas (Canada, Mexico, and the rest of the Western Hemi-

---

[4] See *Migration and Economic Growth*, pp. 130–133.
[5] *Ibid.*, pp. 116–118.

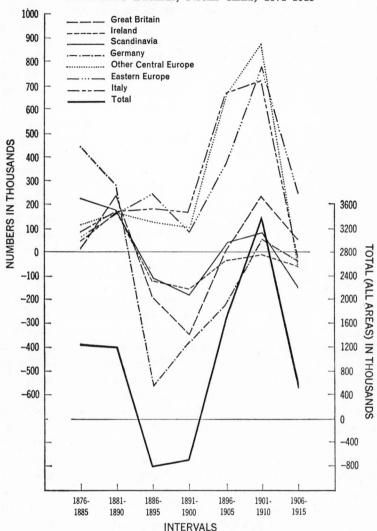

Fig. 8. CHANGES IN IMMIGRATION BY SELECTED AREAS OF ORIGIN, OVERLAPPING DECADES, FISCAL YEARS, 1871–1915

INTERVALS
(Indicated by second of two overlapping decades)

sphere). Despite the variations in the *longer-term trends* in immigration from these several areas and slight discrepancies in timing, the swings in the changes in overlapping decades are quite similar. Since it is highly unlikely that the timing of either the birth cycles or other "push" elements was the same in so many different parts of the world, the similarity must be ascribed to some "pull" factors.

The second relevant finding is the large proportional weight of emigration and the positive correlation of its long swings with the long swings of arrivals or immigration. Since the long swings in population growth in this country are directly produced by the *net balance* of migration, not by immigration alone, the fact that the "push" of this country—which stimulates departures—is an important factor is another way of saying that conditions in *this* country are more important than conditions in countries in which the immigrants originate or to which they return. To support this general point of view we present the evidence of long swings in economic conditions in this country since they should reflect the "pull" element and thus explain the long swings in both the net migration balance and the natural increase.

Flow of goods to consumers, total or per capita, is perhaps the best aggregate measure of changes in economic well-being and would affect both birth and death rates in the country and, particularly, migration from abroad. The question is whether in the comparison with changes in net additions to population, or with the net balance of migration, we should use changes in *flow* of goods or changes in *additions* to flow (i.e., the first or the second derivative, whether in total or per capita flow). Table 11 shows both measures (cols. 5–6 for total flow, and cols. 7–8 for per capita flow). Both measures for total flow of goods and one for the per capita flow are plotted in Figure 9. In general, changes either in total flow or in additions to flow of goods to consumers, and changes in flow per capita reveal long swings of about the same duration as changes in net additions to population and in the net migration balance. There is also a fair similarity in timing, with the interesting and possibly significant difference that changes in the total flow of goods sometimes precede changes in the net migration balance, and, to an even greater degree, changes in the total net additions to population. Before the 1920's, changes in *additions* to flow of goods to consumers and in flow per capita definitely *lead* changes in additions to total population, and by a sufficient margin to suggest that the lead is significant.

In interpreting this comparison we run into some difficulty. We deal here with movements in broad aggregates which are not necessarily indicative of changes in conditions of those groups in the population whose economic success would influence either the native birth and death rates or the net inflow of immigrants. But one may argue that *substantial,* if not moderate, rises in the per capita flow of goods to consumers can be assumed to represent sig-

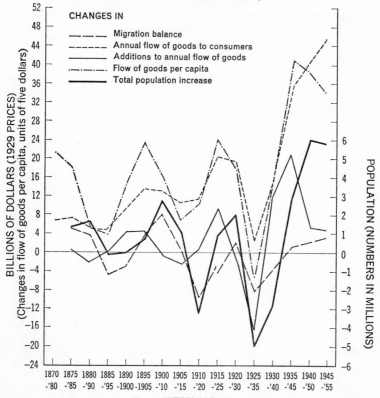

Fig. 9. CHANGES IN THE POPULATION INCREASE AND IN THE MIGRATION BALANCE COMPARED WITH CHANGES IN THE FLOW OF GOODS TO CONSUMERS (1929 PRICES), OVERLAPPING DECADES, 1870–1955

nificant rises in the economic level of the lower income groups. And one may therefore assume that changes in the supply of goods per capita are the telling index, the one which with some delay produces fluctuations in changes in *additions* to population, more quickly *via* the net migration balance and somewhat more slowly *via* the balance of births over deaths. Without holding to this thesis with any firm conviction, I shall use changes in flow of goods to consumers per capita, the index of *quickening* or *slackening* growth of goods, as a measure of the "pull" which economic conditions in this country exercise upon net migration and natural increase balances.

Net additions to population, on the other hand, bring some response on the economic side, particularly in the way of residential housing. We expect long swings in gross and net residential construction (the series used here is limited to nonfarm) to reflect those

345

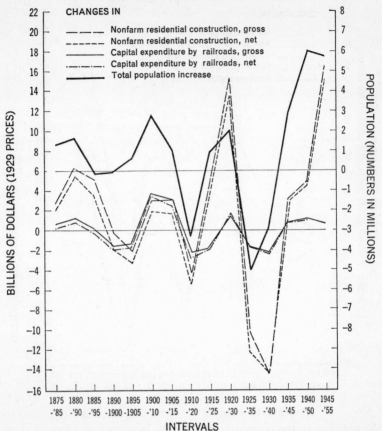

Fig. 10. Changes in Nonfarm Residential Construction and in Capital Expenditures by Railroads Compared with Changes in the Population Increase, Overlapping Decades, 1870–1955

CHANGES IN
— — — Nonfarm residential construction, gross
— — — — Nonfarm residential construction, net
———— Capital expenditure by railroads, gross
.—..—..—. Capital expenditure by railroads, net
———— Total population increase

BILLIONS OF DOLLARS (1929 PRICES)

POPULATION (NUMBERS IN MILLIONS)

INTERVALS
(Indicated by second of two overlapping decades)

in net additions to population; and they do, sometimes with a lag, particularly at the trough points (see Fig. 10, based on Table 12). Another "population-sensitive" component of capital formation is capital expenditures by railroads. These expenditures reflect the long swings in population growth partly because railroads serve the entire population and partly because their volume reflects swings in the volume of *internal* migration, either from the countryside to the cities or across the country. The long swings in capital expenditures by railroads are as conspicuous as those in nonfarm residential construction, and even more closely timed to the long swings in population growth.

The "other" sectors in capital formation (other than the population-sensitive) also show long swings; but, most significantly, these, before the 1920's, are inversely related to the swings in population-sensitive capital formation and in total population growth (see Fig. 11, based on Table 13). Construction other than nonfarm residential or railroad (largely industrial plants, store, and office buildings), producers' durable equipment other than for railroads (largely industrial machinery), changes in inventories (largely in distributive channels), and changes in net claims against foreign countries are these "other" capital formation sectors. This inverse correlation suggests that there were some limits to *total* capital formation in the country, perhaps largely on the savings side, and that when volumes of residential construction and railroad construction and equipment were rising most rapidly, other types of capital formation suffered.

This hypothesis requires further exploration. But its plausibility is supported by the fact that in the 1870's the gross volume of population-sensitive capital formation was over 40 percent of total capital formation; and that even in the first decade of the twentieth century it was still about 25 percent. There is also some suggestion of the mechanism in the changes in the level of yields on industrial stocks, compared with those of yields on railroad bonds and stocks (Table 14). Thus the interval from 1890–99 to 1895–1904, which is marked by a peak change in "other" capital formation in Table 13, is also marked by the greatest decline in yields on industrial stocks, a cheapening of equity money. The same interval saw a decline in the volume of capital expenditures by railroads, and smaller declines in the yields on both railroad stocks and railroad bonds. Further analysis requires study of more detailed components of "other" capital formation for far more sensitive time intervals. The purpose of this comment and of Table 14 is merely to indicate that it should be possible to trace the impact of long swings in population-sensitive capital formation on those in "other" capital formation.

Stretching the same speculative thread further, one may note that the long swings in "other" capital formation are fairly coincident with those in changes in *additions* to flow of goods to consumers or in flow per capita (see Fig. 11). The connection here may operate in one of two ways, or in both. The slackening of additions to "other" capital formation, particularly industrial plant and producers' equipment, may mean slackening in the rate of growth of per capita flow of goods to consumers. Alternately and complementarily, any restriction upon growth in other sectors of the

Fig. 11. Changes in Capital Formation (gross), in Additions to the Flow
of Goods to Consumers, and in the Population Increase,
Overlapping Decades, 1870–1955

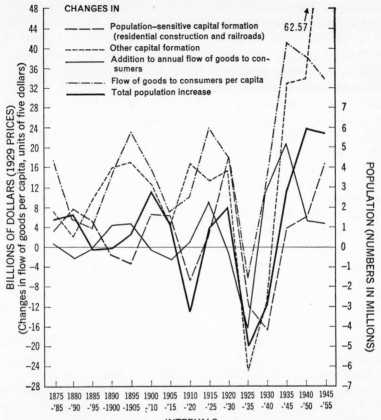

INTERVALS
(Indicated by second of two overlapping decades)

economy produced by acceleration in the volume of residential construction and of capital expenditures by railroads may mean retardation not only of "other" capital formation but also directly of flow of goods to consumers.

On the basis of the foregoing speculation we can now sketch the self-perpetuating long swings in population and product in this country before the 1920's. The long swings in additions to per capita flow of goods to consumers resulted, with some lag, in long swings first in the net migration balance and then in the natural increase, yielding swings in total population growth. The latter then induced, again with some lag, similar swings in population-sensitive capital formation, which caused inverted long swings in "other" capital formation and in changes in per capita flow of goods to consumers. The swings in the latter then started another long swing in the net migration balance and in natural increase, and so on. This, however, is a tentative sketch designed to indicate lines of further exploration and does not claim even rough validity.

If such a self-perpetuating long cycle mechanism—based on the inverted relation between long swings in "other" capital formation and in per capita flow of goods to consumers, on the one hand, and population growth and population-sensitive capital formation, on the other, plus some lags in the reactions—actually operated, the break in recent decades can easily be explained. The two new factors were major wars and a drastic decline in net migration inflow and in the rate of population growth. Even the latter factor alone would have produced a situation in which the productive capacity of the country forged well ahead of its population growth, and a quickening in the rate of population growth or of population-sensitive capital formation would not have induced inverted long swings in "other" capital formation or in additions to per capita flow of goods to consumers. Yet while the lags and the inverted relationship may have disappeared, the long swings have neither ceased nor become milder. Indeed, because of the new synchronism the amplitude of the long swings may have widened.

Gross national product is the most comprehensive measure of the volume of economic product in the country, and when expressed in constant prices is ordinarily considered the best approximation to a country's total economic activity. It is, therefore, most significant to find, as we do in Figure 12 (based on Table 15), that there are long swings in changes in both total gross national product and gross national product *per capita*; and that these swings, particularly in the latter, synchronize quite well with swings in changes in total additions to the population. Thus, as the rate of growth of population accelerates or retards, so does the rate of growth of total product since product is a function of population (which provides the major productive factor, viz., labor) and also that of product per capita.

In Table 16 we calculate product excesses and deficiencies within the "reference" phases of long swings in net additions to total population. This is the technique applied to population in deriving excesses and deficiencies in Table 9. Table 16 is in a sense a recapitulation of much of the earlier discussion. It shows the positive conformity between changes in total and per capita gross national

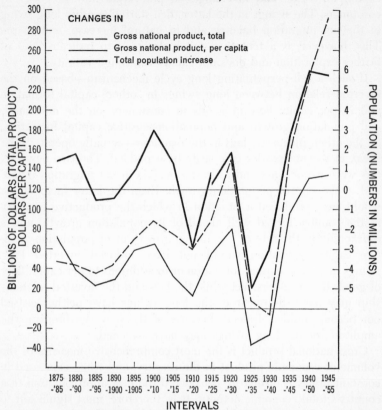

Fig. 12. Changes in the Population Increase Compared with Changes in the Gross National Product, Total and Per Capita, 1929 Prices, Overlapping Decades, 1870–1955

INTERVALS
(Indicated by second of two overlapping decades)

product, and changes in population-sensitive capital formation and in population increase. It shows the negative relationship, until the recent decades, between changes in "other" capital formation and in per capita flow of goods to consumers, and those in population increase. And it shows that the amplitude of the swings in changes in the product flows and in their components is far from negligible.

Table 17 and Figure 13 are largely the result of idle curiosity but they provide intriguing illustrations of long swings in activities in which one might not expect them. The long swings in receipts from public lands, as long as they were fairly widely available for sale, can be explained: the quickening of population growth would involve similar movements in the rate of expansion to new lands. The swings in patent applications can be assumed to reflect fluctua-

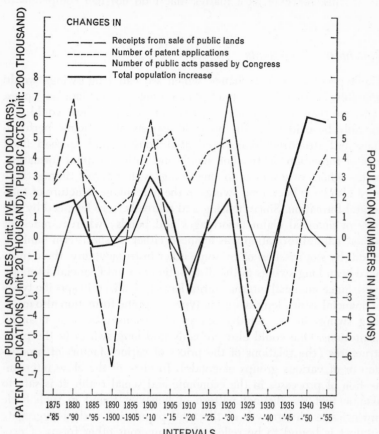

Fig. 13. CHANGES IN THE POPULATION INCREASE COMPARED WITH CHANGES IN OTHER ACTIVITIES, OVERLAPPING DECADES, 1870–1955

tions in the rate of growth of economic activity, particularly of capital formation, which may be expected to stimulate inventive activity. But the number of public acts passed by Congress also fluctuates in long swings that are fairly synchronous with those in net additions to population; this movement is both puzzling and intriguing. Of course, this means synchronism also with the long swings in national product. But why should our additions to the stock of legislation fluctuate in the same way as additions to total population and the flow of total product? Perhaps the answer can be found in the kind of legislation enacted. Perhaps a quickening of the rate of growth of population and national product means also a quickening of some of the tensions that require legislative treatment. This, however, is a matter that I do not feel competent to explore.

Concluding Comments

The type of historical change which we call long swings would probably be found in a much wider range of phenomena, space, and time than was indicated above. For example, they would presumably be evident in the financial aspects of economic performance and structure. Since residential housing and railroad fixed capital formation on the one hand, and "other" capital formation, on the other, were subject to long swings with different timing, there must also have been long swings in the percentage structure of total capital formation. Since housing and railroads were financed by one type of financial claim (mortgages and bonds) whereas much of "other" capital formation was financed either by short-term banking credit, by stock issues, or by some other instrumentality, there must have been long swings in the distribution of total financial assets by type. Since financial intermediaries have specialized in specific types of financial assets, long swings in types of capital formation also mean long swings in the relative shares of various classes of financial institutions. One could also probably find long swings in the price structures (the relations of the prices of various factors of production or of various groups of goods). In view of the close interconnection of processes in the economic and social realm, it is safe to assume that the distinct pattern of behavior found in such basic processes as the growth of the total population and of aggregate product is bound to be reflected in numerous other forms of economic and social behavior.

Second, while our discussion was limited to the period from 1870 to 1955, the few continuous series available for the period before 1870 in this country indicate the existence of these swings in the past. For example, the decennial population census back to 1790 shows that the percentage rate of growth per decade fluctuated regularly up and down from one interval to the next during the seven intervals from 1790 through 1860, a regularity whose probability as a purely random occurrence is low (a similar regularity of successive up and down movements was resumed after the Civil War). And knowing what we do about the nature of the forces at play, we could hardly assume the absence of long swings before the Civil War. What is more important, there is reason to expect this pattern to continue. Births have been rising at a rather remarkable rate since the second half of the 1930's. The *continuation* of this rise at the same rate for much longer is unlikely. But if the volume of births becomes stabilized at the "normal" increase, there will be a downturn in the long swing—a decline in the *change* from one level of births to the next. Will it have the expected effect upon population-sensitive capital formation? What will it mean to the present housing boom? What will its consequences be elsewhere in the economy? While some of the long swings that we have studied are past history in the sense that the specific factors are not likely to recur (for example, the net migration balance in the relative volume of pre-World War I days), much of it is current and future history and germane to the analysis of the changing patterns of the economy.

Third, the long swings are not restricted to this country. Fluctuations of this type, somewhat different in timing and perhaps in duration, can be found in the demographic and economic experience of other countries.[6] There is no reason to assume that countries permitting free migration would escape the effects of long swings in migration opportunities. One may expect to find long-term fluctuations in births and deaths and, if only for that reason, in economic and social activities that respond in various ways to population numbers.

While long swings in the rate of growth of demographic and other social phenomena are widespread, there is little tested knowledge of them. The very profusion of terms employed to designate them—secondary secular movements, trend cycles, long swings, long cycles—is a reflection of lack of assurance as to what they, their established characteristics, and the factors behind them really are. This is partly a result of the obstacles in the way of proper empirical study of such movements: one needs a continuous record over quite a long period, and such records are neither easily available nor easily analyzable. It is partly a result of not being able to translate knowledge into policy. Our policy agencies have a difficult enough time interpreting shorter-term and more obvious changes, let alone swings that may extend over a twenty-year span, although the situation may change with increased awareness and the realiza-

---

[6] In addition to the items cited in footnote 1, see Dorothy S. Thomas, *Social Aspects of the Business Cycle* (London: Routledge & Sons, 1925), and *Social and Economic Aspects of Swedish Population Movements, 1750–1933* (New York: The Macmillan Co., 1941); and A. Lösch, *Bevölkerungswellen und Wechsellagen, Beiträge zur Erforschung der wirtschaftlichen Wechsellagen,* Band 13 (Jena, 1936).

tion that some of the recent errors in diagnosis and projection may have been due to a failure to study the twilight zone between the underlying long trend and the business cycle. And it is partly the case of the usual lag of economic and social analysis behind the accumulation of data; the latter, when properly examined, always reveal findings that call for explanations that are not at hand.

Statistical Appendix

This appendix assembles the basic tables arranged in the order of discussion in the text. When necessary the tables are followed by detailed notes on the sources and methods used in the derivation of the estimates. While complete coverage of sources and methods is not possible, the details provided are indispensable for technical review of the data basic to the discussion; the estimates themselves may be of use to students in the field in other connections.

Table 1. POPULATION ESTIMATES BY NATIVITY AND RACE,
1870–1955 (in millions)

Year	Native white (1)	Nonwhite (2)	Foreign-born (3)	Total (4)
1870	29.36	5.89	5.51	40.76
1875	33.30	6.59	6.43	46.32
1880	37.28	6.86	6.60	50.74
1885	41.79	7.38	8.45	57.62
1890	46.62	7.88	9.15	63.65
1895	51.75	8.62	10.02	70.39
1900	56.85	9.29	10.22	76.36
1905	62.38	9.84	11.54	83.76
1910	68.72	10.32	13.46	92.50
1915	75.53	10.84	14.60	100.97
1920	81.68	11.06	13.65	106.39
1925	89.67	11.88	14.24	115.79
1930	96.70	12.62	13.96	123.28
1935	102.03	13.12	12.53	127.68
1940	107.37	13.59	11.37	132.33
1945	114.41	14.58	10.54	139.53
1950	124.08	16.01	10.11	150.20
1955	135.18	17.90	10.10	163.18

The population estimates for census years (those ending in 0) are based on the census totals. Several adjustments (described briefly below) have, however, been made. Being census totals, the estimates relate to the particular date of enumeration (June 1 for 1870, 1880, 1890, and 1900; April 15 for 1910; January 1 for 1920; and April 1 for 1930, 1940, and 1950). The midcensus data before 1940 are derived by apportioning total deaths during the census interval between the two halves, and estimating the number of children 0 to 4 at a point of time five years before the second of two censuses. The specific date of the estimate for each midcensus year before 1940 is at about the middle of the census interval, and can be calculated from the dates of the census enumerations.

Census Years, 1870–1940

The census year totals for 1870–1940 were adjusted in two ways. (1) Since the number of children 0 to 4 is usually underreported, we estimated this number by applying reverse survival ratios to the population 10 to 14 years of age at the following census. These calculations were carried through separately for males and females, white and nonwhite. For native whites the survival ratios were obtained from a series of life tables prepared by Dorothy Thomas and the staff of the Population Redistribution and Economic Growth Study at the University of Pennsylvania in connection with the Kuznets-Rubin paper cited in footnote 2. For nonwhites, overwhelmingly Negroes, for the period 1900–40, the survival ratios from life tables centering around census years were averaged to approximate decade ratios. For the period before 1900, the ratio of nonwhite to native white ratios for 1900–10 was multiplied by the native white ratios for 1870–80, 1880–90, and 1890–1900, and the resulting products were used as "revival ratios" for nonwhites.

(2) The second adjustment was for the reported census figures of 1870 when total population was underreported. The adjustment was made by applying survival ratios to the more complete enumeration of 1880, using the 1880–90 ratios adjusted for the effect of changing mortality. This adjustment was made for all age groups (by ten-year intervals to the group 65 and over),

separately for males and females, white and nonwhite. The life tables for native whites mentioned above were used to estimate the effect of changing mortality. The ten-year survival ratios for each age group for 1870–80 were divided by the 1890–1900 ratios. The resulting quotients were multiplied by the census survival ratios for 1880–90. The smaller ratios resulting from this operation were then divided into the appropriate 1880 populations to yield 1870 populations for the age groups 5–9 through 50–54. For ages 55 and over in 1870 the unadjusted ratios for 1880–90 were used because of the unreliability of the life tables for these age groups. The age group 0–4 was again estimated by the life-table survival ratios referred to above. The same ratios were used to adjust the nonwhite census survival ratios.

The survival-ratio technique can be applied only to native white and nonwhite population (almost all of the latter are native-born and were so assumed in the calculation). For the foreign born we used the estimates given in Kuznets and Rubin, *op. cit.*, Table B-6, p. 102.

Midcensus Totals, 1875–1935

For the native white and nonwhite population the totals involved (1) apportioning the total of deaths over the census period, derived from application of survival rates, between the two halves of the period and (2) estimating the age group 0–4 at the midcensus date. The former procedure is described in the notes to Table 5, and the latter in the notes to Table 3.

For 1875 a special adjustment had to be made, since the values were affected by the underenumeration in 1870. The computation was as follows. The ratios of five- to ten-year "reverse-survival" ratios obtained from life tables were multiplied by the reverse census survival ratios to yield "five-year census survival ratios." The life-table ratios used were computed from the English life table for 1891–1900 modified in accordance with the ratio of U.S. to English life tables for 1900–10. (The 1901–10 English life-table ratios were divided into the average of the ratios obtained from the 1900 and 1910 life tables.) Next, the "five-year census survival ratios" were multiplied by the ratio of 1880–90 ten-year survival ratios to the 1870–80 ten-year survival ratios. The resulting larger five-year ratios were then multiplied by the appropriate age groups from the 1880 census to yield an estimated 1875 population for all except the 0–4 group, which was estimated by the life-table survival ratio referred to above.

The midcensus figures for foreign-born before 1940 (July 1 totals for 1875, 1885, etc.) were taken from Kuznets and Rubin, *op. cit.*, Table B-6.

Totals for 1945, 1950, and 1955

These were derived by adding to the totals for 1940, the estimated births, deaths, and migration balances—separately for native white, foreign-born white, and nonwhite. The sources are described in the notes to Tables 3, 5, and 6. Although these estimates of births, deaths, and migration are for either calendar or fiscal years, they were added to a census total dated April 1, 1940. However, the minor error involved does not affect the conclusions, and the resulting population totals (in col. 4) are within a fraction of 1 percent of the published Bureau of Census totals (including armed forces overseas) for either January 1 or July 1 of the given years.

Table 2. NET ADDITIONS TO POPULATION, BY NATIVITY AND RACE, OVERLAPPING DECADES, 1870–1955 (in millions)

Period	Native white		Nonwhite		Foreign-born white		Total population	
	Addition (1)	Change in (1) (2)	Addition (3)	Change in (3) (4)	Addition (5)	Change in (5) (6)	Addition (7)	Change in (7) (8)
1870–1880	7.92		0.97		2.55	0.53	9.98	
1875–1885	8.49	0.57	0.79	−0.18	1.09		11.30	1.32
1880–1890	9.34	0.85	1.02	0.23	2.02	0.93	12.91	1.61
1885–1895	9.96	0.62	1.24	0.22	1.57	−0.98	12.77	−0.14
1890–1900	10.23	0.27	1.41	0.17	1.07	−0.50	12.71	−0.06
1895–1905	10.63	0.40	1.22	−0.19	1.52	0.45	13.37	0.66
1900–1910	11.87	1.24	1.03	−0.19	3.24	1.72	16.14	2.77
1905–1915	13.15	1.28	1.00	−0.03	3.06	−0.18	17.21	1.07
1910–1920	12.96	−0.19	0.74	−0.26	0.19	−2.87	13.89	−3.32
1915–1925	14.14	1.18	1.04	0.30	−0.36	−0.55	14.82	0.93
1920–1930	15.02	0.88	1.56	0.52	0.31	0.67	16.89	2.07
1925–1935	12.36	−2.66	1.24	−0.32	−1.71	−2.02	11.89	−5.00
1930–1940	10.67	−1.69	0.97	−0.27	−2.59	−0.88	9.05	−2.84
1935–1945	12.38	1.71	1.46	0.49	−1.99	0.60	11.85	2.80
1940–1950	16.71	4.33	2.42	0.96	−1.26	0.73	17.87	6.02
1945–1955	20.77	4.06	3.32	0.90	−0.44	0.82	23.65	5.78

The sources have been described in the notes to Table 1 (and will also be covered in the notes to Tables 3, 5, and 6). The exact terminal dates of the intervals are explained in the notes to Table 1. Although some intervals are slightly longer or shorter than a decade, the differences are too slight to impair the comparability of the periods, and no refinements were warranted.

Table 3. BIRTHS, BY RACE, OVERLAPPING DECADES, 1870–1955 (in millions)

Period	White Births (1)	White Change in (1) (2)	Nonwhite Births (3)	Nonwhite Change in (3) (4)	Total births Births (5)	Total births Change in (5) (6)
1870–1880	14.69		3.59		18.28	
1875–1885	15.73	1.04	3.66	0.07	19.39	1.11
1880–1890	16.93	1.20	3.75	0.09	20.68	1.29
1885–1895	18.28	1.35	3.91	0.16	22.19	1.51
1890–1900	19.15	0.87	3.95	0.04	23.10	0.91
1895–1905	19.70	0.55	3.92	−0.03	23.62	0.52
1900–1910	21.20	1.50	3.86	−0.06	25.06	1.44
1905–1915	22.72	1.52	3.59	−0.27	26.31	1.25
1910–1920	23.56	0.84	3.27	−0.32	26.83	0.52
1915–1925	24.18	0.62	3.23	−0.04	27.41	0.58
1920–1930	23.46	−0.72	3.26	0.03	26.72	−0.69
1925–1935	21.24	−2.22	3.11	−0.15	24.35	−2.37
1930–1940	20.26	−0.98	3.10	−0.01	23.36	−0.99
1935–1945	22.65	2.39	3.48	0.38	26.13	2.77
1940–1950	27.41	4.76	4.19	0.71	31.60	5.47
1945–1955	31.67	4.26	5.08	0.89	36.75	5.15

The estimates of births, by quinquennia, before 1940, involved two steps: (1) an estimate of the 0–4 group in both the census and the midcensus interval years; (2) an estimate of deaths in the 0–4 group during the period between birth and the end of the fifth year of life.

(1) The estimates of the 0–4 group in both the census and the midcensus interval years were, as indicated in the notes to Table 1, secured by applying "reverse survival" ratios to the population aged 10–14 and 5–9 at the terminal census. These ratios were derived in the following manner. For each life table of the United States from 1900 through 1950 the ratios of the L_x's in the 0–4 to those in the 5–9 group and of those in the 5–9 to those in the 10–14 group were obtained. In establishing the ratio to be used for a particular midcensal population, the ratios from the life tables centering around the initial and terminal censuses were weighted 3 to 1 in favor of the latter. For example, in computing the ratio used for the 1935, 0–4 group from the 1940 enumerated 5–9 group, the reverse survival ratio from the 1940 life table was given a weight of 3 and that from the 1930 life table a weight of 1.

For the period 1870–1900 the English life tables for 1871–80, 1881–90, and 1891–1900 were used to establish a trend. The U.S. ratio for whites for the 1900–10 decade (estimated by averaging the 1900 and 1910 ratios) was divided by the English ratio for 1901–10. The resulting quotient, multiplied by the English ratios for 1871–80, 1881–90, 1891–1900, yielded estimates of the ratios that would have been found in United States decade life tables, had these existed. These were converted into ratios centered around the census years by assuming that the decade ratios applied to 1875, 1885, and 1895, and then interpolating or extrapolating for census years. As before, the resultant ratios were weighted 3 to 1 in favor of the second census year. For nonwhites the corresponding ratios were obtained by dividing the ratio for nonwhites, 1900–10, by that for native whites for the same period, and multiplying the resultant quotient by the native white "revival ratios" for 1900–1895, 1890–85, and 1880–75.

(2) Estimating deaths that occurred in the 0–4 group during half of the

census interval, was part of the calculation of deaths during the whole interval. This calculation, carried through separately for each age group (0–4, and then, by ten-year age classes, through the age group of 65 and over), is described in the notes to Table 5.

Beginning with calendar 1940, direct information on births is available. Birth rates, adjusted for underregistration, are given separately for the white and nonwhite population for 1940, 1945, and annually beginning with 1948 (*Statistical Abstract for 1956*, Table 56, p. 58). Birth rates, again for whites and nonwhites but unadjusted for underregistration, are given annually for 1940–52 in *Historical Statistics of the United States, 1789–1945*, and *Continuation to 1952*, Series C-25 and C-26. Having both at hand, we estimated revised birth rates for the missing years in the 1940–50 decade by simple interpolation, and then applied each to the midyear estimates of total white and nonwhite population, 1940–50 (*ibid.*, Series B-34 and B-35). Beginning with 1948 we have direct estimates of the total number of births in the *Statistical Abstract for 1956*. With the help of these various series, we derived annual estimates of births, white and nonwhite, for calendar years 1940–54. These permitted us to calculate the overlapping decade totals from 1935–45 through 1945–55.

Table 4. NATIVE-WHITE BIRTHS (SURVIVING TO AGE 5), BY
NATIVITY OF PARENTS, 1885–1930 (in millions)

Period	Native parentage (1)	Change in (1) (2)	Foreign or mixed parentage (3)	Change in (3) (4)	Total (5)	Change in (5) (6)
By quinquennia						
1885–1890	5.08		2.17		7.25	
1890–1895	5.47	0.39	2.45	0.28	7.92	0.67
1895–1900	5.72	0.25	2.40	−0.05	8.12	0.20
1900–1905	6.13	0.41	2.42	0.02	8.55	0.43
1905–1910	6.83	0.70	2.73	0.31	9.56	1.01
1910–1915	7.20	0.37	3.03	0.30	10.23	0.67
1915–1920	7.80	0.60	2.98	−0.05	10.78	0.55
1920–1925	8.45	0.65	2.56	−0.42	11.01	0.23
1925–1930	8.51	0.06	2.05	−0.51	10.56	−0.45
By decades						
1885–1895	10.55		4.62		15.17	
1890–1900	11.19	0.64	4.85	0.23	16.04	0.87
1895–1905	11.85	0.66	4.82	−0.03	16.67	0.63
1900–1910	12.96	1.11	5.15	0.33	18.11	1.44
1905–1915	14.03	1.07	5.76	0.61	19.79	1.68
1910–1920	15.00	0.97	6.01	0.25	21.01	1.22
1915–1925	16.25	1.25	5.54	−0.47	21.79	0.78
1920–1930	16.96	0.71	4.61	−0.93	21.57	−0.22

This table shows the number of surviving children aged 0–4 (total births
minus deaths in the first five years of life). This series is presented because
we can estimate, for census years and for midcensus interval years, from
1890 to 1930, the numbers of native whites, by parentage and by age classes,
and can therefore approximate the age group 0–4. To derive total births from
the latter would require life-table or survival ratios that would differentiate
between the mortality of native whites of native parentage and native whites
of foreign or mixed parentage. No such data are available.

The estimates of native whites of native parentage and of native whites of
foreign or mixed parentage were obtained in the same manner as the estimates
for total native whites. The same revival ratios and proportions for deaths occurring in the first five years were used. For 1930 the totals for native whites
by parentage do not add up to the total native whites because there was an
unassigned category in the census of 1930. The midcensus estimates for 1925
were, of course, affected by the omissions in the 1930 census. In other cases,
the age groups for the parentage distributions were different from those for
total native whites. Because the ratios for the parentage classes were computed
for broader age groups, the totals do not add to the native-white total. For
1935 no midcensus estimates were attempted because the 1940 tabulations by
parentage were far out of line with those for 1930, apparently because of
heavy misrepresentation of parentage as native.

Table 5. Deaths (and Disappearances), by Nativity and Race, Overlapping Decades, 1870–1955 (in millions)

Period	Native white		Nonwhite		Foreign born white		Total	
	Deaths (1)	Change in (1) (2)	Deaths (3)	Change in (3) (4)	Deaths (5)	Change in (5) (6)	Deaths (7)	Change in (7) (8)
1870–1880	6.78		2.61		1.12		10.51	
1875–1885	7.25	0.47	2.87	0.26	1.33	0.21	11.45	0.94
1880–1890	7.60	0.35	2.73	−0.14	1.59	0.26	11.92	0.47
1885–1895	8.31	0.71	2.67	−0.06	1.77	0.18	12.75	0.83
1890–1900	8.91	0.60	2.54	−0.13	1.94	0.17	13.39	0.64
1895–1905	9.07	0.16	2.70	0.16	2.14	0.20	13.91	0.52
1900–1910	9.32	0.25	2.83	0.13	2.23	0.09	14.38	0.47
1905–1915	9.57	0.25	2.56	−0.27	2.32	0.09	14.45	0.07
1910–1920	10.60	1.03	2.50	−0.06	2.41	0.09	15.51	1.06
1915–1925	10.03	−0.57	2.19	−0.31	2.46	0.05	14.68	−0.83
1920–1930	8.44	−1.59	1.70	−0.49	2.51	0.05	12.65	−2.03
1925–1935	8.88	0.44	1.87	0.17	2.55	0.04	13.30	0.65
1930–1940	9.60	0.72	2.13	0.26	2.48	−0.07	14.21	0.91
1935–1945	10.27	0.67	2.02	−0.11	2.29	−0.19	14.58	0.37
1940–1950	10.70	0.43	1.77	−0.25	2.14	−0.15	14.61	0.03
1945–1955	10.90	0.20	1.76	−0.01	2.14	0.0	14.80	0.19

For the decades before 1940, the procedure involved applying either life-table or census-survival ratios to determine total deaths during the census interval and then apportioning them between the two halves. The procedures differed somewhat for (1) the age group 0–4, for the "reviving" of which life-table values had to be used; (2) native-white and nonwhite age groups 5 and above, for which census-survival ratios were used for census intervals; and (3) the foreign-born for whom distinctive life-table levels had to be used. Finally, direct information was available on (4) deaths since 1940.

(1) The "revival" of the group 10–14 in the second of two censuses to secure the proper 0–4 group in the first was described in the notes to Table 3. The apportionment of deaths thus estimated for the 0–4 group between the two halves of the census interval used the appropriate life-table values (see 2 below). There was no problem in calculating deaths in the procedure by which the 5–9 age group in the second census was "revived" to yield the 0–4 group in the midcensus interval year. Again, the calculations were made separately for native whites and nonwhites, male and female. The only exception to be noted is the treatment of the 1910–20 decade, described below.

(2) For the age groups for which census survival ratios were used to estimate deaths and disappearances (groups above 14 years of age in the second census, i.e., 5 and above in the first of two censuses), the problem was to devise a procedure by which the uneven distribution of deaths during the decade would be taken into account and which at the same time would provide midcensus estimates in which the biases were in some way proportional to those of both the preceding and following censuses. The solution for all except the 1910–20 decade was to use life tables to estimate the proportion of deaths in each group during the ten-year period which occurred in the first five years, and to apply these proportions to the deaths and disappearances during the intercensus period.

United States life tables including or centered around the census years of 1900, 1910, 1920, 1930, 1940, and 1950 were used in the preparation of the intercensal estimates. In 1900, 1910, and 1920 these life tables were based upon the mortality rates of the registration states of those years—in 1900 of only 10 states and the District of Columbia—but for the last three census years mortality in all the states is represented. The deaths occurring in an age group in the first five years and in a complete decade were obtained by subtracting from the sum of the L_x's for that age group the corresponding sums for the groups five and ten years older. Deaths occurring in the first five years were then divided by those occurring in the complete decade, and these proportions, obtained from each U.S. life table, were averaged for contiguous census years (except for 1910–20) to approximate the proportions which would have been obtained from decade life tables. For example, the ratios used for 1900–10 were the averages of the ratios computed from the 1900 and 1910 life tables.

These ratios multiplied by the deaths and disappearances over the entire intercensus period yielded those which occurred during the first five years (disappearances being treated as if they were deaths). The estimated deaths for the five-year period were then subtracted from the population at the preceding census, yielding the survivors to the midcensus point. This procedure was followed for each age group 5–14 and over, resulting in midcensus population estimates for ages 10 and over.

Because there were no United States life tables for years before 1900 and because deaths were recorded in very few states during that period, the ratios of deaths occurring in the first half of a decade as computed for 1900–10 were used for the three earlier decades. Corresponding life-table ratios were computed from the English life tables for 1871–80, 1881–90, and 1891–1900, but the trends of the English ratios were too different from those of the U.S. life tables for comparable periods after 1900 to warrant their use to extend the U.S. ratios. It was also felt that extrapolation of the post-1900 U.S. trend to the earlier decades, besides being a doubtful procedure, would make little difference in the resulting midcensal estimates.

Estimating the Proportion of Deaths Occurring in the First Half of the 1910–20 Period

Because of the influenza epidemic of 1918, a year not included in the 1919–21 life table, the method employed to estimate the midcensal population aged 10 and over for the other decades could not be used. Instead an attempt was made to compute the number of deaths occurring each year from April 15, 1910, to January 1920, by the age cohorts of the 1910 census. This involved the separation of the deaths occurring in each calendar year into those which occurred in each cohort of persons living at the census of 1910 by 10-year age groups and those which occurred to persons born after that time.

The underlying assumption was a rectangular distribution of deaths within each age group for each year. One twelfth of the deaths in each age group for a calendar year were assumed to occur each month, and one fifth of the deaths in each five-year age group for ages 5–9 and above were assumed to occur to persons in each single year group. Because deaths of native whites were not separated from deaths of foreign-born whites in 1912 and 1913, deaths of native whites in those years were estimated by straight-line interpolation from 1911 to 1914. Since only a fraction of the deaths of native whites occurred within the registration states of 1910, we also assumed that the same proportion of deaths occurred in the entire country in the first 4¾ years of this intercensus period as in the registration states. A similar qualification applies, of course, to the use of the life tables.

An important factor in the estimation of deaths over a long period is migration. Immigration increases the number of deaths in most age groups simply because the population is increased by migration, while emigration has the opposite effect. For nonwhites, the rather small amount of immigration, probably in increasing numbers in the war years, made the proportion of deaths occurring within the age span of a cohort in the registration states in 1910 much too high for the second half of the period. It was necessary therefore to use the ratios for native whites to adjust the nonwhite ratios. The relationship between native white and nonwhite ratios for 1900–10 was used to adjust the native white ratios for 1910–20 for use in estimating deaths in 1910–15 among nonwhites.

A Check on the Method Used for All Periods Except 1910–20

It was assumed that the average of the ratios computed from life tables at the end of each decade adequately represented mortality throughout the intercensal interval. A crude check on this assumption for 1900–40 was made by separating the deaths of native whites in the registration states at the beginning of each decade (i.e., 10 states in 1900 and a larger number at each succeeding decade) as was done for 1910–20. The ratios of deaths occurring in the first five years of each intercensal period were quite close to those obtained by using life tables. The largest difference was just over 4 percentage points, but the ratios obtained in this manner were much more irregular than those obtained from life tables, partly because of the smoothing of life-table values and partly because of the unavoidably crude separation of the deaths. In addition there was the necessity of estimating deaths of native whites in those years when they were not presented separately.

(3) The deaths of the foreign-born were estimated for 1870–1939, annually, in the preparation of Table B-6 in Kuznets and Rubin, *op. cit.*, and the procedure is described on pp. 103–104.

(4) For years beginning with calendar 1940, there are separate, annual death rates for whites and nonwhites (see *Historical Statistics of the United States*, and *Continuation to 1952*, Series C–46 and C–49; and for more recent years in *Statistical Abstract for 1956*, Table 67, p. 65). Applying these rates to July estimates of population (see notes to Table 3), we derived total deaths, white and nonwhite, annually and then quinquennially.

However, these data do not distinguish between the deaths of native and foreign-born whites. For the 1940–50 decade, the difference between the net change in foreign-born whites from the census total for 1940 to the census total for 1950 and the estimate of the net migration balance for the decade (see Table 6) shows deaths and disappearances of foreign-born whites. This total is apportioned equally between the two quinquennia because total white deaths are so divided and because the diminishing base (total number of resident foreign-born whites) can be assumed to be offset by advancing median age. We also assumed that deaths of foreign-born whites in 1950–55 were equal to those in 1945–50, which in view of the constancy of absolute volumes of white deaths cannot involve any substantial error. The deaths of native-born whites are secured by subtracting the quinquennial totals of deaths of foreign-born whites from the parallel totals for deaths of all whites for 1940–45, 1945–50, and 1950–55.

Table 6. Arrivals, Departures, and Net Balance (Aliens or Immigrants), Overlapping Decades, 1870–1955 (in millions)

Period	Arrivals		Departures		Net balance	
	Volume (1)	Change in (1) (2)	Volume (3)	Change in (3) (4)	Volume (5)	Change in (5) (6)
1870–1880	3.01		0.73		2.28	
1875–1885	4.35	1.34	0.80	0.07	3.55	1.27
1880–1890	5.53	1.18	1.05	0.25	4.48	0.93
1885–1895	4.79	−0.74	1.53	0.48	3.26	−1.22
1890–1900	4.13	−0.66	1.59	0.06	2.54	−0.72
1895–1905	5.83	1.70	2.41	0.82	3.42	0.88
1900–1910	9.79	3.96	4.35	1.94	5.44	2.02
1905–1915	10.98	1.19	5.40	1.05	5.58	0.14
1910–1920	5.74 (7.11)	−3.87	2.15 (3.99)	−1.41	3.59 (3.12)	−2.46
1915–1925	3.92 (5.22)	−1.82 (−1.89)	1.40 (2.64)	−0.75 (−1.35)	2.52 (2.58)	−1.07 (−0.54)
1920–1930	4.11	0.19	1.05	−0.35	3.06	0.54
1925–1935	1.69	−2.42	0.67	−0.38	1.02	−2.04
1930–1940	0.53	−1.16	0.46	−0.21	0.07	−0.95
1935–1945	0.48	−0.05	0.18	−0.28	0.30	0.23
1940–1950	1.04	0.56	0.16	−0.02	0.88	0.58
1945–1955	1.95	0.91	0.25	0.09	1.70	0.82

The series on departures and arrivals are from Kuznets and Rubin, *op. cit.*, Table B-1, pp. 95–96, and brought forward by movements of emigrants and immigrants reported in *Historical Statistics of the United States, 1798 –1945*, its *Continuation to 1952*, and the *Statistical Abstract for 1956* (Series B-304 and B-352 in the former, and Table 102 in the latter).

These data are for years ending June 30, so that the first decade runs from June 30, 1870, through June 30, 1880, and the last runs from June 30, 1945, through June 30, 1955. The discrepancy in dating with the decades relating to the movement of native-born components of the population in Tables 1–5 is too slight to matter.

The migration balance, combined with estimated deaths, should check out to net changes in foreign-born population reported in the successive censuses. The series on foreign-born used in Table 1 was based upon a migration and death balance so adjusted. But here we are using the unadjusted series on arrivals, departures, and net balance. It was thought best to leave these components unadjusted in the analysis of the components of the long swings in population growth. The discrepancies are relatively minor (see Table 7).

The figures in parentheses are comparable with the antecedent series of movement of aliens, and the lines divide the earlier series on all aliens from the later series on immigrants and emigrants.

Period	Births minus deaths (1)	Change in (1) (2)	Change in migration balance (Table 6, col. 6) (3)	Change in total pop. increase (2) + (3) (4)	Change directly (Table 2, col. 8) (5)
1870–1880	7.77				
1875–1885	7.94	0.17	1.27	1.44	1.32
1880–1890	8.76	0.82	0.93	1.75	1.61
1885–1895	9.44	0.68	−1.22	−0.54	−0.14
1890–1900	9.71	0.27	−0.72	−0.45	−0.06
1895–1905	9.71	0.0	0.88	0.88	0.66
1900–1910	10.68	0.97	2.02	2.99	2.77
1905–1915	11.86	1.18	0.14	1.32	1.07
1910–1920	11.32	−0.54	−2.46	−3.00	−3.32
1915–1925	12.72	1.40	−1.07 (−0.54)	0.33 (0.86)	0.93
1920–1930	14.07	1.35	0.54	1.89	2.07
1925–1935	11.05	−3.02	−2.04	−5.06	−5.00
1930–1940	9.15	−1.90	−0.95	−2.85	−2.84
1935–1945	11.55	2.40	0.23	2.63	2.80
1940–1950	16.99	5.44	0.58	6.02	6.02
1945–1955	21.95	4.96	0.82	5.78	5.78

This table is a recapitulation of Tables 1–6. The differences between columns 4 and 5 are explained by the fact that in column 4 the unadjusted balance of migration is used, whereas in column 5 the implicitly adjusted balance is used (*via* the foreign born series adjusted to the census totals). On this point see the notes to Table 6. The discrepancy disappears in the quinquennia beginning with 1940–45 because since 1940 the population totals are derived from the entries in Tables 3, 5, and 6.

Table 8. Changes in Population Increase and Flow Expressed as Percentages of Base Population, Averages for Groups of Intervals between Overlapping Decades, 1870–1955

	1875–1885 over 1870–1880 through 1895–1905 over 1890–1900 (1)	1900–1910 over 1895–1905 through 1920–1930 over 1915–1925 (2)	1925–1935 over 1920–1930 through 1945–1955 over 1940–1950 (3)
I. Mean percentage			
1. Native white population			
a. Births (% of native white)	2.37	1.19	1.35
b. Births (% of native white and foreign-born)	1.98	1.00	1.26
c. Deaths	1.07	−0.07	0.48
d. Net increase (a − c)	1.30	1.26	0.88
2. Nonwhite population			
a. Births	0.91	−1.29	2.48
b. Deaths	0.26	−1.80	0.15
c. Net increase	0.64	0.51	2.33
3. Foreign-born population			
a. Arrivals	7.55	1.36	−2.48
b. Departures	3.71	1.67	−1.19
c. Deaths	2.50	0.58	−0.64
d. Net increase	1.34	−0.89	−0.65
4. Total population			
a. Natural increase	0.68	0.91	1.05
b. Migration balance	0.49	−0.08	−0.26
c. Net increase (a + b)	1.17	0.83	0.79
d. Net increase (directly)	1.25	0.80	0.83
II. Mean deviation			
1. Native white population			
a. Births (% of native white)	0.78	0.98	2.43
b. Births (% of native white and foreign-born)	0.66	0.83	2.19
c. Deaths	0.38	0.98	0.16
d. Net increase (a − c)	0.53	0.71	2.52
2. Nonwhite population			
a. Births	0.67	1.25	2.51
b. Deaths	2.05	1.75	1.24
c. Net increase	2.50	2.39	3.75
3. Foreign-born population			
a. Arrivals	12.16	17.28	8.38
b. Departures	2.45	9.15	1.23
c. Deaths	0.68	0.18	0.67
d. Net increase	11.15	9.73	8.03
4. Total population			
a. Natural increase	0.51	0.59	2.45
b. Migration balance	1.63	1.36	0.78
c. Net increase (a + b)	1.56	1.78	3.23
d. Net increase (directly)	1.27	1.69	3.24
III. Coefficients of variation			
1. Native white population			
a. Births (% of native white)	0.33	0.82	1.80
b. Births (% of native white and foreign-born)	0.33	0.83	1.74
c. Deaths	0.36	14.00[a]	0.33
d. Net increase	0.41	0.56	2.86
2. Total population			
a. Natural increase	0.75	0.65	2.33
b. Net increase (by addition)	1.33	2.14	4.09
c. Net increase (directly)	1.02	2.11	3.90

[a] Disregarding sign of mean.

For Table 8 the changes in population increase between overlapping decades or in such flows as births, deaths, arrivals, or departures were converted into percentages of the base population. For native white births, deaths, and natural increase, it was the total native white population (and for births, native white and foreign born also) that provided the base; for nonwhite births, deaths, etc., the nonwhite population totals; for arrivals, departures, deaths, etc., the foreign born population totals; for the balance of all births over all deaths and for the total migration balance, total population served as the base. These base population figures were all taken from Table 1. For every given change, which involves four population stock figures—beginning of the first decade, beginning of the second decade, end of the first decade, end of the second decade—the base figure was the arithmetic mean of the two intermediate stock figures (i.e., the beginning of the second decade and the end of the first decade).

The percentages so calculated for each interval were then averaged; these arithmetic means appear in Section I. There were 15 intervals altogether, and they were grouped into 5, 5, and 5. Arithmetic rather than geometric means of percentages were used in order to minimize calculation.

From the same series of percentages, average deviations around the mean for each group of intervals were then computed. They appear in Section II. For a selected group of items the coefficient of variation is provided in Section III.

Table 9. ESTIMATED EXCESSES AND DEFICIENCIES OF POPULATION, TOTAL AND COMPONENTS, SUCCESSIVE PHASES OF LONG SWINGS IN TOTAL POPULATION GROWTH (lines 1–16 in millions)

	1880–1890 to 1890–1900 (1)	1890–1900 to 1900–1910 (2)	1900–1910 to 1910–1920 (3)	1910–1920 to 1920–1930 (4)	1920–1930 to 1930–1940 (5)	1930–1940 to 1940–1950 (9)
Excesses and deficiencies, total population increase						
1. From Table 2, col. 8	−5.17	+4.27	−9.49	+13.89	−19.05	+20.14
2. From Table 7, col. 4	−6.78	+6.10	−9.33	+11.56	−18.61	+19.83
Contribution of components						
3. Births, native white	−0.03	−0.01	−0.62	−2.00	−3.26	+12.48
4. Births, nonwhite	+0.09	−0.24	−0.68	+0.91	−0.40	+1.50
5. Total births (3+4)	+0.06	−0.25	−1.30	−1.09	−3.66	+13.98
6. Deaths, native white (S.R.)[a]	−0.97	+1.23	−0.78	+5.82	−6.37	+0.39
7. Deaths, foreign-born (S.R.)	+0.25	+0.02	0.0	+0.12	+0.14	+0.32
8. Deaths, nonwhite (S.R.)	−0.17	−0.84	+0.99	+0.93	−2.07	+1.25
9. Total deaths (S.R.)	−0.89	+0.41	+0.21	+6.87	−8.30	+1.96
10. Births and deaths (5+9)	−0.83	+0.16	−1.09	+5.78	−11.96	+15.94
11. Arrivals (S.R.)	−5.68	+9.34	−13.37	+8.16	−6.57	+3.94
12. Departures (S.R.)	−0.27	−3.40	+5.13	−2.38	−0.08	−0.05
13. Migration balance	−5.95	+5.94	−8.24	+5.78	−6.65	+3.89
14. Net, native white (3+6)	−1.00	+1.22	−1.40	+3.82	−9.63	+12.87
15. Net, nonwhite (4+8)	−0.08	−1.08	+0.31	+1.84	−2.47	+2.75
16. Net, foreign-born (7+13)	−5.70	+5.96	−8.24	+5.90	−6.51	+4.21
Relation to base population (Table 1, col. 4)						
17. Date of base population	1890	1900	1910	1920	1930	1940
18. Line 2 as % of base population	−10.7	+8.0	−10.1	+10.9	−15.1	+15.0
19. Line 10 as % of base population	−1.3	+0.2	−1.2	+5.4	−9.7	+12.0
20. Line 13 as % of base population	−9.3	+7.8	−8.9	+5.4	−5.4	+2.9

Percent distribution of total in line 2

	1890	1900	1910	1920	1930	1940	1950
21. Births, native white	+0.4	−0.2		+6.6	−17.3	+17.5	+62.9
22. Births, nonwhite	−1.3	−3.9		+7.3	+7.9	+2.1	+7.6
23. Total births	−0.9	−4.1		+13.9	−9.4	+19.6	+70.5
24. Deaths, native white	+14.3	+20.2		+8.4	+50.4	+34.2	+2.0
25. Deaths, foreign-born	−3.7	+0.3		0.0	+1.0	−0.8	+1.6
26. Deaths, nonwhite	+2.5	−13.8		−10.6	+8.1	+11.1	+6.3
27. Total deaths	+13.1	+6.7		−2.2	+59.5	+44.5	+9.9
28. Births and deaths	+12.2	+2.6		+11.7	+50.1	+64.1	+80.4
29. Arrivals	+83.8	+153.1		+143.3	+70.6	+35.3	+19.9
30. Departures	+4.0	−55.7		−55.0	−20.6	+0.4	−0.3
31. Migration balance	+87.8	+97.4		+88.3	+50.0	+35.7	+19.6
32. Net change, native white	+14.7	+20.0		+15.0	+33.1	+51.7	+64.9
33. Net change, nonwhite	+1.2	−17.7		−3.3	+16.0	+13.3	+13.9
34. Net change, foreign-born	+84.1	+97.7		+88.3	+51.0	+35.0	+21.2
Percent shares in total population of							
35. Native white	73.2	74.4	74.3	76.8	78.4	81.1	82.5
36. Nonwhite	12.4	12.2	11.2	10.4	10.2	10.3	10.7
37. Foreign-born	14.4	13.4	14.6	12.8	11.3	8.6	6.7

a S.R. means signs reversed.

Table 9 requires identification of the phases in long swings revealed by the date of change in the total population increase. The dating of these phases is indicated in the column headings of the table (there being six such phases, three of rise and three of decline). In each case, the decade shown is the second of two overlapping ones, for example, the last phase is the rise from the change of 1930–40 over 1925–35 to that of 1940–50 over 1935–45.

For each interval, we calculated the *hypothetical* addition to the population that would have occurred if the change established in the beginning of the phase had continued to its end. For example, the change for the interval 1880–90 over 1875–85 was 1.61 million, and the addition to population in 1880–90 amounted to 12.91 million. A continuation of such a change in population increments would have meant that in 1885–95, the population addition would have been 14.52 million and in 1890–1900, 16.13 million. Actually in these last two decades the population additions were 12.77 and 12.71 million. The shortage during this phase of the long swing was therefore 5.17 million (i.e., 14.52 minus 12.77, plus 16.13 minus 12.71). This is the figure in line 1, column 1, and the other entries on the same line show shortages or excesses in actual population increase compared with hypothetical, where the latter for each phase of the long swing is based upon the rate of change in the initial interval in the swing.

Although entries in line 1 are based upon the series of direct differences in the census- and midcensus-interval totals, those in line 2 are based upon the series that is a total of the various components. The latter series differs from that used for line 1 largely because the arrivals and departures were not forced to tally exactly with the change in the census series of foreign-born.

The entries in the other lines are based upon similar calculations. For each component distinguished in the table—births, native white; births, nonwhite; deaths, native white; deaths, nonwhite; deaths, foreign-born; arrivals or immigration; departures or emigration (for the phases established)—we again compared the hypothetical change, based on the initial change and the initial volume, with the actual volume in the intervals included in the phase. Thus, in 1880–90, the actual births of native whites were 16.93 million, and the change in the initial interval of the phase (i.e., 1880–90 over 1875–85) was 1.20 million. The expected births in 1885–95 and 1890–1900 were, therefore, 18.13 and 19.33 million respectively. The actual births were 18.28 and 19.15 million. The total shortage was, therefore, 0.03 million.

Such shortages and excesses were added algebraically, with proper regard to the nature of the components (i.e., shortages in deaths or departures meant plus signs in calculating net increase). The algebraic totals for the composite groups therefore check out to the excesses or shortages calculated directly for these more inclusive groups, except for errors due to rounding.

Table 10. CHANGES IN IMMIGRATION, BY SELECTED AREAS OF ORIGIN, OVERLAPPING DECADES, FISCAL YEARS, 1871–1915 (in thousands; second of two overlapping decades indicated in column heading)

Areas	1876–1885	1881–1890	1886–1895	1891–1900	1896–1905	1901–1910	1906–1915
1. Total	1,249	1,185	−852	−707	1,709	3,399	627
2. Europe	1,045	1,419	−432	−746	1,571	3,006	151
3. Great Britain	15	244	−189	−346	6	249	66
4. Ireland	50	168	−118	−149	−43	−6	−63
5. Scandinavia	233	181	−108	−177	47	87	−142
6. Other N.W. Europe	38	44	−33	−66	6	85	30
7. Germany	452	283	−562	−385	−221	57	−39
8. Other Central Europe	116	165	129	110	667	886	−55
9. Eastern Europe	59	161	255	90	373	778	267
10. Italy	82	169	179	166	672	722	−21
11. Other Southern Europe	1	3	16	12	65	148	108
12. America	211	−188	−389	1	49	274	464
13. Europe and America (2+12)	1,256	1,231	−821	−745	1,620	3,280	615
14. Residual (1–13)	−7	−46	−31	38	89	119	12

See *Historical Statistics of the United States, 1789–1945,* Series B-304-330. Line 6 includes the Netherlands, Belgium, Luxembourg, Switzerland, and France. Line 8 includes Austria-Hungary. Line 9 includes Russia, Rumania, Bulgaria, European Turkey, and Poland, except that for 1899–1919, some immigration from Poland is included in Central Europe. Line 11 includes Spain, Portugal, Greece, and Europe not elsewhere classified.

Table 11. Flow of Goods to Consumers, Total and Per Capita, 1929 Prices, Calendar Years 1870–1955 (total in billions of dollars, per capita in dollars)

Volume, (5-year average centered on year indicated)			Additions to flow				
Year (1)	Total (2)	Per capita[b] (3)	Period (4)	Total flow (5)	Change in (5) (6)	Per capita (7)	Change in (7) (8)
1870	6.13[a]	150[a]					
1875	8.75	189	1870–1880	6.92		107	
1880	13.05	257	1875–1885	7.32	0.40	90	−17
1885	16.07	279	1880–1890	5.01	−2.31	27	−63
1890	18.06	284	1885–1895	4.92	−0.09	19	−8
1895	20.99	298	1890–1900	9.13	4.21	72	53
1900	27.19	356	1895–1905	13.71	4.58	116	44
1905	34.70	414	1900–1910	13.15	−0.56	80	−36
1910	40.34	436	1905–1915	10.74	−2.41	36	−44
1915	45.44	450	1910–1920	11.45	0.71	51	15
1920	51.79	487	1915–1925	20.60	9.15	120	69
1925	66.04	570	1920–1930	19.30	−1.30	90	−30
1930	71.09	577	1925–1935	2.40	−16.90	−34	−124
1935	68.44	536	1930–1940	14.05	11.65	66	100
1940	85.14	643	1935–1945	35.11	21.06	206	140
1945	103.55	742	1940–1950	40.50	5.39	193	−13
1950	125.64	836	1945–1955	45.28	4.78	170	−23
1955	148.83[a]	912[a]					

[a] 3-year average.

[b] Col. 2 divided by corresponding figure (for the single year) for total population in Table 1, col. 4.

Entries in column 2 are estimates by the National Bureau of Economic Research recently revised and brought up to date (on an annual basis) in the study of long-term trends in capital formation and financing. The earlier version (annual since 1919 and overlapping decades back to 1869) were published in Simon Kuznets, *National Product since 1869* (New York: National Bureau of Economic Research, 1946).

| Period | Nonfarm residential construction | | | | Capital expenditures by railroads | | | |
| | Gross | | Net | | Gross | | Net | |
	Volume (1)	Change in (1) (2)	Volume (3)	Change in (3) (4)	Volume (5)	Change in (5) (6)	Volume (7)	Change in (7) (8)
1870–1879	6.21		4.56		4.33		2.84	
1875–1884	8.73	2.52	6.50	1.94	4.86	0.53	3.03	0.19
1880–1889	15.04	6.31	11.83	5.33	6.12	1.26	3.89	0.86
1885–1894	20.14	5.10	15.40	3.57	6.22	0.10	3.52	−0.37
1890–1899	19.82	−0.32	13.48	−1.92	4.68	−1.54	1.57	−1.95
1895–1904	17.73	−2.09	10.12	−3.36	3.31	−1.37	−0.11	−1.68
1900–1909	20.70	2.97	11.88	1.76	6.98	3.67	3.23	3.34
1905–1914	23.87	3.17	13.62	1.74	10.01	3.03	5.67	2.44
1910–1919	19.42	−4.45	7.91	−5.71	7.77	−2.24	2.81	−2.86
1915–1924	24.18	4.76	11.76	3.85	6.03	−1.74	0.85	−1.96
1920–1929	39.75	15.57	25.24	13.48	7.60	1.57	2.55	1.70
1925–1934	29.49	−10.26	12.90	−12.34	5.86	−1.74	0.87	−1.68
1930–1939	15.16	−14.33	−1.55	−14.45	3.61	−2.25	−1.48	−2.35
1935–1944	18.24	3.08	1.40	2.95	4.35	0.74	−0.86	0.62
1940–1949	23.18	4.94	5.97	4.57	5.57	1.22	0.22	1.08
1945–1954	39.75	16.57	21.23	15.26	6.27	0.70	n.a.	n.a.

See notes to Table 11. The basic estimates for nonfarm residential construction since 1889 were published in Leo Grebler, David M. Blank, and Louis Winnick, *Capital Formation in Residential Real Estate* (Princeton, N.J.: Princeton University Press, for the National Bureau of Economic Research, 1956). The basic estimates for capital expenditures by railroads are contained in Melville J. Ulmer, *Capital in Transportation, Communication, and Public Utilities: Its Formation and Financing* (Princeton, N.J.: Princeton University Press for the National Bureau of Economic Research, 1960).

Periods	Nonfarm residential construction and Railroad capital expenditures				Other capital formation (excluding war goods)			
	Gross		Net		Gross		Net	
	Volume (1)	Change in (1) (2)	Volume (3)	Change in (3) (4)	Volume (5)	Change in (5) (6)	Volume (7)	Change in (7) (8)
1870–1879	10.54		7.40		16.03		8.50	
1875–1884	13.59	3.05	9.53	2.13	23.31	7.28	12.35	3.85
1880–1889	21.16	7.57	15.72	6.19	25.30	1.99	10.26	−2.09
1885–1894	26.36	5.20	18.92	3.20	34.64	9.34	14.73	4.47
1890–1899	24.50	−1.86	15.05	−3.87	50.42	15.78	25.63	10.90
1895–1904	21.04	−3.46	10.01	−5.04	67.54	17.12	37.61	11.98
1900–1909	27.68	6.64	15.11	5.10	80.22	12.68	43.15	5.54
1905–1914	33.88	6.20	19.29	4.18	84.25	4.03	38.32	−4.83
1910–1919	27.19	−6.69	10.72	−8.57	101.04	16.79	45.40	7.08
1915–1924	30.21	3.02	12.61	1.89	114.41	13.37	50.63	5.23
1920–1929	47.35	17.14	27.79	15.18	130.01	15.60	56.84	6.21
1925–1934	35.35	−12.00	13.77	−14.02	104.46	−25.55	24.99	−31.85
1930–1939	18.77	−16.58	−3.03	−16.80	95.05	−9.41	13.23	−11.76
1935–1944	22.59	3.82	0.54	3.57	128.13	33.08	30.06	16.83
1940–1949	28.75	6.16	6.19	5.65	162.08	33.95	35.42	5.36
1945–1954	46.02	17.27	n.a.	n.a.	224.95	62.87	n.a.	n.a.

Columns 1–4 are derived from Table 12. Columns 5–8 are derived by subtraction from total capital formation estimates. The latter are from the sources indicated in the notes to Table 11.

Table 14. CHANGES IN COMMON-STOCK AND BOND YIELDS, OVERLAPPING
DECADES, CALENDAR YEARS 1870–1914

Period	Railroad bonds (adjusted)		Railroad stocks		Industrial stocks	
	Average level (1)	Change in (1) (2)	Average level (3)	Change in (3) (4)	Average level (5)	Change in (5) (6)
1870–1879	5.56		6.01		5.55	
1875–1884	4.58	−0.98	5.53	−0.48	5.70	0.15
1880–1889	3.89	−0.69	4.59	−0.94	5.50	−0.20
1885–1894	3.65	−0.24	3.94	−0.65	5.61	−0.11
1890–1899	3.45	−0.20	3.68	−0.26	5.58	−0.03
1895–1904	3.26	−0.19	3.53	−0.15	5.14	−0.44
1900–1909	3.41	0.15	3.96	0.43	4.90	−0.24
1905–1914	3.71	0.30	4.53	0.57	4.91	0.01

Historical Statistics of the United States, 1789–1945, Series N-201 (col. 1),
N-208 (col. 3), and N-207 (col. 5). Series N-207 and N-208 extend through
1871 only. The values for 1870 were assumed to be 5.0 for column 5 and 5.5
for column 3—a rough extrapolation based on the movement in Series N-201.

Table 15. FLOW OF GOODS TO CONSUMERS AND GROSS NATIONAL
PRODUCT (EXCLUDING WAR GOODS), TOTAL AND PER CAPITA, 1929 PRICES,
OVERLAPPING DECADES, CALENDAR YEARS 1870–1954

Period	Flow of goods to consumers (in dollars)				Gross national product (in dollars)			
	Total (in billions)		Per capita		Total (in billions)		Per capita	
	Volume (1)	Change in (1) (2)	Volume (3)	Change in (3) (4)	Volume (5)	Change in (5) (6)	Volume (7)	Change in (7) (8)
1870–1879	86.14		186		112.71		243	
1875–1884	123.59	37.45	244	58	160.49	47.78	316	73
1880–1889	157.57	33.98	273	29	204.03	43.54	354	38
1885–1894	178.70	21.13	281	8	239.70	35.67	377	23
1890–1899	210.58	31.88	299	18	285.50	45.80	406	29
1895–1904	265.97	55.39	348	49	354.55	69.05	464	58
1900–1909	335.13	69.16	400	52	443.02	88.47	529	65
1905–1914	400.63	65.50	433	33	518.76	75.74	561	32
1910–1919	450.57	49.94	446	13	578.80	60.04	573	12
1915–1924	523.41	72.84	492	46	668.02	89.22	628	55
1920–1929	641.41	118.00	554	62	818.77	150.75	707	79
1925–1934	686.66	45.25	557	3	826.47	7.70	670	−37
1930–1939	706.72	20.06	554	−3	820.54	−5.93	643	−27
1935–1944	827.69	120.97	625	71	978.40	157.86	739	96
1940–1949	1,023.51	195.82	734	109	1,214.34	235.94	871	132
1945–1954	1,238.05	214.54	824	90	1,509.01	294.67	1,005	134

Columns 1 and 5 are from the source indicated in the notes to Table 11.
Column 3 is column 1 divided by total population in Table 1, column 4 (population multiplied by 10), and column 7 is column 5 divided by total population.

Table 16. Excesses and Deficiencies in National Product Components, Phases of Long Swings in Total Population Growth, 1880–1950

	1880–1890 to 1890–1900 (1)	1890–1900 to 1900–1910 (2)	1900–1910 to 1910–1920 (3)	1910–1920 to 1920–1930 (4)	1920–1930 to 1930–1940 (5)	1930–1940 to 1940–1950 (6)
1. Excess or deficiency in population (Table 9, line 1)	−5.17	+4.27	−9.49	+13.89	−19.05	+20.14
Excess or deficiency in product totals						
2. Changes in flow of goods to consumers	−27.80	+84.30	−26.54	+113.86	−243.44	+377.58
3. Changes in flow per capita	−53.0	+96.0	−77.0	+115.0	−183.0	+260.0
4. Nonfarm residential construction						
Gross	−9.05	−0.25	−7.02	+38.44	−81.56	+54.09
Net	−10.77	+0.80	−7.51	+38.31	−79.57	+53.82
5. Railroad capital expenditures						
Gross	−5.12	+5.55	−7.19	+4.81	−10.44	+9.45
Net	−5.27	+5.83	−8.00	+6.36	−10.81	+9.37
6. Other capital formation (excl. war goods)						
Gross	+28.49	−0.42	−13.19	−8.03	−107.31	+128.34
Net	+26.11	−3.20	−19.20	−4.57	−94.09	+74.30
7. Total capital formation (excl. war goods)						
Gross	+14.32	+4.88	−27.40	+35.22	−199.31	+191.88
Net	+10.07	+3.43	−34.71	+40.10	−184.47	+137.49
8. Gross national product (excl. war goods)	−13.48	+89.18	−53.94	+149.08	−442.75	+569.46
9. Gross national product, per capita	−39.0	+94.0	−119.0	+153.0	−338.0	+405.0
Percent of base value (annual average)						
10. Date of base value	1885–1894	1895–1904	1905–1914	1915–1924	1925–1934	1935–1944
11. Line 8, percent of base	−5.6	+25.2	−10.4	+22.3	−53.6	+58.2
12. Line 9, percent of base	−10.3	+20.3	−21.2	+24.4	−50.4	+54.8

For the technique of calculating the excesses and deficiencies see the notes to Table 9.

The dates of the up and down phases of the long swings are determined by changes in the rate of population growth, not by movements in flow of product. The purpose of the table is to see whether during the periods when the rate of additions to population accelerates or declines, there are similar swings in either the flow of product or in additions to product.

Since the product series are for calendar years, the years included in the first phase are 1880–89 to 1890–99; in the second, 1890–99 to 1900–09, and so on.

Entries in all lines, except 3, 9, and 10–12, are in billions of dollars. Entries in lines 3 and 9 are in dollars.

Table 17. Changes in Volume of Other Activities,
Overlapping Decades, 1870–1954

Period	Receipts from sale of public lands (mill. $)		Patent applications (thousands)		Public acts passed by Congress	
	Volume (1)	Change in (1) (2)	Number (3)	Change in (3) (4)	Number (5)	Change in (5) (6)
1870–1879	18.6		205		1,770	
1875–1884	31.3	12.7	256	51	1,385	−385
1880–1889	65.6	34.3	334	78	1,652	267
1885–1894	58.3	−7.3	383	49	2,120	468
1890–1899	24.4	−33.9	409	26	2,056	−64
1895–1904	32.2	7.8	450	41	2,044	−12
1900–1909	61.4	29.2	538	88	2,511	467
1905–1914	58.0	−3.4	643	105	2,451	−60
1910–1919	32.3	−25.7	697	54	2,058	−393
1915–1924			783	86	2,226	168
1920–1929			881	98	3,655	1,429
1925–1934			823	−58	3,779	124
1930–1939			727	−96	3,391	−388
1935–1944			642	−85	3,951	560
1940–1949			690	48	4,035	84
1945–1954			772	82	3,935	−100

Data are from *Historical Statistics of the United States, 1789–1945* and the
Statistical Abstract for 1956. The series are P-94 (col. 1), P-181 (col. 3), and
P-45 (col. 5). The public act series in column 5 was derived by adding
numbers for successive sessions, counting each as two years, without allowance
for difference in duration of actual sessions.

DATE DUE

~~SEP 3 0 1999~~			
			Printed in USA